A Philosophical Anthropology of the Cross

Indiana Series in the Philosophy of Religion
Merold Westphal, *editor*

A Philosophical Anthropology of the Cross

THE CRUCIFORM SELF

Brian Gregor

INDIANA UNIVERSITY PRESS
Bloomington and Indianapolis

This book is a publication of

Indiana University Press
Office of Scholarly Publishing
Herman B Wells Library 350
1320 East 10th Street
Bloomington, Indiana 47405 USA

iupress.indiana.edu

Telephone orders 800-842-6796
Fax orders 812-855-7931

© 2013 by Brian E. Gregor

All rights reserved

No part of this book may be reproduced or utilized in any form or by any means, electronic or mechanical, including photocopying and recording, or by any information storage and retrieval system, without permission in writing from the publisher. The Association of American University Presses' Resolution on Permissions constitutes the only exception to this prohibition.

♾ The paper used in this publication meets the minimum requirements of the American National Standard for Information Sciences—Permanence of Paper for Printed Library Materials, ANSI Z39.48-1992.

Manufactured in the United States of America

Library of Congress Cataloging-in-Publication Data

Gregor, Brian, [date]
  A philosophical anthropology of the cross : the cruciform self / Brian Gregor.
    pages cm. — (Indiana series in the philosophy of religion)
  Includes bibliographical references (p.) and index.
  ISBN 978-0-253-00671-4 (cloth : alk. paper) — ISBN 978-0-253-00672-1 (pbk. : alk. paper) — ISBN 978-0-253-00704-9 (electronic book) 1. Jesus Christ—Crucifixion. 2. Philosophical anthropology. I. Title.
  BT453.G69 2013
  233—dc23
                                                      2012042031

1 2 3 4 5 18 17 16 15 14 13

For Thomas

Contents

Acknowledgments ix
List of Abbreviations xi

1. Philosophy, the Cross, and Human Being 1

PART ONE
2. The Hermeneutics of the Self 21
3. Faith, Substance, and the Cross 39
4. The Incurved Self 56
5. The Anthropological Question 77

PART TWO
6. The Concreteness and Continuity of Faith 103
7. The Capable Human Being as a Penultimate Good 122
8. The Call to Responsibility 142
9. Reflexivity, Intentionality, and Self-Understanding 156
10. Religion within the Limits of the Penultimate? 176

Notes 199
Select Bibliography 245
Index 257

Acknowledgments

Many people deserve acknowledgment for their help and support in bringing this book to print. I would like to thank Merold Westphal for his interest in my work and for welcoming this book into his series; Kevin Hart for his comments and suggestions on the manuscript; Dee Mortensen, Marvin Keenan, and Sarah Jacobi at Indiana University Press for their support and help; and Drew Bryan for his work as copy editor. I would also like to thank my friends and colleagues in the philosophy departments at Boston College and Fordham University. I owe a great debt to Richard Kearney, my graduate advisor and dissertation director, as well as my readers Jeff Bloechl and Gary Green, who gave me the freedom and support to pursue this project the way it needed to be pursued. Thanks also to Pat Byrne, Vanessa Rumble, and my other friends, mentors, and interlocutors: Jens Zimmermann, Bob Doede, James Taylor, John Manoussakis, Jeff Hanson, Phil Teichroeb, Mike Martens, and Ryan Chace. I must also thank the Fondation Georges Rouault, Annemarie Sawkins and the Haggerty Museum of Art, and Chelsea Radigan at Artists Rights Society, who allowed me to use Georges Rouault's amazing print for the cover of this book; thanks also to Dom Balestra and Nancy Busch at Fordham University for making it possible to cover the permission fees. I also benefited greatly from a series of summer research grants from the Ernest Fortin Memorial Foundation. Thanks to my church family at First Presbyterian Church in Brookline, my mom, and most of all to my wife Meg, whose love and friendship continue to be an immense blessing.

I would also like to thank *Faith and Philosophy* and Indiana University Press for permission to use portions of earlier articles. Portions of chapter 5 appeared as "Formal Indication, Philosophy, and Theology: Bonhoeffer's Critique of Heidegger" in *Faith and Philosophy* 24, no. 2 (April 2007): pp. 185–202; and portions of chapter 8 appeared as "Bonhoeffer's 'Christian Social Philosophy': Conscience, Alterity, and the Moment of Ethical Responsibility," in *Bonhoeffer and Continental Thought: Cruciform Philosophy* (Indiana University Press, 2009), pp. 201–25.

Abbreviations

AB Dietrich Bonhoeffer, *Act and Being: Transcendental Philosophy and Ontology in Systematic Theology,* trans. H. Martin Rumscheidt (Minneapolis: Fortress Press, 1996).
AQ Dietrich Bonhoeffer, "The Anthropological Question in Contemporary Philosophy and Theology," DBWE 10, pp. 389–408.
BT Martin Heidegger, *Being and Time,* trans. John Macquarrie and Edward Robinson (San Francisco: Harper & Row, 1962).
CA Søren Kierkegaard, *The Concept of Anxiety,* ed. and trans. Reidar Thomte and Albert B. Anderson (Princeton, N.J.: Princeton University Press, 1980).
C Dietrich Bonhoeffer, "Lectures on Christology." *Berlin: 1932–1933,* ed. Larry L. Rasmussen, trans. Carsten Nicolaisen and Ernst-Albert Scharffenorth (Minneapolis: Fortress Press, 2009), pp. 299–360.
CF Dietrich Bonhoeffer, *Creation and Fall: A Theological Exposition of Genesis 1–3,* trans. Douglas Stephen Bax (Minneapolis: Fortress Press, 1997).
D Dietrich Bonhoeffer, *Discipleship,* trans. Martin Kuske and Ilse Tödt (Minneapolis: Fortress Press, 2001).
DBWE 10 Dietrich Bonhoeffer, *Barcelona, Berlin, New York: 1928–1931,* trans. Douglas W. Stott (Minneapolis: Fortress Press, 2008).
E Dietrich Bonhoeffer, *Ethics,* ed. Clifford J. Green, trans. Reinhard Krauss, Charles C. West, and Douglas W. Stott (Minneapolis: Fortress Press, 2005).
FM Paul Ricoeur, *Fallible Man,* trans. Charles A. Kelbley (New York: Fordham University Press, 1986).
FN Paul Ricoeur, *Freedom and Nature: The Voluntary and the Involuntary,* trans. Erazím V. Kohak (Evanston, Ill.: Northwestern University Press, 1966).
FS Paul Ricoeur, *Figuring the Sacred: Religion, Narrative, and Imagination,* ed. Mark I. Wallace, trans. David Pellauer (Minneapolis: Fortress Press, 1995).
IM Martin Heidegger, *Introduction to Metaphysics,* trans. Gregory Fried and Richard Polt (New Haven, Conn.: Yale University Press, 2000).
IT Michel Henry, *I Am the Truth: Toward a Philosophy of Christianity,* trans. Susan Emanuel (Stanford, Calif.: Stanford University Press, 2003).

JP	*Søren Kierkegaard's Journals and Papers,* 7 vols., ed. and trans. Howard V. Hong and Edna H. Hong, assisted by Gregor Malantschuk (Bloomington: Indiana University Press, 1967–78). (Cited as JP, followed by entry number).
LPP	Dietrich Bonhoeffer, *Letters and Papers from Prison,* ed. John W. de Gruchy, trans. Isabel Best, Lisa E. Dahill, Reinhard Krauss, and Nancy Lukens (Minneapolis: Fortress Press, 2010).
LW	Martin Luther, *Luther's Works,* 55 vols., ed. Jaroslav Pelikan (St. Louis, Mo.: Concordia Publishing House / Philadelphia: Fortress Press, 1955–86). (Cited as LW, followed by volume and page number.)
OA	Paul Ricoeur, *Oneself as Another,* trans. Kathleen Blamey (Chicago: University of Chicago Press, 1992).
OB	Emmanuel Levinas, *Otherwise than Being or Beyond Essence,* trans. Alphonso Lingis (Pittsburgh: Duquesne University Press, 1981, 1997).
PC	Søren Kierkegaard, *Practice in Christianity,* ed. and trans. Howard V. Hong and Edna H. Hong (Princeton, N.J.: Princeton University Press, 1991).
SE	Paul Ricoeur, *The Symbolism of Evil,* trans. Emerson Buchanan (Boston: Beacon Press, 1967).
SC	Dietrich Bonhoeffer, *Sanctorum Communio: A Theological Study of the Sociology of the Church,* trans. Reinhard Krauss and Nancy Lukens (Minneapolis: Fortress Press, 1998).
SUD	Søren Kierkegaard, *The Sickness Unto Death,* ed. and trans. Howard V. Hong and Edna H. Hong (Princeton, N.J.: Princeton University Press, 1980).
TA	Paul Ricoeur, *From Text to Action: Essays in Hermeneutics II,* trans. Kathleen Blamey and John B. Thompson (London: The Athlone Press, 1991).

A Philosophical Anthropology of the Cross

1 Philosophy, the Cross, and Human Being

> Sustained by philosophy, religion receives its justification from thinking consciousness.
>
> —G. W. F. Hegel, *Lectures on the Philosophy of Religion*

Justifying religious faith through thinking consciousness: this is arguably the highest aspiration of the philosophy of religion. Whether this aspiration is itself justifiable, however, is another question. Can religious faith be grasped and grounded, so that its content is justified by the necessity of the philosophical concept? Does religious faith have its telos in philosophical consummation? Or does there remain some residual opacity that philosophy cannot penetrate, some otherness that philosophy cannot reconcile within its own conceptual scheme? How should philosophy approach a reality that claims to be an irresolvable scandal for philosophical thinking?

This book explores that question with regard to a specific problematic—namely, whether philosophy can think the cross of Jesus Christ, which is central to Christian faith as both a historical event and a fundamental figure of Christian discourse. The cross poses a unique challenge—according to the apostle Paul, a *scandal*—for philosophical wisdom, and during the course of this study we will encounter several cases of philosophical engagement with the cross: in Hegel, for whom the cross is pivotal in the historical development of Spirit; in Nietzsche, who sees the cross as nihilistic, as a curse on human life, strength, and flourishing; in Heidegger, for whom the cross provides an ontic model for the *Destruktion* of the history of metaphysics; and in Ricoeur, who interprets the death of Jesus on the cross as a triumph of life and love over death, as an ethical transfer of love to the lives of his followers. The question, however, is whether these philosophical interpretations preserve the true scandal and offense of the cross, or whether something crucial is lost in them. Our task will be to consider how philosophical thinking can face the cross honestly, so that it is transformed by the cross rather than transforming the cross in order to fit its philosophical agenda. We are investigating, in order words, the possibility of an authentically cruciform philosophy.

No doubt this is a vast undertaking. In order to set the parameters of our investigation, I will focus specifically on the significance of the cross for philosophical thinking about what it means to be human. With the phrase *anthropo-*

logia crucis, I am presenting this book as a contribution toward a philosophical anthropology of the cross. What does the cross of Christ—as both a historical event and a figure of Christian discourse—mean for thinking about the human being and what it means to become a self? How does the cross disrupt philosophical anthropology? How does the cross affect the continuity of selfhood? How does it change the way we think about human capability and responsibility? How does it challenge the way we think about self-reflection and self-understanding? What is the relation between the cross and human religiosity? Does the cross entail a denial or even hatred of life in the world? These are the questions that will occupy us in these pages.

The basic question of philosophical anthropology can be posed several ways. What is the human being? (*Was ist der Mensch?*) That is how Kant approached his *Anthropology from a Pragmatic Point of View*,[1] and since Kant this has been a familiar way to pose the question of human being. Anthropological inquiry can also be pursued in terms of "the human condition."[2] With the hermeneutical turn in philosophy, the quest for a general essence or definition of human being shifted to the question of self-understanding: *Who am I?* and *Who are we?*[3] But whatever form it takes, the anthropological question can be seen as carrying forward the Delphic imperative: *Know thyself.* Like the anthropological question, the oracle's imperative has been interpreted in a variety of ways throughout the Western philosophical tradition. In *The Concept of Anxiety,* Kierkegaard's pseudonym Vigilius Haufniensis laments the fact that German philosophy had misinterpreted "know thyself" as an invitation to an ethereal self-consciousness, which is quite different from the self-knowledge Socrates sought. Socrates understood that true self-knowledge is not absolute, speculative self-consciousness, but rather a truth that must be lived concretely, existentially, subjectively. Kierkegaard argues for a retrieval of the Greek (most significantly, Socratic) model of self-knowledge—but, nota bene, "as the Greeks would have understood it if they had possessed Christian presuppositions" (CA 79). That's not a bad description of what I want to do in this book, though my concern is not so much to reinterpret the Socratic notion of self-knowledge as it is to consider how the anthropological question is altered by one specific Christian presupposition—namely, the cross of Christ. How does the word of the cross alter philosophical thinking about human being?

God on the Cross

> What is this strange and uncouth thing?
>
> —George Herbert, "The Cross"[4]

A running theme of this book will be the tension between philosophy and Christian faith. The cross heightens this tension by exposing the fundamental incommensurability of two rival ontologies—i.e., two competing accounts of human being, identity, and selfhood. As the apostle Paul writes in his first epistle to the Corinthians, the word of the cross is a foolishness by which God destroys the wisdom of the wise (I Cor. 1:18–19). Jews ask for signs and Greeks ask for wisdom, but the word of the cross is a scandal to both (a "stumbling block" for the Jews and "foolishness" for Gentiles) (22–23). It will not accommodate the wisdom of the world; it upsets our expectations and overturns our assumptions about what is good, wise, and strong. The word of the crucified Christ appears as foolishness and weakness—and yet "the foolishness of God is wiser than men, and the weakness of God is stronger than men" (25). The point is not that God, even at his weakest and most foolish, ranks higher than human beings on a shared hierarchy of power and wisdom. Rather, the word of the cross is discontinuous with such a hierarchy; it introduces a new horizon of evaluation, a new reality with a new understanding of power and wisdom.

For philosophical anthropology, the word of the cross is a scandal par excellence. First of all, it is troubling because of its historical particularity. How should philosophy handle the troubling suggestion that, in Kierkegaardian terms, a historical event should be the point of departure for one's eternal happiness?[5] The word of the cross does not have a merely formal significance, and it does not symbolize a general concept like subversion or scandal. It is the proclamation of the singular, historical actuality of Christ's crucifixion—an eminently contingent event that claims to be the locus of true self-understanding for the human being.

In addition to the problem of history and truth, the scandal of the cross also encompasses the offensive thought that this historical event is in fact the crucifixion of *God*. As the Lutheran hymn proclaims, "God himself lies dead/ On the cross he has died."[6] After nearly two millennia of Christendom the figure of the cross has become so familiar as to be innocuous, and thus it is difficult to appreciate how scandalous the crucified God was for the ancient world. As Nietzsche observes:

> Modern men, obtuse to all Christian nomenclature, no longer feel the gruesome superlative that struck a classical taste in the paradoxical formula "god on the cross." Never yet and nowhere has there been an equal boldness in inversion, anything as horrible, questioning, and questionable as this formula: it promised a revaluation of all the values of antiquity.[7]

Martin Hengel confirms this in the primary texts of antiquity, which express a deep aversion to anything associated with crucifixion. The cross was invoked as a gesture of mockery, contempt, and curse, and as the Roman scholar Marcus Terentius Varro observes, even the very word *crux* is phonetically harsh.[8] Similarly, Cicero writes: "Let even the name of the cross be kept away not only from the bodies of the citizens of Rome, but also from their thoughts, sight and hearing."[9] The suggestion of a crucified God was scandalous from the Greco-Roman perspective, but also from the Jewish perspective. As one biblical scholar observes: "On a real cross in this world hangs the long-awaited Jewish Messiah. How can that be anything other than an epistemological crisis?"[10] The word of the cross is a rupture in the framework in which we understand God, ourselves, and our world. Thus "for Paul and his contemporaries the cross of Jesus was not a didactic, symbolic, or speculative element but a very specific and highly offensive matter which imposed a burden on the earliest Christian missionary preaching."[11]

The offense of the cross is one reason for the appeal of Docetism, which provides a hermeneutical principle to interpret the death of God incarnate as an appearance rather than an actual historical event.[12] This is why Paul's readers in the Corinthian church "sought to escape from the *crucified* Christ into the enthusiastic life of the spirit, the enjoyment of heavenly revelations and an assurance of salvation connected with mysteries and sacraments."[13] Just as Docetism was tempting for the early church, it continues to be a temptation in our time. In *The Sickness Unto Death*, Kierkegaard's pseudonym Anti-Climacus comments on the modern version of this heresy: the concrete, individual humanity of Christ is replaced by appearance in that "he docetically becomes fiction, mythology, which makes no claim upon actuality" (SUD 131). We have to consider this point carefully, since there is a way in which symbols, fiction, and myths *do* make a claim on the concrete existence of the self. Paul Ricoeur has convincingly shown that figurative discourse discloses existential possibilities, which are not merely abstract universal possibilities but the contours of a world I might inhabit. This imaginative disclosure of possibility is vital to our understanding and action in the world, and thus it does make a claim on actuality.

On one level this insight applies to the cross as it does to any symbol or image. Like all symbols, the cross gives an abundance of meaning to be thought,[14] and like all symbols it quickens the imagination to disclose new possibilities and a new world for the self to inhabit. But we will need to discuss more carefully what sort of possibilities the cross (and the resurrection) discloses, because the word of the cross claims a unique ontological efficacy insofar as it participates in a concrete historical event—an event that Christian faith interprets as central to the meaning of all history and the condition for the transformation of human being. No doubt the cross changes my self-understanding and discloses a strange new world that I might inhabit. But as I argue in chapters 5 and 10, it is vital that the cross not merely disclose my ownmost ontological possibilities. It brings an eschatological possibility that comes from beyond the immanence of human being in order to transform it.

It is very difficult for philosophy to countenance such a claim. The word of the cross is a scandal for philosophy because it is a limit that philosophy cannot surpass, an excess of meaning it cannot contain, and a power it cannot reduce to human capability. But offense does not always lead to outright rejection. It can also create intrigue. Philosophy tends to become fascinated with its others, that is, with anything that suggests a reality outside philosophical comprehension. Kierkegaard in particular was attuned to the way speculative philosophy dreams of incorporating the otherness of Christian revelation within philosophical thinking. Philosophy is fascinated by the challenge of something that resists conceptual resolution and that threatens to elude objectification and universalization. As Kierkegaard's pseudonym Johannes Climacus observes, this fascination "is the ultimate paradox of thought: to want to discover something that thought itself cannot think."[15] Is the cross a reality that philosophical thought cannot adequately think? If so, what can the philosopher do with the scandalous, unsurpassable, irresolvable reality of the cross?

* * *

Philosophy has employed some shrewd strategies for overcoming and internalizing this otherness. Anticipating the threat of an alterity it cannot fully overcome, philosophy can inoculate itself by injecting a measured, controlled amount of alterity into its system, as a vaccine to build up its internal defenses against an outright invasion. We see this in Hegel's philosophical theology: despite his profound confrontation with the cross and the theme of the death of God, Hegel ultimately rationalizes the historical fact of the cross and reinstates the priority of philosophical speculation. The cross is a pivotal moment in the historical process of Spirit moving toward reconciliation with itself in absolute self-consciousness.

This move appears as early as Hegel's *Faith and Knowledge*, with its famous discussion of the "speculative Good Friday" that is a necessary moment in the development of the supreme Idea. Following the Enlightenment attack on religious faith, European civilization was marked by a feeling of "infinite grief," a sense of loss, that "God Himself is dead."[16] In quoting the Lutheran hymn Hegel draws a connection between the modern experience of atheism and the historical event of Good Friday, aiming to show that both historical events disclose a truth about God—namely, that God includes death within himself. This is why the feeling of modern atheism is "a moment of the supreme idea," and also why philosophy must confront Good Friday—not as a merely historical event but speculatively, "in the whole truth and harshness of its God-forsakenness." The confrontation with this universal and necessary truth makes possible a resurrection in which a true philosophy of the absolute, the totality, can arise.[17]

While Hegel concludes his *Faith and Knowledge* with this provocative suggestion, the speculative interpretation of the cross figures more prominently in his *Phenomenology of Spirit*. There Hegel describes the negative as an essential moment within the life of Spirit, something that is revealed pre-eminently in the crucifixion. Here too the ultimate significance lies not in the historical death of the particular man Jesus, but what it makes known for speculative philosophy:

> The *death* of the divine Man, *as death,* is *abstract* negativity, the immediate result of the movement which ends only in *natural* universality. Death loses this natural meaning in spiritual self-consciousness, i.e. it passes into its true conception ... death

becomes transfigured from its immediate meaning, viz. the non-being of this *particular* individual, into the *universality* of the Spirit who dwells in His community, dies in it every day, and is daily resurrected.[18]

The dead Jesus is resurrected in the spirit of the church-community, and the truth that this community preserves through its religious representations then receives its fullest interpretation in speculative philosophy.

Hegel's philosophical interpretation of the cross is well articulated in his 1827 *Lectures on the Philosophy of Religion*: the phrase "God himself is dead" expresses "an awareness that the human, the finite, the fragile, the weak, the negative are themselves a moment of the divine, that they are within God himself, that finitude, negativity, otherness are not outside of God and do not, as otherness, hinder unity with God. Otherness, the negative, is known to be a moment of the divine nature itself" (p. 326). The concrete, historical event of Jesus' crucifixion gains its full significance when it is grasped by philosophical speculation; religious representation (*Vorstellung*) achieves its telos in the philosophical concept (*Begriff*). The cross becomes a speculative principle of the identity of the finite and the infinite, the human and the divine.[19] What is ultimately significant is not the crucifixion and resurrection of this particular man,[20] but the insight it affords into the universal nature of Spirit: the negation of the negative, the reconciliation of the finite with the infinite, dying in order to live. The kenotic act of God entering history and dying on a cross is not an inscrutable act of divine grace, a contingent act by a God whose ways are not our ways, whose thoughts are not our thoughts; rather, it is a logically necessary moment in the historical development of Spirit. As a result, the cross presents no scandal that philosophical speculation does not ultimately resolve, nor an otherness that is not absorbed by speculative thinking; such an alienation would characterize the "unhappy consciousness" of individual subjectivity that has not yet grasped itself as universal self-consciousness.[21] For Hegel, however, the cross enables a philosophical triumph in which God's thoughts and humanity's thoughts are reconciled. There is no ultimate separation; identity truly is the identity of identity and difference. Whatever the merits of Hegel's interpretation of the cross,[22] it sacrifices the historical particularity and contingency of the crucifixion to the universality and necessity of the Concept. As a consequence, Hegel's *philosophia crucis* is, as Dietrich Bonhoeffer observes, the most brilliant instance of Docetism (C 337).

One might try to answer Hegel by thematizing the cross as a principle of paradox, subversion, or insurmountable alterity. Yet here again the scandal of the cross is compromised, since its significance and potency are verified in reference to an external criterion.[23] This is the danger inherent in a philosophical hermeneutics of the cross, which attends to the poetic power of the cross as a symbol that embodies more fundamental human realities like self-giving and unconditional love. Such a symbol might overturn the world's understanding of what constitutes wisdom, power, goodness, and beauty, but it is a question of where the new power of the cross lies. The cross certainly does have a poetic power to transform the imagination, and it can inspire admirable and even revolutionary deeds; but if this is the full extent of its efficacy, then there is no ultimate difference between Christ and Socrates. The crucified Christ becomes a pre-eminent example of our ownmost existential possibilities. This is what happens in the young Heidegger's hermeneutics of the cross, which sought to render Luther's *theologia crucis* as an *ontologia crucis*. The cross destroys worldly wisdom, but for Heidegger this *destructio* merely provides an ontic model of the more fundamental ontological structure of *Destruktion*. Once again, the true *skandalon* of the cross is lost. The cross of Christ is "made void" (I Cor. 1:17). Whether it is rationalized, poeticized, or ontologized, the philosophical cross has a form of godliness while denying its true power and efficacy.[24] As Hans Urs von Balthasar observes: "Philosophy can speak of the Cross in many tongues; when it is not the 'Word of the Cross' (I Corinthians I, 18), issuing from faith in Jesus Christ, it knows either *too much* or *too little*."[25]

In order to take the scandal of the cross seriously, philosophy would have to resist its impulse to resolve the actual, contingent, historical event of Jesus' crucifixion into some universal or general intelligibility. Is it possible for philosophy to be broken open by the cross and remain open in faith and hope, rather than seeking closure and resolution? Could philosophy be faithful in this way, as a sort of kenotic philosophy?[26] Or maybe something like Luther's description of an apostolic, eschatological philosophy? Or perhaps as a *philosophia crucis*, a cruciform philosophy? In order to preserve the genuine *skandalon*, an *anthropologia crucis* must reckon with the claim that the human being gains true self-understanding in relation to the event of God on the cross. This certainly makes our project of a philosophical anthropology of the cross much more difficult, but we need to be honest about what is at stake.

Interlocutors

In arguing for a cruciform interpretation of philosophical anthropology, our discussion will proceed through the intersection of philosophical and theological anthropology. I will take a hermeneutical approach to philosophical anthropology, drawing primarily on Paul Ricoeur, but with reference to other hermeneutical thinkers such as Martin Heidegger, Hans-Georg Gadamer, and Charles Taylor. This perspective approaches philosophical anthropology as a question of self-understanding: *Who am I?* The question of one's identity encompasses several related questions—questions about meaning, recognition, justification, continuity, capability, and responsibility. Chapter 2 outlines the basic features of the hermeneutics of the self, arguing that the self does not answer these questions in an absolute or self-grounding way, but instead receives answers in being addressed by a word that precedes it. Because the word of address comes from outside of the self, the self is not the absolute origin of meaning. We find ourselves existing in a world that is already given as meaningful.

Moreover, the self is not the absolute guarantor of its own identity. We know who we are not because we have created or constituted ourselves, but because we were first addressed. What I want to consider, then, is what happens when the word of address is the word of the cross. What does the cross of Christ mean for our understanding of what it is to be human, and to be oneself?

From the theological side of things, my primary interlocutor will be Dietrich Bonhoeffer. The pairing of Ricoeur and Bonhoeffer is felicitous for several reasons. Both thinkers interrogate the project of reflexive philosophy and evaluate its capacity to understand the faithful self. Both thinkers offer an important critique of the project of self-reflection and the goal of a self-understanding that is direct, absolute, or indubitable. Each thinker poses a sharp challenge to the *anthropologia gloriae* that characterizes the reflexive tradition—whether it be the *cogito* of Descartes, the absolute *Ich* of Fichtean idealism, the self-thinking *Geist* of Hegel, or the transcendental ego of Husserl. Yet at the same time, Ricoeur and Bonhoeffer both seek to affirm the legitimacy of a certain kind of self-understanding. Finally, both have thought carefully about the status of the self in Christian faith, and as we shall see, the *theologia crucis* is an important factor in their respective critiques of the self as a self-grounding or absolute source of meaning.

This dialogue between Ricoeur and Bonhoeffer will prove fruitful because they challenge and supplement each other in the areas where they each need to be challenged and supplemented. My project is not, however, a comparative exegesis or synthesis of Ricoeur and Bonhoeffer, but a constructive thematic approach to the question of faith and philosophical anthropology. In addition to Ricoeur and Bonhoeffer, then, we will also engage with a strong supporting cast of thinkers. Kierkegaard is an important influence. Luther is also significant, along with several contemporary Lutheran theologians, such as Eberhard Jüngel, Robert W. Jenson, and Oswald Bayer. Our discussion will receive a significant orientation from Luther's *theologia crucis* and several of his early texts, such as the *Heidelberg Disputation*, the *Disputation Concerning Man*, the *Disputation Against Scholastic Theology*, and his early commentaries on the Psalms. That said, my task is not to articulate a specifically Lutheran anthropology, however worthwhile such a project might be.[27] Nor do I present this as a specifically Lutheran philosophy, though that too would be an interesting project.[28] Finally, I do not pretend to be a Luther scholar and do not enter the finer points of Luther interpretation, nor the debates over his interpretation of Paul. While these are important issues, they would take us too far away from our primarily philosophical focus.

With these disclaimers in place, I *do* argue that Luther demands philosophical attention. His impact on the philosophical tradition has been enormous, and it is particularly important for understanding the context in which my project unfolds. Kant, Hegel, Kierkegaard, and Heidegger were all deeply influenced by Luther. These thinkers are all in turn important influences on Ricoeur and Bonhoeffer, who are also related through the family tree of post-Heideggerian

Lutheran theology: Rudolf Bultmann was an important interlocutor for Bonhoeffer and Ricoeur; Gerhard Ebeling was a student of Bonhoeffer, and along with Ernst Fuchs he advanced the post-Bultmannian "new hermeneutic" that influenced Ricoeur's hermeneutics of religious language. Another theologian to come from this context is Eberhard Jüngel, who is a younger contemporary and interlocutor of Ricoeur. There are many connections and relations between these thinkers, and Luther stands in the background of all of them. With this context in mind, I will be attuned to those themes in Luther that have been significant in shaping these thinkers: the human being as addressed and constituted by a prior word, as standing ek-statically outside itself in faith and hope, and as defined by eschatological possibility. These themes proved particularly attractive to the young Heidegger as well as post-Heideggerian theology, but our reading of Ricoeur and Bonhoeffer will lead away from the interpretation of faith as a decision for authentic existence. Such a hermeneutic fails to account for the continuity of faith, and it also compromises the radically eschatological nature of faith, reducing it to a new possibility of human self-understanding.

Such proves to be one of the limits of Ricoeur's hermeneutics of the faithful self, which deliberately remains within philosophical limits. The appeal to limits is an important move, and Ricoeur carries it out with remarkable subtlety, but the philosophical hermeneutics of the self cannot altogether evade the *theological* hermeneutics of the self. This is too often the case; theological anthropology is identified as a regional discourse, an optional variation within the overarching and underwriting governance of a philosophical ontology of human understanding. This is the argument one finds in Heidegger and Gadamer, and while Ricoeur usually manages to avoid this conclusion, he often comes perilously close to arguing for a fundamental ontology of human understanding. The danger in such a view is that a philosophical hermeneutics will compromise the word of the cross, which makes a radical, fundamental claim about reality and cannot be classified as a merely regional word. In chapters 3 and 5 I will argue that the word of the cross is ontologically disruptive, discontinuous with our former way of being in the world and transformative in an ultimate sense. This word introduces a new ontology of the human because the structure of our being is transformed by faith. In short, the word of the cross introduces an ontology of justification by faith, which is incommensurable with our default mode of being in the world—namely, the ontology of self-justification.[29] The self is curved in on itself, seeking to be the origin of its own identity, meaning, and goodness. We will discuss this phenomenon in chapter 4, where I argue that the image of incurvature provides the most compelling figure for understanding sin. The incurved self is driven toward what Jüngel calls "reckless self-actualization."[30] The word of the cross is an address that breaks open this incurved self, destroying the ontology of self-justification. The word of the cross requires that we rethink the ontology of the self in eschatological terms. The self is not defined by its present actuality, by its works, or by any state it has already achieved. The self is defined by an eschatological possibility, and so the cruciform self is always ek-static: it has its being outside of itself, in faith and hope rather than presence.

So concludes part I. Part II takes up the questions that follow from a cruciform ontology of the self. Since the word of the cross is radically disruptive and discontinuous with the prior being of the self, how should we understand the concreteness and continuity of this new selfhood (chapter 6)? The cross reveals the self as fundamentally incapable of establishing itself before God, so what does this mean for thinking about human capability and agency? Does the ontology of justification by faith cripple the self and stifle the call to ethical responsibility (chapters 7 and 8)? Faith is an intentional act that cannot be recuperated and re-presented within self-reflective consciousness, so what does this mean for self-awareness and self-understanding (chapter 9)? The cross pronounces a decisive No to religion, so what does this mean for thinking about the relation and differences between faith and human religiosity? Finally, the cross disrupts the world and introduces a new reality—not just a new humanity but a new creation; given this proclamation, is Nietzsche correct to interpret Christian faith as a nihilistic negation of the world (chapter 10)? I will respond to these challenging questions by drawing on Bonhoeffer's account of the relation between ultimate and penultimate things. Bonhoeffer's model provides a hermeneutical key for understanding the relation between the discontinuity of the eschatological word and the continuity of concrete, historical existence in the world.

Cruciform Faith Seeking Understanding

> Some of the most difficult disputes are all the boundary disputes in the sciences—the boundary between jurisprudence and ethics; moral philosophy and dogmatics—psychology and moral philosophy, etc. Usually a single science is treated by itself; then one has much to say and gives no thought to the possibility of everything suddenly being dissolved if the presupposition must be altered.
>
> —Søren Kierkegaard[31]

> Faith—that too is not a solution but the name of a problem.
> —Louis Mackey[32]

The idea of a philosophical anthropology of the cross might seem to be doubly wrongheaded. From a theological perspective it might seem misguided to talk about an *anthropologia crucis,* since the theology of the cross calls us away from anthropology—away from the human being and its possibilities, away from what Karl Barth calls "the musty shell of the Christian-religious self-consciousness."[33] I agree that the proper subject matter of theology is not merely human religious consciousness, but with Barth's critical corrective in mind we must also recognize that questions regarding human religious consciousness, the hermeneutical question of self-understanding, and the status of the self in faith are nevertheless vital topics of inquiry—especially for philosophy.

From a philosophical perspective the notion of an *anthropologia crucis* might also seem misguided because it transgresses the limits that separate philosophy and theology. Ricoeur is one philosopher who insists on maintaining these disciplinary boundaries. It is therefore particularly noteworthy that he defends this methodological asceticism by appealing to a theology of the cross. In a sermon given at the University of Chicago in 1984, Ricoeur sketches his vision of what cruciform thinking entails. He draws on Jesus' claim that "whoever would save their life will lose it, and whoever loses their life for my sake will find it."[34] What does it mean for the Christian intellectual, "the faithful person who adopts Anselm's *fides quaerens intellectum*," to take up the cross, to lose their life in this way? Ricoeur argues that taking up the cross means "to renounce the representation of God as the locus of absolute knowledge, the guarantee of all my knowledge. It is to accept knowing just one thing about God, that God was present in and is to be identified with Christ crucified. God took up the cross."[35] For the Christian, the task of thinking should be similarly kenotic insofar as it empties itself of claims to divine certainty:

> To take up the cross of Jesus, for me, a member of the university, the community of knowledge, means not to overevaluate my knowledge, caught up as it is in questions of proof and guarantees, before this necessity—higher than any logical necessity: "It was necessary that the Son of Man should suffer and be crucified." For all God's power, God only gives Christians the sign of divine weakness, which is the sign of God's love. To allow myself to be helped by the weakness of this love is, for the question of making sense of my faith, to accept that God can be thought of only by means of the symbol of the Suffering Servant and by the incarnation of this symbol in the eminently contingent event of the cross of Jesus.[36]

Similarly, in his introduction to *Oneself as Another* Ricoeur comments on the place of biblical faith in his hermeneutics of the self. Here too the *theologia crucis* is an obvious influence:

> The dependence of the self on a word that strips it of its glory, all the while comforting its courage to be, delivers biblical faith from the temptation, which I am here calling cryptophilosophical, of taking over the henceforth vacant role of ultimate foundation. In turn, a faith that knows itself to be without guarantee, following the interpretation given by the Lutheran theologian Eberhard Jüngel in *God as the Mystery of the World,* can help philosophical hermeneutics to protect itself from the hubris that would set it up as the heir to the philosophies of the cogito and as continuing their self-foundational claim. (OA 25)

I completely agree with Ricoeur that a philosophical hermeneutics of the self cannot employ the claims of faith as an absolute foundation or guarantee. Such is the model of "Christian philosophy" that Ricoeur resists so strenuously throughout his authorship. Ricoeur is also correct to insist that philosophy respect its limits,[37] because Christian philosophy does face the temptation to transform itself into a sort of philosophical religion. Hegel's philosophical Christianity is the pre-eminent example,[38] and Ricoeur's (Kantian) insistence on philosophical modesty sets a limit to this impulse. However, in chapter 10 I question whether philosophy is capable of setting its own limits regarding the possibility of revelation. According to Bonhoeffer, philosophy only encounters a genuine limit from the *actuality* of revelation, which comes from outside of philosophical reflection. In this regard, a distinctly Christian philosophy is confronted by a limit that philosophy otherwise lacks.

I also want to challenge the assumption that philosophy must remain neutral regarding the crucified God. There is a decisive difference between a Christian philosophy that uses faith to guarantee its conclusions and a Christian philosophy that is genuinely cruciform in character. A cruciform philosophy would not be an impervious, dogmatic philosophy but a faith that seeks understanding in fear and trembling rather than triumph. What would it look like to think philosophically after the cross? Does philosophy have to be Docetic with regard to the cross? What would philosophy look like if it took the scandal of the cross seriously? This would not be a triumphant philosophy, a *philosophia gloriae*, but rather a *philosophia crucis*—a cruciform philosophy.

Of course, the merits of such a philosophy would depend on how it actually plays out. Ricoeur rightly warns against "feeble eclecticism," arguing that the philosophical thinker cannot settle for facile reconciliations of philosophy and the kerygma. The integrity of both discourses requires such vigilance.[39] Barth is similarly suspicious of the enthusiasm of theologians regarding the latest philosophical trends, which results in a "*mixophilosophicotheologia*" that distracts theologians and distorts the word they are called to proclaim.[40] We can appreciate Barth's suspicion, but this need not preclude a fruitful exchange between philosophy and the kerygmatic word. Here we are not concerned primarily with the preacher or theologian, but with another creature—namely, the philosopher who has heard the word of the cross and is called to think philosophically in the light of this word.

But what sort of bizarre creature is this cruciform philosopher? Could we find this oddity in some obscure medieval bestiary, alongside gryphons and unicorns? Not according to Heidegger, who argues that the species "Christian philosopher" is not merely mythical, but rather nonsensical, like a squared circle. Christian philosophy (and Christian thinking) is a contradiction in terms because philosophical thinking must be methodologically atheistic. Faith preempts genuine thinking, which means the Christian, *qua* Christian, cannot *think* in the fullest sense of the word. Defined in contrast to centuries of Christendom, stale scholasticism, and the many varieties of triumphalist theology, it may appear that philosophical questioning is the truly humble, untimely, and difficult path. But if we take the cruciformity of faith seriously, we can hardly be convinced by a story in which philosophy valiantly struggles with questions while faith comforts itself with pat answers. As Louis Mackey observes, faith too is the name of a problem; it is not simply an answer that resolves all questioning.[41] Faith raises questions of its own, many of which are philosophical questions. We therefore cannot conclude that faith immediately transforms philosophy into theology. A philosopher may take revelation as a presupposition or a premise in an argument without this requiring that she is suddenly doing theology. As Alvin Plantinga explains, the argument is philosophical because it wrestles with questions that philosophers ask and does so with philosophical tools.[42] Insofar as the philosopher thinks with honesty and integrity, revelation is not a *deus ex machina* that stops the conversation. It introduces new questions and deepens the philosophical sense of wonder and mystery.

* * *

By entering into these philosophical reflections on matters of faith, one enters into the open discussion of the philosophical community. Philosophical discourse proceeds in a space of *relative autonomy,* such that its conclusions are not dictated by external determinations. Christian thinkers need to respect the *autonomy* of philosophy and relinquish the urge for a sort of theological imperialism that would overthrow the freedom of philosophy. At the same time, philosophers must recognize that the autonomy of philosophy is *relative* rather than absolute. Philosophical rationality is not self-grounding and it cannot absolve itself of all external influence. The philosophical community is constituted through the activity of philosophical discourse, but this is not an absolute, self-founding act. Instead, this act involves a receptive appropriation of a particular tradition, which passes down the texts, thinkers, and problems that shape and guide the course of philosophical debate. These philosophical traditions are not self-contained, since they receive direction from historical, cultural, social, and political factors and are nourished by religious, literary, and scientific sources. Since there is no purely philosophical realm, its autonomy will always be relative rather than absolute. In sum, there is no neutral *Nullpunkt* from which philosophical reflection begins. This has become a widely accepted axiom in contemporary philosophy, but despite the widespread recognition that thinking cannot rid itself of prejudgments, there remains a persistent assumption (in Gadamer's terms, a prejudice against prejudice) that philosophical reason must be secular. Yet advocates of autonomous, secular reason tend to have a selective memory, allowing them to maintain the illusion of theological neutrality by forgetting that their presuppositions draw from theological sources and that their conclusions are often theologically significant.

In order to be consistently hermeneutical, philosophy needs to allow Christian thinking to proceed within this space of relative autonomy. Yet if it is necessary to challenge the presumptuousness of secular reason, this is not to make room for a triumphant Christian system, but to allow for another instance of faith seeking understanding. This form of thinking recognizes its vulnerability and that it has no privileged status. Yet it also seeks to be faithful to its calling as cruciform philosophy: namely, to think through the philosophical implications of faith. In the case of this book, this is a matter of articulating a cruciform philosophy of the faithful self.

Persons, Selves, and Human Beings

Finally, I should make a brief comment regarding the terminology of our discussion. A multitude of terms arise when discussing the human being: "self," "person," "subject," "ego," "I," "spirit," "soul." There are significant convergences but also important differences between these terms, and all of this is complicated by the fact that different thinkers tend to use these terms in different ways. It would likely prove impossible to provide clear and distinct definitions for each of these terms, so I will not try to define all these terms against each other.

That said, each term offers its own advantages and disadvantages. There is a strong case to be made that "person" is the most promising term for a philosophical anthropology. In his essay "Approaching the Human Person," Ricoeur argues that "person" continues to be "the most appropriate term to designate those investigations for which neither the term 'consciousness', nor 'subject', nor 'individual' really apply."[43] None of these terms has the semantic richness to address the multiple layers that constitute a hermeneutic phenomenology of the person, such as the human capacities for language, action, narrative, and responsibility.[44] Furthermore, by framing a philosophical anthropology in terms of personhood, we locate ourselves in a long tradition of theological reflection, stemming from debates over the three persons of the Trinity. Indeed, John Zizioulas argues that the concept of personhood is a distinctly Christian contribution to the history of thought.[45] The Cappadocian Fathers, Boethius, Aquinas, and other medieval thinkers have debated the concept of the person, and a number of contemporary thinkers take this approach to philosophical anthropology, including John Macmurray,[46] Robert Spaemann,[47] and Robert Sokolowski.[48] Moreover, Bonhoeffer's first work, *Sanctorum Communio*, draws heavily on personalist philosophy. Would it be better, then, to orient our discussion around the concept of personhood rather than selfhood?

I will not make a sharp distinction between person and self, and many of my arguments could be framed in terms of personhood. We see a similar flexibility in Ricoeur, who describes human personhood in terms of the capacity for language, action, narration, and responsibility—precisely the capacities he uses to describe the self in *Oneself as Another* and the capable human being in *The Course of Recognition*. As we read a variety of authors and enter a variety of debates, it will be wise to allow a degree of interchangeability between the terms "self," "person," and "human being." Nevertheless, I will focus primarily on the theme of selfhood. First of all, this term has great currency in our contemporary cultural context and as such demands careful and critical evaluation. The notion of a "self" is contested both philosophically and theologically, and there are good reasons to be wary of discourse that centers on the self. "Self" is an unfortunate term because it bears the stigma of the self-help movement and other excesses of late modern therapeutic culture. But instead of discarding the concept, we need to critique it and preserve that which is worth preserving. For example, the term "self" deserves a critical affirmation because it indicates reflexive awareness in a way that other terms do not.[49] The status of self-reflexivity and self-consciousness is a major point of contention in philosophy and theology alike, due in no small part to disillusionment with the exalted claims of self-consciousness in its Cartesian and idealist forms. But one of our tasks will be to determine if there is a legitimate place for self-reflexivity in the life of the human being, and in particular in the life of faith.

* * *

It might also seem that the term "human being" is appropriate for a project of philosophical anthropology, but this term too has its problems. In his "Letter on Humanism" Heidegger argues that we cannot determine what the human being *is* without first thinking through the meaning of this "*is*," and so projects like humanism and philosophical anthropology must be deferred in the interest of thinking Being.[50] This is why Heidegger does not use terms like "man" or "humanity," but instead speaks of *Dasein* to characterize the distinct manner of our being-there as existence. Heidegger's complaint is that philosophical talk about man, or the human being, has already been placed in preconceived categories, e.g. the Aristotelian notion of the rational animal, or the biblical notion of the human created in the image of God. The interpretation of Dasein then proceeds within "a closed context of experience," since we have already subscribed to a certain way of seeing the sort of being that we are.[51] This is also Heidegger's reason for deferring investigations of ethics and theology: we need to think Being before we can give anything else its due.

Heidegger is right to challenge the tendency toward facile statements regarding human nature or essence, and it is true that doctrinaire faith and theological dogmatism can bias our investigation of the human being. Our questioning cannot be truly serious when we prevent ourselves from accessing the genuine questionableness of the human being. Moreover, the self-understanding of faith is also easily distorted because of tacit metaphysical assumptions. One of the best examples of this is the Cartesian lenses through which modern believers so often interpret themselves and their faith. Heidegger's analytic of Dasein in *Being and Time* is a powerful resource to break these lenses and show how they distort our interpretation of our being in the world.

Although Heidegger's expressed desire for radical philosophical openness is admirable, there remains a question of how serious he really is about this openness. It is vital to our discussion that we too allow ourselves to be surprised or even startled by the radical challenge that the cross poses to our preconceived notions of human being. In chapter 3 we will see that it certainly does challenge our metaphysical assumptions about human being; this will be evident in our discussion of Luther. Heidegger saw the radical philosophical implications of Luther's *theologia crucis* and drew considerable inspiration from Luther for his early efforts at a *Destruktion* of the history of metaphysics. However, we will see that Heidegger does not remain open to the full radicality of the cross, instead taking it as an ontic model of a more fundamental ontological insight. This is in keeping with Heidegger's attempt to maintain a methodological atheism: what purports to be a gesture of open questioning is also an arbitrary closure to certain possibilities. We will discuss this further in chapter 5, where it becomes clear that I do not share all of Heidegger's reasons for challenging the project of philosophical anthropology.

I do, however, have other reservations regarding the project of a philosophical anthropology. Following such thinkers as Augustine,[52] Bernard of Clairvaux,[53] Luther,[54] and Calvin,[55] I will maintain that we cannot truly understand ourselves apart from the relation to God. Knowledge of God and knowledge of the self are inseparable. But if true self-understanding of the self depends on true understanding of God, then we must also conclude that true knowledge of the self proceeds by way of the cross, since it is only through the cross that we know God. This is why Luther's *Heidelberg Disputation* argues for the *theologia crucis*, against the *theologia gloriae* that seeks to know God through metaphysical contemplation and establish itself before God through meritorious activity. Analogously, our *anthropologia crucis* opposes the *anthropologia gloriae*, which would seek self-understanding apart from the cross (through an act of self-reflective intuition or spiritual inwardness) or that seeks to constitute itself through self-creative or self-constituting acts. Instead, self-understanding comes through the word of the cross.

What does the word of the cross disclose about the self? The cross is God's *No*—his negative judgment on the sinful, self-constituting human being, but also God's ultimate *Yes* insofar as this is the locus of God's saving love and grace. Moreover, according to Luther the theologian of the cross believes that God is hidden and only knowable through the cross. Analogously, the philosophical anthropologist of the cross believes that the truth about the self is eschatologically hidden and is only known (in faith and hope) through the word of the cross.

The truth that the self can know about itself is not a system of speculative, objective statements about the self or the human being in general. Instead, as Kierkegaard argues so convincingly, the truth of faith is a truth known subjectively; it is truth that can only be known by living it, participating in it existentially rather than merely cognitively. Hence his claim that the Delphic imperative to "know thyself" (*gnothi seauton*) needs to be distinguished from the airy self-consciousness of idealism and reinterpreted "as the Greeks would have understood it if they had possessed Christian presuppositions" (CA 79). As I noted above, one such presupposition is the word of the cross. To this I will add another, which has been well expressed in Bonhoeffer's description of the new humanity, which Christ embodies and inaugurates through the incarnation, crucifixion, and resurrection. Or in the words of Anti-Climacus, another Kierkegaardian pseudonym: "Out of love, God becomes man. He says: Here you see what it is to be a human being. . . . Look this way, he says, and know for certain what it is to be a human being" (SUD 127–28). Following the logic of these claims I will argue that philosophical anthropology is incomplete in itself, not simply for want of a new ontology (contra Heidegger), but because it needs Christology. For it is not ontology that is fundamental, but the word of the crucified Christ. In order to make sense of this claim, however, we will need to enter into the main body of our discussion.

Part One

2   The Hermeneutics of the Self

In Book XI of his *Confessions,* Augustine records his perplexity over the nature of time. What is it? We talk about it all the time in our everyday conversations, as if we know what it is. "What then is time? Provided that no one asks me, I know. If I want to explain it to an inquirer, I do not know."[1] Something similar is true about the self: in late modern Western culture, we talk about selves—and "the self"—all the time. In the natural attitude the idea of the self seems fairly unproblematic, yet if we stop and ask what the self is, we find ourselves at a loss. What then is the self? What *is* it? The question at hand is ontological: what sort of being is the self?

First, we must recognize that the notion of *a* self or *the* self has not always been part of the philosophical tradition. Charles Taylor observes that when ancient philosophers cited the Delphic admonition to "know thyself" (*gnothi seauton*), they did not assume a robust conception of this self as an entity, as *ho autos.* By using reflexive pronouns and verbs we are able to designate self-reference in thoughts and actions, but it is another matter to speak of the self as a noun.[2] That is a modern innovation,[3] and there is no consensus that it is a sign of progress. The modern concept of the self has a strong chorus of critics, whose objections are familiar: the modern self is shaped by false ideals regarding knowledge and ethics; it purports to ground itself through its act of self-reflection; it reifies itself as a substantial thing, a *subjectum* that supposedly remains self-identical through time and its relations to exteriority. As a result, the modern picture of the self is an egocentric, isolated, ahistorical, disembodied, and disengaged thinking subject. These objections have been repeated many times, to the point that critique often verges on caricature, but there are nevertheless good philosophical and theological reasons to be suspicious of the modern concept of the self. This concept distorts our understanding of the human being and its relations—to God, other humans, the natural world, and itself. Critique is therefore necessary, and in subsequent chapters I will show how the cross provides a critique of—and in a certain sense even *destroys*—the self. However, the best way to correct the modern metaphysics of subjectivity is not to discard the notion of the self altogether, but to reorient our inquiry as a *hermeneutics of the self.*

In order to provide some preliminary orientation for subsequent chapters, this chapter will sketch out the basic features of a hermeneutics of the self. Although we cannot conduct a full-length introduction to hermeneutics here, some preliminary discussion will help us locate ourselves. It will also provide us with a working definition of the self. This will not be a comprehensive inventory of attributes or faculties, but an outline of some contested features of the self, such as reflexivity and self-understanding, self-interpretation, responsibility, recognition, and human capability. I will focus on these themes because these are the features of the self that we will interrogate through the word of the cross.

Reflexivity and the Hermeneutical Self

What makes philosophical reflection on the self *hermeneutical*? Traditionally hermeneutics involved the interpretation of texts (particularly biblical and legal texts), but the hermeneutical turn in philosophy brought with it a greater awareness that interpretation pertains not only to written texts but to all meaningful phenomena, including the human self. According to Heidegger, hermeneutics is not first and foremost a doctrine or theory of interpretation, but the self-interpretation of concrete, factical existence. Hermeneutics is concerned with Dasein (the distinctly human way of being), which "has its being as something capable of interpretation and in need of interpretation and that to be in some state of having-been-interpreted belongs to its being."[4] Our being is such that we find ourselves already interpreted, in such a way that our being calls for further interpretation and greater self-understanding. Such is our task in working out the hermeneutics of the cruciform self: we are seeking to encounter, grasp, and express the self-understanding of the faithful self, to lay out the meanings that constitute this self in concrete, lived experience.[5]

Pursued in this way, the hermeneutics of the self is a quest for self-understanding. As Heidegger puts it, hermeneutics develops for Dasein "a possibility of its becoming and being for itself in the manner of an *understanding* of itself." As a possibility of the human being *for itself* (*für sich*), the hermeneutics of the self marks a significant development within the tradition of reflexive philosophy. Reflexive philosophy has a distinguished legacy, initiated by Descartes's reflections on the cogito, passed on through Kant's deduction of the transcendental unity of apperception, variously formulated by post-Kantian accounts of subjectivity (e.g., the absolute idealism of Fichte's *Ich*, Hegel's system of speculative idealism and the science of absolute *Geist*) and the transcendental ego in Husserl's phenomenology. As Ricoeur explains, reflexive philosophy examines the problems and possibilities of self-knowledge, along with the status of the reflexive subject in acts of knowing, willing, evaluation, etc. "Reflexion is that act of turning back upon itself by which a subject grasps, in a moment of intellectual clarity and moral responsibility, the unifying principle of the operations among which it is dispersed and forgets itself as subject."[6] At its most radical, reflexive philosophy aspires to "absolute transparency, a perfect coincidence of the self with itself."[7] Once achieved, this absolute and indubitable self-consciousness would then provide the foundation and unifying center for all possible knowledge. The reflexive self would be fully assured in its intellectual operations, and meaning would be cleansed of any residual opacity. Things would have meaning because I have constituted their meaning, and only in this way are they meaningful for me, the thinking subject. If things "make sense," it is because I have made them make sense by organizing them according to my own categories and concepts. Moreover, this subject is self-grounding, since it is the source and determination of all available meaning. There is no meaning that precedes the subject that it cannot retrieve, and there is no meaning that it might encounter that it does not constitute for itself. In short, if there is meaning it is because the object has been grasped and organized by the thinking subject. This is true not only of its experience of the external world, but for self-understanding as well. Self-understanding is self-mediating. Even when the self encounters external perspectives on itself, the reflecting self always appropriates the meaning of these experiences through its own mediation.

The hermeneutical turn marks an important change in the project of reflexive philosophy, insofar as it dethrones this sovereign thinking subject by showing that its exalted claims to self-knowledge are a ruse rather than a rightful authority. Self-reflection does not provide the self with transparent intuitive access to itself; instead, all self-reflection is self-*interpretation,* and thus we can only speak of self-knowledge in the form of hermeneutical self-understanding. But in order for these claims to be more than sheer assertion, I must explain how we reach them.

The Cogito: Exalted, Shattered, *or* Wounded?

Reflexivity denotes the capacity to refer to oneself, to reflect on oneself, to take responsibility for oneself, and to act upon oneself. These reflexive acts are basic features of selfhood, but as with the notion of the self, the possibilities and limits of reflexivity are highly contested in philosophical and theological discourse. According to critics, the modern emphasis on reflexivity has severely distorted our understanding of human existence, deepening our egocentricity and nurturing the illusion of a self-transparent, self-grounding knowing subject who is also an autonomous lawgiver and self-sufficient moral agent. The most radical expressions of this self have evoked equally radical criticism, to the point of rejecting the ideas of reflexivity and the self altogether.

We find one such critique in Nietzsche's essay *On Truth and Lie in an Extra-Moral Sense.* In a characteristically strident passage, Nietzsche rails against the vanity of human self-reflection:

> What, indeed, does man know of himself! Can he even once perceive himself completely, laid out as if in an illuminated glass case? Does not nature keep much the most from him, even about his body, to spellbind and confine him in a proud, deceptive consciousness, far from the coils of the intestines, the quick current of the blood stream, and the involved tremors of the fibers? She threw away the key; and woe to the calamitous curiosity which might peer just once through a crack in the chamber of consciousness and look down, and sense that man rests upon the merciless, the

greedy, the insatiable, the murderous, in the indifference of his ignorance—hanging in dreams, as it were, upon the back of a tiger. In view of this, whence in all the world comes the urge for truth?[8]

The cogito flatters itself that it can gain a transparent view of itself, that it can set itself on display for reflection, but this self-consciousness is actually self-deception. The human being is an animal who has cultivated the illusions of culture and civilization, but the bestial nature remains, and the bestial is what actually underlies the cogito. Freud will later challenge the cogito along similar lines with his theory of the unconscious.

No doubt there are dangers in the critical interpretation of consciousness that we find in Nietzsche and Freud, particularly if the critique reduces consciousness to a vitalistic power or animal impulses. But Ricoeur argues that while we need not draw the same ultimate conclusions as Nietzsche or Freud, we must confront their critique of the cogito honestly rather than seeking to evade it. Nietzsche and Freud are two key figures who represent, along with Marx and to some extent Feuerbach, what Ricoeur calls the "hermeneutics of suspicion." Individually their respective critiques are often narrow and reductive, but their significance lies in the way they expose false consciousness. As a group, these masters of suspicion embody a general hermeneutic of demystification.[9] This hermeneutic of suspicion originally targeted religious discourse (as each of these critics mounts a severe attack on religion), but it has broader implications as a general critique of the cogito and its delusions of absoluteness and self-transparency.

Ricoeur often speaks of the masters of suspicion collectively, but in *Oneself as Another* he suggests that Nietzsche is the culmination of anti-Cartesian critique and is therefore Descartes's "privileged adversary." Whereas Descartes and the reflexive tradition "exalted" the cogito, Nietzsche "shattered" and "humiliated" it (OA 11–16). In the passage quoted above, Nietzsche poses his challenge: In light of humanity's bestial nature, what accounts for the supposed desire for truth? Nietzsche answers his own question through an examination of language and the formation of concepts. On his account, concepts are forged in dishonesty, being "arbitrary abstractions" that equate what is unequal.[10] Likewise, truth is not the correspondence between sign and reality, because "reality" is only a matter of conventions that we fit to our preferences.[11] "Truth" is therefore merely the obligation to lie according to these conventions.[12] There is no factual reality beyond these conventions, no thing in itself. There are no facts, only interpretations.

For Nietzsche, this phenomenalism obtains in the inner world as much as the outer.[13] There are no "facts of consciousness," but only appearances. As Ricoeur observes, Nietzsche undermines the Cartesian solace of an inner chamber of consciousness that is distinct from the outer. Furthermore, the unified activity of "thinking" is a fiction, since it is interwoven with "the bristling multiplicity of instincts." Finally, thinking does not originate with *res cogitans*. There is no substratum or subject; the assumption of a substantial "I" is merely a habit of grammar—i.e., the habit of attaching an agent to every action, a subject to every verb.[14] Or as Nietzsche contends elsewhere, "there is no 'being' behind doing," no doer behind the deed: "the deed is everything."[15] This actualism is the heart of Nietzsche's attempt to destroy the notion of the substantial self.

In the aftermath of Nietzsche's violent assault, the cogito lies in critical condition. We cannot in good faith dodge or disregard Nietzsche's critique, because he rightly undoes the illusion that reflection can gain immediate access to the self. Our access to the self is always mediated, and is therefore a matter of interpretation rather than positivistic inquiry.[16] Nietzsche's critique provides a forceful push toward a hermeneutics of the self. Moreover, his suspicion is a necessary reminder of the prevalence of self-deception. It is often in one's own interest to interpret oneself falsely.[17] Thus Ricoeur argues that self-interpretation must take a necessary detour through suspicion. But it must not conclude its quest there. For Ricoeur, the challenge is to remove the exalted cogito from its absolute status, yet without allowing suspicion to become an all-consuming abyss. The excesses of reflexive philosophy do not warrant a total rejection of the reflexive self; or as Ricoeur puts it, the false exaltation of the cogito does not require the total shattering of the cogito. Instead, Ricoeur seeks out a middle path, which leads toward a hermeneutics of the "wounded cogito."

What sort of self-understanding is possible for the wounded cogito? Not a transparent self-consciousness, but also not an abyssal lack of meaning. If suspicion is not the last word, the self must be able to speak of itself and its capabilities with a modicum of confidence. Ricoeur designates this affirmation as *attestation*, which is not a declaration of certainty but a gesture of trust. Attestation of self is a matter of identifying oneself, of recognizing who one is, and of taking responsibility for oneself (I am the one who did *x*; I am the one who will keep my promise to do *y* for *z*). Attestation also includes the assurance of oneself as a capable human being: I can speak and designate myself as a self; I can act and bring about changes in the world; I can narrate my story and the story of my community; I can take responsibility for myself, impute myself as the agent of my acts, and respond to the call to live well with and for others in just institutions.[18]

This attestation is not a weak form of theoretical knowledge; rather, it is the lived assurance of the *I can* in its engagements in the world. Here Ricoeur takes an important cue from Maurice Merleau-Ponty's *Phenomenology of Perception*, which contrasts the "I can" with the "I think."[19] The "I think" is the *cogito* of the modern epistemological tradition; it is a subject that relates to the external world through mental representations; it is a disengaged consciousness, registering its experience as a spectator prior to its practical engagement in the world. By contrast, the "I can" finds itself already engaged in practical activity, inhabiting and participating in the world.[20] This engagement, Merleau-Ponty argues, is a thoroughly embodied affair. Whereas the "I think" is a disembodied consciousness, the "I can" is an embodied agent. On this point Nietzsche's critique of Cartesian dualism is apt: the body is not merely an instrument the cogito uses to gather data, because in Gabriel Marcel's terms, I *am* my body, and it is *as* body that I am in the world and engage that which is other than myself.[21] This emphasis on the primacy of engaged, embodied agency in the world will prove to be a vital feature of the hermeneutical turn.

Being in the Lebenswelt

According to Ricoeur, the shift away from idealism and toward hermeneutics was something Husserlian phenomenology could not withstand. In his most idealist moments,[22] Husserl ambitiously pursued the goal of installing the transcendental ego as the origin and unifying center of meaning. The ego actively constitutes the meaning of phenomena, but Husserl was constantly compelled to recognize greater degrees of passivity in the synthesizing work of the ego, such that phenomenology became "caught up in an infinite movement of 'backward questioning' in which its project of radical self-grounding fades away." This backward sliding eventually led to Husserl's recognition of the lifeworld (*Lebenswelt*) as a horizon of immediacy that reflection can never quite reach.[23] The *Lebenswelt* is that primordial, concrete world of givenness from which all reflection arises.[24] Husserl wanted to conduct a transcendental reduction of the *Lebenswelt* so that transcendental subjectivity could discern its *a priori* essential forms,[25] but Ricoeur argues that transcendental subjectivity could never retrieve the *Lebenswelt* and bring it fully into view. And yet the transcendental ego must continue to presuppose this horizon. Given this perpetual frustration of phenomenology's ambitions, Ricoeur describes the *Lebenswelt* as "phenomenology's paradise lost."[26]

By contrast, for Heidegger and post-Heideggerian phenomenology the *Lebenswelt* is not an incomprehensible remainder but a "prior condition" of meaning. We find ourselves thrown into a world, already belonging to it and participating in it. Heidegger describes this in terms of Dasein's *being-in-the-world*, while Ricoeur describes it as a "participatory belonging" to the world.[27] This means that Dasein's most basic interaction with the world is not a "bare perceptual cognition" but understanding (*Verstehen*) (BT 95). Dasein finds the world as already meaningful prior to any intellectual activity of constituting the meaning of things.[28] "Meaning" here is not primarily a question of the semantic content of propositions; rather, the world is meaningful because it matters to Dasein, because it is "non-indifferent."[29] Dasein's world is meaningful, then, because of the totality of its involvements therein (BT 116). Dasein cares about its projects and thus understanding does not originally consist in intellectual grasping but in Dasein's practical engagements in the world. The very structure of Dasein's being-in-the-world, then, is one of understanding.

Dasein understands its being-in-the-world through engaged practical activity, and for this reason Dasein understands the world in terms of its possibilities, its capabilities, its *ability to be* (BT 184). Dasein exists not merely in the here and now of the present, but ahead of itself in its future projects, so particular beings are meaningful because of the way they disclose themselves within the horizon of Dasein's projects. Dasein never encounters naked entities, but rather equipment (*das Zeug*), which it takes along in its work (BT 101). A hammer, for example, is meaningful when I am trying to set up a tent or hang a picture on the wall. Michael Polanyi describes this relation to tools as *indwelling*: "We pour ourselves out into them and assimilate them as parts of our own existence."[30] Our relation with being is therefore one of participation and belonging.

On the basis of this primordial understanding we are able to develop more explicit thematic interpretations of that which we understand. Interpretation (*Auslegung*) is this subsequent task of appropriating and working out one's ontological understanding. Ontological understanding is the more primordial prior condition for interpretation—and likewise for any other intellectual relation, such as assertion and predication.[31] In Heidegger's terminology, understanding provides the fore-structure that we bring to any interpretive venture.[32] Gadamer later describes this fore-structure in terms of *prejudice*. Contrary to the Enlightenment's "prejudice against prejudice," Gadamer shows that prejudice—i.e., prejudgment—is a necessary condition of all understanding.[33] We do not enter into interpretation with a view from nowhere; indeed, we *cannot* interpret in this way. Our prejudgments give us a way into the hermeneutical circle. Moreover, it is crucial to recognize that the hermeneutical circle is productive, that it is a virtuous rather than vicious circle.[34] Thus when we encounter something that is genuinely other than ourselves, interpretation does not simply reinforce our prejudices. The question we will need to confront later, however, is whether the hermeneutical circle actually allows us to encounter that which is genuinely *other*.

Textuality and Selfhood

Once phenomenology began to recognize the importance of this participatory belonging to the world, the path was open for the hermeneutical turn. Philosophical anthropology cannot begin with the transcendental ego, but must take the form of a hermeneutics of the self. There are two important aspects to observe in this hermeneutical turn. First, the self is not known through immediate intuition, but is instead analogous to a text calling for interpretation. Second, self-understanding is only possible indirectly, through the encounter with others. "Self-understanding," writes Hans-Georg Gadamer, "always occurs through understanding something other than the self, and includes the unity and integrity of the other."[35] If self-understanding is only possible through the encounter with otherness, then the interpretive constitution of the self is not the act of an absolute ego, a *Sinngeber*, or a sovereign interpreter ruling over an "empire of sense."[36] Instead, self-understanding requires that we interpret the meanings that precede the self and make understanding possible by giving figurative shape to one's experience and action. The self can only constitute meaning because meaning is already given to it. The self is always spoken before it speaks. Self-understanding is not self-constituted; on the contrary, it is constituted by a prior word, by an address that precedes its activity.

There is no direct route to self-understanding. Self-understanding occurs indirectly, through the mediation of otherness. As Ricoeur was fond of saying, the shortest path from the self to itself is through the other.[37] This other might be another human being, it might be God, or it might be a text. Ricoeur's point is that the self is able to understand itself and its projects—experiences, memories, hopes, feelings, thoughts, actions, etc.—because of the mediation of discourse. "What would we know of love and hatred—and, in general of the feelings and the values which support the Self—if they had not been brought to language and articulated by works of art and discourse?"[38] One finds a similar insight in Gadamer, but whereas Gadamer primarily emphasizes works of art and classic texts, Ricoeur's particular contribution to this hermeneutical principle is to illuminate the indispensable role of figurative discourse (signs, symbols, metaphors, myths, and narratives) in self-understanding.[39] Because self-understanding is not directly accessible in literal discourse, we must reckon with the figurative discourse that constitutes the self and its projects as meaningful.

Ricoeur explains that self-understanding is mediated by *signs* because all human experience is articulated linguistically; language "is the primary condition of all human experience."[40] Further, self-understanding is mediated by *symbols*. Like any sign, the symbol conveys meaning, but it does so via a double meaning and a double intentionality, taking a direct or literal reference and using it to point to another phenomenon *indirectly* (SE 15). This indirect, "second-order" reference[41] gives us access to phenomena that are inaccessible through direct or literal discourse. One example is the experience of sin and evil, a theme Ricoeur examined in great detail. The experience of sin and evil involves a persistent and troubling opacity that resists any attempt at direct or literal communication. Symbols like stain, defilement, guilt, and incurvature (the image I discuss in chapter 4) give voice to these phenomena and are therefore indispensable to understanding these dark aspects of the self. These symbolic meanings are not the achievement of a solitary thinker or speaker, but are given to consciousness through the mediation of culture.[42] They give a horizon within which understanding is possible.

The hermeneutics of symbols marks an important development in Ricoeur's thought, but he later recognized that hermeneutics must expand to include the mediation of *texts* as well. Hermeneutics cannot limit itself to interpreting signs and symbols on their own; it must also confront the broader textual context within which signs and symbols are meaningful.[43] Consequently, Ricoeur later expanded his analysis of metaphor to consider narrative.[44] With metaphor, the locus of semantic innovation (i.e., the creation of meaning) is a single sentence, but with narrative the innovation occurs at the level of the plot.[45] This insight greatly expands Ricoeur's account of self-understanding by showing that human experience needs to be narrated in order to be understood. What Ricoeur calls "emplotment" allows the self to organize the temporal flux of human experience—i.e., characters, events, actions, motives, consequences, goals, hopes, etc.—into a coherent whole. The interpretive work of self-narration is therefore an essential component of self-understanding.

But narration is not the act of a sovereign narrating ego. I am capable of configuring my own story because I already understand other stories, which have given me a sense of how people, actions, and consequences work. With this tacit grasp of narrative sense, I find my experiences are *pre*figured in such a way that they call out for narrative interpretation. Self-understanding is narrative in form, and the work of narration always takes place in relation to the stories that precede me,[46] making it a thoroughly intertextual affair. Through my encounter with other texts, I understand myself differently—not only in terms of past and present circumstance, but also regarding my future. Through the work of narrative *con*figuration, I find myself and my being-in-the-world *re*figured. Ricoeur describes it thus: "To understand oneself is to understand oneself as one confronts the text and to receive from it the conditions for a self other than that which first undertakes the reading."[47] The text discloses a new world: new possibilities, new meaning, and new ways of being-in-the-world open up in front of the text. A hermeneutics of the self is therefore obligated to examine the way self-understanding is figured by the texts—whether fictional, historical, mythical, or biographical—that have informed the world of the self.

In sum, the self finds itself already located in a meaningful world, which is possible because of figurative discourse. Through its ongoing encounters with the otherness of texts, the self is transformed; its being-in-the-world is refigured. And just as the self cannot dispense with these figures and see itself transparently, neither can it get behind these symbols in order to render them transparent. "A hermeneutical philosophy is a philosophy that accepts all the demands of this long detour and that gives up the dream of a total mediation, at the end of which reflection would once again amount to intellectual intuition in the transparence to itself of an absolute subject."[48] But in giving up this dream, the hermeneutics of the self nevertheless wagers that a certain self-understanding is still possible, even though it will always retain some degree of opacity.

The hermeneutical detour through figurative discourse is not, however, a rejection of self-reflexivity. This detour actually gives the possibility for deeper, richer reflection. This is the insight of Ricoeur's famous motto: "the symbol gives rise to thought" (*Le symbole donne à penser*). This motto arose during Ricoeur's early work on symbols, but it could easily be updated to reflect the expansion of his investigations: the metaphor gives rise to thought; the text gives rise to thought; the narrative gives rise to thought. These figures of understanding make a positive contribution to reflection because they offer a surplus of meaning, always giving more than we can grasp conceptually. Rather than trying to begin in an artificial (and impossible) state devoid of presuppositions, hermeneutical reflection deliberately begins in the ontological plenitude of human understanding. This means beginning with the fullness of the speech, symbols, and narratives that figure our self-understanding. By beginning in this way, philosophical reflection avails itself of inexhaustible sources of reflection and greater possibilities of self-understanding.[49]

By approaching our philosophical anthropology of the cross as a hermeneutics of the self, our task will therefore be to examine how the word of the cross figures the self-understanding of faith and reconstitutes one's being in the world. However, a vital question we must confront is whether this semantic refiguration can sufficiently account for the transformative power of the cross and resurrection. That is our topic in chapter 10.

Hermeneutics and Religious Selfhood

Thus far our story will be familiar to those versed in the history of phenomenology and hermeneutics. But the tradition of philosophical hermeneutics has tended to ignore the *theological* contribution to these developments. As Jens Zimmermann observes, philosophical histories of hermeneutics tend to credit Heidegger for undermining the subjectivism of modernist hermeneutics while overlooking Karl Barth's full-scale assault in *The Epistle to the Romans*.[50] Ricoeur is an exception to this oversight, however, since he acknowledges Barth's critique of the sovereign reflecting self, crediting Barth for first teaching him "that the subject is not a centralizing master but rather a disciple or auditor of a language larger than itself."[51] Barth's Romans commentary abounds with striking rhetoric about the radical otherness of God, revelation as *Krisis*, as an interruption that shatters present reality, and the gospel as "the signal, the fire-alarm of a coming, new world."[52] This radical language is typical of Barth's critique of nineteenth-century liberal Protestant thought. In contrast to the latter's preoccupation with religious consciousness, biblical hermeneutics is not an investigation of religious, idealist, or Romantic subjectivity. Yet at the same time, and in contrast to the assumed priority of historical-critical inquiry, biblical hermeneutics is not an objectivist inquiry into a world behind the text. The subject matter (*die Sache*) of biblical hermeneutics is the living word of God, which tells of a new, eschatological world that interrupts our present world.[53] The "strange new world within the Bible" does not simply confirm what we already know, and it does not lie dormant, simply waiting to answer questions. It poses questions in return, such that the interrogating subject finds herself put into question,[54] and the reader finds that the text is reading her.

To interpret well is to participate in the *Sache* of the text, to inhabit and think through the world of the text. In this regard, Barth argues that what is true of the word of God is also true of the human word: in order to understand any text—whether it is the Bible, Lao Tse, or Goethe—one must learn to "consider well"[55] by submitting to the text and allowing it to "lay hold" of oneself rather than trying to control it.[56] Thus a sort of hermeneutical *metanoia* takes place in the life of the subject, with the *master* of the text becoming the *disciple* of the text. Ricoeur takes up this theme of conversion from Barth and makes it a centerpiece of his hermeneutics: the *moi* (the sovereign master of meaning) is transformed into the *soi* (the *disciple* of the text).[57]

With this insight, Ricoeur's philosophical hermeneutics takes a vital cue from biblical hermeneutics—a move that results in considerable ambiguity in his work. If the transformation from *moi* to *soi* obtains as a general philosophical principle for all interpretive activity, it remains to be determined whether Christian conversion is a unique phenomenon or a particular instance of a general model of *metanoia*—whether as a hermeneutical conversion or a moral regeneration. We will return to this question in chapter 10, when we examine Ricoeur's account of religious transformation.

On Self-Interpretation

Human beings are "self-interpreting animals." With this felicitous phrase, Charles Taylor summarizes the hermeneutical conception of the self developed by Heidegger, Gadamer, and Ricoeur.[58] One of Taylor's central premises in this definition is that self-interpretation is ontologically constitutive of selfhood. We become selves through self-interpretation. This is a counterintuitive claim, because we tend to take selfhood for granted, as though we are selves simply by virtue of being *Homo sapiens*. How could I possibly fail to be a self? As Taylor observes, we are accustomed to thinking about the self as something we have in the same way as we have hearts and livers—i.e., as an interpretation-free given.[59]

But if the self is not an interpretation-free given, what does self-interpretation involve? It might suggest a sort of introspective inventory, in which I reflect on myself and catalogue what I find: preferences, commitments, hopes, and fears. This sort of reflection is indeed interpretive, but the hermeneutical model of selfhood involves a more fundamental mode of self-interpretation. According to Taylor, self-interpretation is a matter of evaluative judgment. He distinguishes between *weak* and *strong* forms of evaluation. Weak evaluation includes relatively unreflective judgments regarding such things as the appealing smell of food, the comfort of one's bed, and the dangerous appearance of a wild dog; it can also include more reflective calculations about how I might get some of that food, how to stay in bed as long as possible without being late, and how best to avoid the threatening dog.[60] But however reflective these evaluations might be, they are not self-reflexive in the way that strong evaluation is. Strong evaluation is a *second-order* evaluation in which I evaluate my evaluations. I do not simply evaluate objects in light of my desires and aversions; I evaluate my desires and aversions themselves.[61] I am ashamed when I see greediness or cowardice in myself, just as I value courage and generosity as traits I ought to exhibit. I evaluate these desires according to a sense of the self I *should be*. Through this evaluation the self takes responsibility for itself; it recognizes that it is responsible or answerable to some standard of strong evaluation.

In strong evaluation, I judge my desires and actions according to categories of higher and lower, virtuous and vicious, noble and base, etc.[62] These judgments take place within a horizon of significance, within which I discern that which is good, meaningful, and valuable.[63] But these judgments are not fact-free values; they are *ontological* claims about the way reality is. This horizon gives me an understanding of what it is to be human and what human flourishing looks like; it provides me a vision of the good life, and it shows me the sort of person I should be. Taylor also describes this as a "moral topography," since it is a set of coordinates that locate the self and orient it within the world.[64] In the activity of strong evaluation, we map out our location in moral space, thereby interpreting who we are.[65]

If human beings are self-interpreting animals, this self-interpretation is fundamentally linguistic. Language is not simply a representation of the self and its ontological identity (an ostensive "*This* is who I am"); language reaches deeper, playing a vital role in the very constitution of this identity. Thus Taylor writes that "certain ways of being, of feeling, of relating to each other are only possible given certain linguistic resources." Taylor illustrates this point with the example of someone living a monastic existence: "Without a certain articulation of oneself and of the highest, it is neither possible to *be* a Christian ascetic, nor to *feel* that combination of one's own lack of worth and high calling (the 'grandeur et misère' of Pascal), not to be *part* of, say, a monastic order."[66] In order to live this monastic existence, the self must undergo a transformation of self-understanding. The self starts to undertake disciplines and practices that are meaningful because they are located within a horizon of significance, and this horizon is articulated through linguistic and conceptual resources that have been passed down through the tradition of the order. The self thereby acquires a new grammar of existing. What is true of the monastic life is also true of other forms of life that are passed on communally through social practices and traditions. As a result, self-understanding is not an isolated, individual phenomenon. Who *I* am is vitally shaped by who *we* are, and how we *do* things around here.

Along with the constitutive role of social practice, narrative is also vital to the identity of the self.[67] But the narrative identity of the self is not simply a private story; it is also the larger story in which the self finds itself. It is a story that tells not only my story, but the story of how we have become who we are, and where we are going.[68] Narration occurs, then, against the backdrop of a horizon of significance. Moreover, this narration takes place dialogically. In giving an account of myself, I am accountable to others whose narratives interweave with mine. Granted, it is possible to write an autobiography in isolation, but monological self-narration too easily tends toward pathology because it is cut off from responsibility to others. As such, I can tell the story to suit my preferences and cultivate whatever delusions suit my fancy. Self-narration thereby becomes self-justification.[69]

The sociality of self-interpretation also means that the constitution of the self is not the work of a purely active, sovereign intellect—a hermeneutical *causa sui*. We are self-interpreting animals, but just as we can speak because we are first spoken to, likewise we can interpret ourselves only because we are already interpreted. We begin with a primordial understanding of ourselves and our place in the world. The self finds its existential and ethical bearings within a horizon or topography that is already given; it does not create these coordinates for itself from scratch.[70]

Identity, Recognition, Justification

In the opening pages of *The Sickness Unto Death*, Kierkegaard poses a sharp challenge to the notion of a disengaged, purely active self. Kierkegaard's pseudonym, Anti-Climacus, gives his famous definition of the self as "a relation relating itself to itself." The self is a relation, or synthesis, of the finite and infinite, temporal and eternal, necessity and possibility. But the self is not only the relation between these terms—a merely negative unity; the positive unity arises in the relating of this self to itself (SUD 13). In other words, the self is the reflexive relating of these terms. The self is constituted in the interpretation and reflection of its constituent elements in its thoughts, words, deeds, commitments.

But this is not the end of the story. According to Anti-Climacus, in relating to itself, the self relates to another. The self is therefore not a purely self-positing being, but is established by a power outside of itself. What is this establishing power? As Anti-Climacus explains later, the self is defined by its criterion and goal, by that which gives the self its ideal. In his words: "The criterion for the self is always: that directly before which it is a self" (SUD 79). The category of "existence before" is therefore essential to becoming a self.[71] In Taylor's terms, it is that which gives me my horizon of significance, that to which I find myself responsible, that which shows me who I am and what it means to be a self. For this reason, self-understanding is only possible on the basis of a fundamental passivity. My primordial self-understanding is given to me; I find myself in the middle of things, in a world that is already meaningful, with my self-interpretation already set in motion. My constitution as a self is already under way. On the basis of this prior givenness, I then experience myself as responsible for myself; I am answerable, accountable for who I am and what I do. My existence is subject to strong evaluation.

This strong evaluation takes place before some authority, which is the power that establishes the self. This authority might be another self, a community, an institution. It might be God. It might be a code or principle. It might be my own conscience. Whatever the case, in existing before some authority the self seeks to be recognized; the self needs this recognition as a confirmation of its identity. As Taylor observes, the self does not create its identity in a sheer self-productive act nor discover it as an interpretation-free given; rather, the self discovers its identity in negotiation and dialogue (which is partly overt and partly internalized) with others.[72] We are relational beings, and our continued existence depends on the recognition of others. We need other persons to say Yes to us—to confirm our identity and affirm that our existence is good and meaningful. This basic need for recognition is present from the very beginning of life. The infant needs to be recognized, to be confirmed, welcomed, embraced, and loved simply in order to survive. Moreover, the infant needs to be welcomed with naming. In the event of receiving its name, the child is recognized; this is an important event in the genesis of the child's identity. We need to be addressed by a word from outside of ourselves, a word that recognizes us, that says Yes, that tells us that it is good and right for us to be rather than not to be.

This need for recognition is ultimately a need for justification. I need justification for my actions, for a certain practice or behavior, but most fundamentally, I need justification for my very existence. At a fundamental level, the question of justification penetrates to the heart of my being. To be or not to be—that is the most basic question of strong evaluation. Does my existence matter, or is it a matter of indifference? Does my existence have meaning? Is it a good thing that I exist? By what right do I exist here and now, in the way I do?

The question of justification hearkens back a long way in the philosophical tradition, back to the Anaximander fragment, reputed to be the earliest extant document in Western philosophy. Anaximander writes: "And the source of coming-to-be for existing things is that into which destruction, too, happens, 'according to necessity; for they pay penalty and retribution to each other for their injustice according to the assessment of Time'."[73] The fragment suggests that the question of justice arises with the genesis and destruction of beings. According to Eberhard Jüngel, Anaximander anticipates a concept of justice that will appear in Plato and Aristotle, according to which justice is each person receiving his or her due, and injustice is *pleonexia*—i.e., one person having too much at the expense of others. On Jüngel's reading, *pleonexia* explains the genesis and destruction of beings: "Here the being of existing things as against the non-being of the non-existent is understood as an injustice, the injustice of having too much. So right consists in evening this out: existing things are destroyed so that the non-existent can come into existence. Time brings about this balance."[74] Consequently, nature—*phusis*—is a forensic event. According to Oswald Bayer, the Anaximander fragment describes a world in which the cosmic and the moral order have not yet been divorced; the cosmic order is not yet governed by cause and effect, but through a relation of communication. Everything belongs to a "community of right," and thus "relations in the world are based on the fact that everyone must account for its actions in the face of another." Beings address each other and demand a response, calling into account, accusing each other, protesting against guilt, invoking responsibility.[75] On what basis is it right and just that *I* am, rather than another?

The Jewish philosopher Emmanuel Levinas radicalizes this question, arguing that ethical responsibility is wholly otherwise than ontology. The Levinasian question is this: *Is it righteous to be?*[76] On what basis do *I*, rather than someone else, have the right to be here? This consideration calls into question the basic struggle for life: the way animals compete for food, shelter, and mates; the way plants strain upward to take in sunlight and extend their roots downward to take in nutrients from the soil. Levinas identifies this drive in Spinoza's theme of the *conatus essendi* (the drive to persevere in being) as well as in Heidegger's analysis of Dasein's care for its own being.[77] Ontology consists in this impulse to secure my own being, to claim that this is "my place in the sun." According to Pascal, this claim to one's own place is "how the usurpation of the whole world began,"[78] and Levinas suggests that this is why Pascal goes so far as to write that "the I is detestable." "It is as if, by the fact of being there, I deprived someone of his vital space, as if I expelled or assassinated someone." For Levinas, this is a lesson in ontology, as though "the principle of identity positing itself triumphantly as I contained an indecency and a violence, as if the I impeded, by its very position, the full existence of another."[79] Thus Levinas argues that Dasein's very *being-there* (*Da-sein*) is suspect. The violence of being-there becomes apparent when confronted by the face of the other person, whose visage calls the *conatus* into question. In the face of the other, I encounter vulnerability, nudity, helplessness. This encounter arrests me: I am responsible for this person. I am not called to ensure the continuation of my own existence, to claim my place in the sun, or to insist on my rights. Instead, my first priority is to care for this other person. The face of the other breaks through the closed circle of my being, revealing that ethics, not ontology, is most fundamental.

Is Hermeneutics a Closed Circle?

Ontology concerns that which is meaningful: "the concordant, the permanent, that which remains." Thus the ontology of the I "affirms the fact of remaining in oneself, returning to oneself, positing oneself as oneself, as the sense of the world."[80] The desire to secure one's own justification, right, and recognition is an ontological concern. The self wants closure: it wants a resolved meaning, a finished judgment, a clear conscience. But Levinas maintains that the question of goodness does not belong to the order of being. Goodness comes from beyond, as a rupture of the closed horizon of being; ontology is ruptured when the self is confronted by the face of the other person, which calls the self to surrender its place and perseverance in being and instead take responsibility for the other.

We have seen that the question of identity is inseparable from the questions of recognition and justification. The question *Who am I?* is inseparable from the question *Is it righteous for me to be?* The Levinasian critique of ontology is so radical because he refuses to offer a resolution to these questions. Levinas envisions an anthropology that does not begin with being—with the *conatus essendi*—but with ethics.[81] True humanity consists in my responsibility for the other, and so Levinas writes of a "humanism of the other."[82] This moment of responsibility is a rupture in being; it is the awakening of true humanity within being.[83] Responsibility is the key to understanding the self and subjectivity; only through this radical interruption is the ego converted into a self (OB 50). The self is a subject, in the sense of *subjection* to the other, of bearing a burden of infinite obligation, of assuming a prior debt beyond any possible adequation (OB 88).

What is decisive for Levinas is that responsibility does not afford any return to closure. The rupture remains an open wound. In relation to the other, I can never secure my own justification, because my responsibility (and my guilt) is infinite. Am I righteous in being? Am I justified? For Levinas, the answer to this question is always deferred. On what basis could I be justified in my being? On what basis could I understand my existence as meaningful? Who *am* I? Ethical subjectivity permits no return to self-identity.

Moreover, Levinas does not allow for the resolution that comes from reciprocal recognition between self and other. On this count Levinas is a resolute critic of Hegel. For Hegel, recognition is the means by which the self returns from the other to a greater self-consciousness and sense of identity.[84] We need recognition in order to be, which is why here too Levinas describes ethics as a rupture in being. The other does not arrive to confirm my identity and give me greater self-knowledge. Nor does my responsibility resolve into a clear conscience, with the assurance that I did the right thing and that my actions are justified. Responsibility for the other is not a reciprocal exchange of recognition, but a relation of asymmetry. If we do not insist on the absolute priority of the other, otherness becomes an instrument in service to my own self-identity.

For much the same reasons, Levinas offers an ethical critique of hermeneutics. Despite its epistemic modesty, hermeneutical self-understanding can be a more subtle form of reflective closure. This allegation demands serious consideration. To paraphrase Levinas, it is of the highest importance to determine whether we are duped by hermeneutics.[85] According to Heidegger, Dasein comprehends its world as a meaningful horizon for its practical activity, and this world comprises a totality. Dasein sees beings as equipment for its projects, thereby overcoming them and bringing them into its possession.[86] Levinas objects that this hermeneutical circle is unethical because it is driven by a totalizing impulse, in which the meaning of beings depends on their location in reference to the whole, i.e., to the totality of Dasein's involvements in the world.[87] Beings are significant for me insofar as they belong to the horizon of my projects, which are determined by my care for my own being. As a result, the singularity and alterity of the other is subsumed within totality. One might reply that hermeneutical understanding is not totalizing in the manner of idealism, since interpretation never arrives at a final, self-contained knowledge. Since understanding is ongoing, the hermeneutical circle is not vicious. With Ricoeur, we might suggest a hermeneutical *spiral*.[88] But this response does not appease Levinas, who discerns in this ongoing circle a "notion of totalization that is ever to be resumed anew, an open notion of totality!"[89] Hermeneutics is an ongoing process of totalization and retotalization.

It is therefore a question of whether the hermeneutical circle can be broken open by that which is genuinely other than itself, or whether it is a closed circle of totality. Much the same concern motivates recent critiques of onto-theology, in which the divine becomes an instrument in the service of the self. The self appropriates the authority of divinity and puts it to work in its own projects—whether epistemic, political, or religious. By appealing to the divine, thinking consciousness purports to have an Archimedean point that grounds its claims to absolute knowledge, along with a theoretical mastery and practical control of reality.[90] As such, divine otherness is overcome and internalized within the closed system of thought. For these reasons Kierkegaard critiques Hegelian speculation, and Heidegger critiques technology as an onto-theological method to master Being.[91] But in a somewhat different way than Kierkegaard and Heidegger, Levinas challenges onto-theology with a religion of ethical responsibility. The moment of responsibility is a rupture in being, and it is only here that the voice of God reverberates within being.[92] It is only in responsibility that God "comes to mind."[93] The word of God calls the self to responsibility, and thus into its true humanity. This excludes any religious piety that would seek God for one's own sake—for the sake of securing a meaningful life here and now, or for the hope and assurance of an afterlife. True humanity and true religiosity alike consist in the destruction of this egoistic concern for one's own being.

* * *

Levinas's critique is of vital importance for our investigation of faith and philosophical anthropology. In faith, the self receives the answer to the question *Who am I?* But in conceding the importance of questions concerning self-understanding and identity, are we then led down the wayward path of onto-theology? Is faith instrumentalized, reduced to a means to the end of self-identity? Is the self-understanding of faith a new totality? Does faith internalize divine otherness, so that Feuerbach is correct in diagnosing theology as anthropology writ large? Does the desire for justification amount to a desire to be relieved of the burden of responsibility? Is faith a salve to ease the conscience? Is hope an escape from the concrete reality of this world? Is this self-understanding in fact a case of the *homo incurvatus in se*—the human being sinfully curved in on itself?

These are troubling questions, and it is appropriate that we let them trouble us. In the next chapter I argue that unless our thinking about faith and human being is properly oriented toward the cross, we quickly tend toward these deviations. I therefore argue for a cruciform interpretation of identity, recognition, and justification by faith, in which faith does not resolve itself into a self-contained or self-mediating identity. We will see that this is precisely what faith is not.

3 Faith, Substance, and the Cross

In the previous chapter we discussed Charles Taylor's claim that human beings are self-interpreting animals. As we saw, self-interpretation is a matter of strong evaluation, a second-order evaluation of oneself. Are my desires, goals, and commitments good? Am I living the way I should? Is it good that I "am"? We evaluate ourselves, in this strong sense, within a horizon of significance—i.e., a set of background assumptions regarding what is good, meaningful, and valuable. Moreover, this strong evaluation takes place before some authority. The category of "existence before" is therefore essential to becoming a self. I experience myself as responsible, answerable, accountable to some authority for who I am and what I do. This authority might be another self, a community, an institution; it might be a code or principle; it might be my own conscience. In this chapter, and for much of this book, our concern will be the category of existence before God (*coram Deo*). To begin, then, I offer a few remarks on why this category is the ultimate horizon of strong evaluation, and thus for becoming a self.

* * *

The self exists before others and needs the recognition of those others who are authoritative. This is essential to the self and its sense of identity. As Anti-Climacus puts it in *The Sickness Unto Death*, this authority provides the criterion of the self; it gives the self its goal and the standard by which it is measured. Consequently, those before whom one exists define oneself, and establish one as who one is. Anti-Climacus shows that there is a phenomenological difference between the degrees of self-consciousness, depending on whom one exists before: "A cattleman who (if this were possible) is a self directly before his cattle is a very low self, and, similarly, a master who is a self directly before his slaves is actually no-self—for in both cases a criterion is lacking." There is a criterion for the child who becomes a self before his parents, and as an adult the self gains the community, the polis, as a criterion. In these cases the criterion is human, but there is a qualitative difference between the self whose criterion is the other human and the self who exists directly before God. With God as the criterion, "an infinite accent falls on the self," such that the self becomes aware of itself in a different way. With God as its criterion, self-consciousness is intensified not merely finitely but infinitely (SUD 79–80).

When the self recognizes that its existence is a concern to God, the self is individuated in a new way. This is a disorienting realization—that God is not concerned about oneself through the mediation of an abstract idea like humanity, state, or world, but about the sin and faith of the individual self. This is offensive to human reason because it is so counterintuitive.[1] But the offense is not limited to the theistic idea that the individual exists before God. The offense deepens when it becomes Christological. Not only does the self exist before God; this intimacy is intensified by the claim that God has come to the world for this individual self and has allowed himself "to be born, to suffer, to die, and this suffering God—he almost implores and beseeches this person to accept the help that is offered to him! Truly, if there is anything to lose one's mind over, this is it!" (SUD 85). There is therefore a phenomenological difference between the self before a human criterion, the self before the God of a general theism, and the self before the crucified Christ. It is this last category that will occupy us with our *anthropologia crucis*: How is the self recognized and justified before this suffering God, who became human and died on a cross? What sort of selfhood is constituted before the criterion of the God on the cross?

As we have seen, the need for recognition is a need for justification—for one's actions or a certain practice or behavior, but most fundamentally for one's existence. The question of justification penetrates to the heart of my being. Does my existence matter, or is it a matter of indifference? Does my existence have meaning? Moreover, is it a good thing that I exist? By what right do I exist here and now, and in this manner? The question that concerns us here is this: How do I receive justification for my existence before God? As we will see, there are two possibilities for gaining this recognition and justification, and they reflect two competing ontologies: an ontology of self-justification and an ontology of justification by faith.

With that said we might also ask, with Levinas, whether *any* ontology ought to be our goal. For Levinas the locus of true humanity lies in ethical responsibility for the other, which ruptures ontology and controverts the desire to persist in being, along with the desire for identity, recognition, and justification. Who am I? Am I recognized by the other? Is it righteous for me to be? The encounter with the other calls me to set aside these questions. Ethical responsibility is a rupture that remains an open wound, because I can never secure the closure of identity, recognition, and justification. This also means that I cannot appeal to God as the guarantor or ground of my being. God does not appear to serve my projects. True religiosity therefore means relinquishing my projects and taking up the endless task of responsibility for the other.

Levinas challenges us to consider whether the ontology of justification by faith succumbs to onto-theology and whether the identity and recognition of the faithful self falls back into egoism. But I will argue that we should not relinquish the concern for identity, recognition, and justification altogether. Instead, these phenomena need to be interpreted in a cruciform way. In being addressed by the word of the cross, the self receives its true self-understanding. The word of the cross gives the answer to the question, *Who am I?* The cross is the site at which the self is justified and recognized, but it is crucial that this cruciform recognition not resolve into a self-contained identity. The self has this identity in faith and hope, based on a promise for the future rather than an intuited presence. This is a central insight for our *anthropologia crucis*.

Luther's *Theologia Crucis*

In order to provide the background for our philosophical anthropology of the cross, we need to take a hermeneutical detour through Martin Luther's *theologia crucis*. Despite Luther's many highly critical comments regarding philosophy, his innovative thinking is of great philosophical interest. The purpose of our theological exegesis here is to show how Luther develops the Pauline theme of the cross as a scandal for philosophy and how Luther's account of cruciform faith challenges traditional metaphysical conceptions of human being, substance, identity, and temporality. Luther's treatment of these themes has had a major influence on subsequent philosophy through Kant and post-Kantian idealism, Kierkegaard, and Heidegger,[2] and since this is the context in which we will be interpreting the cruciform self, we need to spend some time in Luther's texts.

The term *anthropologia crucis* is a deliberate allusion to Luther's 1518 *Heidelberg Disputation*, which asserts a fundamental incommensurability between the theology of the cross (*theologia crucis*) and the theology of glory (*theologia gloriae*). Luther's theses and his critique of scholasticism are highly polemical, as his writing can often be, in part because they were written for a disputation, but also because Luther thinks it necessary to make the contrast as stark as possible for the sake of the gospel.[3] The crux of this opposition appears in three theses:

19. That person does not deserve to be called a theologian who looks upon the invisible things of God as though they were clearly perceptible in those things which have actually happened [Rom. 1:20].
20. He deserves to be called a theologian, however, who comprehends the visible and manifest things of God seen through suffering and the cross.
21. A theologian of glory calls evil good and good evil. A theologian of the cross calls the thing what it actually is.[4]

What is at stake in this disputation are the principles of theological thinking. How is it possible to know God—not just that God exists, but to know and be known in a salvific relation? How does one gain access to God? How is one established and recognized before God? Luther suggests two possible answers to this question: a theology of glory or a theology of the cross.

Luther uses the expression "theology of glory" to characterize the errors of scholastic theology and philosophy, which seek to make their way to God in one of two ways—either by metaphysical contemplation (*theoria*) or ethical formation (*praxis*).[5] Both are attempts to reach God from below rather than through faithfulness to the revelation of God, by which God has already made his way to human beings. In metaphysical contemplation, the theology of glory seeks to derive knowledge of the invisible things of God through the visible, i.e., "those things that have actually happened." This could take the form of speculation on the basis of nature, with the assumption that its order, beauty, and intricacy might allow us to determine something of God's being or nature. It could take the form of speculation on the basis of history, which might also seem to display God's work in an unconcealed manner. Or it might derive from reflection on the mysteries of human personality or selfhood, as though the ontological structure of the human being in some way necessitates certain truths about the divine.[6] In each case, the theologian of glory uses the created order as a launching pad for speculation about God and his ways, often with the goal of achieving an immediate vision or union with God through contemplative or mystical ascent.[7]

The theology of glory is also characterized by its attempt to reach God on the basis of good works or merit. This is the reason for Luther's often strident criticisms of Aristotle. How does one become just or righteous? In Book B of *Nicomachean Ethics,* Aristotle argues that "we become just by doing what is just," as is the case with the other virtues: "we acquire them as a result of prior activities."[8] It should be noted that Luther acknowledges Aristotle's genuine insights into ethics and politics, and he understands that Aristotle was not offering a theological soteriology in the manner of the gospel.[9] Moreover, Luther also agrees that on an immanent, worldly level the *habitus* or *hexis* of virtue develops through the practice of virtuous actions; this is what Luther calls civil righteousness.[10] What Luther opposes so vehemently is the scholastic appropriation of Aristotle's ethics in a theological context in order to explain justification before God. In his *Disputation Against Scholastic Theology,* Luther argues: "We do not become righteous by doing righteous deeds but, having been made righteous, we do righteous deeds."[11] According to Luther, the proclamation of the gospel inverts the priority of works over person. The person does not constitute herself through her actions, but is constituted in the unconditional gift of grace. The person is recognized by God apart from any meritorious acts, and thus gains her standing and identity as a person. Only on the basis of this prior recognition does the person perform righteous activities.

Luther will later elaborate on this point by distinguishing between *alien* and *proper* righteousness. Christian faith is a disruptive event, which is given in a decisive moment—the *Kairos,* the *Augenblick*—in which the self is destroyed and re-created. The self receives the "alien righteousness" of Christ and its sin is "swallowed up." Through trust and faith, the self "exists in Christ; he is one with Christ, having the same righteousness as he."[12] This extrinsic, alien righteousness of Christ is the primary constitution of the human being and its standing before God, and it provides the basis for *proper righteousness*—i.e., our works and activity that follow as the fruit of our being in Christ. In faith the self "no longer seeks to be righteous in and for itself, but it has Christ as its righteousness and therefore seeks only the welfare of others." This means (1) crucifying our selfish desires, (2) love of one's neighbor, and (3) devotion to God.[13] The key, however, is that these manifestations of proper righteousness are only possible through our incorporation into the being of Christ; faith means existing in Christ, being one with Christ.[14] In the *Disputation Against Scholastic Theology*, Luther cites Jesus' pedagogical image of the person as a tree: only when the tree is reconstituted as good is it capable of bearing good fruit.[15] No bad tree is capable of bearing good fruit; it might have the appearance of good fruit, but its principles and motives are not genuinely good. The theology of glory mistakenly calls evil good and good evil, because it makes these judgments on the basis of that which is visible, i.e., evident through experience and reason.

Aristotle's emphasis on habituation explains Luther's pronouncement in the next thesis: "Virtually the entire *Ethics* of Aristotle is the worst enemy of grace."[16] The scholastic appropriation of Aristotle implies that good works allow the self to become something before God, to have a legitimate claim to be recognized by God on the basis of merit. Hence the many varieties of religious *askēsis*—exercises, disciplines, and practices that aim to transform the self through habituation. According to Luther, reason is capable of knowing that we ought to be pious, but since it is incapable of knowing what this truly means, reason creates its own methods of piety.[17] However, these methods cannot achieve what they intend, not only because the self cannot reach God via speculation, mysticism, or good works, but because these methods are misunderstood as proper *preparations* for grace. Religion becomes another activity of the egocentric self, and the corresponding idea of God serves to ground one's own needs and desires. Luther undertakes his critique of religion with a severity that matches anything in the masters of suspicion: the only thing the self can contribute prior to grace is "ill will and even rebellion against grace."[18] This is because the self is incapable of wanting God to be God. "Indeed, he himself wants to be God, and does not want God to be God."[19] To let God be God, in Luther's view, is to surrender all claim to merit, to relinquish all attempts to identify God's existence or essence, and to submit oneself to the foolishness of the cross, which discloses saving knowledge of God.

The theology of the cross stands in sharp contrast to the theology of glory, because the word of the cross pronounces a decisive No to self-initiated ways of accessing God. According to Luther, the purpose of God's *descent* in the incarnation is to pre-empt and prohibit any and all human *ascent*.[20] God is not known through metaphysical speculation or by cultivating mystical experience, but only through his acts of revelation. Righteousness before God cannot be achieved through ethical or religious legalism; it has already been achieved by Christ and can only be received as a gift of grace, through faith.

By dealing with fallen humanity in this way, God overturns all our expectations of what God should be or how God should act. As such, God's action (and passion) appears as foolishness. The incarnation of God in flesh—that the Eternal would enter time and physical existence—is a scandal for philosophical thinking. Even more troubling is that God kenotically chose to live the humblest of lives. Christ was born in a manger, lived a life of poverty, had no place to lay his head, and then died the most shameful death of crucifixion, a method of execution reserved for the worst of criminals.

For the metaphysical tradition, perhaps the most troubling aspect of the word of the cross is that God does not redeem us in power and glory, but in suffering and death. God's victory over sin and death appears to be anything but a triumph. From all appearances it seems to be defeat. But Luther argues that God's works are hidden under the opposite appearance of ugliness and evil. God makes himself visible and manifest in suffering and the cross. This is why Paul writes of the weakness and foolishness of God (1 Cor. 1:25), which, contrary to all appearance, is stronger and wiser than what human beings consider strength and wisdom. God's majesty is hidden from view; God is known in the suffering and shame of the cross. This is the basis for Luther's notion of the *Deus absconditus*—the hidden God, which he draws out of Isaiah 45:15: "Truly, You are a God who hides Himself, O God of Israel, Savior!" God cannot be known directly or immediately, but only indirectly through the mediation of the cross. God reveals himself only in concealment. There are two reasons for this: First, because an unconditioned and unconcealed revelation of God's glory and majesty would annihilate us; God is a consuming fire.[21] In order to show himself, God clothes himself in the word. The locus of revelation, and thus saving knowledge of God, is in the word of scripture.[22] Secondly, God's hiddenness is necessary to confront and overthrow human pride and self-sufficiency. Metaphysical speculation looks for omnipotence, omnipresence, and other attributes that seem fitting to the glory of divinity, but God hides himself in human nature, weakness, foolishness, suffering, and the cross.[23] The cross is a scandal, foolishness, an offense to the understanding, and this is necessary to expose the insufficiency of human speculation and works.

Possibility and Actuality

The status of the self before God depends on the source of its justification. There are two options, which entail two competing ontologies. The first possibility is that we justify ourselves on the basis of our activities, through the works and operations by which we actualize ourselves. This is an ontology of self-justification. It is the way of glory. We are what we make of ourselves, and we earn our recognition through our acts. The ontology of self-justification is the natural attitude of the human being, which is why we are so offended by the second possibility—the ontology of justification by faith. This is the way of the cross. The self is what it is on the basis of faith, not because of its activities. In his *Disputation Concerning Man*, Luther argues that Romans 3:28 sums up the definition of human being: "We hold that a man is justified by faith apart from works."[24] The self is justified by faith; this is the basis for becoming oneself.

The self comes to true self-knowledge, and thereby becomes itself, through justification. The self is justified—i.e., it is recognized, given its righteousness and its identity—entirely independent of its own activity. The self receives this justification in the event of being addressed by a word from outside itself: namely, the word of the cross. This is a word addressed to me, and it is through this word that I gain true self-understanding: I am justified by faith, apart from my activity. "Faith" in this word does not mean mere assent to a doctrinal proposition; it means trust in the God who has spoken this word, this promise that my justification is an entirely free gift. This is a thoroughly offensive proposal because it runs counter to our commonsense assumptions regarding what it means to be human. The word of the cross is foolishness because it is a scandal to our understanding of what it is to *be*. According to Luther's *Disputation on Man*, this is a theological rather than a philosophical insight; philosophical wisdom cannot gain this insight on its own, because it would never enter the philosopher's mind to suggest such a thing.

The word of the cross forces us to consider the basis on which we are justified and recognized in our being. As such, it is ontologically disruptive. As Jüngel observes, it requires that we rethink the priority of actuality over possibility. *Either* the self is justified because of its works, activities, achievements—in which case actuality is a necessary condition of recognition; *or* possibility is prior to actuality, so that the self is recognized not on the basis of its actuality, but on the basis of an eschatological possibility.[25] To say that a possibility is eschatological means at least two things: First, it is a new possibility that is not our doing. It is not the outworking of an immanent teleology, and it does not arise from the projection, anticipation, or imagination of the self. It is given from outside of us, in an external word that addresses us and reconstitutes us. Second, it is a new possibility that marks a complete break with the old, leaving the old existence to die so that a genuinely new being begins.[26]

The scandal of the cross must destroy the self-sufficiency of the fallen human being. Here we broach Luther's notion of *destructio*—that the natural human being, the old self, must be put to death and destroyed in order to be raised up as the new self. God takes no pleasure in this destruction; it is God's alien work (*opus alienum*) rather than God's proper work (*opus proprium*). Luther draws this distinction from I Samuel 2:6: "The Lord kills and makes alive; He brings down to Sheol and raises up." The alien work of God, which is foreign to his nature, is the *destructio* of all self-righteousness, pride, and every attempt to establish oneself before God through one's own activities.[27] God enacts this *destructio* by giving the law, which reveals the magnitude of one's sin and unrighteousness and crushes all attempts to merit one's standing before God.[28] Religious activity therefore contains an inner logic of despair: the more progress one makes, the greater one understands the degree of one's shortcomings; the more pious one becomes, the more one recognizes the depths of one's unrighteousness. This is not simply hyperbolic self-effacement, but a genuine recognition that the closer one comes to holiness, the more one's unworthiness comes into view. Only through God's *destructio* is true self-understanding possible, for here the self begins to understand itself as it really is before God (*coram Deo*), with no claim to merit.[29] But even this recognition of one's own unrighteousness must surrender its claim to merit. The pious self might presume to deserve grace by cultivating humility, as though this humility is a worthy preparation for grace, but this humility could be the final plea of self-justification, as a polymorph of Socratic wisdom. To paraphrase the *Apology*,[30] I am the most righteous of human beings because I recognize that my righteousness counts for nothing. This claim is the last, but often the most difficult, self-righteousness to be rooted out.

What the cross demands is complete submission and passivity before God; we need to be decentered by grace, taken out of ourselves, taught to stop saying "I, I, I."[31] Only through this alien work of *destructio* can God enact his proper work, which is the justification of the sinner. This activity is an event of *creatio ex nihilo*. Destruction is followed by a new creation, as the proper work of God effects an ontological reconstitution of the self.

Destroying Substance

What exactly does the cross destroy? It destroys the substance of the sinful self. But what does this mean? If we understand the self as a thinking substance, a *res cogitans*, it might seem that the cross obliterates the immaterial soul substance in order to recreate it in a new form. We might also wonder what this destruction entails for our capacities of thinking, feeling, and willing; it might seem to entail a violence that destroys the self psychologically. In order to understand Luther on the cross and its destruction of substance, then, we need to examine his redefinition of substance.

On Substance and the Self

The history of substance ontology is long and varied, and there is no univocal definition or concept of substance. The substantial definition of being originates with Aristotle, who employs *ousia* as a generic term for being. According to Book Z of the *Metaphysics*, *ousia* is used in multiple senses: as the matter of a thing, as the form of a thing, or as the composite of matter and form.[32] Moreover, in the *Categories* Aristotle defines substance as a subject of predication; it is the *hypokeimenon*, i.e., that which underlies predication as the bearer of qualities, and as the substrate that underlies change (1029a).[33] In medieval thought the Greek word *ousia* was translated into the Latin *substantia*. Along the way, Aristotle's understanding of substance underwent important modifications, many of which were meant to accord with the metaphysical commitments and implications of Christian faith.[34] But critics have argued that this modification is not radical enough, because the concept of *substantia* is problematic in its own right. According to Heidegger's version of the story, the translation of *ousia* into *substantia* was a fateful decision that would distort the subsequent history of metaphysics. "Substance" came to denote that which subsists, that which endures continuously through the dynamics of time and change, and "Being" came to mean constant presence and presentness, just as beings are present-at-hand objects (IM 96, 206–208).

The metaphysics of substance also had a significant impact on Western conceptions of human being. We see this in Boethius's influential definition of the person as the "individual substance of a rational nature."[35] This definition of personhood became a standard point of reference for the concept of personhood through medieval scholasticism,[36] carrying with it Boethius's emphasis on individuality and rationality as defining features of human substance. The substantialist ontology of human being, along with its emphasis on individual rationality, would come to an even sharper point with Descartes, whose *Principles of Philosophy* defines substance as "nothing other than a thing which exists in such a way as to depend on no other thing for its existence." In the most precise sense of the term only God counts as substance, and we cannot apply the term univocally to God and his creatures. All other substances exist only through God's concurrence. These created substances fall into two distinct categories: corporeal substance and thinking substance,[37] *res extensa* and *res cogitans*. The *cogito*, the thinking substance, is metaphysically dependent upon God, but otherwise the cogito exhibits the usual features of substance: an independent, individual, self-contained being that exists prior to its relations with the external world. Leibniz would later take this conception of individual substance to a further extreme with his monadology.[38]

While it is true that substance may depend on a metaphysical ground for its existence, it is nevertheless a self-contained entity that subsists in itself, bears qualities, and endures over time. If the self is conceived as a substantial entity, then, it is a *subjectum* that underlies and endures through accidental changes. Substance preserves the unity of the self through the flux of experience and ensures the continuity of personal identity over time and through change. This notion has a certain commonsense appeal, because it seems to work well when distinguishing between one's unchanging existence (e.g., my existence as a mammal) and changeable attributes (e.g., hair color, body weight, etc.).[39] But this advantage comes with a heavy price, because it distorts our understanding of human being.

First of all, substance is that which persists or stands under qualitative change. Despite its commonsense appeal, we will see below that this idea presents a major obstacle for understanding sin and faith and their ontological impact on the self. The concept of substance emphasizes self-subsistence. Moreover, by virtue of its unifying form, substance is unitary and/or simple.[40] As a result, the self is taken to be a self-contained entity, which first exists and then enters into relations with others. The substantial self maintains an essential integrity and self-possession independent of other substantial selves. Thus while relations with other selves may be an inescapable feature of human experience, they are not constitutive of human being. Relations with others may change the self in its accidents, but not in its substance; the substantial reality of human being remains the same regardless of its relations.[41]

John Zizioulas has argued that this understanding of substance has confused reflection on the Trinity, particularly in Western theology insofar as it has assumed that substance has priority over relation. At its worst, this creates a tendency to conceive of the persons of the Godhead as individual substances who stand in relationship with each other. In turn, this substantialist doctrine of the Trinity also distorts our understanding of human beings made in the image of the Triune God. By contrast, Zizioulas commends the Greek Fathers—particularly the Cappadocian Fathers—for their relational ontology, arguing that their relational understanding of the Trinity also provides better guidance for anthropological reflection. The being of persons is not substantial but relational. This means, first of all, that personhood must be understood in terms of ek-stasis—as a movement from one's own being toward communion with an other.[42] Personhood consists in this movement beyond one's own boundaries toward others. The person is an ek-static being, not a self-contained substance.[43]

Secondly, personhood must be understood as *hypostatic*—albeit according to a new definition of *hypostasis* that developed in the fourth century. Whereas *hypostasis* had previously been identified with *ousia* as substance, it came to connote personhood as distinct from substance.[44] Basil of Caesarea presented the first and most famous distinction[45] between *ousia* and *hypostasis* in order to understand the unity and diversity of the Trinity. Basil uses *ousia* to describe the common divine essence or substance of the Trinity, and *hypostasis* to describe the distinct, particular persons.[46] Here Basil adopts the classical metaphysical distinction between the one and the many, unity and plurality, but with a crucial difference. The metaphysical tradition gave priority to the one over the many, unity over plurality, universal over particular, nature over person—in Platonism, an overarching *genos hyperkeimenon* that is the ideal of which particular beings are images, and in Aristotelianism a *genos hypokeimenon* that is the substratum from which particular beings emerge. From that perspective nature or substance must precede person, which would lead one to expect that the unity of the divine nature has priority over the particular persons or *hypostases* of the Trinity; yet Basil and the other Cappadocians reject this view, insisting that God's being does not involve priority of either the one or the many, but involves both simultaneously. This means that personhood is ontologically primary and not a derivative mode of a prior, impersonal substance. It also shows us a unity that is constituted by relations between distinct persons rather than a self-existing, self-contained individual substance. As Zizioulas observes, the Trinity is a philosophical scandal that can only be accepted if personhood replaces substance as the first principle of ontology.[47]

The anthropological consequence of the Cappadocians' Trinitarian ontology is that the identity of human beings does not reside in their being individual substances, but in their ek-static personhood, which moves beyond the boundaries of self-contained existence toward communion with others. If this relational conception of personhood is ontologically primary, then relations are not secondary features added onto already existing substances. The person does not first exist and then subsequently enter into relations with others. Instead, relations constitute persons in their very being.

Luther's Redefinition of Substance

Zizioulas makes a lot out of the difference between Eastern Orthodoxy and the Latin West on the themes of substance and personhood, but for our purposes here we must also note significant developments in Reformation thought that diverge from substance ontology.[48] In his early *Lectures on the Psalms* (in particular Ps. 69), Luther does not simply discard the notion of substance, but instead redefines it. Rather than taking it according to its philosophical definition, Luther points to its scriptural use—particularly in the Vulgate, where *substantia* refers metaphorically to one's "standing," i.e., that by which one subsists. For example, the wealthy subsist by riches, the honored by honor, pleasure seekers by pleasure. These examples reveal a fundamentally relational concept of substance: the self subsists in relation to some thing or quality that is external to itself. According to Luther, substance is therefore a qualitative rather than quidditative concept: "'substance' properly is a quality or something from the outside rather than the very being of a thing. For Scripture is not interested in the quiddities of things, but only in their qualities." The scriptural view is not concerned with an intrinsic *what*-ness of the person, but with the *how*, with the manner in which the person exists and acts. This qualitative *how* is the scriptural understanding of substance.[49]

Whatever is the source of one's subsistence, then, is the substance of one's existence. And of course, there are true and false sources of subsistence. The worldly form of subsistence is to prosper according to the examples cited above—health, wealth, honor, human wisdom, beauty, pleasure, good fortune, and so forth. These substances have the appearance of stability, since they are easily recognized and identified by the world. They are well esteemed by the standards of human wisdom. The faithful, however, do not have this sort of substance. Hebrews 10:34 reminds the faithful that they have "a better and a lasting substance," and Hebrews 11:1 recalls that "faith is the substance of things to be hoped for."[50] The faithful have their source of hope, security, and identity elsewhere. The writer of Hebrews thereby reminds the faithful of Jesus' teaching that one's life does not consist in the abundance of one's possessions.[51]

So far this does not seem to pose any great philosophical challenge. So what if Luther gives an idiosyncratic definition of substance? We can easily ignore this, especially since Luther's account of substance is not consistently thematized and articulated throughout his works. Moreover, there is nothing particularly novel in suggesting that the faithful have a better hope because they do not subsist on the fleeting goods of the world. In that case, Christ and Socrates don't seem so far apart after all. But Luther takes his point further in his concluding remarks on the psalm. Paraphrasing 1 Cor. 1:27–29, Luther writes: "But all these substances Christ has destroyed by His own non-substance, so that the faithful may not subsist on them nor trust in them but be without substance. But instead of these they should have faith, which is another substance, the substance of God. So also Christ's death destroyed the life of glory and of riches, so that they may neither live nor subsist on it."[52] The life of glory takes different forms: "Glory" can denote honor, beauty, pleasure, and other delights in this world. On this count Socrates is a vigorous ally against glory. But the life of rational contemplation and/or ethical action can be a more subtle form of glory. "Glory" in the sense of the *theologia gloriae* denotes any form of self-righteousness—that is, any attempt to subsist on one's own merit. One might try to subsist in relation to wealth and power, or one might try to subsist by contemplating the Good, the True, and the Beautiful. The point is that this substance presumes to provide the self with *standing*, i.e., standing before God, and standing that will sustain the self and uphold it from falling into the abyss of sin and death.

What grounds this standing? Who is able to keep us from falling, and who is able to make us stand before God (Jude 24)? According to the Christian kerygma, it is the crucified and resurrected Christ. That is what is at stake in this contested notion of standing. Consequently, false substances must be destroyed by the cross because they are attempts to stand apart from total faith and trust in Christ. The attempt to find one's subsistence apart from God is idolatry, and the attempt to subsist before God through oneself is works righteousness. The cross destroys both of these forms of false substance.

When the cross destroys the substance of the sinner, this is not a physical, biological, or psychological destruction, but a soteriological destruction of self-willful efforts to establish one's own subsistence before God. It is an ontological destruction, in that the cross destroys the ontology of self-justification. The crucifixion of the old self is the destruction of the illusion that one can stand before God in the self-contained substance of one's own being. Thus the life of the new being is "soteriologically de-substantial."[53] The substance of the human being is not in herself, but in another. The faithful self subsists not intrinsically but extrinsically, in the being of Christ.[54]

This poses a radical challenge to the traditional bond between substance and presence. Faith is the substance of things that are hoped for but not visible—in the Vulgate, the evidence of things that appear not (*argumentum non parentum*). The substance of faith is not visible by physical senses, but neither is it present for the vision of metaphysical contemplation. Faith is necessary because we have this substance in faith (*in fide*) and hope (*in spe*), not as a present reality (*in re*).[55] The self has died, and its life is hidden with Christ (Col. 3:3).

Toward a Philosophical Anthropology of the Cross

The substance of faith does not appear in visible presence, in the present moment. It has a different phenomenality: it is given in promise, as a word for the future. This conviction drives Luther's critique of philosophy and its desire for the presence of metaphysical vision. In contrast to the theology of glory, Luther describes the theology of the cross. But the cross is not only a matter of theological interest, since it raises important questions for philosophical reflection. What would a cruciform philosophy look like? Although Luther never attempts to develop a full Christian philosophy, he does offer some indications pointing in this direction. While it would be hasty to conclude that Luther envisioned any sort of constructive project along these lines, these remarks are nevertheless highly suggestive of what a cruciform philosophy might look like.

In the *Heidelberg Disputation,* Thesis 29 states: "He who wishes to philosophize by using Aristotle without danger to his soul must first become thoroughly foolish in Christ," and Thesis 30 states: "Just as a person does not use the evil of passion well unless he is a married man, so no person philosophizes well unless he is a fool, that is, a Christian." Beyond these provocative suggestions, Luther spends little time developing this notion of foolish philosophizing. In his commentary on Romans,[56] however, Luther writes of an "apostolic philosophy,"[57] which is best exemplified by the apostle Paul: "The apostle philosophizes and thinks about things in a different way than the philosophers and metaphysicians do." Philosophers typically seek to understand reality by attending to the essence and accidents of things, but are blind to the "expectation of creation" and deaf to the groaning and travail that sound through nature.[58] A foolish, apostolic, cruciform philosophy must therefore be thoroughly *eschatological* in orientation.[59] Philosophy must be reconfigured in an eschatological mode. It must be oriented toward the future of reality rather than its present, visible manifestations. According to the ontology of justification by faith, possibility is prior to actuality, and because this eschatological possibility is given through a word of promise, it calls for faith and hope. Against all appearances, we have the promise that creation will be set free.

Likewise, a cruciform philosophical anthropology—an *anthropologia crucis*—must also be eschatologically oriented. The being of the self is not defined by static essences, but by faith and hope. Our substance is radically futural; it is not yet apparent what we will be (1 John 3:2). The self is not a finished reality, a stable achievement. Thus there is no resting point—no intuition, no actualized virtue, no piety—on which the self can rest. The faithful self is restless because it is "*res*-less."[60] The self has an impulse to locate itself as a thinking thing, a virtuous thing, a spiritual thing, or even a faithful thing—because this would allow it to judge itself. The self has an impulse to locate itself reflexively and thereby stabilize itself as a self-subsisting substance—in other words, to see itself and be able to say before God, *this is good.* Through the reflexive act I hope to locate a state of being in which I am established before God.

But the faithful self is always in transit. The present life of faith is never a stable presence; it is always between contraries, simultaneously "in a point of departure and a point of destination." Thus faith is never fully actual, never finished in such a way that one can locate the act of faith and rest on it. Luther draws this insight from Ecclesiastes 1:9 ("What is what was? That which is still to be done") and Ecclesiasticus 18:6 ("When man has reached the end, then will he begin"). The life of faith is always in movement. "Thus he who is confident that he is just in the present moment and stops has lost his righteousness, just as movement is lost when one stops. The point to which we have come in the present moment is a point of departure in the succeeding moment. The point of departure is sin, from which we are always to be going, and the point of destination is righteousness, to which we are always to be going."[61] This means that the life of faith does not consist in the acquisition of a *habitus* on which I can rest or an act that I can reflexively grasp. The faithful self is *simul justus et peccator*—at once justified and sinner. In itself, my being remains in sin; in Christ, it is justified.[62]

If the life of faith is substantiated in the present because of this hope for and from the future, there is a sense in which this hope and faith is also grounded in the past. Faith and hope depend on *memoria*. Our hope for the future is nourished by our memory of the past, by giving thanks, praise, and narration of God's works in concrete historical existence.[63] We see this, for instance, throughout the Psalms, where the psalmist attests to the grounds for Israel's hope by remembering God's deliverances in the past. The pre-eminent memorial source of Christian hope is the crucifixion and resurrection. As we discuss in chapter 10, the being of the faithful self depends on the historical actuality of these events.

Because the hope of one's own resurrection depends on the particular historical resurrection of Christ, it is not an inherent or innate attribute of our nature. It is an eschatological possibility—something that does not fit the Aristotelian framework of possibility and actuality. In the *Nicomachean Ethics* Aristotle describes two possibilities: (1) Regarding powers that we have by nature (such as sensation), possibility precedes activity. (2) But regarding the virtues, activity precedes possibility; we acquire the power to act virtuously through performing virtuous acts.[64] The possibility of resurrection fits neither of these options, because it is an eschatological possibility given from outside and beyond the self. It is not gained by any kind of habituation, activity, or practice, nor is it given at birth as an innate or essential attribute of soul-substance. The latter is a common metaphysical view, according to which the soul is like a sort of spiritual battery containing an inherent *dunamis* for immortal, disembodied existence. But the promise of resurrection is a new possibility, which has no origin in the immanent potentiality of the human being. If the human being is to be raised imperishable (1 Cor. 15:42), this is only as a gift that comes from outside. The promise of resurrection is only possible because the self has been claimed by Christ.

* * *

Instead of thinking of the self as an individual substance, these apostolic insights demand a relational ontology of the self. The self is not a substance, a *sub-*

jectum, but a being that is constituted relationally. The self is not a being subsisting in itself, which subsequently steps out into relations with the rest of the world. The self has its being outside of itself (*extra se*) in another. The self subsists in Christ. Our righteousness, our identity, our meaning, is not intrinsic but extrinsic.[65] These implications are metaphysically disturbing because they are so counterintuitive and because they upset our expectations for what the integrity of the self should look like.

A Relapse into Substance Abuse

With this account of transformation in faith, Luther breaks with classical metaphysics and pushes us to think beyond the tradition of substance ontology, and yet the consequences of this break have never been fully appropriated by subsequent theological and philosophical reflection. This is due partly to the fact that Luther did not develop his thinking systematically, let alone work out anything like a full-fledged ontology. Luther may not have seen constructive ontological reflection as a pressing need, but we cannot avoid the ontological questions indefinitely. What sort of beings are we, if the word of the cross can address us? How do sin and faith affect our being?[66] It is not satisfactory to propose a simplistic Athens/Jerusalem dichotomy and conclude that the kerygma cannot raise ontological questions. Instead of keeping these Greek/pagan/philosophical concerns in brackets, this suspension only ends up leaving one tacitly committed to an earlier metaphysics,[67] which is less suited to the demands of the kerygma.

This is what happened with the Protestant scholasticism that followed in Luther's wake. Rather than developing the radical ontological implications of Luther's insight, these theologians resumed thinking within the conceptuality of *substantia* and *accidens*. But their attempt to fit Luther's account of sin, faith, and justification into the old substantialist account of human being resulted in unnecessary confusion and controversy. One example of this is the debate between Matthias Flacius Illyricus and Victorinus Strigel over the metaphysical status of original sin. Is sin a substance or accident? Strigel maintained that sin is an accident, while Flacius insisted that the genuinely Lutheran conclusion is to define sin as the formal substance or essence of the sinner. Although the sinner's material substance retains its creaturely structures and capabilities (thereby remaining human), the fallen human is sinful in essence. Flacius even goes so far as to assert that the sinner exists in the image of Satan (*imago satanae*) rather than the image of God (*imago Dei*).[68] The Flacian position was eventually rejected, with the Lutheran *Formula of Concord* asserting that sin is assuredly an accident because it cannot subsist on its own.[69] What this conclusion leaves unchallenged, however, is the assumption that Aristotelian categories of substance and accident are sufficient to account for such things. We need to ask whether a substance ontology is the best way to understand the human being and the transformation of its status in sin and faith.

Despite the commonsense appeal of the distinction between substance and accidents, this model is not up to the task of locating sin. To speak of sin as an accident is to risk superficiality. As Robert Jenson observes, "accidents can come and go without ontologically deep disruption, which does not seem to be the case with original sin as Christian theology and piety otherwise treat it." If we define sin as an accident, "it should be more easily eradicated than Christian teaching allows to be the case." Particular malefactions would therefore seem to take hold in the subject "only loosely," such that counseling, medication, or some other therapeutic technique could prevent further misbehavior. Yet if we follow Flacius and define sin as substance, we render it "ineradicable" and cannot account for the genuine transformation that takes place in faith.[70]

This problematic is not merely a theological peculiarity. It also affects philosophical anthropology insofar as it engages the question of human corruption and evil. Kant wrestles with this problem in his interpretation of radical evil in *Religion Within the Limits of Reason Alone*,[71] and it also arises for Heidegger's interpretation of fallenness and inauthenticity in *Being and Time*.[72] In chapter 4 I will argue that we need a relational ontology to understand sin as well as faith, and that we find a cue in Luther's description of sin as incurvature—as the self curved in on itself. Sin distorts the relationality that is ontologically constitutive of humanity: rather than being for God and the neighbor, the self tries to bring all exteriority within the domain of its power.

Conclusion

Luther's redefinition of *substantia* and his concept of *destructio* run counter to the received metaphysical tradition as well as our commonsense intuitions—which are what they are because of this received metaphysical tradition. Our commonsense intuitions are tacitly substantialist, and we are therefore accustomed to understanding ourselves as individual substances that possess such essential attributes as rationality and freedom.

New wine requires new wineskins, and the subsequent tradition of German theology and philosophy did not realize the ontological implications of Luther's insights as fully as it might have. This is true of Reformation theology, and it is arguably true of Kant, Fichte, Schelling, and Hegel.[73] Kierkegaard is an interesting case, since he belongs in many ways to the traditions of both Lutheranism as well as post-Kantian German philosophy. In Kierkegaard we also find something of the reformer's zeal for retrieving the radical implications of the cruciform gospel, in opposition to the philosophical metaphysics of glory. Whereas Luther's target is medieval scholasticism, Kierkegaard's target is German Romanticism and Idealism. It is noteworthy that Jaroslav Pelikan once suggested that Kierkegaard provides the best model for a genuinely Lutheran philosophy.[74] Pelikan is on to something with this argument, but he underestimates the elusive nature of Kierkegaard's texts; Kierkegaard's strategies of indirect communication, irony, and pseudonymous authorship pose a considerable challenge for any attempt to base constructive work on his authorship. This is certainly not to suggest that Kierkegaard cannot help the task of constructive philosophical and theological reflection, but it is at least clear that the task of articulating a cruciform ontology of the self is unfinished. In the next two chapters I attempt to make some contribution to such a task, drawing primarily on Bonhoeffer and Ricoeur. In chapter 4 I argue for an interpretation of sin according to the image of incurvature. Then in chapter 5 I focus primarily on Bonhoeffer as a resource for articulating an ontology of the self in faith. Through our reading of Bonhoeffer, we will be able to see how faith involves a cruciform ontology, in which identity and justification do not return to the self-enclosure of the incurved self.

4 The Incurved Self

> Perhaps that is what put Des in such a thoughtful mood—honest and self-critical—that afternoon.
> "Do you know the Shakespearean admonition 'To thine own self be true'?" he asked.
> I nodded, of course.
> "It's premised," he said, "on the idea that 'thine own self' is something pretty good, 'being true' to which is 'commendable.' What if 'thine own self' is not so good? What if it's 'pretty bad'? Wouldn't it be better *not* to be true to thine own self in that case? You see, that's my situation."
>
> —Whit Stillman, *The Last Days of Disco,
> with Cocktails at Petrossian Afterwards*

The purpose of this chapter is to work out two related claims regarding how to think about the fallen self, i.e., the self in sin. First, following on the relational ontology we sketched in the previous chapter, we need to think about sin relationally rather than in terms of substance and accidents. Second, in order to understand sin, we need recourse to figurative discourse. Taking Ricoeur as a point of departure, in the first section we will see why reflection on sin and evil requires a hermeneutics of figurative discourse. Sin and evil cannot be explained, but must be described. Phenomenological description will not, however, render sin and evil transparent, because theirs is an irreducibly opaque phenomenality. Consequently we need a *hermeneutics* of sin and evil in order to gain some understanding of them. In the second section I give a hermeneutical investigation of the incurved self—i.e., the self curved in on itself in sin. The image of incurvature is helpful regarding both of our aims: to think fault figuratively, and to figure it relationally.

Interpreting Sin and Evil: Opaque Phenomena and Hermeneutics

There are philosophical as well as theological reasons why reflection on sin and evil needs to be hermeneutical in nature. First, sin and evil cannot be adequately conceptualized or illuminated through direct reflection; they are phenomenally opaque. This is a central insight in Ricoeur's early trilogy on the *Philosophy of the Will*, which will be our first point of departure.

Bracketing and Figuring Fault

Freedom and Nature, the first volume of Ricoeur's trilogy, aims at an eidetic description of the essential "meanings or principles of intelligibility" of willing—a sort of "keyboard of human nature." These eidetic principles are not Platonized Ideas or forms, but they are essential elements in a schematic understanding of the will and therefore precede any empirical description of particular actions (FN 3–4). In the interest of this eidetic description, Ricoeur finds it necessary to bracket two constitutive features of human activity: first, he brackets *transcendence,* which "hides within it the ultimate origin of subjectivity" (FN 3). Second, he brackets *fault,* which is the "corrupt state" of self-division and self-bondage that "profoundly alters" the intelligibility of human action (FN 3, 20 n. 9). Ricoeur believes that fault is an indispensable feature in any robust account of human agency, but it is necessary to bracket it because (1) phenomenology is incapable of treating it adequately, and (2) eidetic description limits its inquiry to essential structures, whereas fault is a concrete actuality rather than an essential structure of the human being. Fault is "alien," "an accident, an interruption, a fall." Eidetic inquiry can disclose certain principles of intelligibility regarding the interaction of the voluntary and the involuntary, but there is no such principle of intelligibility for the contingent disruption that is fault. "The *fault is absurd*" (FN 24). It must therefore remain in brackets.

Ricoeur's next volume, *Fallible Man,* shifts from a general eidetics of the will to an *empirics* of the will. Ricoeur considers the specific question of fallibility, but here too the actuality of fault remains in brackets. Instead, Ricoeur investigates the structures that make human beings uniquely capable of fault: Why is fault an existential possibility for human beings but not animals, plants, and minerals? Since fallibility is the possibility of fault (FM 143), there is a qualitative gap that separates this investigation from the next volume, *The Symbolism of Evil.* This is the gap in which evil is posited. However, at no point does Ricoeur try to explain or account for the "leap" that actually posits evil. This is a crucial and deliberate omission, attesting to the opacity of evil (FM 142f.). Instead, *The Symbolism of Evil* starts from the other side of this gap, after sin has been posited, in order to think through the actuality of fault. Ricoeur finally removes the earlier phenomenological brackets, and his empirics of the will gives way to a *poetics* of the will, which reflects on the various symbols that shape human understanding of evil: first defilement, then sin, and finally guilt. Rather than proceeding with abstract ideas, Ricoeur wants to let the believing soul speak (SE 19), and this means attending to the figurative discourse that gives voice to these religious phenomena. The philosopher might be tempted to take a "shortcut" to religious psychology and direct descriptions of religious phenomena like sin, evil, and pardon, but they are only accessible by taking the long route through symbolic discourse (SE 266, 274). In *The Symbolism of Evil,* Ricoeur fixes his attention on figurative discourse at the level of the symbol; in later works, however, he will expand this insight to include texts and narratives, and speak in terms of hermeneutics rather than poetics.[1] Ricoeur seeks to give figurative discourse its due by reflecting on the full semantic scope of lived experience. If we hope to hear what the believing soul has to say, we cannot reduce these figures of meaning to allegories or rationalized concepts.[2]

The indispensability of figurative discourse is already evident in Ricoeur's introduction to *Freedom and Nature*. Even the apparently simple task of outlining fault in order to bracket it ends up being deeply figurative. Fault is the bondage that Paul laments in his epistle to the Romans: "For what I am doing, I do not understand; for I am not practicing what I would like to do, but I am doing the very thing I hate" (Rom. 7:15; cf. FN 21). Ricoeur describes this as a *passion*, by which he means not an intense affectivity or emotional passivity, but an "aberrant principle" in which the self is divided within itself, and binds itself to itself (FN 21, 23). However, in binding itself to itself, the self effectively binds itself to nothing. The self binds its own freedom and projects this bondage "into an intentional *Nothing*" (FN 24). This "Nothing" is not the negativity or limitation that is endemic to and inseparable from finite existence. Fault is therefore not reducible to finitude. Fault is the nothingness of *vanity*; it is "a lie of the soul," a "chasing after the wind." It is the perverse self-regard of "reproach, suspicion, concupiscence, envy, hurt, and grief" (FN 23). Taking vanity further, this passion for Nothing also introduces a "bad," "unhappy," "painful infinite" into the act of willing. The self tries to deify itself. But this self-deification—the apotheosis of one's own will—"is in fact its demonization" (FN 24).

Ricoeur's description echoes Karl Barth's commentary on Romans, which describes this movement of self-deification as "the madness of the devil—*Eritus sicut Deus* (*ye shall be as God*)." This mad infinite may not look directly demonic or destructive; indeed, it often manifests itself "in our devotion to some romantic infinity, some No-God of this world, which we have created for ourselves."[3] Whatever its form, this self-deification is a transgression of human limits. In *Church Dogmatics* IV/1, Barth identifies sin as paradoxical, inexplicable, and absurd because it contradicts our humanity. Sin is absurd because we have no warrant for this desire to be like God. Consequently, in sin the human "loves and chooses his inner nothingness," which can only manifest itself in an impotent self-contradiction. It is absurd, and as such no principle can explain it. "It cannot be deduced or explained or justified. It is simply a fact."[4] In his Romans commentary, Barth writes: "We see all men doing what Adam did, and then suffering as Adam suffered. We see men sin, and then die. We see men wresting from God what is His, and then being brought to shame. We know that the 'then' is really 'therefore'. We are, however, unable to see the causal relationship; only the concrete facts are visible to us."[5] As such, our only apprehension of this absurd fact can be descriptive.[6] What Ricoeur demonstrates is that this description needs to take the long hermeneutical detour through the otherness of symbols, myths, narratives, and texts.

Sin Loves to Hide Itself

In addition to their irreducible opacity and absurdity, sin and evil are also elusive. As Eberhard Jüngel observes, "What Heracleitus once said approvingly of nature (φύσις), is true of evil and sin, but true in a very evil sense: 'Nature likes to hide'."[7] As a result, sin and evil are hidden from the self-reflective gaze. This is why Anti-Climacus writes that there needs to be a revelation in order to know what sin is (SUD 89, 95–96).[8] To paraphrase Pascal, the heart has sins that consciousness does not know. This requires a certain realism regarding sin, for as Ricoeur observes, "the consciousness of sin is not its measure." Rather, sin is one's "true situation before God," and no self-consciousness is sufficient to comprehend the breadth or depth of one's sin. This is why the self needs an other—such as the prophets—to expose and denounce sin.[9]

Sin loves to hide itself, and therefore revelation is necessary in order to expose it. This is true on a theoretical level as well as an individual level. Sin and evil elude theoretical comprehension. Kierkegaard's pseudonym Vigilius Haufniensis confronts the problem of thinking sin in his book *The Concept of Anxiety*: What can explain original sin? How is sin possible? What can account for its origin? Sin poses a deep provocation to philosophical psychology, which would seem capable of accounting for a psychic fact like sin. But a psychological explanation, like all scientific discourse, deals with essential *possibilities,* and in order to account for a psychological possibility one must have recourse to the universality and ideality of the concept. Sin, however, is a concrete, particular *actuality.* "Sin does not properly belong in any science," Haufniensis writes, because sin is a singularity that concerns the existing individual. The only discourse that is the proper domain for talk about sin is the sermon, for in the sermon "the single individual speaks as the single individual to the single individual" (CA 16). Haufniensis will later propose that *dogmatics* is the only theoretical discourse that can explain sin, but it can only do so retroactively by presupposing sin as actual, and dogmatics hears about this actuality in the proclamation of the *kerygma,* that is, in scripture and in the proclamation of the sermon (CA 19). Similarly, in *The Sickness Unto Death* Anti-Climacus maintains that sin cannot be raised to the level of a universal concept: "Sin cannot be thought" (SUD 119–20). To understand sin properly is not to articulate a universal essence, but instead to recognize oneself as complicit in sin.

Sin and evil love to hide themselves, and yet they do show themselves. They are phenomena insofar as they appear, and yet they never appear transparently. They exhibit a troubling sort of phenomenality. Theirs is a problematic appearing: they are hidden, strange, foreign. This is why the self-recognition of the sinner is a matter of faith rather than transparent intuition.[10] But as Richard Kearney shows in *Strangers, Gods, and Monsters,* this alterity is not a purely alien reality. This hiddenness and otherness are within the self. It is tempting to identify sin and evil as that which is an external entity, through scapegoating, vilification, demonization, etc. These strategies give us a tangible source of evil, sin, and suffering—for example, personal and political enemies, demonic forces or the devil, the body, or evil substance as in Manichaeism. But this externalization creates a blind spot within the self, since it ignores one's own complicity in evil. As Ricoeur argues, evil involves an active as well as a passive dimension: evil precedes me, such that I find myself the victim of something I did not begin; but evil is also something I initiate, for which I am responsible and culpable.[11]

* * *

Although the actuality of fault is not transparently available to eidetic description or the introspective gaze, neither Kierkegaard nor Ricoeur take this limitation of thought to demand utter silence. One of the guiding aims of Kierkegaard's pseudonymous authorship is to plumb the depths and test the limits of communicating that which cannot be mediated by the universal. That which cannot be mediated by the universal cannot be communicated directly, so Kierkegaard writes with the hope of communicating to the existing individual in the only way possible: *indirectly*. And Kierkegaard never stops trying; his voluminous literary output warrants Ricoeur's observation that Kierkegaard is not a mystic or an intuitionist, but a reflective thinker.[12] Granted, sin cannot be grasped reflectively, and it cannot be "thought" or mediated by the universal, but it certainly gives rise to a great deal of thinking, reflecting, writing, and intellectual struggle. As we observe Kierkegaard's voluminous authorship, we recognize the truth of Ricoeur's dictum "the symbol gives rise to thought" (*Le symbole donne à penser*). Just as Ricoeur brackets fault from his eidetic phenomenology in order to return to it with a *hermeneutics* of the symbolism of evil, so Kierkegaard denies direct communication in order to struggle with indirect communication.[13] In keeping with this hermeneutical insight, our task in the second section of this chapter is to reflect on a particular symbol of sin: *incurvature*.

Being in Adam

As we reflect on the opacity and hiddenness of sin, the ontological question returns: What *is* sin? In chapter 3 we observed the problems that arise from thinking about sin in the terms of substance metaphysics. Is sin a substance or accident? A similar problem arises when we try to think of sin in terms of act and being. Bonhoeffer addresses this problem in his *Habilitationsschrift*, the aptly titled *Act and Being*. We could interpret sin as an individual act, but like the Protestant scholastic definition of sin as accident, this does not go deep enough. "If sin were no more than a free act of the particular moment, a retreat to sinless being would in principle be possible" (AB 145). No, the particular sins arise out of a deeper ontological source. As Anti-Climacus puts it, particular sinful acts are like puffs of smoke coming from a locomotive; they do not move the train, but manifest something much deeper (SUD 106). But what is the status of this something deeper? It is tempting to historicize, psychologize, naturalize, or ontologize original sin, but these strategies obscure the character of sin as breaking forth in a contingent act, thereby opening up excuses for that which is inexcusable (AB 145). The challenge, then, is to reconcile act and being in our understanding of sin.

According to Bonhoeffer, the New Testament provides the right concept with its notion of Being in Adam. But how do we interpret this ontological participation in Adam? Here we can benefit by considering the case of Augustine. From the *Confessions* we know that the ontological status of evil was a question of great perplexity for Augustine, and an obstacle on his way to faith. *Unde malum?* Augustine's famous conclusion is that evil has no positive ontological status; it is not a substance but a wound in being.[14] It is a nothing. Hence Augustine's definition of wickedness, which is not "a substance but a perversity of will twisted away from the highest substance, you O God, toward inferior things."[15] Sin and evil cannot be defined in terms of substance or nature, but must be understood as a defective movement, as Augustine puts it in *De libero arbitrio*. Evil occurs when the will turns away from God and from that which truly is, toward that which is in fact nothing.[16] With this interpretation, Augustine makes an important contribution to the image of sin as incurvature.[17] Sin is a refusal of the relations that constitute the human self; it is a proud and willful turn away from God, leading to inappropriate self-love (*amor sui*), as well as a misdirected and inordinate love of creation rather than Creator.[18] Sin is an *aversio a Deo*[19]— a sinful turn away from God, as a sort of perverse conversion (*conversio*) to oneself, which in turn distorts one's relations with others.

With this concept of sin in place, Augustine makes a major break with Manichaeism. But Augustine was then compelled to distinguish his position from the Pelagians, who embraced Augustine's voluntarism because it allows for a strong affirmation of individual responsibility and thus exonerates God for punishing sin. On the Pelagian view sin is a voluntary act, and so our relation to Adam is merely one of imitation. But this account was clearly unsatisfactory for Augustine, who had a more profound sense of the existential anguish of the servile will, and of evil as an involuntary penetrating to "the very heart of the voluntary."[20] Augustine seeks to maintain individual responsibility for sin, arguing contra Manichaeism that sin is willed rather than a nature or substance, and contra Pelagianism that evil somehow precedes and corrupts individual acts. Augustine tries to reconcile these concerns with his concept of original sin as an inherited guilt, transmitted from Adam. But how is Adam's original sin transmitted? As Ricoeur observes, Augustine posits a quasi-biological concept of original sin, transmitted like a contagion through the generation of subsequent human beings.[21] As a result, Augustine's leaves us with an inconsistent concept of sin as a "quasi-nature."[22]

Ricoeur argues that it is necessary to "deconstruct" (*défaire*)[23] Augustine's concept of original sin. The concept must be *destroyed* as false knowledge—i.e.,

The Incurved Self 61

as quasi-juridical and quasi-biological knowledge—so that we might understand its true meaning as a symbol. In other words, this interpretation destroys abstract speculation and scholasticism in order to recover the meaning that is given in the lived experience of preaching and the confession of sin.[24] The narrative of Adam provides a rational symbol, but we must avoid the false rationality that renders this a speculative concept, as well as the false historicizing that renders it as a dogmatic mythology. Instead of venturing into the thin air of abstraction, we need to return to the surplus of meaning contained within the symbolism of Adam's sin. Rather than explaining the origin and transmission of sin, this symbolism describes and discloses the way we experience and understand evil—as something that binds us as captives, that precedes us, and which we perpetuate but do not inaugurate. We confess our sins not only as individuals, but communally, confessing to a "transbiological and transhistorical solidarity of sin," which "constitutes the metaphysical unity of the human race."[25] In this way we understand ourselves as Being in Adam.

Ricoeur's essay makes a strong case against trying to reduce this figurative understanding to explanation, so when he talks about the unity and solidarity of humanity we should not take this as a starting point for metaphysical speculation or conceptual explanation. Bonhoeffer's notion of "Being in Adam" is helpful in this regard. In *Sanctorum Communio*, Bonhoeffer argues that we must maintain both individual culpability and the universality of sin, while avoiding Augustine's false biological concept of sin and the species (SC 110–12). Being in Adam is not a matter of participating in a Platonic form or *eidos* of human being, nor is it an Aristotelian participation in a nature. Instead, Bonhoeffer draws on Max Scheler's notion of collective personality to interpret Adam as the collective person (*Gesamtperson* or *Kollektivperson*) of fallen humanity.[26] According to Scheler, the concrete, finite person is a social being—living, experiencing, and acting with other persons. Against this background, the person discovers herself not only as an individual agent among others, but as belonging to "a totality of interconnections of experience" which is concentrated in a social unity. This collective person is a center of experience and action. Moral subjectivity is not given strictly individually. The moral subject does not merely experience herself as an individual; rather, "as a moral subject in this whole, everyone is *also* given as a 'person acting with others,' as a 'man with others,' and as 'coresponsible' for everything morally relevant in this totality."[27] Scheler argues that every concrete finite person consists of an individual and collective person. Both factors (individual and collective personality) belong to the concrete finite person and are reciprocally related. This collective personality is not a synthesis, an artificial construct, or an abstraction, but an experienced reality of the concrete person.[28]

Following Scheler, Bonhoeffer argues that the human being is always both individual and humanity (AB 120). "I am I and humanity in one." In the act of sin, "for which I hold myself utterly responsible on every occasion, I find myself already in the humanity of Adam. I see humanity in me necessarily committing this, my own free deed. . . . The I 'is' not as an individual, but always in humanity. And just because the deed of the individual is at the same time that of humanity, human beings must hold themselves individually responsible for the whole guilt of humankind" (AB 146). With this description, Bonhoeffer holds together the conflicting aspects that problematize Augustine's concept of original sin: namely, individual responsibility along with the awareness of sin as the condition of all humanity, as something that precedes me but which I perpetuate in my individual act. However, this insight derives neither from metaphysical speculation nor from a causal explanation that would conceive of sin as an entity. Instead, it is phenomenologically descriptive. This description is, however, hermeneutical because this collective personality is given *as* the figure of Adam. Bonhoeffer does not thematize the role of figurative discourse to the extent Ricoeur does, but he shares Ricoeur's emphasis that our self-understanding as Being in Adam arises through preaching and through the confession of sin in the church.[29] I understand myself in Adam not through an immediate intuition gained by reflecting on my own acts, because, as Bonhoeffer observes, "we remain opaque to ourselves" (AB 142). Self-understanding requires the mediation of another—namely, the proclamation of the word that discloses the self to itself. The self needs the external word of preaching and the sacraments to break open its incurvature.

Incurvature and the Fall

> The thirst of the ring lives in you: every ring strives and turns to reach itself again.
>
> —"On the Virtuous," *Thus Spoke Zarathustra*[30]

Our task in the remainder of this chapter is to unpack this image of sin as incurvature. I will focus on this image because it is particularly helpful for thinking about sin in a relational sense, thereby moving out of the framework of substance ontology. This image also suggests itself because it informs the works of Ricoeur, particularly in his critique of the self-enclosed ego that needs to be decentered by a prior word. Our main guide through this discussion will be Bonhoeffer, who interprets Being in Adam with the image of the heart curved in on itself (*cor curvum in se*).

Bonhoeffer draws this image from Luther's *Lectures on Romans*, which describe the human being as "deeply curved in upon itself,"[31] such that we are only concerned with what appears good and useful for us.[32] The self is curved inward, cut off from God and from the neighbor, and therefore ultimately cut off from true self-understanding as well. The incurved self is opaque to itself, despite its impression that it knows its own good. This is true of secular and pious selves alike. In Luther's words, the human being is so curved inward that he "uses not only physical but even spiritual goods for his own purposes and in all things seeks only himself."³³ The self takes "the finest gifts of God in upon itself and enjoys them" and "even uses God Himself to achieve [its] aims."³⁴ As we already noted in our discussion of the onto-theological condition, religious piety is all too often a manifestation of incurvature. Luther reminds us that the *homo religiosus* can also be a *homo incurvatus in se*.³⁵

The Beginning

Although the figure of incurvature appears throughout Bonhoeffer's authorship, I will focus our discussion on *Creation and Fall*, which originated as a lecture course in the winter semester of 1932–33 at the University of Berlin. There Bonhoeffer offers his fullest treatment of incurvature, giving a hermeneutically rich description of human being in Adam. In these lectures Bonhoeffer pursues his descriptions in a decidedly theological voice. Bonhoeffer thereby reflects the influence of Barth, departing from the assumption that historical-critical analysis is the only way for biblical scholarship to be truly *wissenschaftlich*, in favor of a decidedly theological-kerygmatic reading of the text.³⁶ Bonhoeffer does not present the narrative of Genesis 1–3 as a literal historical record,³⁷ yet neither is he content to dismiss it as a *mere* myth or fairy tale. He affirms the need for figurative language, especially when narrating that which is fundamentally mysterious. Genesis 1–3 narrates a beginning that is impenetrable to us. We cannot speak of it adequately, nor can we discern its why or how: "Where the beginning begins, there our thinking stops; there it comes to an end." Thinking is thrown back upon itself. The fact that the Bible speaks of this beginning is deeply provocative to thinking: "the desire to ask after the beginning is the innermost passion of our thinking" (CF 25). But for those who inhabit the ambiguous middle between banishment from Eden and the advent of the Eschaton, this beginning is a destination that is continually deferred. The sufficient reason always slips away. As those who occupy the twilight (*Zwielicht*) between the primal state of creation and the fulfillment of all things (CF 104), we live in a circle. The thinking of fallen human beings "lacks a beginning because it is a circle. We think in a circle. But we also feel and will in a circle. We exist in a circle" (CF 26). The beginning is closed off from us. The point of origin is inaccessible.

One might try to deem this circle infinite. This is the strategy of idealism, which declares this circle of thinking to be the beginning itself, and posits itself as its own object, "as an entity over against itself" (CF 27). But this is the vicious circularity of thinking curved in on itself. Here Bonhoeffer iterates his critique of idealism and the self-reflective, self-positing subject. This subject strives to be its own origin, its own foundation, and its own guarantor—a striving that Bonhoeffer identifies as the impulse of the incurved self. This theme later appears in the work of Ricoeur, who likewise critiques "the tendency of the 'I' to close a circle with itself" (FN 20).³⁸ Ricoeur describes reflection as having a threefold wish to be absolute consciousness: (1) the reflecting I wishes to be total rather than limited to a finite perspective; (2) it wishes to be transparent, such that self-consciousness coincides perfectly with intentional consciousness; and (3) it wishes to be self-sufficient, so that it does not depend on any necessity, involuntary, or ontological belonging that might precede its acts.[39]

But the beginning frustrates this ambition. Thinking needs to locate and mediate the beginning—an impulse Ricoeur observes in the psychoanalyst seeking the origin of psychic life, the historian seeking the birth of a regime, the anthropologist seeking the beginning of humankind, the biologist seeking the beginning of life, or the cosmologist seeking a "big bang."[40] But the beginning is irretrievable, immemorial.[41] Thus Bonhoeffer writes: "Thinking pounds itself to pieces on the beginning. Because thinking wants to reach back to the beginning and yet never can want it, all thinking pounds itself to pieces, shatters against itself, breaks up into fragments, dissolves, in view of the beginning that it wants and cannot want" (CF 27). Turned in on itself, thinking divides against itself; it wants, and yet cannot want, this beginning.

In addition to idealism, Bonhoeffer also critiques critical philosophy, calling it "a systematic despair of its own beginning—indeed of *any* beginning. Critical philosophy may proudly renounce what it lacks the power to attain, or else lapse into a resignation that leads to its complete destruction; either alternative stems from the same human hatred of the unknown beginning" (CF 27–28). The beginning is inaccessible, and yet scripture claims to speak of this beginning. This presumption provokes many objections,[42] but our only access to the beginning is by *hearing* and submitting ourselves to this text that precedes us (CF 30). To hear the proclamation of this word—"in the beginning"—is to be decentered. As Ricoeur observes, the self can seek the beginning from its "own self-centered awareness," or one can start with the proclamation of "the beginning itself, which decenters consciousness and imposes itself as being there already before consciousness starts to look for it."[43]

There is a circularity in hearing and believing, but it is not the circularity of idealism, which seeks to close the circle of its own reflections. The account of Genesis does not give reflection an absolute *archē* from which to understand the genesis of being. Rather, it narrates an event that decenters reflection. To be guided by a prior narrative, Ricoeur writes, "would be to break out of the enchanted enclosure of consciousness of oneself, to end the prerogative of self-reflection."[44] There is no intuition of the origin. Neither is there evidence that would give a foundation. But there is a legitimate hermeneutical circularity. This knowledge is not an achievement of onto-theological speculation, nor is it information that we can commandeer and control, nor does it allow us to escape the circular middle and occupy the position of God, becoming the beginning ourselves (CF 31). It is impossible to discover why the world was created, whether this creation was necessary, or what the inner logic of God's plan might be. The proclamation ("In the beginning God created heaven and earth") does not answer these questions. It simply declares that God created. God the Creator is the beginning, and we cannot speculate our way back behind this (CF 31–32).

Temptation and Fall

In a similar manner, speculation about the *ratio* of the fall into sin also runs into impenetrable mystery. The biblical account of Adam's sin does not speculate about the origin of sin and evil, but instead witnesses to its incomprehensible reality (CF 104). There is no psychologistic explanation here, nor is there a *diaboli ex machina* that would explain the fall by blaming the devil. Such an explanation would in principle exonerate Adam, providing an excuse for that which is inexcusable. The event of the fall is opaque, and we must admit that here the biblical narrative is not explanatory in nature.

While forswearing the explanatory approach to sin and evil, Bonhoeffer does offer a powerful interpretation of Adam's sin and a description of the consequences of this inexplicable primordial event. It is entirely appropriate, Bonhoeffer argues, to narrate the chain of events leading up to an evil deed, but it is crucial that this narration not present itself as an explanation. The narration can carry us right to the brink of the deed, but here "the chasm opens, where it becomes completely incomprehensible how the evil could have been done" (CF 117). The narrative does not explain the qualitative leap in which evil is posited. With regard to evil, genuinely theological reflection must relinquish the speculative question of "Why," which presupposes that it is possible for us to get behind our being as sinners: "If we could answer the question why, then *we* would not be sinners." The genuinely theological question, therefore, "is not a question about the origin of evil but one about the actual overcoming of evil on the cross; it seeks the real forgiveness of guilt and the reconciliation of the fallen world" (CF 120).

The biblical account narrates the temptation that precedes the fall. Bonhoeffer notes that the possibility of becoming *like God* emerges from a religious question—from the "pious question" posed by the serpent. God commanded that Adam and Eve not eat from the tree in the center of the garden, but the serpent asks, "Did God really say . . . ?" The serpent exploits the hermeneutical situation.[45] What did God *really* mean? Surely God didn't mean *that*. And so begins "the era of suspicion." As Ricoeur observes, "a fault line is introduced into the most fundamental condition of language, namely, the relation of trust, what linguists call the sincerity clause."[46] With this interpretive cunning, the serpent invites the human being to look behind the given meaning ("so badly misrepresented in this human word"!) to find the deeper knowledge, "of a more exalted God, a nobler God, who has no need to make such a prohibition." By showing what the command "really" means, one is actually performing a service to God by removing the offense of the prohibition.

Thus opens "a new possibility of 'being for God,'" a new piety, a more profound obedience, a more perfect *gnosis*.[47] But it is precisely this pledge to be for God on one's own terms that is "the primal evil in the pious question of the serpent" (CF 106–109). With this reading of the text, Bonhoeffer shows the human religious impulse as already implicated in this primordial transgression. One cannot simply blame sensuality or the human desire to know, as has too often been suggested. No, as Ricoeur observes, it is a "sudden mutation in human desire,"[48] the corruption of a good desire. The serpent appeals to the look of the tree, to the desirability of its fruit. But the serpent does not simply appeal to a biological taste or hunger. Rather, "the tree was desirable to make one wise" (Gen. 3:6). Yet this was not the desire for a wisdom befitting humanity, but rather "the desire for infinity, which implies a transgression of all limits."[49] On this point Ricoeur and Bonhoeffer concur with Barth, who describes the sinful desire to be *sicut deus* as the madness of the devil, which aims to rob God, to cross the boundary between Creator and creature.[50] According to Bonhoeffer, the human being was created to recognize *limits*. First, Adam recognized the inherent limits of finite creatureliness, as distinguished from the Creator (CF 86–87). These limits were not a source of frustration, because Adam knew them as signs of grace. Similarly, Adam recognized the limit of the other human. Adam experienced the woman as a limit, yet he loved her as a limit (CF 97–99). After the fall, however, Adam does not perceive his limits as grace but as frustration. He hates his limits. He "no longer regards the other person with love," and thus "the limit is now the mark of dividedness" (CF 122). Where Adam previously lived in freedom for the other, the bonds of this freedom are severed. The self cuts itself off from others and curves in on itself.

Likewise, through the fall Adam goes from being in the image of God (*imago dei*) to being "like God" (*sicut deus*). As the serpent promised, human beings became *like God* by transgressing the tree of the knowledge of good and evil. Bonhoeffer distinguishes between being "in the image of God," and being "like God" as follows:

> Imago dei—humankind in the image of God in being for God and the neighbour, in its original creatureliness and limitedness; sicut deus—humankind like God in knowing out of its own self about good and evil, in having no limit and acting out of its own resources, in its aseity, in its being alone. (CF 113)

In coming to be *sicut deus,* human beings also come to know about death. Now humankind "lives in a circle" (CF 90–91).

The fallen Adamic self cannot want God to be God. It wants to be God. Bonhoeffer agrees with Luther, Nietzsche, and Sartre regarding the ego's desire to be God. The problem is that any *imitatio dei* ends up being a travesty rather than a genuine likeness. This becomes evident in Adam's attempt to mimic God's aseity: the aseity that results from becoming "like God" is in fact a distorted image of the Godhead. To be created *imago dei* means to image God's relationality, such that relationality is constitutive of selfhood. It means being free for others, so that one embraces the fact that others are *other* than oneself. To bear the image of God also means that one sees the freedom of others as a good thing. God shows this in the act of creation, when "the Creator denies [the Creator's own self]" (CF 39). God also shows this in the kenotic love expressed in Christ's incarnation. By contrast, in becoming *sicut deus* the fallen human cannot abide anyone or anything independent of itself. At its worst, the fallen human refuses "to recognize any limit at all" in relation to the other, giving rise to obsessive desire and the lustful ambition to possess the other (CF 123). No longer is the limit of the other a blessing; the limit is a source of frustration and resentment. The self covets the good of others, wanting everything for itself. The self "no longer needs any others, it is the lord of its own world." Or so it believes. In reality, the self "is the solitary lord and despot of its own mute, violated, silenced, dead, ego-world [*Ichwelt*]" (CF 142). The purported independence and autonomy of the self is actually moribund isolation.

Sensing that we are unable to live without others, Adam seeks to retrieve, replace, or replicate the presence of the other with the voice of *conscience*. Conscience is vital to one's attempt to be like God, to know good and evil out of oneself, because it allows the self to feign alterity by mimicking the voices of God and the neighbor (CF 142). In conscience, the self attempts to be its own other. It is important that the self prevent a truly *other* voice from intruding upon its isolation, because this otherness would pose a threat to it. In *Ethics*, Bonhoeffer observes that the voice of God is a threat to human beings who presume to be the origin of good and evil and the source of their own unity and identity:

> They do not deny their own evil. But in the voice of their conscience those who have become evil call themselves back to their authentic self, their better self, to the good. This good, which consists in the unity of human beings with themselves, is now considered the origin of all good. It is God's good, it is the good for the neighbor. Bearing the knowledge of good and evil within themselves, human beings have now become the judge of God and others, just as they are their own judge. (E 308)[51]

Thus conscience is actually a defense against the voice of others (CF 128), insofar as it allows the self to preserve the illusion of being the origin of good and evil, and of being properly related to others: "Conscience claims to be the voice of God and the norm for relating to other people. By relating properly to themselves, human beings think to regain the proper relationship to God and to others" (E 308). But conscience is the voice of the self addressing itself, determining its own responsibilities, showing remorse for the failings that it recognizes, and determining its own justification. Ultimately, the pseudo-alterity of conscience keeps the self locked within itself, impervious to the interruption of the other—whether God or the neighbor.

And so incurvature results in a paradoxical condition of living death. It is the despair that Anti-Climacus diagnoses as the *sickness unto death*, the torment of which is precisely being unable to die (SUD 18). At the same time, the despair of incurvature also consists in being unable to live. Humankind "lives out of its own resources, yet it cannot live. It is compelled to live, yet it cannot live" (CF 135). Death means "no longer being able to live before God, and yet having to live before God" (CF 90). Death "means to have life not as a gift but as a *commandment.... To be dead means to-have-to-live.*" There is no escape from this imperative to *be*. It "demands from me something that I am not in a position to fulfill. It obliges me to live out of myself, out of my own resources" and this is precisely what I cannot do (CF 90–91). This dividedness therefore means an ongoing, self-renewing revolt against one's own Dasein; "it is a quarrel with life, a grasping at the life that would put an end to *this* life, that would be the new life. What Adam wants under any circumstance is *to live*" (CF 142–43). Yet this is impossible.

Bonhoeffer describes the internal division that tears Adam between death and life: "It is therefore essentially a desperate, an unquenchable, an eternal thirst that Adam feels for life. It is essentially a thirst for death; the more passionately Adam seeks after life, the more completely he is ensnared by death." Adam yearns for death; he "wants to die—which of us wants to live forever? Yet in this very act of dying Adam hopes to rescue his life from the bondservice and drudgery [*Frohn*] of having to live without life" (CF 143). This is not a nihilistic hatred of life. It is a desire for life, but a desire that cannot escape its very inability to live.

Bound Freedom and the Ontology of Self-Justification

The desire for autonomous freedom results in a similar paradox: Adam has the semblance of freedom, but is in fact unfree. Prior to the fall, the human being existed in the image of God. In order that God might recognize the *imago dei* in creation, God created a free creature. "Only in that which is itself free could the free Creator behold the Creator" (CF 60–61). But the biblical conception of freedom is not a quality or attribute that a human being possesses in isolation, in and of itself. Freedom is a relational phenomenon; it only appears in relation to others. "Being free means 'being-free-for-the-other,' because I am bound to the other. Only by being in relation with the other am I free" (CF 62–63). But with the fall, freedom curves in on itself, longing to be free from otherness and unlimited in fulfilling its desires. True freedom, by contrast, is not being free *from* others, but being free *for* them. This definition is counterintuitive insofar as we are accustomed to thinking of freedom as a capacity of choice through which we select from one of an array of possibilities, which we then realize through our action. But the arbitrary liberty of indifference is, as Kierkegaard puts it, a *chimera* (JP 1241).[52]

Charles Taylor also helps to expose the inadequacies of the strictly negative concept of freedom, according to which freedom means being free *from* external constraints or limitations. In short, I am free if nothing stops me from doing what I want. But the concept of freedom is incoherent without a stronger sense of what I am free *for*—in other words, freedom is inseparable from strong evaluations regarding what is desirable and what I should do. If we suppose that freedom means being able to do what I want, a host of other questions arise: *What* do I want? How do I *know* what I really want? *Should* I want it? Once we pay attention to the complexities, conflicts, and confusion that arise with these questions, we can better understand how freedom can be bound.[53] The fallen (*sündig*) self exists in self-division and self-bondage. This is what Ricoeur characterizes as *fault*, evoking the Pauline description of the incapacity that disrupts our fundamental human capabilities. In Barth's words, "an abyss is disclosed between myself and—myself."[54] I observe, "with evident horror," myself doing the very thing I hate. Here a dark, impenetrable mystery arises within the self. In Paul's words, "what I am doing, I do not understand."

Philosophers have often bristled at the suggestion of the will being bound by sin. There is something deeply offensive about the idea of a self-binding freedom: it offends advocates of negative conceptions of freedom; it offends the determinist, who wants to deny freedom altogether by appealing to physical/material causality and therefore chafes at (1) any notion of freedom and (2) the idea of letting a religious notion like sin interfere or have any significance in philosophical argumentation; it also offends the intellectualist, who maintains that one cannot know the good and yet act contrary to it. But Ricoeur insists that philosophy must not disregard this troubling phenomenon:

> It might seem humiliating to the philosopher to admit the presence of an absolute irrational in the heart of man, not merely as a *mystery* quickening the intelligence, but as a central and in a sense elementary opacity which obstructs the very access to intelligibility as much as to mystery. Might not the philosopher take exception to introducing the absurd on the pretext that it is dictated by a Christian theology of original sin? Yet if theology opens our eyes to an obscure segment of human reality, no methodological *a priori* should prevent the philosopher from having his eyes opened and henceforth reading man, his history and civilization, under the sign of the fall. (FN 25)

There is undoubtedly a deep mystery, even opacity in sin and its impact on the self. As we have seen, philosophical reflection must relinquish its desire for conceptual transparency in favor of a hermeneutics of evil. In this region there is a surplus of meaning to be thought, and philosophical anthropology can only ignore this to its own detriment.

Once we move beyond a merely negative conception of freedom *from* and recognize that freedom requires the more determinate notion of freedom *for*, we can better understand Luther's infamous treatise on *The Bondage of the Will* (*De servo arbitrio*), which has too often been interpreted as a defense of psychological determinism. The incurvature of sin is a situation of bondage, and therefore we cannot speak of a properly free will. But this does not mean that the self cannot deliberate and decide what to have for dinner, whether to quit a job, etc. Luther maintains that we are free with regard to that which is below us, but we are not free regarding that which is above us.[55] In other words, we are free with regard to our mundane, worldly activities (*coram mundo*), but we are not free before God (*coram Deo*). This means we are bound to try to establish ourselves before God—compelled to posit ourselves, to establish our own position before God, to seek to ensure our recognition and thus our identity. This is the situation that Anti-Climacus describes as despairingly willing to be oneself (SUD 67). The self desperately and despairingly strives to constitute itself, to give itself meaning, to justify itself within its horizon of significance, and to be recognized as a self.

* * *

In Adam, the self is bound in an ontology of self-justification. In other words, the self constitutes the meaning of its existence through its own acts and operations. It may be objected that the question of justification is no longer a live issue in late modernity, since it presupposes an outdated forensic concept of the self. Perhaps it made sense to Luther, but anxiety over sin, like the fear of divine judgment, death, and the devil, was a symptom of a lingering medieval mindset and can no longer be taken seriously. Perhaps people have become more enlightened. Or perhaps the leveling effects of modernity have lowered the expectations and aspirations of the self, such that the self no longer holds itself to a transcendent standard. After the death of God, the self no longer exists before God—or any other horizon of the Good, for that matter. Hence our crisis of meaning and value. We see the problem of nihilism in the rise of senseless destruction, as well as in the banal political correctness in which the *nice* has supplanted the *good* as our horizon of evaluation.[56]

And yet the question of justification nevertheless remains an inescapable issue for the self. If Nietzsche's madman is correct and the death of God wiped away our entire horizon,[57] this does not mean there is no longer any horizon at all. After the death of God, we late moderns cannot assume the common horizon of Christendom, and given the fact of religious and cultural plurality we can no longer assume a single shared horizon of the good. Yet strong evaluation remains, even if the horizon has been fractured and fragmented. What counts as a meaningful life? How do I determine whether my life was a success, or even worthwhile? What is the good life, and how do I know that I have lived it? The question takes many forms, but fundamentally it is the question of justification. What justifies my existence? If late-modern selves no longer seek justification before a divine horizon, they still continue to evaluate themselves according to some horizon. As Taylor has shown, these horizons are inescapable.[58]

In fact, after the death of God the need for justification has in many ways acquired greater urgency and even desperation.[59] Jüngel observes that the modern emphasis on individual freedom and self-determination has created a deeper unfreedom. The self is bound because it is driven to justify itself, to prove that its existence is warranted and meaningful.[60] The self has a greater liberty of self-determination and is free to pursue its own happiness. More than ever the self can achieve greater heights of accomplishment, but it can also sink even deeper into despair over itself. We inhabit, in Miroslav Volf's poignant phrase, a culture stripped of grace.[61] In late modernity, the economic logic of exchange governs more severely, and thus the self is under greater pressure to exert more effective mastery and control—of nature, others, and itself. The self is constituted ontologically through its performance. "Be somebody!" is the imperative that summons the self to responsibility.

This ontology of self-justification can take a variety of forms. Perhaps I evaluate myself on the basis of a universal moral law (Kant, Fichte). Or I might evaluate myself according to a law of my own devising, as I create my own new tablets of values (Nietzsche). I might find myself as an existing being, devoid of essence and therefore responsible for defining and making myself through my actions (Sartre).[62] Whatever the law of evaluation, the self is forced to justify itself through its activity. Sartre is more right than he knows: the human being is condemned to be free.[63] But Sartrean freedom is condemnation because nothing comes freely. Were life devoid of all grace, it would be always and only Monday morning. In such a situation the self must take itself up—summon itself and raise itself from its lethargy in an act of self-positing, so that it can undertake the work of self-definition once again. There is no Sabbath for the self.[64] This is why the self, despite its formally "free will," is unfree. Nothing is given freely, nothing can be taken for granted. I must earn in order to receive. Consequently, I cannot be truly free for the other. I am locked in a struggle for recognition, and thus cannot act freely with and for the other because my need for recognition always lingers in the background. The self cannot forget itself; it cannot help but consider everything and everyone in relation to itself.[65] The incurvature of the self deepens. The closed circle tightens.

* * *

Human beings therefore live in accord with their humanity to the extent that they recognize others—and are themselves recognized—unconditionally on the basis of their personhood as prior to their works, on the basis of possibility prior to actuality. As Jüngel observes, this unconditional recognition disrupts the society in which works, actuality, achievement define one's person, one's being. Such a society denies its own humanity and is oblivious to the ontological structure of human being, which does not originate through self-creating, self-realizing activity. The ontology of justification by faith reveals this basic truth about our being: "Being born, like being raised from the dead, is a process in which the human person participates only as all his or her own activity is excluded. One cannot call oneself to life." Consequently, all of our activity has its origin in "being and letting-be," in receiving the gift of our existence with joy and gratitude.[66] This also entails an unconditional recognition of those others who cannot so easily pretend to justify their existence through their achievements—children, the elderly, the disabled, and those at the fringes of society. Human dignity consists in the irrevocable priority of person over works. This is even true for those who appear to have forfeited their humanity and personhood through crimes and atrocities and have no illusions about deserving grace. At the same time, it is also true for those whose achievements appear to define them, as though their success has allowed them to surpass or overcome themselves as passive recipients of being.[67]

This recognition of the unconditional dignity of the person disrupts the ontology of self-justification, which governs the achievement-oriented society. This recognition witnesses to the truth of the ontology of justification by faith; it is a penultimate expression and anticipation of the ultimate word.[68] This insight should not, however, be taken as a starting point for a natural theology, but instead as evidence of God's gracious preservation. Contra the Flacian view, the fall into sin did not pull humanity down into the *imago satanae,* nor does the incurvature of our Being in Adam mean that we act like devils at every moment. As Bonhoeffer argues, God does not abandon humanity, but instead upholds and preserves the fallen creation—not so human beings can remain broken, but in anticipation of Christ coming to restore true relations between God, the self, other human beings, and creation (CF 139–40, 146). We will return to this theme in chapter 6.

Appendix: Revelation, Sin, and Gender

As an addition to our discussion in this chapter, I would like to recall Anti-Climacus's claim that there must be a revelation to show what sin is. It is worth recalling this point because it might seem that our description of incurvature could function as a natural theology of sin—a sort of natural hamartiology, as it were. By observing the countless examples of human selfishness and egocentricity, we would seem to have a wealth of empirical evidence from which to construct a doctrine of sin. Perhaps we could attempt a deduction of a transcendental guilt, or perhaps we could inductively infer something like a sinful human nature. This seems to be the point of G. K. Chesterton's famous statement that original sin "is the only part of Christian theology which can really be proved,"[69] and Reinhold Niebuhr's even bolder claim that "the doctrine of original sin is the only empirically verifiable doctrine of Christian faith."[70] More modestly, perhaps we could use a description of incurvature to illustrate particular instances of sin—manifest as egocentricity, selfishness, vanity, etc.

But we must reiterate the assertion that there must be a revelation to show what sin is. *Why?* To be sure, unaided human reason is constantly judging between good and evil, right and wrong, and these judgments often overlap significantly with biblical judgments regarding sins like theft, lying, murder, and adultery. But revelation is not necessary simply to give us the correct list of prohibitions. That might be the case if sin were reducible to misbehavior; yet sin is not only a matter of particular vices and misdeeds, but about the misrelation to God. As Anti-Climacus puts it, "what makes sin so terrible is that it is before God" (SUD 80). Sin is a misrelation, the broken and refused relation to

God. This is why Anti-Climacus argues that the opposite of sin is not virtue but faith—i.e., the restored relation to God (SUD 82). Revelation is necessary to expose the misrelation for what it is. We cannot know what the corruption is unless we understand how things are supposed to be. The misrelation is therefore only evident from the perspective of the right relation; or to say the same thing in different terms, sin is only evident from the perspective of faith.

There is another reason not to use incurvature as the basis for a natural theology of sin. It requires that one assume the misguided task of trying to show that human beings really are as bad as Christianity seems to suggest. This strategy employs a hermeneutic of suspicion that depicts the self in the most pessimistic terms possible in order to make the description of the *status corruptionis* more compelling and convince people they really do need grace. This task takes on a greater urgency in late modernity; in order to get people to take sin seriously, it seems necessary to expose the ugly underside of the human condition.

Bonhoeffer was highly critical of apologetic and evangelistic techniques that tear down the human being—its strength, ability, and maturity—in order to create a sense of need for grace (LPP 450–51). This strategy could be particularly tempting for an *anthropologia crucis*: to depict the human being in the darkest terms possible, to emphasize the cross as the destruction of human pride and presumption, and thus envision faithful existence as one of severe self-denial and sacrifice. But a hyperbolic rhetoric of human depravity can be destructive in an unedifying way and can stifle the genuinely liberating efficacy of the good news. This has been a common objection of feminist theologians against traditional theological conceptions of sin and redemption. Another feminist objection is that the figure of incurvature depicts a very masculine vision of sin. On this view, separation from others and the desire for self-sufficiency, power, and dominance may reflect male sin, but they do not accurately depict feminine modes of sin. Moreover, it is dangerous for women to think of sin as incurvature because this perpetuates destructive patterns of domination and oppression. Women in harmful and abusive relationships, for instance, should not be encouraged to cultivate submissiveness, passivity, and kenotic self-giving. Instead, they need to be strengthened, to have their subjectivity recognized, and to have clear boundaries between themselves and others who would come to steal, kill, and destroy. This problem is exacerbated when the theology of the cross teaches that the proud, self-protecting ego needs to be broken or even destroyed by a heteronomous transcendence. The violent rhetoric of the cross is not good news for such women, and the call to self-denial is not liberating for those whose selfhood or subjectivity is already denied by a powerful other.[71] Consequently, we need to recognize and affirm the legitimacy of notions like self-actualization and self-realization, which are not reducible to Sartrean subjectivity or Fichtean egology.[72]

This is a serious objection and needs to be taken as such, but the way forward is not to drop the language of incurvature altogether. Instead, we need to draw out the full semantic expanse of this image. If incurvature encompasses such stereotypically "male" sins as pride, the *libido dominandi,* and refusal of relationality, it can also encompass the sort of terms that some feminist theologians suggest, like "triviality," "hiding," "anguish," "sloth," "violence," and "abuse of the vulnerable."[73] Incurvature is not simply reducible to a supposedly male hubris. We must also realize that pride too can appear in manifold ways—as cowardice,[74] as vanity, or as the envious refusal to recognize the good or success of others. These are not exclusively male sins. Incurvature cannot be reduced to a supposedly male exertion of power. Moreover, after Nietzsche we should be more aware of the subtle ways in which human beings exert the will to power. Incurvature is not simply reducible to a refusal to submit to others; it is also the sin of the self that seeks to protect itself in the wrong way—through sloth,[75] by ignoring one's responsibilities in a given situation, through manipulation, cruelty, resentment, or by seeking to control or undermine others. This recalls Luther's description of incurvature as covetousness, as the desire to have every good for oneself.[76] These manifestations of the *homo incurvatus in se* are not exclusively male.

Furthermore, discourse about sin needs to observe the difference between *committing sin* and being *sinned against.* When people are suffering in concrete situations of oppression, abuse, and domination, they are being sinned against. The appropriate response here is to confront this sin and its perpetrators (whether individuals, groups, practices, or structures); this sin goes unchallenged if we tell the victims that they are incurved sinners who must learn to submit. Traditions of religious piety that focus on the individual self are often particularly blind to the fact that collective persons (e.g., communities, societies, and institutions) can also curve in on themselves and perpetrate sin. Incurvature is not merely individual; it is a social and structural phenomenon. That said, it does not follow that sin is exclusively social. One finds this non sequitur in some forms of liberation theology, and it is a premise in the feminist project of discarding the language of individual sin altogether. We create a major blind spot for ourselves if we ignore the fact that each of us is not only a victim of sin but a perpetrator. One may be a victim in one situation or relationship, and yet perpetrate sin against someone else in another situation or relationship.

For this reason, Deanna Thompson observes that "the world is not split neatly into static categories of oppressor and victim," and we oversimplify the complex identity of selves if we uncritically confer one status on a person. Moreover, we should not discard the language that allows us to understand our status as perpetrators of sin. Given the therapeutic orientation of so much contemporary religious discourse and practice, we have developed an allergy to terms like *sinner* or *wretch.* But Thompson suggests that "we lose a critical insight into human existence" if we discard such words. To this point, she cites Kathleen Norris: "Who never lies awake regretting the selfish, nigh-unforgivable things that he or she has done? . . . It seems to me that if you can't ever admit to being a wretch, you haven't been paying attention."⁷⁷ In sum, the point of retaining the language of individual sin is not to retreat from the critique of structural or social evil, but to be honest about the full scope of the incurvature of sinful persons, whether individual or collective, male or female.

* * *

As we come to this end of our discussion of incurvature, we cannot help but wonder what it would mean to be free for the other. How can the self be broken out of its incurvature and set free for others? What could overturn the economic logic of exchange and destroy the ontology of self-justification? To respond to these questions, we must begin another chapter.

5 The Anthropological Question

Who am I? This is the question of the human being seeking self-understanding. It is also a question the incurved self cannot ultimately answer, because it seeks to answer this question itself through reflection on its own possibilities and acts. In order for the self to be put into the truth about itself, it must be addressed by a word from outside of itself. This external word constitutes the self and opens it toward the future. Following our discussion in chapter 4, we can distinguish between two different ways of relating to the future: (1) According to a conditional word, which establishes a logic of exchange and an ontology of self-justification, or (2) according to a word of promise, which is unconditional and inaugurates an ontology of justification by faith. The latter is the word of the cross, which breaks open the incurved self and sets it free for others.

I begin this chapter by discussing the word of address, taking as my point of departure Bonhoeffer's treatment of the theme in his inaugural lecture on "The Anthropological Question in Contemporary Philosophy and Theology." This will lead us to evaluate Bonhoeffer's critique of Heidegger. Despite Heidegger's significant contribution to contemporary philosophy and theology (including Bonhoeffer's own thought), I will argue that Heidegger's attempt at an *ontologia crucis* does not provide the best model for thinking about the being of the cruciform self. Instead, I draw on Bonhoeffer's work in *Act and Being*, his 1933 Christology lectures, and his *Ethics* to articulate a more thoroughly cruciform anthropology.

Being Addressed

In July 1930 at Berlin University, Bonhoeffer fulfilled his postdoctoral requirements by delivering his inaugural lecture,[1] which focused on the anthropological question (*die Frage nach dem Menschen*) in contemporary philosophy and theology: What does it mean to be a human being? Bonhoeffer's treatment of this question makes it clear that he has taken the hermeneutical turn: the anthropological question—*Was ist der Mensch?*—is not a quest for an abstract universal essence of humanity, but for self-understanding (*Selbstverständnis*). Who am I? Who are we? These are the questions that drive philosophical and theological anthropology. What is at stake in them is the possibility of true self-understanding: is the autonomous self capable of placing itself into the truth by reflecting on itself, or does the self need to be given the truth about itself from an outside source, from beyond its self-mediating reflections and immanent possibilities?

Bonhoeffer argues that self-understanding requires a point of unity (*Einheitspunkt*). There are two reasons for this: First, the self must be addressed from a point—a ground, a source, a principle, an essence—that discloses the truth about the self. The anthropological question finds its answer in this point of unity. Second, the point of unity is necessary to establish the continuity of self-understanding; in other words, the point of unity establishes the identity of the self through the flux of temporal experience (AQ 389). In reference to my point of unity, I know who I am.

I would like to look more closely at the theme of being addressed as ontologically constitutive of the self. This theme allows us to bring Bonhoeffer into closer dialogue with Ricoeur, since both thinkers argue that true self-understanding requires an address that precedes the self. The theme of being addressed is not peculiar to Bonhoeffer and Ricoeur. In fact, their treatments of the theme are situated within a much larger discussion. This discussion has been prominent in contemporary phenomenology, most notably in the phenomenology of the call as treated by Jean-Luc Marion and Jean-Louis Chrétien,[2] who draw deeply from the resources of Husserl, Heidegger, and Levinas. According to Marion, who follows Levinas in this regard, the call precedes the active operations of subjectivity. Supposing itself to be the origin and constituting agent of phenomena, the subject instead finds itself constituted by a prior givenness. The call constitutes human consciousness (and self-consciousness).[3] In addition to the phenomenological discussion, the theme of being addressed has also been prominent in theology, particularly among theologians influenced by the Heideggerian appropriation of Luther's theory of language—e.g., Rudolf Bultmann, Ernst Fuchs, Gerhard Ebeling, and Eberhard Jüngel. Our present task is not, however, to conduct a full survey of this theme and its significance for Continental philosophy and theology. Instead, I would like to present Bonhoeffer's contribution to the discussion. To establish the background of Bonhoeffer's view, I begin with a few remarks on Luther's notion of the effective word of address.

* * *

Luther originally held an Augustinian view of language, according to which words refer to things. Linguistic signs designate objects, ideas, states of affairs, etc., but the sign is distinct from the reality it designates. In considering the role of language in the sacrament of penance, however, Luther expanded his view to include insights that have more recently been developed in speech act theory. From the Augustinian perspective, when the priest says "I absolve you of your sins!" these words are a statement about a distinct fact. The penitent's sins are forgiven, and the priest's words declare this reality, but the sign is not the reality. Luther's "great hermeneutical discovery" was to see that "the linguistic sign is itself the reality, that it represents not an absent but a present reality." The word is the note of a present thing (*notae praesentis rei*). Thus the utterance "I absolve you of your sins!" is a speech act that effectively creates the reality it declares.

The speech act is an active, effective word (*verbum efficax*) that "does what it says" and "says what it does."[4]

The word is creative. Commenting on God's creative act in Genesis, Bonhoeffer writes that God's word "summons that which comes to be out of nonbeing, so that it may be" (CF 43). The word creates *ex nihilo*. God speaks into the nothing: "Let there be light." This *nothing* (*das Nichts*) is not a "primal possibility or a ground of God." It is a sheer nothingness. It is not the *Khora* of deconstructive religion. God's creative word is an utter beginning, which calls being out of absolute nothingness.[5] It is the nothingness of God in the grave: "The fact that Christ was dead did not provide the possibility of his resurrection but its impossibility; it was nothing itself, it was the nihil negativum. There is absolutely no transition, no continuum between the dead Christ and the resurrected Christ" (CF 35). Likewise, the sickness unto death, the living death of the incurved self, is not the negative possibility of justification, a negative moment to be sublated by a higher unity. The incurvature of sin is not a happy fault (*felix culpa*), but the impossibility of communion with God. The only possibility of escape is that a creative word might speak into this tomb and create a new being.[6]

This word is not simply a command and it is certainly not a conditional contract. It does what is says, and says what it does. As Bonhoeffer writes, "the word does not have 'effects'; instead, God's word *is* already the work. . . . With God the imperative is the indicative. The indicative does not result from the imperative; it is not the effect of the imperative. Instead, it *is* the imperative" (CF 42). The word is creative; it creates what it indicates.

This view of language requires a relational ontology. First of all, what is created by this speech act is not a self-subsisting spiritual substance, but a relational reality. It creates a new being who relates to God in faith rather than self-justification. It sets the self free to love the neighbor as itself. It creates community, in the form of the church. This intersubjective context is necessary because the self needs to hear the creative word of grace spoken from outside of itself (*extra se*). The promise is not a word the self can give to itself; the self needs to hear it from others,[7] and as we will see in chapter 6, this is why Bonhoeffer argues that God's self-disclosure occurs in the intersubjective context of the church. Oswald Bayer makes a similar argument, arguing that we do not know God through abstract metaphysical speculation, because "God's truth and will are not abstract attributes, but that which is orally and publicly related as concrete words of comfort to a particular hearer in a particular situation."[8] On the basis of this interlocution, in which I am addressed by a word of promise, I understand myself.

This word of address is ontologically constitutive of the self, which is to say that the being of the self is constituted by what is said to it. Human being is not a substantial entity that precedes community, but, as Robert Jenson argues, it is a reality that "happens in the event of communication, *in* the speaking and hearing of the word." The word we hear calls us into being. "The word—the actual, ordinary human word—is the active initiation of human reality. What I am is not defined in advance by some set of timelessly possessed attributes; it is being defined in the history of address and response in and by which you and I live together." Thus: "The word is the locus of the creation of humanity."[9] The word I hear opens up the possibilities of the future for me and constitutes the sort of being I will be. Consequently, what we *hear* and what we *are* cannot be separated.

It is possible to conduct a strictly phenomenological inquiry into the address, or the call, as a universal structure,[10] but we must also consider the specific content of the address. What sort of future the word opens up depends on what sort of word is spoken. Different words initiate different structures. When someone says to me "I love you," "I trust you," or "I forgive you," this word constitutes or reconstitutes our being in relation to each other. If someone curses or condemns another person, he is striking at the very heart of his being, at his sense of identity. The curse is therefore a type of misrecognition (or *mal*-recognition) that seeks to determine, deny, or close one's possibilities for the future.[11] If the self hears only the conditional word of the law, then its being depends on the fulfillment of these conditions.[12] Much of the time this is the word the self hears pronounced in its world, which is why the everyday self is so oriented toward self-actualization through works. And as Bonhoeffer observes, the evaluation of works is one of the main strategies by which the self seeks to understand itself. The self seeks its point of unity in its works—its actualities and its possibilities—in order to determine the meaning of its existence, that is, what makes it count. Self-understanding on the basis of one's works is a pledge for self-justification, such that my existence is meaningful based on the transactions I perform in the economy of exchange that seems to govern the world.

The word of the cross, by contrast, brings something entirely new to consciousness.[13] It discloses a new ontology, in which eschatological possibility is prior to actuality. Paul asks the Corinthians to consider what they were when they were called: not many were wise, powerful, or noble according to the standards of the world (I Cor. 1:26); according to the ontology of self-justification, they were nothing to speak of. Yet God has not chosen the things that *are* according to that ontology (the wise, strong, and noble), but has instead chosen the things that are not (*ta mē onta*) (the foolish, weak, base, and despised) in order to "nullify the things that are, so that no one may boast before God" (27–29). The word of the cross destroys the ontology of self-justification. This call is not based on God's recognizing some achieved actuality, nor on some innate human possibility for good that might suggest this as a prudent investment. God gives life to the dead and calls into being that which does not exist (*ta mē onta*) (Rom. 4:17). But the incurved self is blind to this possibility, and even becomes hostile when it is addressed by it. Yet the word of the cross undermines this hostile nothingness because it is the self-disclosure of God's love for fallen humanity. God demonstrates his love toward humanity, in that Christ dies—

not for the righteous, for those that *are* just and good, but for sinners curved inward in revolt against God (Rom. 5:7–8).

Note, however, that this new, eschatological possibility does have its grounding in actuality. The promise of the *not yet* is grounded in the *already* of Christ's cross and resurrection. The word of the cross is not reducible to the disclosure of new ethical or religious possibilities that the self must actualize.[14] Christ calls the self to take up the cross and follow after him, but this imperative is based on the indicative of what is already accomplished.[15] The word of the cross is not a conditional contract; it is a word of unconditional promise that creates a different sort of being by opening a different sort of future.[16] The gracious logic of the gift disrupts the economy of exchange and overturns the ontology of self-justification, inaugurating the ontology of justification by faith.

In the kenotic word of the cross, God discloses himself to human understanding. The word of the cross reveals God as love,[17] as the gracious, creative, justifying, self-giving God. From this word we know God, and on this basis we know ourselves. A new self-understanding emerges, of which there are two aspects: the faithful self understands itself as being determined through the future (the new humanity of Christ) as well as the past (the old humanity of Adam, which remains in effect) (AQ 406–407). The word exposes the incurvature of the self, its Being in Adam, and so the self is called to confession. But this confession is not a self-mediated recognition of sin, in which conscience seeks to judge and justify itself, since self-mediating confession seeks to remain a law unto itself by recognizing its sin autonomously. Instead, the word requires that the self recognize its sin on the basis of revelation rather than its own immanent criteria. In surrendering every claim to self-mediation, the incurved self is broken open. This is the true *via crucis*: the cross destroys the self-justifying ego, putting it to death. "The humanity of Adam is overcome by the humanity of Christ" (AQ 406). The self understands itself in relation to the story of Christ's incarnation, cross, and resurrection.

Toward an *Ontologia crucis:* Heidegger and Bonhoeffer

In chapter 3 we discussed Luther's notion of *destructio,* as well as his redefinition of the notion of substance. Luther redefines substance according to scripture rather than philosophical principles, so that "substance" designates that by which one subsists in life. In this account substance is therefore a relational category, since this subsistence comes from outside the self (*extra se*). But the subsequent tradition of Protestant thought has not fully appropriated Luther's insight, and as Robert Jenson proposes, the task of thinking through Luther's critique of substance remains unfinished.[18] Before we can concur with Jenson, though, we must consider the case of Heidegger, since it has been suggested that Heidegger in fact completed Luther's destruction of substance ontology.[19]

In his early work, during the period of roughly 1919–1927, the young Martin Heidegger saw himself as a sort of philosophical counterpart to the young Martin Luther and assumed the task of articulating the ontological significance of Luther's *theologia crucis*.[20] Heidegger was fascinated by the interpretation of concrete Christian existence in such thinkers as Paul, Augustine, and Kierkegaard, and he used their texts as raw material in developing his project of a fundamental ontology.[21] One of the most important thinkers in Heidegger's development was Luther, who inspired Heidegger to envision his fundamental ontology as an *ontologia crucis*. Heidegger was inspired by Luther's interpretive retrieval of Paul and Augustine and his confrontation with late medieval scholasticism, but Heidegger also saw that the subsequent tradition of Reformation theology "succeeded, only in a very small measure, in providing a genuine explication of Luther's new fundamental religious position and its immanent possibilities."[22] As John van Buren has shown, "Heidegger wanted to use these possibilities to rethink not only theology, but also ontology. Neither Luther nor the theological and philosophical movements he inspired finished the deconstructive commentary on Aristotle and Aristotelian Scholasticism that the young Luther had started."[23] It is clear that Luther deeply influenced Heidegger's early thought: the critique of substance and the metaphysics of presence; the emphasis on ek-static, eschatological temporality; the theme of the kairological moment (the *Augenblick*); and the emphasis on constantly beginning anew[24] all exhibit Luther's well-documented influence on Heidegger.[25] But according to van Buren, Heidegger not only took up Luther's destruction of substance ontology, he "finished it."[26] If that is the case, we might expect Heidegger's project to provide an apt philosophical framework for thinking about the being of the self in faith. Indeed, Heidegger himself suggests his ontology is capable of directing theological reflection on faith.[27] Consequently, we need to look more closely to determine whether or not that is the case. I argue that it is not.

* * *

The problem begins with Heidegger's formalization of theological categories. Heidegger gives a de-theologized, formalized version of Luther's *destructio*, which *Being and Time* transposes into the *Destruktion* of the history of metaphysics. According to Heidegger's famous account, philosophy has complacently assumed that it knows what 'Being is, and so the most fundamental, originary philosophical question has been obscured and forgotten. But the meaning of Being is far from self-evident. The history of metaphysics is a long lineage of misguided interpretations of Being (as *substantia*, presence-at-hand, subjectivity, etc.), and therefore the history of metaphysics must be destroyed so that we can gain access to the primordial experiences that first determined philosophical thinking about Being (BT 43–44).[28] Heidegger's *Destruktion* aims to remove the falsifications and received interpretations that obstruct a genuine understanding of Being, so that we can retrieve the originary experience of Being. To put it in Luther's terms, the alien work (*opus alienum*) of philosophy is to destroy inauthentic thinking, stripping "commonly used concepts and expressions of the veneer of self-evidence" and uncovering "once again what is 'genuine' about these expressions as a possibility for the future."[29] This philosophical destruction thereby discloses the possibility of an authentic understanding of Being.

For Luther, *destructio* is not directed at inauthentic forms or concepts of Being, but at sin. For Heidegger, by contrast, sin is an ontic, theological concept rather than an original ontological determination of Dasein. The more fundamental ontological structure is *guilt,* which has no moral or religious connotations. Instead, moral and religious phenomena like culpability and indebtedness depend on the more primordial ontological "*Being-guilty*" (BT 328–29). The same can be said regarding Heidegger's ontological analysis of fallenness (*Verfallenheit*). Again, Heidegger insists that these terms do not imply any moralizing or negative evaluation (BT 211, 220), because he is offering an ontological rather than ethical or theological analysis. "Fallenness" therefore makes no ontic claims regarding Adam's "fall" into sin:

> Ontically, we have not decided whether man is "drunk with sin" and in the *status corruptionis,* whether he walks in the *status integritatis,* or whether he finds himself in an intermediate stage, the *status gratiae.* But in so far as any faith or "world view," makes any such assertions, and if it asserts anything about Dasein as Being-in-the-world, it must come back to the existential structures which we have set forth, provided that its assertions are to make a claim to *conceptual* understanding. (BT 224)

Heidegger insists, however, that the better we grasp the structures of guilt and fallenness, the better we can articulate the theological concept of sin. Philosophy can thereby "correct" and "co-direct" theology by pointing it in the right ontological direction.[30]

The same point applies to faithful existence. Like sin, faith is an ontic event; it is a rebirth and transformation that alters Dasein ontically, but not ontologically. According to Heidegger the ontological structures of Dasein are pre-Christian, so that they remain what they are through the rebirth of faith and are included in one's faithful existence.[31] Instead of faith, then, Heidegger's *Daseinanalytik* describes authenticity (*Eigentlichkeit*), which means taking hold of one's ownmost possibilities and resolutely taking responsibility for oneself and one's potentiality-for-Being.

But Dasein's everyday existence is one of inauthenticity, of fallenness (*Verfallenheit*), forgetfulness (*Vergessenheit*), and lostness in the anonymity of the "they" (*das Man*). The "they" prevents Dasein from taking hold of its ownmost possibilities by making existence appear easy and comfortable. It does this through anonymous opinion and ambiguous, "commonsense" notions that lead Dasein to be complacent in its understanding of itself and its world, thereby relieving Dasein of the burden of taking responsibility for itself (BT 312–13). Idle talk keeps Dasein in its fallenness by circulating an average, superficial interpretation of Being. It does not disclose Being in any primordial way, and yet it gives Dasein the illusion of understanding. "Idle talk is the possibility of understanding everything without previously making the thing one's own" (BT 213). These thoughtless interpretations obscure Dasein's authentic understanding of its ownmost possibilities—most significantly, death. Death is Dasein's final and definitive possibility, which limits and determines the scope of Dasein's totality, its being-a-whole (BT 277). But in its everyday existence Dasein flees the awareness of death. The idle talk of the "they" helps to keep one's own death covered over. One is aware that everyone dies, and the "they" talk about it euphemistically (BT 296–99), but Dasein has to reckon with the fact that it will have to die its own death. Death is a nonrelational possibility, which means that no one else can relieve Dasein of this possibility or take its place (BT 284, 308). Yet within itself Dasein has the possibility of authentic Being-towards-death. When Dasein lays claim to its own death in anticipatory resoluteness, it is wrenched away from the everyday fallenness of the "they" (BT 307, 345). Dasein must respond to the call of conscience, recognizing its Being-guilty, fallenness, and inauthenticity so that it can authentically take hold of its own death.

* * *

The purpose of Heideggerian *Destruktion* is to destroy inauthenticity for the sake of an authentic understanding of Being. But whatever his fascination with the *theologia crucis*, in the end Heidegger's *ontologia crucis* is insufficiently cruciform. To paraphrase Paul, Heidegger's ontology has the form of the cross, but denies its true power.[32] The problem with Heidegger's project is the way he conceives the relation between the cross and ontology. Heidegger's analysis must treat the historical cross of Christ in the same way it treats sin and faith—namely, as a particular ontic phenomenon rather than a fundamental *ontological* concern. One might reply that Heideggerian *Destruktion* is the formal structure of Lutheran *destructio* and that the two categories are therefore compatible, but Lutheran *destructio* and Heideggerian *Destruktion* involve very different, and finally incommensurable, claims. According to Luther, God destroys false forms of substance (pride, self-justification, self-glorification, etc.) in order to create the proper substance in which the self has its being in relation to God. The cross kills in order to bring life. Heidegger transposes this theme into a critique of metaphysics and its complacency, self-satisfaction, and pride, but the point of this critique is to get back into the concrete, historical, and factical—away from idle conceptions of Being so that an authentic interpretation of Being might take its place. The cross is therefore ontologically significant because it provides an ontic model to destroy the *ontologia gloriae* of traditional metaphysics. As van Buren puts it, traditional metaphysics is crucified "on the cross of facticity," so that it is "resurrected through the *skandalon* and 'foolishness' of historicity."[33] In short, the cross is ontologically significant because it indicates concreteness, historicity, and facticity; it teaches us to stop thinking about Being as substance, to think in terms of absence and hiddenness as opposed to pure presence, temporality as opposed to static eternity. The cross is therefore an ontic model of this ontological insight. The historical cross of Christ and its work of *destructio* point toward the more fundamental ontological structure of *Destruktion*.

With this formalization, Heidegger loses the real scandal of the cross. His emphasis on the concrete and factical is good as far as it goes, but he does not take the concrete and factical far enough, because he will not consider the possibility that the fundamental ontological question is in fact the question of the particular historical human being Jesus of Nazareth, just as he later refuses the possibility that the *logos* should be identified as this particular human being. But what if the most fundamental question is in fact *Christological*? What do we make of this man Jesus, who claims to be the crucified and resurrected God? Granted, from a philosophical perspective it is difficult to see how such a word could be anything but a regional, ontic concern; if anything, Heidegger's hermeneutic concedes more than most philosophers by allowing philosophy to admit the significance of Christ as a regional, ontic concern. Nevertheless, for Heidegger, Christ and his cross are philosophically significant insofar as they disclose a more fundamental ontological insight—namely, that Being cannot be understood as substance or presence. But the question we must consider is this: what if Heidegger's ontology is not fundamental?

In arguing that the ontological structures of Dasein are more fundamental than regional categories like sin, faith, and the cross, Heidegger implies that there is such a thing as Dasein in itself. To be sure, this is not an abstract, universal form or *eidos*, a metaphysical essence, or human nature. Ontology is a hermeneutical science, so its investigations are inseparable from concrete, factical, historical existence.[34] These fundamental ontological structures are not formal in an abstract universal sense, but they nevertheless have an authority and fundamental claim that ontic, *existentiell* realities lack. In this regard Heidegger exhibits an urge toward the transcendental and to the privileging of form over content. Despite his appeal to Christian sources against traditional metaphysics, he does not go far enough to recognize that for biblical thought there is no fundamental Dasein that underwrites sinful and faithful existence.

Bonhoeffer critiques Heidegger on these grounds, arguing that there is no Dasein in itself; there is only *Dasein in Adam* or *Dasein in Christ*. In this way Bonhoeffer takes Luther's critique of substance further toward its radical implications, presenting a more consistent *ontologia crucis* than Heidegger. Granted, Heidegger is deeply influenced by Luther's conception of *substantia* as radically relational, extrinsic, and ek-static. As we have seen, Luther argues that human being is not constituted by an intrinsic *what* or *quidditas*, but by its *where* (*Da*-sein) and the *how* (*Wie*-sein) of its being[35]—a point that reappears when Heidegger insists that ontology is only possible as a hermeneutics of factical being. Yet by insisting on the distinction between the ontological and the ontic, Heidegger is prone to the same error as natural theology, which appeals to a fundamental ontology of natural or created being. According to Bonhoeffer, the problem with both strategies is that they want to identify an ontological level that is undisturbed by sin and faith. Yet from the perspective of revelation, the realities of sin and grace determine Dasein's being (AB 32). Neither the structures of creatureliness nor Dasein can provide a theologically neutral ontology of the human being, because the "'there' ['Da'] of human beings is not to be defined independently of the 'how' ['Wie']." Da-sein cannot be understood apart from "how" it is, because Dasein "only 'is' in Adam or in Christ, in unfaith or in faith, in Adamic humanity and in Christ's community" (AB 152, 153). We have no archaeological access to original creaturely being, nor do we have access to a theologically neutral ontology of Dasein.

The ontological is not outside the jurisdiction of the cross, which is God's judgment of Being. Sin is an ontological violation of Dasein, which is in the power of its Adamic "how." Because of sin, the "concrete being-how-it-is [Wiesein]" violates the created form of Da-sein and relativizes such distinctions as ontic/ontological, *existentiell/existential*, and there/how (AB 137–38). By appealing to the ontological difference, Heidegger attempts to subordinate revelation to the structures of ontology, but Bonhoeffer rejects this strategy: "The letting go of the ontic by retreat into the ontological [unity of Dasein] is considered futile by revelation." Heidegger is correct that revelation appears within the horizon of Dasein as an ontic, existentiell event, but it does not stop there. It goes *all the way down*. In this event "the existential structure of Dasein is touched and changed. There is no second mediator, not even the existential structure of Dasein." The ontological is not outside the jurisdiction of revelation, because "[f]or revelation, the ontic-existentiell and ontological-existential structures coincide" (AB 78 n. 89). Contra Heidegger, then, pre-Christian existence differs from faithful existence on an ontic as well as an ontological level.[36] Like sin, faith is a disruption of Dasein's being. Being in Christ is not only an ontic, existenti*ell* concern, and Christ is not simply an ontic model of a more fundamental ontological structure, an example of authenticity or a new mode of self-understanding. Christ is the new humanity. He is not a word that signifies some other, more fundamental reality; Christ is the creative Word that embodies and inaugurates this new humanity in his incarnation, crucifixion, and resurrection. Moreover, the significance and efficacy of the cross and resurrection extend into the very roots of the ontological, inaugurating a new Being.

* * *

None of this amounts to a direct philosophical refutation of Heidegger's *Daseinanalytik*. One might object that the appeal to Christology entails more of a transcendent, external critique than an immanent, internal critique.[37] But our question here is whether Heidegger provides an apt ontology for understanding the cruciform self. I maintain that this is not the case, because faith requires a significant reinterpretation in order to accommodate Heidegger's ontology. By allowing Heidegger to correct and guide its work, Christian thinking must operate at a significant loss. To be sure, Heidegger does remarkable things with his interpretation of Luther's *theologia crucis,* and his attention to concrete, historical existence has greatly expanded the possibilities of philosophy and theology alike.[38] But he does not fulfill the radical ontological promise of the cross. Despite his celebration of concrete, historical, factical existence, Heidegger translates the concrete historicity of the cross into the ontological structure that is *Destruktion.* Therefore we can only conclude that Heidegger successfully "finished" Luther's destruction of substance metaphysics if we presuppose that Heidegger's ontology is indeed fundamental and that a formalized concept of *Destruktion* is the philosophical telos of Luther's *destructio.* But this formalization eviscerates Luther's insights and ultimately reveals its inaptitude for understanding the reality of faith.

The inaptitude of Heidegger's ontology is particularly apparent insofar as its notion of futurity is insufficiently eschatological. Heidegger's approximation of eschatology is oriented toward the futurity of Dasein's own death. But death belongs to Dasein's "*ownmost* potentiality-for-being"—a possibility that wrenches Dasein from the anonymous mass of *das Man*. Authentic Being-towards-death is nonrelational. Death individualizes Dasein. It also precludes any possibility of substitution; no one can take Dasein's place in death.[39] But according to Bonhoeffer, such an orientation toward death only deepens Dasein's incurvature. The future that Heidegger describes is not a genuine future, because in being defined by our own possibilities we succumb to the past—to sin, despair, and death. We need an eschatological possibility, given from beyond our ownmost possibilities. "There is a genuine future only through Christ and the reality, created anew by Christ, of the neighbor and creation. Estranged from Christ, the world is enclosed in the I, which is to say, already in the past" (AB 157). That is the condition of "being in Adam." Dasein is estranged from God, the neighbor, and all creation. Dasein is curved inward, divided within itself. Dasein's present state is death, that is, being unable to live, yet being forced to live from one's own resources (CF 90–91, 135, 142–43). This is the basic truth of the ontology of self-justification.

We have seen that one of the basic strategies by which the self seeks to understand itself is through its works—its possibilities and its acts. The self possesses its own potentiality for true self-understanding. Bonhoeffer's primary target here is the tradition of reflexive philosophy, which reached its apotheosis in idealism, but he extends his critique to the hermeneutical model of Heidegger's *Being and Time*. No doubt there are significant differences between Heideggerian hermeneutics and German Idealism insofar as Heidegger's hermeneutics of Dasein significantly departs from subject-centered philosophy. But Bonhoeffer argues that both identify true self-understanding as an immanent possibility. For Heidegger, self-understanding is one of Dasein's ownmost possibilities. Dasein is therefore capable of "being a whole" out of its own resources. In the call of conscience, Dasein summons itself to take up its guilt, to be toward death authentically, and in taking up its own death authentically Dasein establishes its own wholeness. Dasein addresses itself. There is no genuinely exterior address to give a point of unity beyond oneself. Dasein therefore remains curved in on itself, closed to otherness, addressing itself on the basis of its own possibilities and works.

Futurity, Works, and Limits: Asking the Anthropological Question, Seriously

For Bonhoeffer and Heidegger alike, it is a matter of how the question of human being can be asked with true seriousness. Heidegger acknowledges the fundamental problem of human self-questioning, but ultimately Dasein answers its own question. Or as Bonhoeffer puts it, for Heidegger "the question becomes the answer" (AQ 397). Dasein remains alone in its self-established totality. Dasein is not genuinely open to being addressed, and thus for Heidegger the question of human being "has no ultimate seriousness."

With this brazen critique Bonhoeffer aims directly at the heart of Heidegger's project—namely, the assumption that ontology is truly fundamental. Heidegger is similarly concerned with how the question of human being can be seriously asked, and he makes much ado about this in his *Introduction to Metaphysics*, where he argues that the question of human being remains alien to us. However many books pose the anthropological question (*Was ist der Mensch?*), their questioning cannot be taken seriously. "The question is not asked . . . because one already possesses an answer to the question" (IM 151–52). According to Heidegger, the question of human being is not strictly an "anthropological question, but a historically meta-physical question" (IM 149). We cannot genuinely ask the question of human being without retrieving the essential meaning of Being, which has been obscured by the history of Western metaphysics. Heidegger makes a similar criticism several years later in his "Letter on Humanism," claiming that the problem with philosophical anthropology and humanism alike is that they assume a faulty interpretation of Being, which has been passed down through Christian theology and exacerbated by modern philosophy. This distortion is evident in the modern metaphysics of subjectivity, which interprets human being as substance, as a bearer of properties, and as the subject of epistemic acts. Alternately, the human being is defined zoologically, "as *zōon logon echon, animal rationale,* rational living thing," according to the misinterpretation of *logos* as rationality (IM 151). Heidegger seeks to return to the pre-Socratic philosophy of Heraclitus and Parmenides in order to retrieve the primordial meaning of Being and *logos,* to think the "gatheredness" of the Being of beings, apprehension, and the "sway of *phusis*" (IM 142, 148). Only in this way can the question of human being be asked seriously.[40]

But here again we meet the ontology of self-justification. The human being is not genuinely addressed, but instead brings itself into the truth about itself. Now, from a Heideggerian perspective such an objection might seem patently false. Heidegger maintains that we need to be addressed by the world of Heraclitus, Parmenides, and Sophocles, and by Hölderlin's echo of this world—which is far from a self-sufficient, self-actualized world. In stark contrast to the modern view, Heidegger wants to retrieve a sense of Being that exceeds the impulse for control and the technological grasping that characterizes modern subjectivity. Being is "the gatheredness" of a conflicting unrest, of *polemos*, of "that which contends and strives in confrontation" (IM 142). Accordingly, the human being is not a self-transparent entity—something that becomes clear in *Antigone*, where Sophocles shows the human being as the uncanniest of beings. In short, Heidegger emphasizes the unfamiliarity of the address of this world, stressing that it is our responsibility to hearken to it. Genuine hearkening is not merely hearing, but "obediently following what *logos* is: *the gatheredness of beings themselves*" (IM 137).

However, it is precisely Heidegger's interpretation of this obedient response that exposes this as an ontology of self-justification. For the gathering of Being is "not a heap or a pile where everything counts just as much and just as little"; it is not the false harmony that eliminates all tension through leveling. Being, as *logos*, is a "gathered harmony" that depends on "rank and dominance" (IM 141). It requires discipline.[41] "Because being is *logos, harmonia, alētheia, phusis, phainesthai* . . . it shows itself in a way that is anything but arbitrary. The true is not for everyone, but only for the strong" (IM 142). The truth of being is only disclosed to the strong. This is a flattering thought for the incurved self, but with this logic of strength and struggle, the logic of self-justification holds sway.

Heidegger does not present his view of justification in a theological or typically moral sense, but there is certainly a horizon of strong evaluation involved. We see this in his interpretation of the theme of *dikē* in *Antigone*. *Dikē* has traditionally been translated to denote justice, the judicial, the normative, but Heidegger translates it as "fittingness" (*Fug*). "Being is a fittingness that enjoins: *dikē*." We are not enjoined to achieve this fittingness before a moral, legal, or theological horizon, but before the horizon of Being. We are enjoined to relate fittingly to Being. In his later thought Heidegger envisions this in a more pastoral way, as poetic dwelling, as *Gelassenheit*, letting Being be,[42] but in his *Introduction to Metaphysics* Heidegger characterizes this in terms of violence—as the violent interpretations and irruptions of human being within Being, understood as *phusis,* as the sway and the originary gatheredness of the overwhelming. On his account the Greeks understood this violence well, which is why they achieved "the fundamental condition of historical greatness." Dasein is justified—i.e., is *fitting*—according to its heroic works. We see this in Heidegger's description of death, which restates his analysis in *Being and Time.* Death is the one and only thing against which this "violence-doing" shatters. "It is an end beyond all completion, a limit beyond all limits." This is essential and definitive of human being. Death is the deepest mark of the un-canniness (*Unheimlichkeit*) of human being. "With the naming of this violent and uncanny thing, the poetic projection of Being and of the human essence *sets its own limits for itself.*"⁴³

It is therefore a question of limits, and Dasein sets its own. Dasein is the breach, the "*in-cident*" in which Being discloses its truth.⁴⁴ To put this in more familiar terms, Dasein is constituted in being addressed, and it is Being that addresses Dasein. But there is no genuine limit here—there is nothing otherwise than the closed circle of being, to put it in Levinasian terms. Dasein justifies itself, makes itself fitting, according to its own strong, heroic, violent, or poetic works. It's good work if you're strong enough to get it, but it is clear how far Heidegger has departed from the ontology of the cross toward an ontology of self-justification: human being sets its own limits, and is fitting on the basis of its works.

On Limits

The alternative to a selfhood based on works (*Werk*) is that the self is defined in the act of relating (*Aktbezug*) to genuine limits (*Grenzen*) (AQ 390–91). The self loses itself in the encounter with its limit, but then finds itself through this loss. In Ricoeur's terms, the egocentric *moi* is replaced by the other-oriented *soi*. Bonhoeffer will argue for this second alternative, but the question is this: if the self only gains true self-understanding in relation to its limits, where can a true limit be found? As Bonhoeffer writes, "everything depends on whether the I misappropriates transcendence and draws it into itself or instead acknowledges this limit" (AQ 391). The thinking I curves in on itself and seeks to preserve its incurvature by encompassing everything exterior within its cognitive grasp. The self mediates its own understanding of itself and its relation to all of external reality. This is true of systems like Hegel's, but also of transcendental thought, despite its pledge to respect the limits of its finitude. Bonhoeffer echoes Hegel's critique of transcendental philosophy: "By limiting my own possibilities in thought . . . I demonstrate through the very possibility of limitation the infinity of my possibilities, from which I can no longer go back" (AQ 399). The thinking ego can transcend these limits, because these are limits that thinking has determined itself.

Bonhoeffer will also critique dialogical personalism for its failure to provide a genuine limit for the thinking I. We can appeal to a Thou that supposedly eludes reflective consciousness, but the relation to this Thou can still be mediated by the self-reflecting I. Thus, as Gadamer argues, the infinite reflection of Hegel's system will always gain the upper hand over dialogical philosophy:

> The formal superiority of reflective philosophy is precisely that every possible position is drawn into the reflective movement of consciousness coming to itself. The appeal to immediacy—whether of bodily nature, or the Thou making claims on us, or the impenetrable factualness of historical accident, or the reality of the relations of production—has always been self-refuting, in that it is not itself an immediate relation, but a reflective activity.⁴⁵

The other person introduces something new into my horizon, but it is only through my own mediating operations, my own constituting acts, that this alterity has meaning for me—indeed, that I can even appeal to it as a supposed instance of immediacy.

Thus for transcendental philosophy and dialogical personalism alike, the limit succumbs to the activity of the thinking I (AQ 404). In this way, the otherness of the other is overcome by the act of the thinking I and the self achieves true self-understanding through its own works. Alterity is absorbed into the sameness of my own projects. Otherness is like a vitamin pill that makes the reflecting self stronger and more vigorous, the elements of alterity like nutrients that nourish the identity of the reflecting self. As a result, the relation to the other is not a genuine limit because it arises from within the possibilities of the self. The relation to the other is self-mediated,[46] and therefore the act of relating to the other is merely another operation of the self. My limits are reduced to my acts. I am not defined in relation to a limiting other, because the other is defined in relation to me, through my acts. This limit poses no ultimate limit.

This drive for closure is also true of hermeneutical thought. Here Bonhoeffer anticipates Levinas's critique of Heidegger. For Heidegger, Dasein's self-understanding is that of its being in the world, and the world is Dasein's totality of involvements. For Bonhoeffer and Levinas alike, totality is the problem. While it may be even more modest than transcendental philosophy, hermeneutics nevertheless locates the meaning of every phenomenon, every *other* that appears, within the projects and possibilities of the self. Death is the limit of these possibilities, but by taking hold of its own death in anticipatory resoluteness, Dasein can achieve an authentic self-understanding. The limit allows Dasein to achieve totality and hold its own unity within itself (AQ 395).

In short, the thinking (and understanding) self is curved in on itself and cannot break free. Thinking is incapable of transcending itself by and through itself. To paraphrase Luther, incurved reason is unable to want the transcendent to be transcendent. So what can break this incurved self open? Where does the true limit, the true point of unity lie? Where is an alterity that the incurved self cannot sublate or enclose in its circle of self-reflection? What can limit the self-mediating I?

According to Bonhoeffer, the human being only encounters its true limit before God. Only in relation to God does the question of human being not contain its own answer. The self can only understand itself through revelation. The Word is the true address in which the self is placed into true self-understanding. The point of unity for self-understanding "resides with God," and this means that "the human being experiences his foundation not through himself, but through God" (AQ 400).

On its own this argument is far from convincing, because the appeal to God does not ensure a genuine transcendence. The self can always employ God, or revelation, as an Archimedean point to ground one's own reflections. With God on its side, the self gains more certitude than ever. As we noted in chapter 2, this is the basic onto-theological move. This is also the problem with idolatry, which simply reinforces the incurvature of the self through the delusion that one is actually in contact with some transcendent point of unity.

Bonhoeffer fully recognizes the fact that religious consciousness (including theological reflection on revelation) is a way for the self to secure itself on the basis of its own acts. But he does not try to overcome the self-mediating self by finding some instance of transcendence—such as the ethical injunction of the face of the other (Levinas) or the radical otherness of divine revelation (Barth's *Der Römerbrief*)—that would escape mediation altogether. Instead, Bonhoeffer will argue for a different form of mediation, a mediation that is otherwise than self-mediating, so that the self-mediating ego is broken open through the mediation of another. Self-understanding is mediated Christologically.[47] The anthropological question—*Who am I?*—is dislocated and reoriented by the Christological question: *Who do you say that I am?* Now the primary question is not my own, but the question that Christ poses to me. This is a question the self is unprepared to answer. Instead, the self responds with crucifixion.

A Phenomenology of the Crucified Logos

God's word of revelation is the personal Word, the incarnate *Logos*. Bonhoeffer describes the encounter with the transcendent *Logos* in his 1933 Christology lectures, which he opens with a phenomenology of the encounter with Christ. This phenomenological Christology does not conform to the Husserlian ideal of a pure or presuppositionless phenomenology, but is instead a decidedly theological phenomenology, consciously conducted in the hermeneutical circle of scriptural and theological thinking. If it differs from the Husserlian variety, this phenomenological Christology also differs from Hegelian phenomenology by challenging the Docetism of Hegel's Christology.[48] Here we recall a question we anticipated in our introduction—namely, whether philosophy can take the word of the cross (and with it the crucified Word) seriously, without trying to rethink it according to its own immanent logic. As Bonhoeffer argues in *Ethics*, given what Christ claims about himself, philosophical reflection cannot ignore his claims and the reality they contain.[49] Philosophy may demur or disagree, but as Anti-Climacus argues in *The Sickness Unto Death*, one must have an opinion. In order to appreciate how this Word disrupts philosophical thinking, then, our investigations in this section will follow a hermeneutical detour through some scriptural and theological terrain.

In his Christology lectures, Bonhoeffer describes the encounter between the human *logos* and Christ, the divine *Logos*. In order to approach the phenomenon in the right way it is necessary to pose the right question, and the basic Christological question is not *What?* or *How?*, but *Who?* (C 302–304). As Bonhoeffer observes, Christology is essentially Logo-logy, the word about the Word (C 301). In the Christological question, however, we have a confrontation between conflicting *logoi*. The *modus operandi* of the human *logos* is to classify phenomena according to their proper regions by asking questions like *What?* and *How?* Through these objectifying operations, the human *logos* seeks to maintain its autonomy and the finality of its judgments.

But the *Logos* is a living person and cannot be reduced to an object of cognition in this way. A genuine encounter with the *Logos* requires the question *Who?* How can human thinking countenance this revelation? Here, if anywhere, we encounter offense and scandal. Not only did the eternal God enter human history, but this particular person is the *Logos*. He is the center of human existence, history, and nature (C 324).[50] Bonhoeffer will therefore argue in *Ethics* that talk about reality apart from Christ is an abstraction. Christ *is* reality—the one Christ-reality (*Christuswirklichkeit*) inaugurated by the reconciliation of God and the world (E 58). Thus there is no question of getting behind or beneath Christ to find some more fundamental *logos*. Christ, the *Logos*, is ontologically fundamental. The world was created through him, toward him, and has its being in him (E 68). All created being exists through and for him, just as all created being has its origin, essence, and goal in him (E 54, 402).[51]

How can the human *logos* countenance this claim? This claim unsettles the various ontic, regional *logoi*, but it also confronts the philosophical *logos* that aims to disclose Being. Here philosophical ontology finds itself confronted with Christology. By considering this confrontation, we begin to see the full implications of Bonhoeffer's critique of Heidegger. In his *Introduction to Metaphysics*, Heidegger complains that Christianity first misinterpreted Heraclitus's notion of *logos* by identifying it with "*one* particular being"—namely, Christ. In the New Testament (particularly John's gospel) the Christic *logos* is a person, a point that stands in marked contrast to Heraclitus, for whom *logos* means "the Being of beings, the gatheredness of that which contends." For Christianity, the *logos* comes to mean the word, the announcement, the imperative, the word of the Cross (*logos tou stauros*), and the meaning that ties these together is the person of Christ. "The announcement of the Cross is Christ Himself; He is the *logos* of salvation, of eternal life, *logos zōēs*." Heidegger therefore concludes that "a world separates this from Heraclitus" (IM 133, 143). Heidegger is indeed correct about that, but it is another question whether this innovation is good or bad.

Returning to Bonhoeffer's phenomenological sketch, we can note that his description recalls an earlier phenomenology of the incarnate *Logos*—that of Anti-Climacus in *The Sickness Unto Death*. Anti-Climacus argues that the self cannot avoid the Christological question (SUD 129).[52] It is impossible to remain neutral about this question, since even neutrality involves a decision. One must have an opinion. God entered into history, and he did so *for me*. But this incarnation is an irresolvable paradox for thought. The paradox of the God-man is Christianity's weapon against speculation, against the thinking ego and its drive for closure. Here is a phenomenon that permits no system of thought, because this is not a general or universal insight to be appropriated reflectively or speculatively. When confronted with this claim, the self is brought to the apex of its responsibility for itself. Thus the incarnation makes a phenomenological difference: the self is intensified immensely by the recognition that one exists as an individual before God, but this intensity increases even more when the self hears that it exists before Christ—that is, that God was born, suffered, and died *for this particular self* (SUD 79, 113). About this, Anti-Climacus insists, one must have an opinion.

That said, the example of Hegel's phenomenology shows that it is not enough simply to introduce the incarnation, because "the Incarnation" can indeed be conceptualized philosophically and serve as a useful tool in the repertoire of speculation—even providing a keystone for one's philosophical system. The same is true regarding the word of the cross, which Hegel also puts to profound philosophical use. For Hegel the phenomenality of Christ is the necessary manifestation of the idea as it unfolds in history; idea and appearance (*Erscheinung*) are related to each other by necessity rather than the contingency of God's freedom, and the impossible and inconceivable is thereby conceived as a principle. Thus Bonhoeffer objects that Hegel's philosophy is the most brilliant form of Docetism, since the phenomenal appearance of Jesus Christ is significant as the necessary manifestation of this principle (C 337). Consequently, Bonhoeffer argues that in the strictest sense talk about "Incarnation" or "God becoming human" is too abstract, too speculative. We should instead speak of "the God *who* became human" (C 354, emphasis mine), not "the Incarnation," but "the incarnate one."[53] To push the point further, it is also misleading to employ the paradox of the incarnation as an anti-systematic principle. "Paradox," like "incarnation," is also an abstraction that can allow thinking to remain self-enclosed.[54] Talk of the incarnate one must not remain in a third-person, theoretical perspective because its truth depends on the interlocution between the first and second person, when I am addressed by the living person of Christ, who asks me: *Who do you say that I am?*[55]

Bonhoeffer argues that this question is ontological, since it concerns "the being of Christ's person as clearly being the revealed Logos of God." It is a matter of bringing out "the ontological structure of the *who*," which requires that we engage the *Logos* as irreducibly personal in its being (C 304). Because the *Logos* is personal, he can act freely, out of love rather than necessity. This personal *Logos* can perform speech acts, addressing me with the *Who?* question. The Christological-ontological question thus cannot be reduced to the questions of *What?* and *How?*, nor can it be traced back to a more fundamental thinking of an impersonal (or prepersonal) being and *logos*, as in Heidegger. Personhood is ontologically primary, and the fundamental ontological question is the Christological question: *Who do you say that I am?*

The *Who?* question brings the human *logos* to its limits. The transcendent, personal *Logos* exposes the limits of the human *logos*, thereby relativizing it (C

304). Christ is the *counter-Logos* (*Gegenlogos*) who inverts the objectifying gaze of the human *logos*. The transcendent counter-*Logos* has appeared and entered the horizon of the immanent human *logos,* which now finds its authority challenged by a claim that it cannot resolve with its own questions of *What?* and *How?* Confronted by the claim of the counter-*Logos,* the human *logos* seeks to evade, deny, reduce, or destroy this otherness. "The logos cannot bear the presence of the counter Logos, because it knows that one of them must die." This confrontation leads to the cross, and either the incarnate *Logos* of God must be crucified by the human *logos* or the human *logos* must be crucified.

This description might seem unduly stark, overly harsh, or even simply false. How does it fit the gospel accounts of Jesus, who shows God's love, heals the sick, and forgives the sinner? Jesus' love clearly appeals to a desire for this divine love and life, and for the promise of the coming kingdom. Thus, as Jeffrey Bloechl observes, "it is the unique and defining appeal of Jesus Christ to *propose* the love of God to us" and to instruct the faithful on the meaning of this divine love. "It is by love and to love that the Christian is called, and Christ is the possibility of both of these movements at once."[56] Bloechl is right to describe the encounter with Christ in terms of the appeal and proposal of divine love, and nothing of our discussion should minimize this point. The point we must take from Bonhoeffer and Kierkegaard, however, is that there is no direct continuity from the desire for divine love to the life of faithfulness; at some point in the encounter the self will confront the scandal of the cross. Christ draws us to himself, but he also offends our understanding of what the divine love and life must entail. Hence W. H. Auden's famous remark that none but Christ "arouse *all* sides of my being to cry 'Crucify Him.'"[57]

In order to preserve itself, then, the human *logos* crucifies the counter-*Logos* "and goes on living with the unanswered question of existence and transcendence" (C 305–306). The human *logos* might even conclude, with Heidegger, that living with the unanswered question is the only way to truly think, to truly question, and to be truly human. With Heidegger, for instance, questioning becomes the answer (AQ 397). But the conscious exclusion of the Christological question suggests that this questioning lacks true seriousness. As Anti-Climacus argues in *The Sickness Unto Death,* to defer judgment and remain neutral is to stumble over the offense; about this man one must have an opinion (SUD 130). Heideggerian questioning remains curved in on itself.

This incurvature is the basic situation of the human being in Adam. Alienated and hostile in mind (Col. 1:21), the human *logos* determines that it must put Christ to death in order to protect itself.[58] But this confrontation is not merely an intellectual dispute. The human *logos* is not only an intellectual faculty, but the locus of our understanding, which encompasses our entire being in the world. This is how being is disclosed to us.[59] The counter-*Logos* confronts us in the fullness of our being. To borrow once more from Auden's confession, Christ arouses "*all* sides of my being to cry 'Crucify Him.'"

The Cross and the Elemental

The incarnate counter-*Logos* also challenges the sovereignty of the *stoicheia* that Paul describes in Colossians 2:15. *Stoicheia* are the rudimentary or elementary principles of the world (*tou kosmou*). These principalities and powers were created through Christ and for Christ; they hold together in Christ (Col. 1:16–17) and are meant to serve him by providing the necessary structures and limits of the created order. In terms we will define in chapter 6, they are *penultimate* realities. However, instead of serving Christ, the *stoicheia* have curved inward, seeking autonomy rather than christonomy. Like the groaning of creation in Romans 8, the *stoicheia* groan in their attempt to deny that they are not complete in themselves, to imply that they are absolute rather than relative to Christ.

Could it be that the groaning of the *stoicheia* is what Heidegger describes when he commends the Heraclitean *logos*? The gatheredness of Being, in its violent sway, the overwhelming, the churning violence and turmoil of *phusis*—these elemental realities belong to the *stoicheia*. Commenting on Sophocles' *Antigone*, Heidegger discusses the sea, the "wintry swells in which it constantly drags up its own depths and drags itself down into them." The human being surveys this seascape, gives up his place, and heads out, "ventures to enter the superior power of the sea's placeless flood" (p. 164). In the face of the elemental sway and swell of the sea, the human being experiences itself as without place, homeless, the uncanniest of beings.

The disciples of Jesus, being fishermen, understood the power of this elemental swell and sway firsthand. But in Jesus they also encounter the one who rules over the elemental. The Gospel of Luke records one particular journey by sea, during which the disciples come into a violent storm that threatens to destroy them. They wake up Jesus, who was asleep, in order to warn him that they are in mortal peril. In response, Jesus is perplexed by their lack of faith, then rebukes the wind and surging waves so that the storm subsides. The disciples look at each other in fear and amazement, asking: "Who is this, that he commands the wind and the waters, and they obey him?" (Luke 8:22–25).

Who is this? This is the question that arises when one is confronted with the incarnate *Logos*. It is the question that follows the confrontation between the *Logos* and the *stoicheia*, when the elemental is revealed to be subservient to a more fundamental reality. The *stoicheia* are not the most primordial or fundamental realities; they have their Being in Christ, but they cannot bear this subservience and so they contend against him in rebellion. The *stoicheia* cannot abide the authority of the counter-*Logos*, so they lash out in violence, crucifying Christ.[60] To borrow Bonhoeffer's vivid description: "The world exhausts its rage on the body of Jesus Christ" (E 83).

Yet the counter-*Logos* rises, alive and victorious as God's final Word. When the crucified *Logos* appears as the resurrected *Logos*, the question *Who?* is focused to its sharpest point. Now the *Logos* stands as a living question, "over and around and within humanity." Struggle as it might, the *logos* is powerless against the risen counter-*Logos,* who reverses the questioning: "Who are you, that you ask this question? Do you live in the truth, so you can ask it?" (C 305). Here the human *logos* is convicted, exposed in its untruth. The human *logos* must itself be crucified—not in an act of revenge, but because this is the way of grace; the risen counter-*Logos* puts the incurred human *logos* to death, destroys it, in order to restore and justify it. In the cross, Christ makes peace, reconciling all things to the Father (Col. 1:20); he disarms the *stoicheia* and makes a public display of them (2:14–15). The risen one forgives the world its sins. In Christ, the abyss of God's love "embraces even the most abysmal godlessness. . . . Now there is no more godlessness, hate, or sin that God has not taken upon himself, suffered, and atoned" (E 83). The grave reality of death, God has taken upon himself.[61] The sin of the human being, curved in on itself in despair, God has taken upon himself. The overwhelming, the uncanny, the violent sway of *phusis*—all of this has been assumed and redeemed by Christ.

In the counter-*Logos,* that is, in the person of Christ, the self finds its true limit and point of unity. In Christ the self discovers that the anthropological question—*Who am I?*—follows after the Christological question: *Who do I say that Christ is?* Here the human being encounters its true limit. The counter-*Logos*, the counter-Word, exposes the self as curved in on itself. He reveals the self as being in Adam, as closed and hostile to God. He even arouses this hostility.[62] But the counter-*Logos* breaks open this incurvature in order to transform the self ontologically, conforming the self to the likeness of Christ.

Christ as Dasein for Others

In order to answer the Christological question *Who?* we must also consider the question *Where?* We cannot understand the identity of Christ apart from the place (*der Ort*) of Christ (C 324). Where does Christ stand? He stands there in the center (*der Mitte*), as the mediator (*der Mittler*) of reality. The being of Christ is that of being-there for others: *Dasein-für-Andere.*[63] The being of Christ is that of standing in the place of others. The German term here is *Stellvertretung*, which is usually translated "substitution," though this lacks the spatial connotations of the German term. Christ stands in my place, where I should be standing but cannot. According to Bonhoeffer, this statement is ontological, and not merely psychological, historical, factual, or ontic. The "very core" of Christ's personhood "is the '*pro-me*' structure. The being of Christ's person is essentially relatedness to me. His being-Christ is his being-for-me" (C 314, 324). This relation is vital to my knowing who I am: Christ is there for me (*pro me*), as *Dasein for me.*

First of all, this means that Christ stands between the self and God. I do not stand there in and by myself, but in another. I do not *in-sist;* I *ek-sist*, existing *ek*-statically outside of myself in Christ.⁶⁴ Christ "stands at the boundary of my existence and nevertheless in my place." Before God, Christ stands there for me, where I should stand but cannot.

Christ is also the mediator between the self and itself. "I am separated, by a boundary that I cannot cross, from the self that I ought to be. This boundary lies between my old self and my new self, that is, in the center between myself and me." In this limit I come into the place of judgment; it shows me who I should be and exposes me in my old, incurved being; I recognize myself in Adam rather than Christ. At this place of judgment, I cannot stand on my own. But Christ stands here for me, between my old and new being, as both my limit and my center: "Thus it is important that we human beings, in recognizing that our limit is in Christ, at the same time see that in this limit we have found our new center" (C 324).

Further, Christ also stands between the self and the neighbor. There is no immediate relationship of I and Thou. True community with the other is not an intimate union or fusion, but an encounter mediated by Christ. In other words, I do not constitute the meaning of other beings, nor do I determine my responsibility for them autonomously, because I receive them as they are for Christ, prior to my own projects, desires, and ambitions regarding them. In Christ, the other is given as the neighbor. I encounter the other as one for whom Christ became human, was crucified, and resurrected, and this sets them free to be who they are.⁶⁵

Christ is the new humanity, and I participate in this new reality through my being in him. But if Christ is the center of reality, this means that this ontological transformation does not merely register at the level of the individual self. The recognition of Christ there *pro me* is not the inauguration of a new religious egoism. Christ stands there as the center and mediator of human existence (*das Dasein für den Menschen*), as the center and mediator of history (*das Dasein für die Geschichte*) as well as nature (*das Dasein für die Natur*) (C 324–27). This Christological horizon decenters the self, opening us to something beyond our individual selves.⁶⁶ Faithful selfhood is not merely a matter of one's personal religious journey or the egoistic concern of the individual self for its own private salvation. Rather, the self is a participant—both patient and agent—in the much larger narrative of God's reconciliation of the world to himself through Christ. Christ is the center of human existence as well as history and the entire cosmos. As Paul writes in his letter to the Ephesians, God put all things in subjection to Christ, "and gave Him as head over all things to the church, which is His body, the fullness of Him who fills all in all."⁶⁷ This is the one Christ-reality (*Christuswirklichkeit*).

* * *

All of this might sound like high triumphalism, yet Bonhoeffer's Christology remains consistently cruciform throughout these claims. Christ is the center (*Mitte*) and mediator (*Mittler*)—but what sounds like glory and triumph must be interpreted kenotically, through the cross. Christ is Dasein *for-others*. This is not an onto-theological principle by which the self theologically mediates its own triumph. The being of the cruciform, Christomorphic self therefore consists in being-there for others. Likewise the church is only the church in being for others;[68] it does not exist for itself, and it does not exist to implement theocratic rule of the world. It is a disastrous mistake to conclude that because Christ has conquered the rebellious *stoicheia* through the cross, the church is now called to subdue the world by means of these same *stoicheia* (e.g., money, political power, etc.).[69] Christ overcame these *stoicheia* through the cross, and it is through the cross that the church must engage the world. Just like the self, when the church seeks to establish and preserve its own standing, it is no longer itself.

Conclusion: On Cruciform Philosophy

We can now understand Bonhoeffer's claim that the anthropological question only becomes truly serious in Christ. By following Bonhoeffer to this conclusion, we find our position clearly distinguished from Heidegger's. From Heidegger's perspective, our project of a philosophical anthropology of the cross is misguided in multiple ways. In his view, we cannot genuinely think human being without rethinking the question of Being, and this requires philosophy to break with Christian thinking. We need to get back to the unsettling, uncanny questionability of the human being, before Christianity obscured the original meaning of Being and identified the *logos* with Christ. Without this radical departure, the anthropological question never becomes truly serious; it always has its answer in view.

Here Heidegger echoes his earlier argument against the very idea of Christian philosophy. On his account, the basic question of metaphysics—"Why are there beings rather than nothing?"—is a question the Christian (or "anyone for whom the Bible is divine revelation and truth") cannot genuinely ask. Faith preempts genuine philosophical thinking because it always has the answer in its back pocket. There are beings because God created them (IM 7). The Christological aspect adds to this answer: there are beings because they were created by God in and for Christ. Nevertheless, Heidegger will still argue that this answer forestalls genuine philosophical questioning.

Heidegger is correct that human beings are prone to forget the wonder and mystery of being and take it for granted that they know what being is, but it is not clear that an atheistic thinking of being is necessarily more amenable to wonder than a faithful thinking of creation. There are beings rather than nothing. But why is it not even more thought-provoking that at one point there was a *beginning* in which beings came into being through the creative word of God? The Heideggerian may suppose this notion of creation satisfies the principle of sufficient reason and thereby cuts off authentic thinking, but such a facile view of creation fails to confront the sheer contingent grace of creation, the mystery of the new, of the beginning. This is something that thinking consciousness cannot get behind or master. In the beginning, God spoke into nothingness and through his word called beings into being: one can present this word as an "answer" in a facile, inauthentic way, but is it not also possible to encounter this mystery authentically?

Heidegger acknowledges that "one can thoughtfully question and work through the world of Christian experience—that is, the world of faith." But this sort of thinking does not succeed in squaring the circle by yielding a Christian philosophy. It is simply theology (IM 8). From the perspective of faith, the fundamental question of metaphysics is "foolishness," and so the very idea of a "'Christian philosophy' is a round square and a misunderstanding." Yet there is a choice irony in Heidegger's portrait of philosophy, which proudly wears its foolishness like a badge of distinction. There was a time when the word of the cross was foolishness to the philosopher. True, God used the folly and weakness of the cross to make the wisdom of the world foolish (I Cor. 1:20), but this is not the reversal of fortune (or transvaluation of values) that it might seem. The foolish wisdom of the cross cannot become a triumphant, world-conquering wisdom without compromising itself. Insofar as cruciform thinking resists this sort of compromise, the cross is a perennial scandal. If that is the case, then Heidegger's atheistic philosophy is in no position to claim the exclusive privilege of being the poor, outcast, vulnerable, foolish, weak, marginalized other—as though faith does nothing but forestall the difficult and untimely work of thinking (IM 8–9).

It is therefore misleading to suggest that atheistic philosophy alone is truly serious in its questioning. Moreover, can philosophy be truly serious if it refuses in advance to face the Christological question: *Who do you say that I am?* What if this *Who?* turns out to be the most fundamental question of Being and *logos*? What does this mean for philosophy, and for our understanding of human being?[70] Heidegger has precluded this possibility in advance. But we must confront this possibility: What if the *Logos is* Jesus Christ? Once this possibility has entered our horizon, we must have an opinion about it.

Here the anthropological question acquires a new gravity, because here human being and human *logos* are addressed by their true limit. What could inspire more wonder than the possibility that the *Logos* is a person, who was born as a human being in history, was crucified and resurrected, thereby inaugurating a new humanity and a new creation? What if the violence of the gathering is not the end of the story of being? What if being is addressed by a genuine futurity, rather than being governed by ontocratic violence and the self-justifying logic of authentic being-towards-death? Rather than resolving our questions, we find our sense of mystery deepened. As one theologian remarks, "the human person becomes mysterious in the light of Christ."[71] If this story is true, then this is where the human being finds its point of unity and the answer to the anthropological question. But this answer opens up a whole new set of questions.

Part Two

6 The Concreteness and Continuity of Faith

In chapter 5 we saw how the self is constituted through the address of an external word, which gives the self its point of unity (*Einheitspunkt*). But if the self is constituted in the event of being addressed, how does the self have continuity from moment to moment? Does this event have any concrete extension in the life of the self, or does this account lead in the direction of an actualistic or punctual (*Pünktlich*) self?

Charles Taylor uses the term "punctual self" to describe the highly influential modern assumption that the self is pointlike in nature, with no extension in space, time, or corporeality. The punctual self is a disengaged consciousness, defined by its power to objectify external reality through its epistemic acts and to remake this reality through practical activity. This self is pointlike because it is really "nowhere"; it exercises these powers remotely,[1] and in its most extreme form the punctual self defines itself entirely through its acts, which are unconditioned by any ontological claims regarding the way things are apart from these acts.

We find an analogue to the punctual self in certain dialectical accounts of the eschatological event—the Moment, *Kairos, Augenblick*—of faith. In a radically disruptive event from beyond the closed world of the self, God justifies the sinner by grace and faith alone. The self constituted in this event is not the disengaged, punctual self of modernity, insofar as the faithful self does not define itself through unconditioned epistemic and practical acts. Instead, it is the revelatory, justifying act of God that is punctual in nature. The faithful self is sheer passivity, defined by a divine act that has no ontological location or extension. Does this pointlike eschatological event have any continuity in the concrete, historical existence of the self? There are two questions at stake here. First, what is the ontological status of revelation, that is, what sort of being does it have? Second, what sort of ontological continuity does the self have as the recipient of revelation? Is the self a bundle of these constituting moments? Is there any unity or continuity between the concrete, historical existence of the self and the self as it stands in this moment of justification? In an important sense the new reality of faith is hidden, but does this mean it is entirely absent from the horizon of self-understanding? In short, what difference does God's ultimate word of address make in concrete existence? As Bonhoeffer puts it, we must consider "whether we can live by the ultimate alone, whether faith, so to speak, can be extended through time," and "whether the word, the gospel, can be extended in time" (E 151–52). If the moment has no extension, then it would seem that the faithful self is a purely punctual or actualistic self.

In this chapter I examine how Ricoeur and Bonhoeffer diagnose this challenge, which they perceive as a danger of dialectical and existential theology. I also show how this debate is framed by a long-standing theological dispute over the capacity of the finite to bear the infinite. I conclude by proposing Bonhoeffer's category of the penultimate as a promising way to think about the relation between finite and infinite, immanence and transcendence, ontology and eschatology.

Hermeneutics and the Moment

An important reference point for both Bonhoeffer and Ricoeur is the early theology of Karl Barth. The theme of the eschatological moment punctuates Barth's commentary on Romans, which describes the "Moment" of justification in which God acts and the human being does not. The error of religion is to assume that this moment depends on some prior or subsequent act—some behavior, feeling, or practice, but justification occurs entirely apart from the works of the law (Romans 3:28).[2] We are habituated by religion, ethics, and metaphysics to assume that the moment occurs along a continuum, as an immanent telos actualized once certain conditions are established or a certain threshold is crossed. But the moment has no such continuity. It is *Krisis*. Thus Barth famously writes, "if I have a system, it is limited to a recognition of what Kierkegaard called the 'infinite qualitative distinction' between time and eternity."[3] The moment does not extend itself within the known world of historical existence; eternity touches time the way a tangent touches a circle—namely, at a point with no extension.[4] As a result, the moment is irreducible to any historicizing or psychologizing account of religious consciousness.

Barth's dialectical description of the moment has been highly influential, but he was not alone in emphasizing the moment of rupture in this way. Following Kierkegaard as well as Heidegger, other mid-twentieth-century thinkers interpreted faith in terms of an existential moment or event. Most notable are Bultmann, who was influenced by Heidegger's early hermeneutics of the moment (*Augenblick*), and the "New Hermeneutic" of Bultmann's students Gerhard Ebeling and Ernst Fuchs, who followed the later Heidegger's thinking of the event (*Ereignis*) in their respective accounts of language as a Word event (*Wortgeschehen*) or speech event (*Sprachereignis*).[5] Ricoeur acknowledges a significant debt to all of these thinkers (Barth, Bultmann, Ebeling, Fuchs), but he also discerns some significant problems with a concept of faith as an existentially definitive moment. I will mention two of them here. *First*, this idea of the moment tends to be lacking in content. As a result, it runs the risk of evacuating eschatology of the rich temporal, historical, communal, political, and cosmic dimensions that belong to the hope of resurrection—tending instead toward a philosophy of the eternal present and a subject-centered, interiorized understanding of faith.[6] The eschatological moment opens the self toward the future. But *what* future? And *whose* eschaton?[7] One of the dangers of privileging the eschatological Word event is that it can reduce revelation to the "slender thread of eschatological speech."[8] An overemphasis on the eschatological Word event plays out as a monotonous tune, failing to reflect the polyphony of biblical discourse, with its multiplicity of genres and forms. Such an emphasis also tends to be monotone in its depiction of faithful existence, failing to reflect what Bonhoeffer calls "the polyphony of life."[9]

The *second* difficulty that follows is whether this moment makes any difference in historical existence. How does it take shape concretely? According to Barth's description, the moment manifests itself like a "crater made at the percussion point of an exploding shell."[10] This image evokes the moment's negative judgment on religion, ethics, and humanistic subjectivity as a capacity for the ultimate. There is no point of contact (*Anknüpfungspunkt*) between the event of revelation and the immanent horizon of the human being.[11] Barth's dialectical rhetoric in these early texts is highly polemical, but if the divine Yes to humanity is overshadowed here by the No it is because Barth perceived the critique of religious possibilities as the most needful thing for that context. Liberal Protestantism had exalted humanity at the expense of God,[12] proclaiming an optimistic view of human religiosity and ethics. Yet despite its preoccupation with ethics, it was an ethical failure—something that became painfully evident to Barth in 1914 when all of his teachers and mentors endorsed the war policy of Kaiser Wilhelm II.[13] A corrective was therefore necessary, but when the corrective becomes the norm (as it did with the caricature of "Barthianism" that continues to obscure Barth's legacy), the danger is that humanity will be diminished in order to secure the majesty of God. In later writings Barth places a greater emphasis on God's gracious affirmation of human being, culture, and action—the gracious Yes that is the ultimate goal of the No.[14]

In his early essay "The Critique of Religion," Ricoeur sees himself as being "thoroughly faithful" to Barth in maintaining that the kerygmatic word, the word of the cross, is deeply disruptive.[15] But Ricoeur insists that we must straightaway add "that this kerygma has only become visible by becoming itself a fact of culture. Not only has it ruptured into our culture, but it has appeared as a fact of culture." There is therefore both discontinuity and continuity between the transcendent word and the immanence of human understanding,[16] since the disruptive, kerygmatic word inevitably comes to be heard within the living world of discourse.

This desire for balance between discontinuity and continuity is a constant throughout Ricoeur's work on religious discourse. Word events, or speech events, introduce something new and unfamiliar into discourse, and they initiate a genuine semantic shock, impertinence, and innovation. We see this in the paradoxical logic of parables,[17] in "the irruption of the prophetic word," and in "the kerygmatic explosion of the message of Christ."[18] But the novelty of these events occurs within the system and structure of discourse.[19] Thus Ricoeur writes: "If salvation is a word-event, the communication of this word-event does not take place without an interpretation of the whole symbolic network that makes up the biblical inheritance, an interpretation in which the self is both interpreter and interpreted."[20] With this point Ricoeur opposes the literalism of fundamentalism as well as Romantic hermeneutics and its distinction between explanation (*Erklären*) and understanding (*Verstehen*). Ricoeur objects that Ebeling and Fuchs (like Bultmann and Gadamer) follow Dilthey down this path.[21] By contrast, Ricoeur wants to investigate both explanation and understanding. Hence his motto: to explain more is to understand better. Ricoeur's hermeneutics does not only consider the existential self-understanding given through the word of address; it also concerns the systemic and structural features of the discourse within which this word is given.

Ricoeur is quick to acknowledge the dangers of explanation—namely, that the semantic and ontological novelty of the kerygmatic word might be reduced to mere epiphenomena of structure and thereby explained away. Ricoeur wisely resists these reductionist tendencies in structuralism, which would result in a word that is all continuity and no discontinuity. At the same time, we must also avoid the opposite error and acknowledge that the disruptive word takes concrete shape in the structures of our human, all too human discourse; otherwise we would end up with a hermeneutics more Docetic than incarnational.[22]

We find a similar concern in Bonhoeffer, who shares Ricoeur's commitment to maintaining the discontinuity as well as the continuity between the transcendent word and the immanence of human thought and culture, as well as between the word of address and the self-understanding of faith. It is a question of whether consciousness can receive and communicate this event. Or to put it in terms of another significant debate, it is a question of whether the finite is capable of bearing the infinite.

Finitum (Non) Capax Infiniti?

Bonhoeffer was deeply influenced by Barth, but one of his persistent questions for Barth concerned the concrete manifestations of faith.[23] Bonhoeffer identified this problem during his formative encounters with dialectical theology in the 1920s, and it occupied him throughout his authorship. We find him grappling with these questions in an early seminar paper on Luther's doctrine of the Holy Spirit. According to Luther, faith is not an act of the self but the act of the Holy Spirit, in which I receive the transforming revelation of Christ's death and resurrection for me (*pro me*) and for us (*pro nobis*).[24] The Holy Spirit actively creates a new self; faith is therefore not simply the assertion of an external forensic judgment, but a real transformation of the self. Yet a difficulty arises when we consider how to interpret Luther's insistence on the hiddenness of this new self, which does not show itself to objective scrutiny. This difficulty becomes a problem in Barth's dialectical account of the new self, because Barth describes the new self as hidden in an eternal, timeless reality. The problem Bonhoeffer sees in this bifurcation is that Barth posits a heavenly *Doppelgänger* of the self,[25] thereby problematizing the unity of the concrete, historical self.

What is at stake in Bonhoeffer's critique of Barth is the question of *capacity*. For Barth, the moment of justification remains supratemporal because no historical moment is capable of bearing the infinite, just as no empirical human act such as faith or obedience is capable of bearing the infinite. The historical act can only *refer* to the infinite in faith, without being faith itself. Hence the dialectical nature of Barth's understanding of the self in faith: since we can never speak directly of the new self, and since the act of faith is never identical with an empirical act of the historical self, we must qualify our statements about the believing *I* with a *not-I* (AB 84–85). Moreover, the subject of faith is the Holy Spirit, and this divine activity comes from beyond any human capacity and is therefore discontinuous with the life of the subject. Strictly speaking, then, a psychology or phenomenology of religion can never locate the act of faith, since faith is not an act of human consciousness.[26]

Bonhoeffer's divergence from Barth on this point is prefigured by an earlier debate in Protestant thought between the Reformed view that the finite is incapable of bearing the infinite (*finitum non est capax infiniti*) and the Lutheran view that the finite is capable of bearing the infinite (*finitum capax infiniti*). This difference comes out of Reformation debates over Christology (regarding the relation between the divine and human natures in the person of Christ) and sacramentology (regarding the presence of Christ in baptism and the Lord's supper).[27] The Reformed position seeks to preserve the difference between Creator and creation, emphasizing the majesty of God along with the incapacity of finite creaturely being to bear this majesty; the Lutheran *finitum capax* maintains that God acts "in, with, and under" worldly reality and not alongside it as a parallel spiritual reality.[28] In what follows I will not presume to resolve this doctrinal dispute, but will instead seek to compare and contrast the strengths of these two positions for thinking philosophically about revelation. As we will see, they have had a significant influence in subsequent philosophical thought.

In taking his position in this debate, Barth is not concerned with perpetuating some arcane scholastic debate. For Barth this is an urgent question with real-life implications. The Lutheran *finitum capax* has had a significant legacy in German philosophy and theology: Romanticism, idealism, and liberal Protestant theology all drew their lifeblood from the Lutheran *finitum capax*,[29] which they interpreted as an affirmation of the finite human spirit (expressed through art, poetry, culture, ethics, and philosophical concepts) as capable of mediating and containing an intuition of the infinite. This high estimation of human consciousness led to the optimistic humanism that Barth came to see as ethically disastrous. But he found a kindred spirit in Kierkegaard, who vehemently insisted on the infinite qualitative difference between God and humanity; when the finite tries to bear the infinite through itself, it will always end up with something less than truly transcendent. Barth also found an ally in another great critic of idealism: Ludwig Feuerbach, who sought to expose theological discourse as anthropology writ large. According to Barth, Feuerbach was all too often correct in this evaluation. One could fault modern theology for selling its birthright for a mess of Romantic-idealist pottage, but in Barth's view the roots of this error run all the way back to the Lutheran *finitum capax*,[30] which leaves theology wide open to Feuerbach's hermeneutic of suspicion. An atheist like Feuerbach might seem an unlikely ally for Barth, who wants to affirm the transcendence of God over against human consciousness, but Barth commends Feuerbach's critique of theology because it shows us why the *finitum non capax* must be defended: without it, we cannot maintain any sense of divine transcendence.[31]

Another way of looking at this debate is in terms of the objectivity of revelation. Barth insists on the nonobjectivity of revelation in order to preserve its transcendence. God is never given as an object, as an entity at the disposal of the thinking subject. On this count Bonhoeffer shares Barth's concern, and he similarly rejects every view that reifies revelation as a fixed entity—in Heidegger's terms, as present-at-hand, technologically manipulable information; in Levinas's terms, as a saying reduced to a said; or in Woody Allen's terms, as a meaning I can carry around in my wallet.[32] While sharing Barth's concerns, Bonhoeffer also insists on the concrete givenness of revelation. Barth is correct to resist the historicist or psychologistic reduction of faith, but his solution comes at the expense of the concrete historicity of the human being and the act of faith. The existing self is thereby divided into a duality of I and not-I, and the faithful self is spirited away into a supratemporal realm (AB 99–100).

Is it possible to reconcile the transcendence of revelation with the immanence of human understanding? How might we understand the being of revelation without treating it as an entity at our disposal? How does revelation retain its transcendence, so that it remains a reality that confronts my existence "from outside" (AB 111) and does not come under the control of my thinking? Bonhoeffer wants to show that the being of revelation is "ob-jective" (that it stands over and against the subject—AB 106) without being irreducible to an objective, present-at-hand thing, yet also without sacrificing its concreteness and continuity in historical existence.

The Concreteness of Revelation

In his 1933 Christology lectures, Bonhoeffer seeks to clarify his position in the *capax/incapax* debate, concluding that *finitum capax infiniti, non per se sed per infinitum!*[33] The finite is not capable, in and by itself, of the infinite. Rather, the infinite bestows this capacity on the finite. This clarification excludes the idealist appropriation of the *finitum capax,* as though the activity of religious, Romantic, or transcendental subjectivity includes the *a priori* conditions to receive and contain revelation. The receptive capacity for divine truth is not an immanent capacity, because this capacity itself is a gift. In the words of Kierkegaard's *Philosophical Fragments,* the teacher must give the condition that allows the learner to know the truth.[34]

What would this condition be? In order to answer this question we need to think carefully about the concept of truth and consider what it means to be in the truth. It does not mean impersonal, theoretical cognition but rather a relational knowing, because for Christianity the teacher and the truth coincide. The truth is a person. Consequently, the self participates in the truth not through strictly objective intellectual assent, but in a subjectively engaged relation of participating in and following after (*Efterfølgelse, Nachfolge*) this person.

In order that we might know the truth in this way, the truth enters the world— the eternal entered time, the infinite entered the finite, God entered history, and did so for us (*pro nobis*) and for me (*pro me*). For Bonhoeffer, it is only through God's promeity that we can interpret God's aseity.[35] God discloses himself to us by entering into the world and transforming it from the inside out. God makes himself vulnerable and available to human beings, yet this divine self-giving is never reducible to an *es gibt,* an objective "there is." As Bonhoeffer writes in *Act and Being*: "*Einen Gott, 'den es gibt,' gibt es nicht*"—"there is no God who 'is there'" (AB 115). God does not give himself in such a way that we can make direct statements that would capture God's being as a fixed object of cognition. According to Bonhoeffer, we encounter this revelation—at once transcendent and concrete—in the person of the incarnate, crucified, and resurrected Christ. As we saw in chapter 5, the resurrected *Logos* continues to put me in question, ever anew: *Who do you say that I am?* Kierkegaard refers to this relation as becoming contemporary with Christ. Faith is not a matter of detached, objective cognition but an engaged, existential relation to the living person of Christ.

These Christological insights provide the clue for thinking about the being of revelation: (1) Revealed truth is not *objective,* which is to say, it is not a static entity at my disposal. In his appeal to the *finitum capax,* Bonhoeffer adamantly maintains that the thinking subject is incapable of bearing (or sublating) the fullness of revelation as an object of cognition. Contra idealism, the *finitum capax* does not mean that philosophical or theological reflection becomes capable of bearing the fullness of revelation through conceptual mediation or representation. Bonhoeffer emphasizes the personal, social nature of revelation because it confronts the idealist subject with a reality it cannot adequately cognize. Thus revelation, as the event of God's self-giving in the person of Christ, can never be captured as an objective, manipulable idea or meaning.[36] (2) Yet at the same time, revelation is not simply *nonobjective*—contra dialectical theology. (3) Revelation is both concrete and transcendent. It does not disappear in nonobjectivity. It is "ob-jective" (*Gegen-ständlich*). It stands over and against the thinking self as genuinely other, different, transcendent, while remaining irreducible to the objectivity of fixed, manipulable entities.

Embodied Revelation: Community, Word, and Sacrament

In the relation of faith, the self is continually broken open rather than returning to the closure of a self-mediating, reflective consciousness. The intentionality of faith is an *actus directus*, not an *actus reflexus*. On these points we find strong agreement between Bonhoeffer and Kierkegaard, but they differ regarding the site of the encounter with Christ. Whereas Kierkegaard tends to stress interiority and the hidden inwardness of faith, Bonhoeffer argues that we encounter Christ in the church, in the proclamation of the word, and in the sacraments. In this regard Bonhoeffer is closer to Luther, while Kierkegaard is closer to Lutheran pietism. The danger of pietism is that one's intentional gaze turns inward, seeking the assurance of faith in subjective experiences, emotions, and inner experience of transformation. But this interiority, with its cultivation of self-conscious earnestness, is a perilous site for faith. The inward paths of self-reflection are labyrinthine—fraught with darkness and self-deception and inhabited by a conscience that ravages like a minotaur. The self needs to be broken out of the winding corridors of self-reflection, which so often lead into the despair of self-justification.

Kierkegaard would surely oppose the pietistic attempt to attain some sort of intuitive certainty of one's own faith, but his emphasis on interiority obscures the degree to which we need an external word (*verbum externum*) to break us out of self-reflection and destroy the ontology of self-justification. Granted, Kierkegaard stresses that the self is constituted through being addressed by an external word,[37] but he does not go far enough in stressing the corporeality of this external word. This might be because of Kierkegaard's emphasis on interiority, along with his heightened suspicion of Christendom. But Bonhoeffer insists, following Luther, that we need to encounter the word of revelation in external, embodied form—in the church, in the word, and in the sacraments. The risen *Logos* is there for me, not as a manipulable entity but as a concrete person who addresses me from outside of myself. The Word became flesh and dwelt among us (John 1:14). There are (at least) two implications to note here:

First, we must note the unremitting corporeality of this divine self-giving. The *Logos* became flesh. This is God dwelling among us, dwelling in us—not as passionate inwardness, nor as pious stirrings in disembodied souls, nor as conceptual ideality in a transcendental subject, but as the embodied presence of God in flesh. Revelation is a deeply corporeal phenomenon. In Christ, in the proclaimed word, in the sacraments, God is really *for us* in all the fullness of divinity. Revelation is God's self-giving, "God's coming out of God's own self" (AB 90). This self-giving occurs in God's *given* Word, in which God binds himself to finite, concrete, historical reality. Thus, "Christ is the word of God's freedom. God *is* present, that is, not in eternal nonobjectivity but—to put it quite provisionally for now—'haveable', graspable in the Word within the church" (AB 91). This Word is given in the proclamation of the gospel and in the sacraments. Whereas Barth wants to preserve divine transcendence by stressing God's freedom *from* human beings, Bonhoeffer wants to preserve God's transcendence by stressing that divine freedom is freedom *for* human beings (AB 91). Thus God's transcendence and God's freedom are ensured precisely by God's intimate dwelling among us. This is the sense in which Bonhoeffer will later write, in his prison letters, that "God is the beyond in the midst of our life" (LPP 367). Divine transcendence must be interpreted in this-worldly terms.

Similarly, Bonhoeffer argues against a formal understanding of divine freedom as an absolute, unconditioned will (e.g., nominalism's emphasis on the pure contingency of revelation). That is not the God who reveals himself in the Incarnate One. Christ reveals a God whose freedom is not abstract and arbitrary, but a freedom that is determinately *for us*. God makes himself available to us, vulnerable to us. As Luther writes: "It is the honour of our God, however, that, in giving the divine self for our sake in deepest condescension, entering into flesh and bread, into our mouth, heart and bowel and suffering for our sake, God be dishonourably handled, both on the altar and the cross."[38] This is God "deep in the flesh."[39]

The exteriority of the word becomes apparent when I hear the word spoken by another person, and in the sensible experience of the bread and wine. This corporeality assures me that the gospel addresses me from outside myself. The word became flesh and dwelt *among* us, and not just *in* me. This word occupies space and time in the external world.

The second implication we must note is that God dwells among *us*, and not just in *me*. Christ is after all *pro me* (for me) as well as *pro nobis* (for us). If revelation were solely a disclosure of information, then it would be accessible to the solitary self, but if God gives himself in the proclamation of the gospel and in the sacraments, then the phenomenon of faith is inescapably intersubjective. Bonhoeffer criticizes Barth (and Kierkegaard) for conceiving faith and revelation individualistically, arguing that the faithful self has its continuity in the church community. In the church there is unity between the act of faith and the being of the faithful self. It is crucial that the being of the self is prior to the act of faith—in other words, that the self does not create itself in the act of faith. Bonhoeffer insists, contra idealism, that the being of the new, faithful self does not depend on the act of faith. The act of faith is not a self-positing, self-creating act. Rather, the being of the faithful self is ontologically prior to the act of faith. Therefore in the first instance the faithful self is not active but passive. In relation to God, the human being is defined "as being acted upon" (*pati*) (AB 116)—i.e., of being encountered, being addressed by Christ, by a reality that is already there prior to my individual act of faith—in the church, in the proclaimed word, and in the sacraments.[40] Insofar as faith, too, is an act of consciousness, it can fall prey to an ontology of self-justification, according to which I merit God's recognition on the basis of this act. But the ontology of justification by faith maintains that I am recognized, justified prior to any self-positing act that might merit recognition. With regard to faith, the new being constituted by this eschatological promise is prior to my act.

The faithful self is therefore a synthesis of act and being (*Akt-Sein-Synthese*) (AB 120). The faithful self "is" only in reference to Christ; there is no being without this act of reference. In other words, being only discloses itself in the act of faith (AB 122). But if the self "is" only in this referential act of being toward Christ, this is not a self-positing act. The act presupposes a prior being (i.e., being-in-Christ). The act of faith does not create its being-in-Christ; it is neither self-positing nor self-sufficient, but is only justified in reference to Christ. The act is *aufgehoben* in being (AB 120). In its acts of believing, praying, and proclaiming, the faithful self bears the new humanity of Christ; yet the self knows that it only bears this new reality insofar as it is already borne in its acts "by the community of faith, by Christ":

> I hear another human being truly tell me the gospel. Someone offers me the sacraments: you are forgiven. Someone along with the community of faith prays for me. And I hear the gospel, join in the prayer, and know myself bound up in the word, sacrament, and prayer of Christ's community of faith, the new humanity, whether it is here or elsewhere. Bearing it, I am borne by it. Here I, the historically whole human being—individual and humanity—am encountered, and I believe, that is, know myself borne. (AB 121)

Bonhoeffer sums up the relation between the act of faith and the being of the faithful self as follows: "I am borne (*pati*), therefore I am (*esse*), therefore I believe (*agere*)." The act of belief is possible because of this prior being, which in turn depends on a prior passivity.

* * *

To draw these themes together, then, in *Act and Being* Bonhoeffer argues that the ontological continuity of the self does not reside in an immanent substratum or the punctual acts of a solitary faithful self, but in the community of faith.[41] In this community I hear a word that precedes my own acts—in proclamation, in prayer, in the sacraments.

There are, however, some points on which Bonhoeffer's account needs to be supplemented. First, I would suggest that we enrich Bonhoeffer's account by taking a cue from Ricoeur's account of narrative identity. We understand ourselves—our past, present, and future—according to a narrative structure. This is a vital element of the continuity of the self, though this too needs to be understood in a relational and communal context. Our stories are not solitary affairs, since we understand our own stories as they are taken up into the story of God's relation to the world. This is the story we hear in the church, the story of God's promise to Abraham, the hopes of Israel, the life, death, and resurrection of Christ, the story of his coming kingdom.

Secondly, Bonhoeffer's appeal to the church as the locus of continuity leaves numerous questions unanswered. We need to reflect further on the relation between revelation and such basic features of human being as ethical responsibility, capability, rationality, and intentionality. Bonhoeffer's account in *Act and Being* in many ways echoes Luther in that the acts of the faithful self are *simul justus et peccator*.[42] The act cannot justify itself autonomously, because in itself it remains a human possibility that is bound by sin. The act must be justified by faith, and not by any inherent or immanent merit. But this dialectical structure inevitably raises further questions: Does this mean that it makes no difference how one acts, since ultimately every act is justified by faith? Does the dialectical logic of faith eliminate the possibility of making relative distinctions between acts? Moreover, does it preclude growth and formation of character? In order to address these questions, we must turn to Bonhoeffer's *Ethics* and its theme of the penultimate.

Ultimate and Penultimate Things

With the typology of the ultimate (*das Letzte*) and the penultimate (*das Vorletzte*), Bonhoeffer provides a model for thinking through "perpetual polarities"[43] that perplex philosophical and theological discourse: transcendence and immanence, grace and nature, act and being, revelation and reason, other and same, eschatology and ontology, difference and identity. For Bonhoeffer the ultimate designates the eschatological word—the proclamation of the incarnate, crucified, and resurrected Christ. It should not be understood along the lines of Tillich's notion of ultimate concern,[44] since it is not a formal category. The ultimate word is the self-announcement, self-witness, and self-revelation of God in Jesus Christ (E 49). The human being participates in this ultimate reality through the eschatological event of justification by grace alone and faith alone.

The eschatological event of justification is ultimate in both a qualitative and temporal sense. It is *qualitatively* ultimate because it is a decisive break with everything that claims to be ontologically prior. Here Bonhoeffer agrees with Luther, Kierkegaard, and Barth,[45] as the ultimate is an ontologically disruptive event, the new creation coming from beyond the horizon of our own immanent possibilities and actualities, breaking in and interrupting the world as we know it. It does not arise from any native ontological conditions, nor is it the *telos* of any immanent human potential. No method or program and no moral or religious potentiality are capable of reaching the ultimate. The ultimate interrupts the self and its capacities. It is a moment of rupture that stands in judgment on everything penultimate (E 149–50).

This moment is also *temporally* ultimate. The declaration of justification is God's final word. This word is the *kairos*, the fullness of time, the day of salvation.[46] However, the fact that this word is temporally ultimate means that the eschatological moment is given at the end of a stretch of time. It is a complete break, and yet it is nevertheless preceded temporally by the *pen*ultimate. If the ultimate designates last things, then the *penultimate* designates the *next-to-last*—i.e., that which comes before the ultimate. Prior to the moment of justification there is always "some action, suffering, movement, intention, defeat, recovery, pleading, hoping—in short, quite literally a span of time at whose end it stands" (E 150–51). The ultimate is preceded by the penultimate, and in order to reach the ultimate it is necessary to traverse the penultimate. In a letter written during his imprisonment, Bonhoeffer argues that we must not speak the ultimate word before the penultimate (LPP 213). The penultimate is the road that one must travel to reach the ultimate. Within its proper limits, the penultimate serves to "prepare the way" for the eschatological word of grace (E 161), and once it has preceded the ultimate in this way, the penultimate *follows after* the word of address, in order to precede it again (E 159). In this way, the penultimate provides the temporal extendedness of the word.

Although the ultimate is ontologically disruptive, Bonhoeffer wants to avoid the conclusion that it annihilates everything penultimate. He also wants to avoid the implication that the ultimate is a pointlike event with no concrete extension, because the ultimate impacts the historical existence of the self. The ultimate makes itself known in the penultimate, which is the ontological structure of human being in the world. Or as Jean-Yves Lacoste puts it, the penultimate is the "pre-eschatological site" that is our concrete, historical existence.[47] It is the horizon within which the ultimate shows itself.

Being Human and Being Good

As we have seen, in *Act and Being* Bonhoeffer locates the continuity of faith in the church community. In chapter 8 we will see that Bonhoeffer's book *Discipleship* (*Nachfolge*) examines the theme of following after Christ as a way in which faith is extended in space and time. This theme provides an early version of Bonhoeffer's description of the penultimate, but one of the major developments in *Ethics* is its deeper recognition of the *worldly* character of revelation. Through Christ's incarnation, the reality of God is disclosed in the reality of the world. There are no longer two separate realities, realms, or kingdoms. The ultimate word announces that God and the world are reconciled in the one realm of the Christ-reality (*Christuswirklichkeit*). In faith the self encounters the world as "always already borne, accepted, and reconciled in the reality of God." Consequently, being-in-Christ means participating in the reality of God and the world at the same time (E 55).

The church is the site at which this ultimate word of reconciliation is proclaimed, but the purpose of this proclamation is neither triumphalistic nor imperialistic, as though the word absorbs the world into itself. The word addresses the world and destroys its false self-understanding—its incurvature, despair, and sense of God-forsakenness—in order to call the world to a *genuine* worldliness (E 60, 63–64). By recognizing itself as penultimate, the world is set free from its burden of self-justification and enabled to be the world—created, preserved, and reconciled in Christ.

According to Bonhoeffer, two basic ontological features of this penultimate, worldly humanity are "being human" (*Menschsein*) and "being good" (*Gutsein*) (E 159). Questions of humanity, selfhood, and identity are penultimate concerns. The question *Who*—the basic question with which we identify the existing, historical self—is a penultimate question. We identify the self through its bodily comportment in the world, through its actions, its relations, its situation in space and time, its capabilities, its cares and its commitments, its relations and responsibilities, its story and its hopes. Moreover, we have seen that the ontology of the self is inseparable from what Charles Taylor calls a moral ontology: we can understand who we are because we can locate ourselves in moral space; we have convictions regarding what it is to be human, what it is to flourish, and what it is to do the good. These ontological commitments give us our bearing in the world, they form the horizon through which we perceive reality, and they are the topography by which we locate ourselves in moral space. These concerns fall within the domain of what Bonhoeffer calls being good (*Gutsein*).

The ultimate disrupts all of this. It is a word spoken from beyond our horizons, overturning our self-understanding and our sense of what goodness, humanity, wisdom, and power are. The self no longer has its identity in itself, but has its new being—its new *substantia* or standing—before God in Christ. Here the self is fundamentally passive; the ultimate is a gift rather than a wage. There is no way to anticipate it, initiate it, or hasten its advent. As such, penultimate realities like *Menschsein* and *Gutsein* are not transcendental conditions of the ultimate. The ultimate is an impossibility that makes itself possible. It gives its own conditions. Yet at the same time, Bonhoeffer insists that these penultimate conditions are still relevant to the coming of the ultimate. They serve to "prepare the way" for the ultimate word. To be sure, the ultimate makes its own way to us, so we cannot reach it through any moral or religious program nor through any rational or mystical ascent. The ultimate is a negative judgment on every method that aspires to reach the ultimate from within the penultimate. But "preparing the way" is the path that leads from the ultimate to the penultimate (E 167). In cultivating and nourishing the penultimate, we prepare the way for the ultimate word to address us.

In order to understand the relation between the ultimate and the penultimate, it is crucial to see that there is a dialectical logic at work here. For example, *being human* is penultimate with regard to justification, because only human beings are justified. To paraphrase Luther, the kingdom of God is not proclaimed to geese.[48] The human being is addressed by the Word and yet remains a concrete, historical, embodied person with basic human capacities for thinking, feeling, relating, and acting in the world. In this sense, Bonhoeffer maintains that "being human precedes being justified" (E 159). But this does not imply that *Menschsein* is therefore an autonomous condition for justification. With a keen sense of the paradox involved, Bonhoeffer writes: "Only the human being can be justified, simply because only the one who is justified becomes a 'human being'" (E 160).[49] *Menschsein* is not a self-sufficient reality, because it is only properly understood in reference to the ultimate word of justification. It is a penultimate reality, and the penultimate does not exist in and for itself. "There is no penultimate as such, as if something or other could justify itself as being in itself penultimate." The identity of the penultimate is not self-contained, but is only given in relation to the ultimate. By definition the penultimate is the next-to-last, so it would be impossible to designate the penultimate without reference to that which is ultimate, or last. Thus "the penultimate becomes what it is only through the ultimate, that is, in the moment when it has already lost its own self-sufficiency" (E 159). The penultimate is the horizon within which the ultimate shows itself, but it must relinquish any claim to earn or make possible the ultimate.

For these reasons Bonhoeffer maintains that human being does not exist whole and sufficient unto itself, as if we simply need one last attribute—the crown of justification—to fulfill our humanity. After the fall into sin, the human being lives in disunity with itself, in isolation from God and others. Sin ruptures the original created relation with God, resulting in a fall away from our origin (E 300ff.). This fall would have resulted in a descent into utter corruption and chaos, except that God does not abandon humanity. God affirms the fallen creation, upholding it and preserving it—not in order that human beings might persist in their brokenness, but for the sake of Christ's coming to restore true relations between God, the self, other human beings, and creation (CF 139–40, 146).

In the same manner the penultimate does not exist for its own sake, but only as directed toward the ultimate. This is how Bonhoeffer understands the concept of nature. Because of sin we cannot access a pure ontology of creaturely being, nor can we appeal to a creaturely goodness that is untouched by sin; yet Bonhoeffer also resists the radical Protestant conclusion that the fall obliterated the goodness of creation altogether. Creation remains good not because sin had a merely superficial impact, but because God has preserved and sustained creation for the coming of Christ (E 174). After the fall, we need to speak of *nature* rather than *creation*, though this is no more a pure nature than it is a pure createdness. Instead, the natural is God's gracious preservation of creation, for the sake of the coming grace of the ultimate: "We speak of the natural as distinct from the created, in order to include the fact of the fall into sin. We speak of the natural as distinct from the sinful in order to include the created." In other words, the natural is a penultimate reality, preserved and directed toward the coming of the ultimate (E 173).

The fallen human being is therefore upheld and preserved in its penultimate *Menschsein* for the sake of the new humanity revealed in Christ.[50] This is what Bonhoeffer has in mind when he argues that the ultimate determines the penultimate and not vice versa: the penultimate cannot dictate the terms on which the ultimate is given, nor can it compel its coming; the ultimate cannot be negated, bound, or forced by the penultimate, and nothing immanent to *Menschsein* can determine the ultimate. But the freedom of the ultimate is not simply a freedom *from* humanity; it is fundamentally a freedom *for* humanity. Hence Bonhoeffer's claim that the freedom of the ultimate "empowers the penultimate," and hence his simultaneous insistence that "the penultimate must be preserved for the sake of the ultimate" (E 160). This means that the Christian must work for everything that preserves, deepens, and enriches human being at a penultimate level.

Penultimate conditions of humanity and goodness are relevant to the advent of the ultimate because they can make it difficult for us and others to come to faith.[51] There are conditions of the heart, conditions of life, and conditions in the world that oppose the advent of grace and hinder its reception. When people are suffering from disgrace, desolation, poverty, and helplessness, they find it difficult to believe in a good and just God. When people have lost self-discipline and are living in disorder, it is difficult for them to hear God's commands in faith. When people are living lives of material abundance and worldly power, it is difficult for them to understand God's judgment and God's grace.[52] Although conditions such as these cannot finally prevent the advent of grace, they can nevertheless oppose it (E 162).

Penultimate concerns like justice, peace, human dignity, and human flourishing do make a difference before God (E 166). They do not establish one's ultimate righteousness, but they matter nonetheless: "The hungry person needs bread, the homeless person needs shelter, the one deprived of rights needs justice, the lonely person needs community, the undisciplined one needs order, and the slave needs freedom" (E 163). By attending to these penultimate needs, one does not proclaim the ultimate, yet these are indispensable concerns in anticipation of and as a witness to the ultimate.[53]

Radicalism and Compromise

In chapter 5 we discussed Bonhoeffer's account of the one Christ-reality (*Christuswirklichkeit*). One of the major advantages of this account is that it undoes the dualisms that slip so easily into Christian thinking. Static oppositions of sacred/secular, church/world, eternity/time, faith/works, and revelation/reason, ultimate/penultimate follow from thinking in two realms,[54] but the Christian message proclaims a unified reality: "*the one realm of the Christ-reality [Christuswirklichkeit]*." Because of Christ we see that the world, the natural, the profane, and the rational are "included in God from the beginning. All this does not exist 'in and for itself.'" The two realms are one in Christ. This has major consequences for understanding faithful being in the world: "Just as the reality of God has entered the reality of the world in Christ, what is Christian cannot be had otherwise than in what is worldly, the 'supernatural' only in the natural, the holy only in the profane, the revelational only in the rational" (E 58–59). But note well that this unity is not a simple identity, since Bonhoeffer does not want to erase these distinctions. The unity is polemical in nature, so that the categories "worldly" and "Christian" exist in a relation of mutual limitation. This polemical relation prevents us from viewing either in static, independent terms (either as an otherworldly religiosity or a trivial worldliness that is unchallenged by faith),[55] thereby witnessing to their common reality and unity in Christ (E 59–60).

This polemical unity will also characterize Bonhoeffer's account of the relation between ultimate and penultimate things, since he seeks a middle course between the matching errors of *radicalism* and *compromise*. According to Bonhoeffer, "Christian life neither destroys nor sanctions the penultimate" (E 159). This can be an uncomfortable relationship to maintain, since it would be easier if the penultimate were either rejected as ungodly or left alone as self-sufficient. We could then choose one or the other. But such a choice would only result in a false resolution, since neither radicalism nor compromise can sufficiently account for the complexities of faithful existence.

Radicalism, Bonhoeffer writes, "sees only the ultimate." Christ and the penultimate stand opposed as mortal enemies, because everything penultimate is "sin and denial." Eschatology annihilates ontology. All relative distinctions are abolished; "it is a matter of all or nothing. The ultimate word of God, which is a word of grace, becomes here the icy hardness of the law that crushes and despises all resistance" (E 153). Radicalism amounts to a condemnation of existence. Whether it wants to flee the world or revolutionize it, radicalism "comes from the hatred of creation. The radical cannot forgive God for having created what is." The radical feels "bitterness, suspicion, and contempt for human beings and the world" (E 155). Bonhoeffer cites Ibsen's character Brand, with his principle of "All or Nothing!," as an example of this world-negating radicalism.[56]

Compromise, at the opposite extreme, wants to protect the autonomy of the penultimate from any interference from the ultimate. "The ultimate stays completely beyond daily life and in the end serves only as the eternal justification of all that exists" (E 154). Compromise hates the ultimate, hates its demands, hates its offensive claim that the penultimate is fallen in sin and can only be justified by grace alone. "One must manage the world only by worldly means. The ultimate is to have no say in the formation of life in the world."[57] Rather than taking the ultimate word seriously, compromise accommodates itself to worldly wisdom, which it passes off "as genuine Christian openness to the world and love" (E 156). For example, the eschatological disruption of the self is eclipsed by an overriding concern with human subjectivity, which includes such possibilities as religious consciousness, cultural formation, or social and ethical projects. On this view faith is a subjective phenomenon, and the transcendent realities to which faith refers are relative to the conditions and capacities of religious subjectivity. Barth traces the genealogy of liberal Protestant theology along these lines.[58] Insofar as faith appears in cultural objectivity, it is governed by the authority of the reigning social and ethical norms. Eschatology is a domestic product.

Bonhoeffer juxtaposes the opposite extremes of radicalism and compromise as follows:

> Radicalism hates time. Compromise hates eternity.
> Radicalism hates patience. Compromise hates decision.
> Radicalism hates wisdom. Compromise hates simplicity.
> Radicalism hates measure. Compromise hates the immeasurable.
> Radicalism hates the real. Compromise hates the word. (E 156)

Or in another formulation: "One absolutizes the end, the other absolutizes what exists" (E 154). One wants eschatology without the concreteness and continuity of ontology, the other wants ontology without the disruption of eschatology. According to Bonhoeffer, what both extremes fail to recognize is that the unity of the ultimate and penultimate is established in Christ, and it is essential to the Christian life that what God has reconciled not be torn asunder (E 157). Radicalism and compromise are therefore both abstractions from the concrete unity of the ultimate and the penultimate in Christ.

This points toward an important caution for our *anthropologia crucis*. We should not identify the ultimate as the word of the cross in isolation from the incarnation and resurrection. All three aspects belong to the ultimate word. Commenting on the incarnation, Bonhoeffer writes that God becoming human means that we might become human before God (E 157). Or as Anti-Climacus writes in *The Sickness Unto Death:* "Out of love, God becomes man. He says: Here you see what it is to be a human being" (SUD 127). The cross is also necessary for understanding the faithful self. "The ultimate has become real in the cross," Bonhoeffer writes, "as judgment on all that is penultimate, but at the same time as grace for the penultimate that bows to the judgment of the ultimate" (E 158). The cross is the judgment on the incurved self. It destroys the ontology of self-justification. If justification by faith is a *creatio ex nihilo*, however, the cross "does not simply mean the annihilation of creation" (E 158). The cross does not entail a sheer obliteration of the self and its penultimate capabilities. Instead, the judgment of the cross discloses an eschatological possibility, a new self, a new being in Christ. This is why resurrection is also necessary for understanding the faithful self. The human being "remains human, but in a new resurrected way that is completely unlike the old." The break is decisive, and yet "[e]ven the resurrection does not abolish the penultimate as long as the earth remains; . . . eternal life, the new life, breaks ever more powerfully into earthly life and creates space for itself within it" (E 158). The resurrection initiates and effects a re-creation of the self, one that originates from beyond any penultimate potentiality.

Conclusion

Through Bonhoeffer's interpretation of the *finitum capax* and his later account of the penultimate, we can better understand how the cruciform self avoids being a punctual self. The word of the cross is ontologically disruptive, marking a fundamental discontinuity within the life of the self. Yet this word does not obliterate all continuity because the penultimate prepares the way for the word, and in turn follows after it—so that it might precede it again (E 159). As a result, the ultimate word has its concreteness and continuity in the penultimate.

With this account of the penultimate in place, we are now in a position to examine the questions we posed in chapter 2. What does the word of the cross mean for philosophical discourse about human capability and self-understanding? This word introduces a radical rupture within philosophical discourse, breaking apart and even destroying its worldly wisdom. But does this mean that philosophical anthropology—and the phenomena to which it attends—are simply annihilated by the word of the cross? Or is a philosophical anthropology of the cross in fact possible? Over the next three chapters, I will show how the category of the penultimate allows us to retrieve and affirm human capability and self-understanding after they have undergone the *destructio* of the cross. A correct understanding of the penultimate does this by avoiding both radicalism and compromise. From the perspective of theological radicalism, philosophical anthropology as a whole is a misguided, disobedient discourse that should be overcome by theological anthropology. The cross leaves no place for fallen reason and worldly wisdom. Likewise, themes like human capability and self-understanding are also misguided notions that lead us to misunderstand the nature of faith. I will argue that the category of the penultimate allows us to discern the proper place of philosophical anthropology and its concerns in a discourse that has been transformed by the word of the cross. In other words, it establishes the theological legitimacy of *philosophical* anthropology.

At the same time, the fact that the penultimate has its identity in relation to the ultimate guards against a philosophical anthropology that would compromise the word of the cross. An anthropology of compromise would fix the word of the cross within a general or fundamental philosophical framework, interpreting it solely in terms of religious symbolics or semantics, as a figure of transcendence and otherness, or perhaps even an instance of a more general idea of paradox or rupture. Philosophy might then be interrupted and decentered by the word of the cross, just as it is interrupted by its other *others* (literature, poetry, religion, the natural sciences), but the philosophical *logos* retains its prerogative to identify and classify the *logos* of the cross, because philosophy has the truly fundamental anthropology and/or ontology. In other words, the philosophical *logos* is not ultimately transformed through its interrogation by the counter-*Logos*. Whatever upheaval it undergoes, philosophical reflection always regains its composure. This raises another problem, which we have already noted: How can a philosophical anthropology of the cross avoid returning to systematic closure? Is it possible that Christian thinking can remain decentered, *ek*-static, and eschatologically oriented? How does the intentionality of faith relate to reflexivity and self-understanding? Further, in what way is the cruciform self also a capable human being? And finally, what is the relation between cruciform faith and religion? Over the remaining chapters I put Bonhoeffer's category of the penultimate to work, showing how it provides a hermeneutical key for thinking through these questions.

7   The Capable Human Being as a Penultimate Good

In chapter 6 we saw that the cruciform self is not a punctual self. In this chapter I demonstrate the sense in which the cruciform self is a capable self, since capability is one of the central themes of philosophical anthropology. On Ricoeur's definition, capability is a power or potentiality that the self is able to exercise—most basically, "the power to cause something to happen."[1] So our question is this: What place do human agency and the power to act have in the life of faith? What does the word of the cross mean for our understanding of the self as a capable human being, as an *I can*?

In the first section I argue that a distinction between ultimate and penultimate possibilities is vital in order to avoid a religious radicalism that would deny human capability altogether. This is followed in the next section by a critical analysis of Michel Henry's proposal for a Christian philosophy of action. In the third section, I examine the relation between the call and response of faith. This theme provides a focal point for our discussion of human capability, since it leads us to consider what sort of capability or agency is involved in the response of faith. After locating capability as a penultimate good and a vital component of being human (*Menschsein*), in chapter 8 I bring Ricoeur and Bonhoeffer into dialogue with Levinas in order to discuss conscience as a penultimate capacity for hearing and receiving the call of the other, in ethical responsibility as well as faith.

Ultimate and Penultimate Possibilities

From a certain perspective it might seem that a philosophical affirmation of *l'homme capable* is simply incommensurable with an *anthropologia crucis*. The word of the cross destroys the human presumption of being capable of the ultimate; this is why Bonhoeffer argues on several occasions that the concept of possibility has no place in theology or theological anthropology.[2] One might also appeal to textual support against the capable human being—such as Galatians 2:20, which describes the *I* as having been crucified with Christ: if it is therefore no longer I that live, but Christ that lives in me, does this amount to a complete denial of human agency and the power to act? Can the cruciform self no longer designate itself with the words *I can*? A radical interpretation might take this in the direction of a metaphysical occasionalism, as a psychological transformation in which divine agency commandeers human agency, as though the crucifixion of the I means that the faithful self has no agency, efficacy, or proper sphere of action.[3]

Radicalism's interpretation of the cross often tends toward a misanthropy that seems to confirm Nietzsche's judgment regarding Christianity—namely that it heaps contempt on the human being, demanding "a sacrifice of all freedom, all pride, all self-confidence of the spirit," along with an accompanying "enslavement and self-mockery, self-mutilation."[4] The word of the cross destroys and humiliates the self, making a significant contribution to the development of nihilism through its negation of everything human and this-worldly. This annihilation of the self also has serious ethical consequences. Numerous feminists have argued that a cross-centered anthropology (particularly one that employs the violent rhetoric of *destructio*) has too often valorized passivity, submission, suffering, and even victimhood. This rhetoric is a luxury that certain privileged people can afford, but it is not good news for those who are oppressed, powerless, disabled, or living in abusive relationships and other situations in which they need to be strengthened.

Radicalism's rejection of human capability also distorts the nature of faith, obscuring the fact that the cross calls us to an active response and responsibility for others. Kierkegaard observes that the wrong emphasis on passivity and incapability often serves to justify apathy and irresponsibility[5]—a problem he saw as endemic to Lutheran Christendom. Although Luther was correct to stress justification by grace and faith alone, his "Reformation discovery" gave way to a travesty of the gospel in which people presumptuously took grace for granted and saw no need for works to follow.[6]

With these interpretations in view, it is clear that the hermeneutics of the cross is a subtle art and must be practiced with care, because not every interpretation of the cross is good news. If we insist on the wrong sort of passivity we fall into a theological radicalism that would extinguish all sense of capability. We therefore need to ask what sort of possibilities and capacities are at stake. The word of the cross is a negative judgment on all human projects of reaching God, whether via religious piety, ethical activity, or metaphysical speculation. To stand justified before God is not a human possibility nor the realization of any human teleology. In relation to the ultimate we can therefore only speak of human *im*possibility and *in*capability.

Although the word of the cross is indeed radical, it must not be carried into a false radical*ism*. We therefore need to distinguish between ultimate and penultimate capabilities. The word of the cross does not destroy or nullify every penultimate capacity and possibility. Thus in rejecting possibility as a category of theological anthropology, Bonhoeffer is primarily referring to justification by faith; he does not deny the proper role of possibility as a philosophical or psychological category. I can move; I can think; I can speak; I can respond to the demands of my situation. I have the capacity to perform these acts and do these deeds. The point is that I can*not* determine the ultimate standing of these actions before God, whether by appealing to a principle, ideology, the practiced wisdom of *phronesis*, the purity of my motives, or the good consequences of my actions.

The cross pronounces God's No over incurved life, over the self as fallen away from the origin, essence, and goal of its life. The cross takes the incurvature of the self with dead seriousness, and therefore its No means "dying, suffering, poverty, renunciation, surrender, humility, self-deprecation, and self-denial" (E 352). Yet if we abstract this No from the Yes, we confirm Nietzsche's suspicion that the cross is a word of negation that leads to a nihilistic cult of suffering and death. If that is the case, then whence comes the Yes? The self has its life outside of itself, and in recognizing Christ as its life the self hears God's Yes to its life as a human being—"to what is created, to becoming, to growth, to flower and fruit, to health, to happiness, to ability, to achievement, to value, to success, to greatness, to honor, in short the Yes to the flourishing of life's strength." Radicalism's interpretation of the cross cannot abide this word of affirmation, whereas the way of compromise cannot abide the word of negation, but the life of faith consists in the Christological unity of this No and Yes (E 251–52).

To put it another way, in Christ the self encounters the unity of the ultimate and the penultimate. By wrongly obliterating the penultimate, radicalism distorts the liberating power of the cross. As Bonhoeffer argues in one of his prison letters, Christ does not only make human beings "good"; he also makes them strong (LPP 516). Human strength and capability is a penultimate good and must be defended against these distortions—not for the sake of celebrating human achievements, but "primarily for the sake of those who have never achieved these penultimate things, whom no one has helped to gain them, for whom no one has prepared the way" (E 164). This recognition is good news for the poor, the weak, the suffering, the disabled, and the marginalized.

* * *

The category of the penultimate also guards against the radicalism that would interpret faith in terms of theological occasionalism or determinism. Within the scope of the penultimate we can affirm a proper sphere of human agency and capability. We will discuss this more in the third section, but for now I would like to highlight a few of Bonhoeffer's observations regarding the self's capacities for acting effectively in the world.

The first point concerns what Kierkegaard calls "works of love." As we will discuss in the next section, Bonhoeffer argues that love is never autonomous and independent of God's love, since it requires the passive reception of God's love. This passivity does not, however, erase human freedom and activity. On the contrary, the prior gift of election [*Erwählung*] liberates the self to love others freely, and this freedom involves a genuine creativity: "To be loved by God certainly does not prohibit human beings from thinking powerful thoughts and doing joyful deeds. It is as whole human beings, as thinking and acting human beings . . . that we love God and our brothers and sisters" (E 336–38). In this sense the faithful self is an agent (and not simply a passive conduit) of divine love.

The second point concerns the discernment of God's command or will in concrete ethical situations. According to Bonhoeffer, discernment requires the trans-formation (*Umgestaltung*) of one's mind and the con-formation (*Gleichgestaltung*) of the human being to the form (*Gestalt*) of the new humanity, Christ. Ethical discernment is therefore not an immanent possibility or autonomous act; it is given ever anew in the concrete situation. Yet this does not obviate the role of human discernment, which is a hermeneutical task rather than an immediate intuition.[7] It requires "the entire array of human abilities," including heart, intellect, conscience, cognitive ability, attention, observation, and prior experience (E 321–24). These capacities are vital conditions of responsible action.[8]

The third example concerns the status of reason as a penultimate capacity. This point is particularly important because the *theologia crucis* can easily be interpreted in fideistic or irrationalist terms. To be sure, the word of the cross is a decisive critique of reason. It is a word that incurved reason cannot abide; reason can only revolt against that which appears to be impossible, foolish, weak, absurd, abominable, and even diabolical. According to Luther, faith "slaughters reason," that "bitterest and most pestilential enemy of God."[9] Luther's severe rhetoric is not, however, a fideistic dismissal of rationality in general, but a critique of autonomous, incurved reason.[10] In the *status corruptionis*, the impulse of reason is to dominate rather than serve. Incurved reason seeks mastery in its concupiscent desire to bring everything *other* under its dominion. But reason is also part of the preserved world, and within its proper scope the natural light of reason is integral to being human. A proper recognition of reason can therefore be seen as preparing the way for the ultimate. By contrast, irrationalism (which Bonhoeffer saw vividly expressed in Nazi ideology) opposes the advent of the ultimate. Revelation does confront incurved reason with an alterity that it cannot master,[11] yet it is also true that revelation has entered the world in and through the rational (E 59). Reason is not capable, in and of itself, of bearing the fullness of the infinite, yet it is nevertheless a pre-eschatological site at which revelation enters our horizon of understanding. Reason must not be nihilistically dismissed or devalued;[12] it must be brought into obedience to revelation and thereby set free to serve. Incurved reason must be broken open by an external word, which reveals the proper identity of reason as penultimate, as directed toward a word beyond itself. Reason is not self-justifying, but surrenders its operations to be justified by faith.

A Christian Philosophy of Action? Michel Henry

We find a provocative contrast to Bonhoeffer's description of penultimate human capability in Michel Henry's book *I Am the Truth*, which deals at length with the status of the *I Can* in Christian life. Like Bonhoeffer, Henry maintains that genuinely Christian ethical action does not originate from the autonomous self, but from the participation of the self in Christ, who is Life itself.[13] As we will see, though, there are considerable differences between how they interpret this participation, and it soon becomes clear that Henry presents a highly sophisticated philosophy of Christianity that manages to be at once both a *philosophia gloriae* and a variety of radicalism.

Henry argues that Christianity entails "an entirely new philosophy of action" that "breaks decisively" with both classical and modern accounts of action (IT 171). On those accounts, to act is to move from an interior, subjective intention, project, or desire to an exterior, objective reality, which means that "reality resides in the product of the action," which shows up in the world. Henry argues that Christianity overthrows both this concept of action and of reality (IT 172), citing the example of fasting: the true act of fasting does not consist in external conduct, which is visible in the light of worldly objectivity; instead, it is entirely invisible, immanent within subjectivity (IT 176). This is why Christ denounces the hypocrisy of those who perform their religious duties for the sake of being seen by others; the true act of fasting does not show up in the world, but is hidden in interiority.

Henry is not merely making the familiar point that Christianity is concerned with purity of heart and motives, but more significantly that Christianity introduces a radically novel conception of subjectivity. This concept of subjectivity is in turn vital to understanding Christianity's philosophy of action. Henry argues that the essence of the self is *life,* and that life is a distinctive phenomenon unlike anything in the world. Life is distinctive because its essence is *self-affection,* which is to say that life *affects* itself, and this self-affection is phenomenologically different from the way life is affected by anything else. Henry explains: "Affection generally implies a manifestation. If a being of the world affects me, it makes itself felt by me, shows itself to me, gives itself to me, enters into my experience in some way or other. . . . In self affection, what affects me is no longer anything foreign or external to me who am affected, and consequently no object belonging to the world or the world itself" (IT 105). The self affects itself, experiences itself, and this self-experience is what constitutes the self (IT 107). This means that the essence of life does not consist in being related to persons and things in the world; prior to being affected by anything exterior, life affects itself. The essence of life is an "acosmic," nonworldly reality that is entirely prior to and independent of any possible world. Life cannot be understood in terms of the world, regardless of whether we understand the world in the naturalistic sense of the sciences or in the transcendental sense of philosophers like Kant, Husserl, or Heidegger. Life is not a worldly phenomenon, but "comes about in itself in the absolute sufficiency of its radical interiority" (IT 105).

Christianity's radical conception of subjectivity is accompanied by an equally novel conception of phenomenality. In fact, Henry argues that Christianity is itself a phenomenology, since it does not merely disclose the truth about particular phenomena, but about phenomen*ality* itself—that is, it concerns the manner in which phenomena are accessible to us. Christianity challenges virtually the entire philosophical tradition (including the phenomenological tradition) and its conception of phenomenality, which derives at its most basic level from the "immediate perception of mundane objects," and at more sophisticated levels from "the appearing of the world."[14] This conception of phenomenality derives from Greek thought, according to which "to appear" means a phenomenon shows itself by coming into the light of a world, an ek-static "outside" beyond the immanence of life.[15] The philosophical perpetuation of the Greek conception of phenomenality has resulted in a "disastrous confusion of the appearing of the world with the essence of all conceivable appearing."[16] Henry's complaint is that the world's light is "indifferent" to the particular beings it illuminates, so that all phenomena must appear in a worldly manner. This "ontological monism" (Henry's term for the homogeneous phenomenality of the world) has influenced phenomenology, starting with Husserl's "principle of all principles," which posits intuition as the source that gives knowledge and intentionality as the structure of consciousness that makes phenomenality emerge in intuition.[17] Henry contends that this manner of appearing "deprives each thing of its substance in order to deliver it to us," in a "making-seen that destroys" and that annihilates "everything it exhibits" (IT 18–19). The phenomenality of *life*, by sharp contrast, is entirely unlike the world. Life is "*grasped in its pure, phenomenological essence as self-revelation.*"[18] Life is not on display as a thing in the world, because it can only be grasped in the immanence of living itself.

If life is as radically immanent as Henry suggests, then the relation of the self to itself must be unmediated by anything outside itself (*extra se*). This does not, however, mean that the self is a nonrelational, solipsistic monad. On the contrary, Henry contends that the self is generated by being addressed by Christ. This is why Henry often speaks of the self in the accusative "Me" rather than the nominative "I" (IT 107). I discover myself through the encounter with Christ, who issues a "Commandment to Life" to me, thereby calling me to the true source of Life (IT 183, 185). Christ mediates between me and myself (IT 116). Here Henry might sound close to Bonhoeffer, who also argues that the self-relation is mediated Christologically, but unlike Bonhoeffer[19] Henry locates this mediation within the radical immanence of subjectivity. The self-relation is not mediated by anyone or anything outside of the self.

According to Henry, the life of the self takes place within the Life of Christ. What does Henry mean by this? Developing his definition of life as self-affection, Henry argues that the human self only lives—i.e., affects itself—within the self-affection of absolute, divine Life. God the Father experiences and enjoys himself in absolute self-affection, which occurs through his engendering the Son. Christ is therefore the "First-Living."[20] Our own self-affection is then possible insofar as it takes places within the process of the divine self-affection. Taking a cue from Meister Eckhart, Henry writes that "I myself am this singular Self engendered in the self-engendering of absolute Life, and only that. *Life engenders itself as me*" and likewise "*Life engenders me as itself*" (IT 104–105). As such, we human selves are Sons of God, living within Christ the "Arch-Son." In short, my self-affectivity is "nothing other" than Christ's self-affectivity as the Father's self-affectivity.[21]

Although this description might seem to make human life and divine Life identical, Henry rules out this conclusion by distinguishing between God's "strong" self-affectivity, which produces its own content absolutely, and humanity's "weak" self-affectivity, which does not affect itself absolutely but rather finds itself self-affected. My self-affectivity is not self-engendering such that I engender myself. "I have not brought myself into this condition of experiencing myself. I am myself, but I myself have no part in this 'being myself': I experience myself without being the source of this experience. I am given to myself without this givenness arising from me in any way" (IT 107). Human life is defined by a radical passivity, and the self is given to itself in its self-affectivity—not by any external source in the world, but from a source that is entirely immanent within the self.

The radical passivity of the self is pivotal to Henry's philosophy of action, since it means that the human being is never the absolute origin of its own capabilities and acts. By showing this, Christianity decisively alters the phenomenology of the *I Can*. The *I Can* designates the self who has taken possession of its powers to act, and by exercising these powers lives them as its own. As Henry observes, "[t]here is an incontestable experience that leads the 'I' to say, specifically: *I* take, *I* walk, *I* feel, *I* imagine, *I* want, *I* do not want." The *I can* enacts these possibilities when and how its chooses, yet it is also vital to recognize that the I is not itself the source of these powers, any more than it is the source of its own life. Just as life finds itself self-affected, so the *I Can* finds itself capable of acting. In brief, the I is a passive recipient of the power to act (IT 137).

Nevertheless, the *I Can* tends to forget this primordial passivity and imagine itself to possess this power in a radical way: "the more the ego exercises its power, the more profound the experience it has, in the concreteness of its effort, of effecting this power, the more it attributes this power to itself, and the more it forgets the Life that gave it" (IT 142). This forgetfulness results in what Henry calls "the transcendental illusion of the ego" (IT 140). The ego forgets its true condition as a Son of God and imagines itself to be the absolute source and origin of its own active power. To be sure, this forgetfulness is possible because the true source of this power conceals itself so well; the divine Life is invisible, radically immanent, and never shows itself in the world. The things of the world, on the other hand, are so readily apparent and familiar that the ego forgets its true condition and loses itself in the things of the world. The self does not, however, become preoccupied with worldly things for their own sake, but from an egocentric care for itself. Everything outside the self becomes a means to its own egocentric ends. This is similar to the condition we have described as the incurved self, though for Henry it is a condition of *forgetfulness* rather than a corrupt or perverse will. The ego curves in on itself, making a closed circle or system of its egoism, drawing everything back into the orbit of its own projects. Yet despite its illusions of absoluteness, this ego is in truth merely a "phantom," "a ghostly and unreal Self," because the more the ego curves in on itself, the more it forgets its true essence and condition (IT 141–44). Henry therefore distinguishes this false self-relation from the true self-relation, in which the self relates to itself within the divine Life. The self-relation of incurvature is entirely distinct from the self-relation of Christian life; indeed, the two are mutually exclusive.

What the incurved ego requires, then, is a transcendental rebirth. The ego must be reborn, which for Henry means overcoming this forgetfulness and remembering one's true condition as a Son of God, a living self in absolute Life. This remembering is not, Henry insists, a process in consciousness or an achievement of thinking (IT 153). The new Self is "neither constituted by nor the object of thought"; it is a radically immanent, interior self, yet an interiority without a reflexive inward gaze. The true self-relation is entirely non-intentional, since it relates to itself in a radically passive immediacy by rejoining and uniting with the absolute Life of God (IT 148–151, 160, 165). The self is addressed by the Word of Life, a Word that engenders its hearer and frees her from nothingness to call her into life (IT 226). Salvation consists in this relation to oneself and to God; it is only a matter of coming into one's life in the divine Life—"the unspeakable happiness of experiencing oneself and of Living" (IT 227). This is a relation that cannot be grasped intellectually, but can only be lived.

* * *

Henry's interpretation of Christianity requires careful critique on several points,[22] but given the topic at hand I will focus on his proposal for a Christian philosophy of action. On his account, the reborn Christian self is the true realization of the *I Can*, a capable human being acting in the power it has received passively from the divine Life. Henry seems to echo some key points we have drawn from Bonhoeffer, but there are vital differences that highlight problems in Henry's account.

To begin, both thinkers describe the self as a passive recipient and participant in the divine Life—that is, Christ, who is the ground of human life and selfhood. Moreover, both thinkers emphasize that the roots of action are in some sense inscrutable. For Henry, this means human self-affection within divine self-affection is a non-intentional relation, which is prior to any worldly light and cannot be represented in thought. For Bonhoeffer, the inscrutable is the "pre-ethical (*vorethisch*) flow of life," which cannot be taken up and comprehended within ethical reflection:

> The motives of actions are inscrutable, everything we do is interwoven with something conscious and unconscious, natural and supernatural, with inclination and duty, with the egotistical and the altruistic, the intended and the inevitable, the active and the passive, so that each deed is simultaneously an act of enduring, something done to oneself, just as each deed is simultaneously also a doing. (E 384)

This means that "the roots of human life and action are hidden in darkness," a realization that decisively undermines the ontology of self-justification and the ethical reflection it entails. Ethical reflection cannot dissect "the knotted growth of life," and since activity and passivity are "inextricably intertwined," there is no possibility of determining the true origin and justification of one's actions.

What is vital here is that for Bonhoeffer, the life and action of the self are passively rooted in the divine *as well as* in one's worldly, historical, natural existence. For Henry, on the other hand, the advent of the true self requires "the elimination of the worldly self shown in the world," along with its egocentric care for worldly things, so that the self "experiences itself within the Ipseity of absolute Life and is nothing other than that" (IT 169). The encounter with the divine Life is an entirely acosmic reality, immanent within the self rather than outside in the world. As Henry puts it, "God's revelation as his self-revelation owes nothing to the phenomenality of the world" (IT 25).[23] By contrast, Bonhoeffer rejects such oppositions as Henry's between the world and "life" because Christ has united such opposing terms in the one Christ-reality (*Christuswirklichkeit*), so that "the world, the natural, the profane, and reason are seen as included in God from the beginning." These realities do not exist in and for themselves, but in the reality of God in Christ. Consequently, "[j]ust as the reality of God has entered the reality of the world in Christ, what is Christian cannot be had otherwise than in what is worldly, the 'supernatural' only in the natural, the holy only in the profane, the revelational only in the rational" (E 59). This does not mean that divine revelation is reducible to worldly processes, nor that the world is identical with the divine. In itself, in its own autonomous self-understanding, the world is curved inward and resistant to Christ, but through the incarnation, crucifixion, and resurrection of Christ the world is reconciled to God (E 66–67). One of the tasks of Christianity, then, is to understand the world better than it understands itself, and thus to reveal a genuine worldliness (E 400–401).

The reason Henry will not accept that life is passively received from any natural, worldly reality is that he does not want it to be reducible to naturalistic explanation (which he sums up as "Galilean science"). For this reason, Henry would also not countenance Bonhoeffer's emphasis in *Creation and Fall* that "the human being created in God's image—that is, in freedom—is the human being who is taken from earth." As Bonhoeffer puts it, not even Darwin or Feuerbach could affirm matter more strongly than Genesis does in locating Adam's roots in the dust of the earth. Human life and freedom are rooted in the earth, and this is the source of our essentially embodied being (CF 76). The human being *is* its body—not as a mere physical thing, the Cartesian *res extensa* (*Körper*), but the living flesh (*Leib*) of the capable human being.[24]

This distinction between objective body and subjective flesh is central to Henry's phenomenology of the *I Can*, which he identifies as an embodied, fleshly self. Yet Henry radicalizes this distinction so that this fleshly *I Can* is a transcendental ego absolutely distinct from the empirical person belonging to the world (IT 240). Action is invisible. The I who acts is "an invisible transcendental me" and "if it is its body that acts, it is its living body, its invisible transcendental body. The exterior 'action' is just the representation of this originally subjective and living interior action" (IT 173). This is in keeping with Henry's proposal for a Christian philosophy of action, which depends on the nonworldly character of action. We can agree with Henry's claim that the acts of the *I Can* are not objective, worldly processes that can be studied, reduced, or explained in naturalistic terms, but it is not clear why this requires such a radical denial of the world and the natural sciences. Henry surpasses even Heidegger in his tendency to reduce the natural sciences to crude scient*ism*. But as Drew Leder observes, this radical opposition between phenomenology and natural science actually perpetuates the Cartesian dualisms of *res cogitans* and *res extensa,* subjectivity and objectivity.[25] This methodological dualism also derives from Dilthey's distinction between the explanation (*Erklaren*) of the natural sciences and the understanding (*Verstehen*) of the human sciences, and Henry presents this dualism in a highly concentrated form.[26] But such a dualism fails to recognize the ways in which our subjective, first-person understanding of the lived body is enriched by the objective, third-person insights of scientific anatomy and physiology. As Leder observes, "once relativized within a broader phenomenological reading, scientific references need not be reductionistic; they can open up a rich experiential domain."[27] Ricoeur makes the same point with his maxim "to explain more is to understand better." The natural sciences should not be surrendered to scientism, any more than the world should be surrendered to sin, death, and the devil.

Henry's denial of the world leads toward a variety of the punctual self, which has no extension in concrete, historical existence. In chapter 6 we discussed the punctual self in terms of dialectical theology, and whatever Henry's differences from that position, he too creates a dualistic opposition between the true self and the empirical self. Since the world's truth and Life's truth are so radically opposed, the reality of action involves a radical duality of its visible, exterior, objective appearance in the world and its invisible, interior, subjective movement as life (IT 174–75). Henry goes on to suggest that these are ultimately dual aspects of one reality, but rather than seeing these aspects as reconcilable he suggests that one is in fact "an appearance, an image, a copy of reality, but not that reality itself" (IT 195). Yet if this is true, it threatens the meaning and value of the faithful self in its concrete, historical being in the world, including the worldly consequences of one's actions in relation to others.

Henry's denial of worldly reality is in keeping with his rejection of the theological idea of creation, which he rejects because it implies a world that is exterior to the divine essence. Instead, Henry prefers the idea of *engendering,* by which God gives the human his own essence and enables a radically immanent self-experience that includes "neither 'outside' nor 'world'" (IT 94, 103). Yet one might wonder what this denial of creation means for thinking about the relation and distinction between divine and human agency—something that is much better accounted for by the idea of creation than the idea of engendering. According to Henry, the *I Can* is engendered within the self-affection of divine Life. As he writes, "there is no 'I Can' except in Life" (IT 170). But is there a genuine *I Can* in Henry's philosophy of action? He certainly claims there is, but the question arises with his interpretation of Galatians 2:20, in which Paul describes his condition as having been crucified with Christ, so that it is no longer Paul that lives, but Christ that lives in him. In Henry's rendition, the passage becomes "It is no longer me who acts, it is the Arch-Son who acts in me" (IT 169). There are different ways to interpret this passage, but Henry elaborates on his interpretation by claiming that the action of the *I Can* is "nothing but" the divine acting in me. It is telling that Henry can describe human action or "doing" as belonging to life "to the point—when it has become 'thy will be done, on earth as it is in heaven'—of being nothing but the self-achievement of absolute Life" (IT 171). The words "nothing but" are a problem because they threaten the distinction between divine and human agency and suggest that human action is a passive conduit of divine Life.

The distinction between divine and human agency is also endangered by Henry's idea of *engendering*, which is meant to preclude any life outside of the divine Life. If, however, the world and the human being have been created, and have a creaturely integrity as different from—yet ontologically dependent on—God, then it becomes possible to conceive of genuinely free human action. God's creative act brings about a distinct world and free human beings, suggesting that God is not threatened by creatures that have their own integrity as distinct from himself. On this point Kierkegaard provides a highly instructive discussion, which is worth quoting at some length:

> The greatest good, after all, that can be done for a being, greater than anything else that one can do for it, is to make it free. In order to do just that, omnipotence is required. This seems strange, since it is precisely omnipotence that supposedly would make [a being] dependent. But if one will reflect on omnipotence, one will see that it also must contain the unique qualification of being able to withdraw itself again in a manifestation of omnipotence in such a way that precisely for this reason that which has been originated through omnipotence can be independent. . . . Only omnipotence can withdraw itself at the same time it gives itself away, and this relationship is the very independence of the receiver. God's omnipotence is therefore his goodness. For goodness is to give away completely, but in such a way that by omnipotently taking oneself back one makes the recipient independent. All finite power makes [a being] dependent; only omnipotence can make [a being] independent, can form from nothing something that has its continuity in itself through the continuous withdrawing of omnipotence. . . . It is incomprehensible that omnipotence is able not only to create the most impressive of all things—the whole visible world—but is able to create the most frail of all things—a being independent of that very omnipotence. Omnipotence, which can handle the world so toughly and with such a heavy hand, can also make itself so light that what it has brought into existence receives independence. Only a wretched and worldly conception of the dialectic of power holds that

it is greater and greater in proportion to its ability to compel and to make dependent. No, Socrates had a sounder understanding; he knew that the art of power lies precisely in making another free. But in the relationship between individuals this can never be done, even though it needs to be emphasized again and again that this is the highest; only omnipotence can truly succeed in this. Therefore if a human being had the slightest independent existence over against God (with regard to *materia*), then God could not make him free. Creation out of nothing is once again the Omnipotent One's expression for being able to make [a being] independent. He to whom I owe absolutely everything, although he still absolutely controls everything, has in fact made me independent. If in creating man God himself lost a little of his power, then precisely what he could not do would be to make a human being independent. (JP 1251)

God is able to create out of nothing a being that is at once ontologically dependent and yet has a genuine creaturely integrity, with its own independence and worldly continuity. God is not threatened by human strength, freedom, and action, and can therefore allow the creature to exist outside of himself. Kierkegaard is describing a noncompetitive understanding of divine and human action, such that their relation is not a zero-sum game.[28] God creates beings out of nothing, and to borrow the language of *The Sickness Unto Death*, releases them from his hand (SUD 16), withdrawing himself in an act of love that allows the creature to exist in its own creaturely integrity.

It might seem that Henry also has a notion of God withdrawing and holding himself back, insofar as he describes God as so radically immanent and interior to be invisible in the world, but that is not the withdrawing that Kierkegaard is describing. Henry's position does not allow for the same noncompetitive relation between divine and human agency, since he refuses the idea of creation and with it the idea of a creature who is distinct from God, with its own integrity and agency in the world. For Henry human life and action are engendered within the spiraling movement of divine self-affection, but this concept of engendering simply does not provide the same degree of ontological differentiation and creaturely integrity that is possible in the concept of creation.

One of the advantages of this concept of a spiraling self-affection, on Henry's account, is that it provides the human self with the power to love others. Consider Henry's description of the Christian commandment to love:

> Only because it is joined to itself in life's *pathētik* embrace, edified in the love in which Life eternally loves itself, embracing itself and loving itself within this love, having become an ego in it and taking its power from it—for this sole and unique reason is the ego, constituted by this Commandment of love and drawing its condition of Son from it, able eventually to obey it. (IT 187)

Henry maintains that the self is only able to perform works of love because of its prior, passive reception of divine love. The key passage here is 1 John 4:19—"we love because he first loved us."

This passage from John also inspires Kierkegaard's reflections on love. *Agape*, the self-sacrificing love for the neighbor, is not a result of pure human spontaneity but a gift received passively. As Kierkegaard writes in *Works of Love*, human love is like a quiet lake, whose source is a gushing spring hidden at its bottom. God's love is the mysterious origin and ground of human love.[29] Similarly, Bonhoeffer argues that human love is never autonomous and independent of God's love, since it requires the passive reception of God's love. "Love means to undergo [*Erleiden*] the transformation of one's entire existence by God; it means being drawn into the world in the only way in which the world is able to live before God and in God alone" (E 336). By participating in God's love we are able to love others. Henry, Kierkegaard, and Bonhoeffer agree on this point. But what Bonhoeffer in particular emphasizes is that Christian love is a thoroughly *worldly* affair. Love is not a purely interior, immanent phenomenality, but shows up in the exterior phenomenality of the world.

This does not mean that Christian love will accord with the world's prevailing opinions of love. The radical difference between worldly and divine conceptions of love is particularly pointed in the event of the cross. But the cross is a problem for Henry.[30] As Kevin Hart observes, Henry's philosophy does not allow for deep reflection on the Passion; his notion of the divine life has no telos, so his Christology makes no mention of the plan of salvation in the divine economy nor of the soteriological significance of the Passion.[31] This is an excellent point, as the cross plays no significant role in Henry's thoughts—an omission that is at once surprising insofar as Henry purports to give a phenomenology of Christianity, yet unsurprising given his conception of sin and salvation. If sin is forgetfulness of one's true condition as a Son of God, and salvation is the overcoming of this forgetfulness, it is not clear what role the cross might have in Henry's system. It is telling that Henry's paraphrase of Galatians 2:20 ("It is no longer me who acts, it is the Arch-Son who acts in me") omits the clause about having been crucified with Christ.[32] It is also striking, given his affinity for the Gospel and epistles of John, that Henry does not engage John's claim that God loved the world and sent his Son to save it (John 3:16). Henry leaves us with remarkable ambiguity regarding the question of God's love for the world—not to mention the question of whether the world[33] came into being out of divine love, and ultimately the question of what the point of the world might be.[34]

Of course, such a question implies intentionality, and Henry describes the self-affection of life as entirely non-intentional. As Hart points out, this is another reason why Henry's philosophy does not allow for deep reflection on the cross as the revelation of divine love: without an account of intentionality, and the counter-intentionality of the divine gaze, it is impossible to give a satisfactory account of love.[35] The divine love expressed in the intra-Trinitarian drama of the crucifixion and resurrection—as well as the eschatological hope these events promise—becomes unintelligible if the economy of divine life is an entirely immanent, non-intentional self-affection. We will return to the question of intentionality in chapter 9, as well as in the third section of the present chapter, where we will examine the dynamic relation of call and response in the life of faith.

In sum, whatever insights might be gleaned from Henry's phenomenology of Christianity, it does not offer much for our understanding of the cruciform self and its capacity for action in the world. Granted, there is a prima facie affinity between Henry's critique of worldly phenomenality and the Pauline-Lutheran claims regarding the divine hiddenness and the worldly folly of the gospel, but Henry does not engage the *skandalon* of the cross. This is evident not only in his neglect of the cross as an explicit theme, but also in his diluted interpretations of sin and salvation. Henry's phenomenology of the self is a *philosophia gloriae* rather than a *philosophia crucis*—and yet it also manages to be a form of radicalism, characterized as it is by its denial of the world. As we have seen, this denial of the created world is a problem for any Christian philosophy of action worthy of the name.

The Call and Response of Faith

At this point I would like to consider the theme of human capability as it pertains to the call and response of faith—a theme that has received considerable attention in recent phenomenologies of religion (including Henry's). The call is individuating, constitutive of the self, and in being called the self is summoned, invited, or perhaps compelled to give some sort of response. The call-and-response structure takes a variety of forms in the life of faith, such as the call to worship, the call to confession and repentance, the call to a vocation, and the prophetic call, which we read about in the calling of Samuel or Isaiah, who responds with the phenomenologically striking "here am I!"[36] Ricoeur suggests that the call and response is perhaps the closest that phenomenology of religion can come to a universal structure of religious phenomenality. But like language, which is only realized in particular languages, we cannot locate a universal religious phenomenon in naked immediacy. Since religion is always mediated linguistically, culturally, historically, and textually, the phenomenology of religion must therefore "run the gauntlet" of a specifically textual or scriptural hermeneutics.[37] In this section I offer some hermeneutical observations regarding the call and response of faith. Given our theme of the cruciform self, the most pertinent figure for our interpretation is the call of Christ: *take up your cross and follow after me.*[38] The notion of *taking up* one's cross suggests a positing of the self, the taking of a position; the self is called to gather itself up beneath the cross and follow after Christ. Since this response suggests some sort of activity or spontaneity, we need to look more closely at the status of capability in responding to this call.

The word of the cross is an indicative insofar as it proclaims the finished work of Christ, which is an unconditional gift. But this indicative also entails a call, an invitation, even an imperative: take up your cross and follow after me. This call is an election. The self is passive prior to any active response, and yet this election nevertheless calls for an active response from the self. However, the suggestion of such a requirement quickly raises suspicions of Pelagianism or synergistic co-operation, as though the self contributes to its own justification. Any demand on human activity or agency would seem to put a condition on the unconditional word, thereby reinstating the ontology of self-justification. How then could we affirm the necessity of an obedient response?

Bonhoeffer addresses these concerns with a textual interpretation, drawing on the Gospel accounts of the calling of the disciples. The call initiates a situation in which the possibility of faith enters the horizon of the self. Here Bonhoeffer echoes Kierkegaard, who insists on the need for a "decisive act" whereby the self ventures forth into the setting or situation (*Bestedelse*) in which faith is possible.[39] But while Kierkegaard's emphasis falls on the need for decisive action, Bonhoeffer brings into sharper focus the significance of the call in creating this new situation. This call does not simply proclaim a doctrine. It "creates existence anew" (D 62). This word reconstitutes the world for the disciples, who are called to "step out" out of their former existence, to *ex-ist* in the ecstatic sense of the term (D 58). For this reason, the call itself is a gift of grace (D 66). It is radically other, sounding from beyond the self and creating an entirely new situation.

Bonhoeffer develops this point with reference to the calling of Peter.[40] There is no suggestion of Peter calling himself. The call is novel, disruptive. Yet the call also requires a response, and there is one thing Peter can (and must) do: he can leave his nets (D 64). Likewise, when Christ calls Peter to come to him on the water,[41] Peter needs to step out of the boat. Granted, this "first step of obedience is itself an act of faith in Christ's word. But it would completely misrepresent the essence of faith to conclude that the step is no longer necessary, because in that step there had already been faith" (D 66). Note the worldly appearance of Peter's faith, which is manifest in the world as this first step: while this external movement is not sufficient in itself, it is nevertheless necessary. There is therefore a unity (but not an identity) of faith and obedience in this first step.[42] The call creates the situation in which faith becomes possible, but only by responding with the first step can the self enter "the situation of being able to believe." The self is called out of its old situation "into a situation in which faith can begin" (D 62). This first step is necessary in order to avoid cheap grace and "pious self-deception." Without it, the call "dissipates into nothing" (D 63).

From a phenomenological perspective the figure of the first step is interesting for several reasons. First, the text does not offer a psychological explanation of the response, but instead witnesses and testifies to the disruptive nature of the call. Walking by the Sea of Galilee, Jesus sees Peter and Andrew fishing and says to them, "Follow me, and I will make you fishers of men." Their response is as abrupt as the call: "Immediately they left their nets and followed Him" (Mark 1:16–18). Behind the text we might be inclined to postulate a horizon of anticipation that prepared the way for this call: the prophetic tradition, messianic expectation, the teaching of John the Baptist, the cultural practice of following a rabbi, etc. Or perhaps this call was the culmination of prior instruction. But in seeking the continuity of explanation, we obscure the text and its witness to the fundamental *dis*continuity of this call. According to Bonhoeffer, reason wants to mediate this event, to account for it historically or psychologically, and yet the text does not engage in explanation (D 57). The lack of an interval between call and response testifies to the decisive fracture[43] that the call initiates. In a certain sense this call is irresistible (D 60). The self needs to take a first step, but this free response is not the arbitrary fiat of a naked will faced with two equally compelling alternatives: *Should I stay or should I go?* The call creates a new situation; it is arresting; it is an election that penetrates to the heart of the self. The self is *summoned,* and this summons does not leave the self in a state of disengaged deliberation.

Second, on this point Bonhoeffer might seem to agree with Henry's phenomenology of the call, according to which the call does not leave the self with the "license to respond or not. To be able to respond to the call, to hear it in an appropriate listening, but equally to turn away from it—it is always too late for all that" (IT 227). Henry distinguishes the call of Life from every worldly call, in which call and response are distinct from each other. In the call of Life there is no difference between call and response, Word and Hearing. This identity of call and response follows from the fact that my Hearing is in fact my condition as a Son, which is already immanent within me prior to my activity. Thus while Bonhoeffer describes a transcendent, disruptive call that initiates an *ek-static* existence, such that the self has its life outside itself, Henry describes a call that initiates from within one's own true condition and initiates an entirely *in-ecstatic* existence, such that one's life takes place entirely within the immanence of divine Life (IT 159, 195).

This is a significant disagreement, but the point we need to focus on here is Henry's claim that "this hearing has no freedom at all with respect to what it hears" (IT 227). There is some phenomenological warrant for the claim that the call is prior to one's own spontaneity. Levinas has done much to illuminate this point. Yet is there not also an aspect of our experience in which I hear the call summoning me to *respond,* such that this call throws me into crisis as I see the gap between my hearing and my response? Henry would concede that this experience can characterize worldly calls, but not the call of Life. Yet here again such a duality makes it very difficult to understand the lived experience of faith. Bonhoeffer's description is more illuminating, since it recognizes the concrete, worldly response to the call as a penultimate act. The first step is a free act of the *I can*. This is not a causal explanation, but a description of the worldly experience of being addressed by the call. The self is disclosed to itself as capable of taking this first step. Peter can stand up and leave his nets; he can step out of the boat onto the water. In Ricoeur's terms, the self is capable of acting and causing something to happen in the world. Bonhoeffer cites another example: I can leave my house, walk to church, and hear the word proclaimed. I am capable of doing this and culpable insofar as I do not, since I would thereby willfully exclude myself "from the place where faith is possible" (D 64–65). In *Ethics* Bonhoeffer describes these first steps as penultimate actions, as the last act of preparing the way for the word. The hearing of the word also presupposes a self endowed with such penultimate capacities as "the external possibility, the physical ability, and enough inner concentration and ability to think" (E 166). When penultimate capacities such as these are threatened, the hearing of the word is impaired. In this penultimate horizon we can also recognize the truth of Heidegger's analysis of *hearing* as a possible openness to Being,[44] as well as Gadamer's theme of *linguisticality* as a capacity for understanding. Contra Henry, these penultimate capacities do not need to be radically distinguished from the hearing of the ultimate Word, since they are the horizon within which the Word is extended in the concrete, historical existence of the self.

These observations about *hearing* might bring the reader to notice that the penultimate plays a role akin to the transcendental (or fundamental-ontological), insofar as it involves certain conditions of possibility. There are, however, crucial differences between the penultimate and the transcendental as it has often been understood. There are good reasons to be wary of designating the penultimate as a transcendental capacity or openness for the ultimate. First, the project of deducing transcendental conditions for a possible revelation is not unaffected by the incurvature of the thinking I, which has a vested interested in protecting itself against any revelation it perceives as a threat. This problem is evident when we consider how Kant's and Fichte's philosophies of religion treat the claims of Christian revelation: by appealing to the transcendental or fundamental-ontological, the incurved self retains its authority to reject any word that threatens its autonomy.

Of course, transcendental thinking need not proceed in a rationalistic way. Karl Rahner, for example, rejects the attempt to determine the content of a possible revelation "from below" (according to the standard of human spirit—whether reason, religious disposition, or experience),[45] but he nevertheless attempts to deduce the a priori conditions for a possible revelation. Rahner identifies a fundamental human openness that he describes as an "obediential potency for revelation,"[46] arguing that the human spirit has an absolute, unlimited openness for being, and along with this openness the human spirit is, by its "innermost being, always already referring to the absolute being of God" (140). In short, Being is always already implicitly oriented toward God. But this brings us to another problem facing a transcendental philosophy of religion: namely, the ambiguity of human being-in-the-world. In his book *Experience and the Absolute,* Jean-Yves Lacoste argues that it is not possible to locate and identify a natural openness for revelation, as Rahner maintains. Rather than an implicit, prethematic orientation toward God, Lacoste finds a "transcendental ignorance of God," such that what is most proper to human being is hidden from it.[47] Following Husserl and Heidegger, Lacoste argues that phenomenological analysis discloses our everyday being-in-the-world as atheistic. There may be aspects of human experience that seem oriented toward some sort of divine transcendence—the wonder inspired by nature, the sense of futility described in Ecclesiastes, the restless heart narrated by Augustine's *Confessions*—but these experiences are ambiguous as well and need not point to our true relation to God. As Lacoste observes, "the immanent sacred of the earth can also deceive *restlessness* and offer to make up the deficit."[48] Without the proclamation of the ultimate word, the most we can discern in our experience of Being are manifestations of this immanent sacred, which gives rise to paganism. In this regard we must acknowledge a certain merit to Heidegger's insistence on the methodological atheism of philosophy.[49]

It may be that experiences of wonder in nature, a desire for the infinite, or existential restlessness reflect the fact that human beings are created to know the true God, but these experiences only receive their true hermeneutical inflection after the ultimate word has been disclosed. The experience of manifestation must be refigured by proclamation.[50] Or as Lacoste puts it, "God must be named beforehand for the heavens to sing his glory."[51] Likewise, the penultimate is only able to recognize itself as next-to-last in relation to the ultimate. This is why we need to be careful not to hastily identify the penultimate with the transcendental. The transcendental purports to deduce the conditions of revelation as a *possibility*, yet on its own it cannot truly assume the posture of the penultimate. The transcendental cannot recognize itself as next-to-last unless the ultimate is disclosed in *actuality*.[52] Genuine openness is only possible a posteriori, when the transcendental subject is open*ed* and its autonomy has been relativized by the self-disclosure of the ultimate.

Although the call discloses me to myself as capable, my self-attestation as an *I can* is not the focal point of my awareness. In taking the first step the self attends to Christ, rather than reflectively trying to determine the adequacy of its response. Thus Bonhoeffer describes the intentionality of faith as an *actus directus* rather than an *actus reflexus*.

We will discuss the question of reflection and the intentionality of faith in chapter 9, but for now I want to address a potential problem in Bonhoeffer's distinction between these two acts. If we take this sharp opposition between the *actus directus* and the *actus reflexus* as the two fundamental modes of intentionality,[53] it would seem that either I intend the other directly with no self-awareness, or I intend myself reflexively. But this does not do justice to the complexity of intentionality, specifically the interrelation between what Michael Polanyi calls subsidiary and focal awareness.[54] Bonhoeffer's model must therefore be enriched with some phenomenological observations regarding intentionality.

First of all, intentionality is not merely intellectual or perceptual. As Merleau-Ponty has shown, the *I think* is an abstraction from the embodied *I Can*, which means that intentionality is most primordially a matter of my motility as a lived body (*Leib*); intentionality begins in my embodied agency, which involves a vast array of structures and capacities that make possible my comportment in the world and with others. But as Drew Leder writes, these structures and capacities *disappear* from our explicit thematic awareness. Indeed, it is only by disappearing into the background that these capacities enable me to engage in the world. Thus Leder observes:

> I have a tacit command over my body, accomplishing without the slightest difficulty actions I could not begin to comprehend or carry out in a reflective fashion. If I attempted to walk by consciously manipulating all the proper muscles I would soon find myself incapacitated.[55]

The genius of the lived body is precisely its ability to disappear from focal awareness. In hearing the call, I do not focus on my capacity to hear or to concentrate, and in taking the first step I do not reflect on my capacity to walk. Such reflexive awareness would be distracting, even crippling. Intentionality is therefore always a matter of attending ek-statically *from* a subsidiary background of capability *to* a focal point. But at the same time, I remain tacitly aware of this subsidiary dimension, and this tacit self-awareness and sense of capability allows me to respond and engage when I am addressed by various calls and cues in the world.

In my everyday engagement in the world and in my comportment toward the other, I tacitly understand myself as capable, and in stepping forward I tacitly attest to myself as capable. But for the sake of my projects this self-attestation remains a subsidiary rather than focal mode of awareness; capability requires this disappearance, because otherwise I would be unable to proceed. This is also true of the first step of faith. In taking the first step, the self attends to Christ from a subsidiary background of capability. The first step is a self-effacing act. The urgency of the call takes the self out of itself. The self is ek-static, standing outside of itself; it is ab-sent, being away from itself.[56] The self and its capabilities disappear from focal awareness so that the self can focus on Christ.

For Bonhoeffer, the intentionality of faith is closely related to the question of justification. He insists that faith is an *actus directus* that only sees Christ (D 66), with no attempt to ground one's justification through a self-reflexive act. In the first step of response, the self attends directly to the call and does not reflect on its own act. The self does not attempt to thematize its relative capability or incapability, the purity of its motives, or any other question of merit. The text in Matthew 14 illustrates this point vividly: in responding to the call, Peter steps out onto the water and begins to walk toward Christ; yet when Peter sees the wind and becomes self-aware in the danger of his situation, he starts to sink. Similarly, when reflection tries to thematize one's own capabilities or determine the nature and extent of one's own contribution, the self falls back into the ontology of self-justification. But in taking the first step in faith, the self does not turn back on itself reflexively in order to locate its act and determine its worth. The first step is self-effacing insofar as it does not posit itself as a meritorious act. In itself, the first step is nothing: "as an external deed [it] is and remains a dead work of the law, which can by itself never lead to Christ. As an external deed, the new existence just remains the old existence. At best, a new law of life, a new lifestyle, is reached, which has nothing to do with the new life in Christ."[57] As long as the first step attempts to establish its own position before God, it is not faith. The first step has its telos outside of itself; it is not self-justifying, but is instead justified by faith. Consequently, the free response of the self—the first step—is not a *syn-ergon,* a co-working or co-operation in which the self contributes to its own justification (D 64–65).[58] The first step is never the ultimate in itself, but it is always a penultimate act performed by a capable human being.

8   The Call to Responsibility

As a result of the preceding chapter, we can see how the category of the penultimate allows us to affirm human capability yet also discern the limits of human capability and avoid a synergistic confusion of divine and human agency. The ultimate word is pronounced from beyond the self and its immanent possibilities and capacities, but within the horizon of the penultimate the self is *homo capax*. We can therefore identify the capacities that Ricoeur discusses in his phenomenology of *l'homme capable*—speaking, acting, narrating, and assuming responsibility—as penultimate capacities. If time permitted it would be worthwhile to examine how Ricoeur's investigations of these themes are manifest in the life of the faithful self. I will limit our analysis, however, to one aspect of Ricoeur's ontology of the self, namely conscience, arguing that conscience should be interpreted as a penultimate capacity, both with regard to the call of faith as well as the call to ethical responsibility. In particular I focus on two of Ricoeur's arguments regarding conscience: first, that it is an ontological presupposition of ethical responsibility; second, that it is the anthropological presupposition of justification by faith.

Ricoeur's Phenomenology of Conscience

In *Oneself as Another*, Ricoeur develops a phenomenology of conscience that situates him between Heidegger and Levinas. The influence of Heidegger is evident in two aspects of Ricoeur's description: First, conscience is a voice in which the self addresses itself, and this reflexive structure is integral to the self and its care for itself. Second, in conscience testimony has priority over accusation. That is, in the call of conscience the self attests, or bears witness, to its ownmost power to be, and this self-attestation is prior to the judgments of the good or bad conscience.[1] Both of these features have a distinctly Heideggerian echo. According to Heidegger, ontology is more fundamental than ethics, and thus the ontological call of conscience—in which Dasein calls itself to authentic being—is prior to the call of the other. Authenticity precedes ethical responsibility and makes it possible.

Here Ricoeur's appropriation of Heidegger is altered by the critical perspective of Levinas, who shows the inadequacy of a strictly ontological (and ethically neutral) interpretation of conscience (OA 355). Levinas counters Heidegger (and Husserl) by arguing that responsibility is initiated asymmetrically by the absolute exteriority of the other. In order to keep responsibility uncompromised by ontology, Levinas leans toward an ethical radicalism that is structurally similar to theological radicalism: the election to responsibility is a *creatio ex nihilo*—an apocalyptic, punctual event[2] that is entirely otherwise than being. The election to responsibility is otherwise than the *conatus essendi* and the inter-*est*-edness of being, beyond every horizon, capability, or intention that might prepare the way for the coming of the other (OB 86). I am elected by a prevenient call, making my responsibility prior to any voluntary decision to assume it. This call is "absolutely heteronomous" (OB 53); it does not activate any autonomous capacity for mediation or receptivity, nor does it appeal to an existing ethical potentiality, desire, need, or natural tendency. My response comes from a hyperbolic passivity—a passivity more passive than all receptivity—that is prior to every potentiality and act.[3] There is no prior will to responsibility (OB 51), no voluntary decision to assume it (OB 54); it is not an act of spontaneity (OB 56) or capability (OB 89, 118). Faced by the other, I respond "despite myself" (OB 53).

Ricoeur agrees with Levinas that the ego (*moi*) only becomes a self (*soi*) through the address of the other, but he has reservations about the severity of Levinas's description. Ricoeur objects that the call cannot be completely externalized, because if the other were as radically other as Levinas suggests, the self would be unable to hear and respond to this call (OA 354–55). The call is indeed necessary to break the ego from its incurvature, but the self must possess some capacity for openness and discovery, along with a capacity for reception, discrimination, and recognition (OA 339). Thus Ricoeur asks: "Would the self be a result if it were not first a presupposition, that is, potentially capable of hearing this assignment?" He recognizes that the appeal to potentiality and capability is precisely what Levinas tries to avoid: "The slightest admission of a capacity that is one's own, correlative to this assignment, would ruin everything gained from a philosophy of passivity relentlessly carried through." Yet Ricoeur insists that we need a hermeneutics in which the attestation of the self and the glory of the absolute are "co-originary."[4]

In Ricoeur's view, ethical responsibility requires a self who is at least minimally capable of hearing and responding to the call of the other. This capacity is conscience, which enables the self to recognize the voice of the other, to take it up and make the call its own in the form of a conviction (OA 339). If there is no point of contact in the self, the call of the other will simply not register or initiate a response. To paraphrase Luther once again, the call to responsibility does not address geese. It addresses human beings who have a proper range of capability.

Ricoeur therefore maintains that conscience is the ontological presupposition of ethical responsibility. This does not mean that the self is there already equipped and waiting to showcase its capability by responding to the needs of others. The self is capable only insofar as it has already been formed through its encounters with others. Thus the formation of habits, dispositions, and practical wisdom provides a horizon within which the call of the other is voiced. This call might catch me off guard, it might be deeply troubling and inconvenient, and I might find myself at a loss, ill-equipped to respond adequately. In this regard the Aristotelian *phronimos* and the great-souled, magnanimous man must lower the flag of triumph.[5] In defending human capability, Ricoeur's description of responsible action is also marked by vulnerability, suffering, and tragedy.[6] This is not an anthropology of glory, and *l'homme capable* is not the exalted cogito. The capable self is wounded, fragile—and yet capable of such basic human activities as speaking, acting, remembering and narrating, assuming responsibility for itself and others, making promises and remaining true to its word.

In Bonhoeffer's terms, it is precisely because capability is so fragile that we must defend it as a penultimate good—not merely for ourselves, but first and foremost for those who suffer from incapability, and who therefore need our help to develop their capabilities. Being-there for others also means caring for others in this way, helping to restore the capacity for self-esteem and self-attestation, so that they too can become capable of living well with and for others. Self-esteem and self-attestation are not celebrations of the power-to-be or the will-to-power. We would do well to recall the closing lines of Georges Bernanos's *Diary of a Country Priest*, which Ricoeur cites in *Oneself as Another*:[7] "It is easier than one thinks to hate oneself. Grace means forgetting oneself. But if all pride were dead in us, the grace of graces would be to love oneself humbly, as one would any of the suffering members of Jesus Christ."[8] This proper self-love, or in Ricoeur's terms self-esteem and self-attestation, is a grace that allows the self to forget about itself. After all, what locks the self into self-consciousness more fixedly than an unremitting sense of incapability?

Ricoeur thereby situates himself between Heidegger and Levinas, advocating an ontology of the self that includes attestation and care of self as well as openness and receptivity to the call of others. The call of conscience is ontological *and* ethical, since it discloses the ontology of the self in terms of "being enjoined to *live well with and for others in just institutions and to esteem oneself as the bearer of this wish*" (OA 352, 354). Unlike the Levinasian description of the ego as fundamentally egocentric, Ricoeur describes the self as "defined by its openness and its capacity for discovery." Consequently, on the ethical level Ricoeur opposes the description of human being as strictly egocentric and allergic to alterity. This is not simply optimism or wishful thinking, but follows from a hermeneutical wager regarding the original goodness of creation—that it has not been entirely effaced by sin[9] and that fault has not completely obliterated the capacity to be free for others in responsibility, justice, and love.

Bonhoeffer on the Structure of Responsible Life

How does Ricoeur's description fit with Bonhoeffer's description of responsibility and the penultimate? It is fruitful to bring Bonhoeffer into this debate because he engages many of the same questions regarding the self-other relation. There is much to say about Bonhoeffer's approach to this topic, but I will focus on two of the relative merits of his view, which describes ethical responsibility as structured by two basic determinations: (1) I am primordially bound to others (both God and the neighbor), and (2) responsibility occurs in the freedom of my life as a human being.

(1) The self is responsible because it is already bound to the other person. According to Bonhoeffer, responsibility consists in vicarious representation (*Stellvertretung*), acting on behalf of others and standing in their place—working, intervening, struggling, and suffering for them (E 257–58). On this point there are parallels with the Levinasian theme of substitution, but whereas Levinas develops this phenomenologically, Bonhoeffer develops it Christologically. As we saw in chapter 5, Christ stands there for me, where I should stand but cannot. On this basis Bonhoeffer defines *Stellvertretung* as a basic anthropological and ethical concept and as a basic structure of faithful existence. In his prison letters, Bonhoeffer describes faith as participation in the being of Christ, and being-in-Christ means being-there-for others (*Für-andere-Dasein*). This being-for-others then provides the hermeneutical starting point for thinking about transcendence, as well as such classical divine attributes as omnipotence, omniscience, and omnipresence. "Faith," Bonhoeffer writes, "is participation in this being of Jesus (incarnation, cross, and resurrection). Our relation to God is not a 'religious' relationship to the highest, most powerful, and best Being imaginable—that is not authentic transcendence—but our relation to God is a new life in 'existence for others', through participation in the being of Jesus." Transcendence is therefore "not the infinite, unattainable tasks, but the neighbor within reach in any given situation" (LPP 501).

Given the Levinasian interpretation of responsibility as *infinite*, it is striking to read Bonhoeffer's description of transcendence in terms of a responsibility for the neighbor—but a responsibility that is *not* infinite. According to Levinas, it is precisely the concrete neighbor who presents one with an infinite and unattainable task, yet Bonhoeffer suggests that there are limits to one's responsibility for others. First, he warns that responsible life is corrupted if we absolutize either the self or the other (E 259). The self must not be absolutized, because responsibility requires the self to surrender its autonomy and devote itself to the other selflessly,[10] but neither should the other be absolutized. On this point Bonhoeffer's thinking reflects a shift from his earliest work, where he gives a one-sided description of responsibility as a complete submission to the other, and as loving the other *instead of* (not *as*) oneself (SC 170–71). In *Ethics* he qualifies this asymmetry by arguing that selflessness "must never be confused with destroying and annihilating the self, which would then also no longer be able to take on responsibility" (E 281). The self-denial of responsibility also involves a proper form of self-assertion—albeit a "selfless self-assertion" that consists in surrendering oneself to God and other human beings (E 254). The being of faith is not an incurved being-for-oneself, but a being-for-others.

Bonhoeffer also shares Ricoeur's conviction that ethical responsibility presupposes some basic and proper degree of capability—including the capacity of conscience as a call to unity with oneself and a limit of responsibility. Unlike Levinas, then, Bonhoeffer does not describe responsibility in terms of trauma, persecution, obsession, and the hemorrhaging of the self. According to Levinas, these vivid terms describe a certain "good" violence, but the perplexing question is whether this traumatic alterity redeems its violence by virtue of "being Good"[11] (just as we cannot assume that every interpretation of the cross as *destructio* is redemptive). Granted, the incurred self is always quick to find an excuse to protect its own rights and interests, and all manner of egoism tries to justify itself in the name of a legitimate self-esteem. But we need to ask whether the rhetoric of destruction and violence might celebrate something more akin to *ir*responsibility.

It is therefore not an inadmissible consideration to ask whether responsibility *requires* a proper understanding of limits. Bonhoeffer argues that responsibility is not infinite but is instead limited by the fact that we are creatures (E 267). We are not God, and we are not Christ, so our responsibility is not the ultimate source of redemption and reconciliation in the world. We are called, even bound to responsibility for others, but the other is not a black hole of infinite responsibility; instead, responsibility is mediated by faith, in which the self surrenders its responsible action to God's grace and judgment (E 268). Of course, the notion of responsibility as limited by justifying faith could easily be a self-justifying excuse to ignore one's responsibility, so we will return to this problem at the end of this chapter. For now, however, I will outline some other ways in which Bonhoeffer demarcates the limits of responsibility.

My responsibility is limited by the fact that the other is responsible as well (E 269). Against this Levinas will object that I am responsible for the other regardless of his response to me. The other's response is not my concern: I cannot wait for the intimacy of Buber's I-Thou relation or Hegelian mutual recognition in order to assume responsibility for the other. Nevertheless, Bonhoeffer argues that the recognition of others as *also* responsible is necessary to prevent the self from violating others—whether in the name of its own agenda of responsibility or by stunting the development of their own responsibility. In many of its roles (such as parent, teacher, or friend), the self has the responsibility to help others recognize and take up their own responsibilities. Thus Bonhoeffer interprets responsibility in terms of mutuality and recognition in a way that Levinas does not.

Further, Bonhoeffer argues that responsibility does not mean absolutizing the demand of the other, because responsible life involves a multiplicity of demands (E 259). The Levinasian answer to these objections is that one's infinite responsibility for the second person is corrected by the entrance of a third person. The absolute, asymmetrical demand of the other is mediated by the third; I must measure and compare competing demands. This conflict of responsibility situates me in a society and opens me to the order of justice, law, and other reflective institutions. Thus as a responsible self I am granted a certain "grace" insofar as others approach me as their responsibility: "'Thanks to God' I am another for the others" (OB 158–59). In this way Levinas acknowledges the mediation that characterizes human existence in the world while insisting that this mediation is *posterior* to the immediacy of the other's face. The mediating concern for justice does not, however, permit the closure of the good conscience, or the promise of an ultimate justification. Instead, Levinas advocates a religiosity without such promise.

(2) As we have seen, Ricoeur argues that the responsible self would not be possible if it were not in some way already an ontological presupposition—i.e., if the ontology of the self did not already consist in being enjoined to live well with and for others in just institutions, and to esteem oneself as the bearer of this wish. In conscience the self attests to this orientation to the good life, and this ethical aim mediates the injunction to act responsibly for others. On this point Bonhoeffer's description of responsibility is closer to Ricoeur than to Levinas. For one thing, Bonhoeffer does not share the Levinasian allergy to ontology; being-human and being-good are basic ontological characteristics of life in the penultimate, and they form the horizon within which the call of the other appears. This brings us to our second point regarding the structure of responsibility.

For Bonhoeffer, the call to responsibility is not a *creatio ex nihilo*. What is true of the ultimate is not necessarily true of the penultimate. Granted, the call of the other is a disruptive event, and it rarely sounds when we are expecting it or when we feel ready to assume responsibility. But such disturbances arrive in the horizon of life. It is no accident that Bonhoeffer writes about the structures of responsible *life* instead of punctual events of responsibility. As we noted in chapters 4 and 6, God has not abandoned the world to its own devices, but has preserved it for the sake of Christ. Central to this preservation is the theological concept that human beings have received divine mandates or commissions, which include the church, marriage and family life, work and culture, and government (E 388–89). Ethically responsible life is played out in the context of these concrete tasks, forms of life, and institutions; these mandates give concrete structure to the call to responsibility.

Responsible life also requires that we "learn to live with others," and this life together includes not only the imperative of the ought, but also the plurality and richness of life's many impulses and motivations. Life is polyphonous and should not be reduced to one note or key. But when the ethical is interpreted as an event of absolute rupture, we cannot account for the continuity of life. Such an ethics can only consist in making life questionable to itself; it cannot approve anything penultimate, anything "pre-ethical" (*vorethisch*), just as it can only interpret the freedom of justifying faith as cheap grace. But faith liberates the self to live a genuinely human, worldly life—to "eat, drink, sleep, work, celebrate, and play" with vigor, without constantly interrupting and confronting oneself with questions over whether this freedom is permitted or whether there are at every moment more urgent demands (E 384–85). We must give up the "humorless hostility against the art of living [*Lebenskunst*]" (E 370). This does not mean embracing a hedonistic or self-absorbed lifestyle, but rather learning to find and love God in the good that he gives us. Everything has its season: there are times of responsibility and times of rest, and we should not try to be "more pious than God" by second-guessing the times of happiness and joy (LPP 168). The teleological aim of living a good life and flourishing as a human being is a genuine penultimate good, and the horizon within which the call of the other appears.

Responsibility is therefore not a punctual moment of sheer discontinuity. It is not the radical decision of the anguished, heroic individual, as in existentialism, nor is it a strictly formal and universal judgment, as in deontological ethics; both of these models detach the ethical from its concrete determination. This is much the same reason why Ricoeur situates a Kantian deontology within the context of an Aristotelian account of virtue.[12] Bonhoeffer agrees with Ricoeur: the injunction appears within the aim of a good life, with and for others, in just institutions. Responsibility is not "a principle that levels, invalidates, and shatters all human order. Instead, it inherently involves a certain order of human community and entails certain sociological relationships of authority. Only in their context does the ethical manifest itself and receive the concrete authorization that is essential to it." Responsible life also requires the formation of selves. Genuine ethical discourse cannot subsist on the punctual moment, but requires "repetition and continuity; it demands time.... The authorization of ethical discourse proves itself in loyalty, trustworthiness, duration, and repetition" (E 373–75). The responsible self needs to be formed in virtues like loyalty, trust, and reliability, and to develop the capacity for memory. As Bonhoeffer observes, the course of Luther's life was forever altered by a flash of lightning; such was the power of this memory. But in modern society the power of memory has gone into decline, and with it the capacity for love, marriage, friendship, loyalty, as well as the accomplishments of truth, justice, and beauty—all of which require memory and continuity through time (LPP 284).

Like memory, conscience is also a penultimate good. Its mediating power makes responsible life possible, since it has a proper competence in judging relative degrees of being good (*Gutsein*). Conscience is an essential feature of any basic moral ontology, as a capacity for strong evaluation and a compass for locating oneself within the topography of the Good. Through this formation, the way is prepared for the coming of the neighbor. Conscience is also significant for being human (*Menschsein*). At one level Bonhoeffer agrees with Ricoeur that conscience is ontological, and that it runs deeper than specific moral prohibitions. In strictly formal terms, conscience is a call to unity. The self calls itself to unity with itself, and this unity is ontologically vital. To disregard the call of conscience is a destructive, even suicidal act that disintegrates one's existence as a human being. Considered in this strictly formal sense, it is never advisable to defy the authority of one's conscience (E 276–77).

However, things become complicated when we consider the *content* of this formal call to unity. Here Bonhoeffer's description of conscience adds a critical perspective that we need to consider. As we saw in chapter 4, the incurved self uses conscience in an attempt to be like God (*sicut deus*), determining good and evil autonomously. Conscience is the voice of the self-justifying ego; it springs from the impulse to address oneself, to provide one's own point of unity. Additionally, in conscience the incurved self tries to determine its own limits. Conscience limits my responsibility for the neighbor, because it allows me to judge whether I have done everything I can reasonably be expected to do. This judgment can easily become self-justification: faced with the demands of responsibility, conscience resolves its tensions by establishing its own limits and justification. This is why conscience cannot be the ultimate arbiter or guide to the good.[13] The self would prefer to establish clear limits of responsibility, thereby ensuring a clear conscience, yet according to Bonhoeffer genuine responsible action sometimes requires that one surrender the justification of one's own conscience. Then responsibility entails *becoming guilty* for the sake of others. In fact, Bonhoeffer argues that the responsible self cannot avoid taking on guilt (E 275). In this, conscience meets its limits, when the responsible self must surrender its good conscience and its desire for self-mediation and self-justification to God's grace, in order that it might be justified by faith. This is a difficult saying, so we need to look more closely at the relation between conscience and justification.

The Call of Conscience and the External Word

Let us return to Ricoeur. We have looked at his argument that conscience is the ontological presupposition of ethical responsibility. Now we need to examine his argument that conscience is also the anthropological presupposition for understanding and appropriating justification by faith. Ricoeur makes this case in his essay "The Summoned Subject," where he gives a more religious inflection to the phenomenology of conscience he develops in *Oneself as Another*.

In presenting conscience as the anthropological presupposition of justification by faith, Ricoeur follows Bultmann's reading of the apostle Paul. Conscience (*suneidesis*) is a religiously neutral capacity of humanity in general, common to Jews, Christians, pagans, and barbarians alike. It is a dialogue of the self with itself, a knowledge shared with oneself, the self standing in judgment before itself (*coram seipso*).[14] But the interiority of conscience is disrupted by an external word—the word of justification by faith, which comes from outside of the self. Without some capacity of reception, however, the event of justification would remain radically extrinsic. Ricoeur argues that this word must "be able to be received within the intimacy of a conscience that already offers by itself the dual structure of a voice that calls and a self that responds," and that this capacity "is already constituted as an instance of testimony and judgment."[15]

Conscience is therefore necessary for the word to enter the horizon of human self-understanding, so that the self might appropriate the word as its own conviction.

On this point Ricoeur cites his agreement with Gerhard Ebeling, who interprets justification by faith as a Word-event (*Wort-Ereignis*). According to Ebeling, conscience also has a call structure, so it too is a Word-event. Without the call of conscience (and thus the word of the law), we would lack the hermeneutical horizon within which the new word of the gospel appears.[16] Ricoeur agrees with the general contours of Ebeling's description, but he qualifies it in two ways. First, he agrees that the kerygma is an efficacious Word-event, but he wants to expand the horizon of its reception, which is not only law but the entire symbolic network of the biblical inheritance.[17] Second, Ricoeur sees less continuity than Ebeling does between conscience and the word, between the *coram seipso* and *coram Deo*. He therefore points to the *dis*continuity—the paradoxical, dialectical tension between the inner call of conscience and the call of the external word.[18]

This tension between the autonomy of conscience and the obedience of faith is the condition of the "summoned self" in post-Enlightenment culture. "It is to the extent that the self is capable of judging itself 'in conscience' that it can respond in a responsible way to the word that comes to it through Scripture."[19] There is a paradoxical tension between interiority and exteriority, and it is tempting to resolve it by choosing one pole or another, reducing the external word to conscience (e.g., identifying the voice of God with the immediacy of conscience), or else resorting to the heteronomy and positivism of the fundamentalist. But rather than choosing between autonomy and heteronomy, continuity and discontinuity, ontology and alterity, Ricoeur argues that this tension must be preserved. This also means avoiding a premature theoretical synthesis between conscience and the external word.[20] Such a synthesis is not given; it remains a wager, a risk that belongs to faith.

* * *

There is a clear continuity in Ricoeur's transposition of conscience from the discourse of ethics to that of faith, but how far does this continuity extend? If the ethical self is defined by openness, a capacity for discovery, and a capacity of receptivity (OA 339), is there a similar capacity for openness to the ultimate word?

While Ricoeur is right to insist on the dialectical tension (or paradox) between conscience and the external word, we need to push his emphasis on discontinuity further, emphasizing more sharply that the *homo capax* is also *incapax* before God. In other words, we need to show more clearly the extent to which the external word disrupts and conflicts with conscience. In showing how conscience prepares the way for and receives the external word, Ricoeur understates the incurvature of conscience and its complicity in the ontology of self-justification—and thus the degree to which it presents an *obstacle* to the external word. More pointedly still, we must confront the fact that conscience is also a means of self-defense against the word I cannot bear. If the self is characterized by a capacity for openness, discovery, and receptivity, there is also a frightening capacity for hostility and violence against threatening others, including the word of God. This is, after all, how the counter-*Logos* became the *crucified Logos*.

Ricoeur contends that the receptivity of conscience prevents justification by faith from remaining a radically extrinsic event. Whereas the prophetic call and the call to follow after Christ involve a call from outside, in conscience the transcendent caller is internalized and transmuted into an inner voice.[21] It is true that the self needs to appropriate the external word such that it becomes one's own conviction, but we must also recognize the danger that a certain sort of appropriation and internalization can render the external word as static, manipulable information, as an entity at my disposal that allows me to judge myself. This is why the external word must always be spoken anew, so that the *saying* is not reified as a *said*. Yet even if conscience concedes this point, it would prefer to rehearse this saying by itself and for itself, apart from the encounter with an other.[22]

Conscience is therefore marked by a deep ambiguity. Ricoeur acknowledges this in *Oneself as Another*, describing conscience as "that place par excellence in which illusions about oneself are intimately bound up with the veracity of attestation" (OA 341). But we need to push this point further in the context of Ricoeur's theological interpretation of conscience to reckon with Bonhoeffer's observation that conscience can just as easily "be the ultimate prop of human self-justification as the site where Christ strikes home at one through the law" (SC 108). If conscience is an organ of receptivity, it is also an organ of self-mediation, self-justification, and self-deception.[23] Cut off from the other, frustrated by the other as limit, the self tries to construct its own alterity within itself, from which it can call itself to unity with itself. The incurved conscience wants to establish its own limits; it wants to constitute its own point of unity within itself; it wants to speak its own word of justification to itself. Conscience wants to stand where Christ stands, as the mediator between me and myself.

The self needs to surrender the autonomy of conscience, which ultimately aspires to be like God (*sicut deus*) by knowing good and evil for itself. But when conscience relinquishes its impulse to self-justification and surrenders the finality of its judgments to the external word, it can then perform its proper penultimate operations. Ricoeur is correct that there is no final synthesis given in which my verdict is identified with that of the external word; the self only has its ultimate justification in faith and hope, trusting in a word from outside of itself. Bonhoeffer argues something similar, but with a more pronounced Christological orientation: "the unity of human existence no longer consists in its own autonomy, but, by miracle of faith, is found in Jesus Christ, beyond one's own ego and its laws." In following after this external word, "conscience in the formal sense still remains the call, coming from my true self, into unity with myself. However, this unity can now no longer be realized by returning to my autonomy that lives out of the law, but instead in community with Jesus Christ." Thus the "godless self-justification" of the natural conscience is "overcome by the conscience that has been set free in Jesus Christ, calling me to unity with myself in Jesus Christ." The unity and identity of the self lie outside of the self. Christ becomes my conscience. Therefore "from now on I can only find unity with myself by surrendering my ego to God and others" (E 278). We cannot describe the call of conscience as "co-originary" with the call of Christ, but must instead describe conscience as following after his prior call. When one surrenders one's self-judgment to Christ in this way, the faithful conscience is not obliterated, but rather liberated for responsibility.

Justification and Responsibility: *Either/Or* or *Both/And*?

With Bonhoeffer's interpretation of the liberated conscience, we see once again the incommensurability between two competing ontologies: justification by faith versus self-justification. But as we saw in chapters 2 and 3, Levinas poses a considerable challenge for our interpretation of faith by rejecting the ontology of justification altogether. On his reading, both self-justification and justification by faith are instances of egocentricity, and both are obstacles to genuine responsibility because both seek the resolution of a clear conscience. According to Levinas, my responsibility for the other is infinite. Therefore I can never do enough. I cannot mediate my ethical relation to the other via some principle, maxim, norm, law, rule, or practical wisdom that would allow me to conclude, "Yes, I've done my duty; I can rest assured with an easy conscience that I did what was required of me. I cannot be held responsible for anything beyond what I did, because these are the proper limits of my action. Anyone would agree that I did everything that could be done. I did the right thing. I am justified. I am righteous. I am not guilty. I am exonerated." My encounter with the other is now reconciled within my own self-understanding; I grasp the meaning of the encounter and close the circle of self-understanding. I get back to work on my projects, and ontology—i.e., my *conatus essendi*—remains fundamental.

But Levinas objects that the proximity of the other does not permit this sort of closure; it is deeply troubling, even traumatic—an open wound that cannot heal. Levinas describes an ethics with no return to self-identity and sameness. Once we permit a return to the horizon of justification, we have lost the radical alterity of the other. Instead, ethics consists in *an-archic* responsibility—an ethics without *archē* and thus without justification.

Bonhoeffer shares Levinas's opposition to the closure of self-understanding and self-mediating, self-justifying autonomy. The question of ethics is usually posed in two ways—"How can I be good?" and "How can I do something good?" (E 47)—but these questions betray a decision about ultimate reality: namely, an ontology of self-justification. Like Levinas, Bonhoeffer rejects this aspiration to autonomy, but he does not reject justification altogether. It is crucial to recognize that justification by faith is not a self-mediating closure, since faith does not furnish a principle or *archē* that would allow the self to give itself the justifying word. Instead, the self understands itself outside of itself, as having its mediation in Christ. It is also crucial to appreciate that Christ is not a principle or an Archimedean point that grounds ethical action and thereby ensures the goodness of the self. In that case the mediation of Christ would only provide onto-theological (or onto-Christological) leverage to the self-mediating ego. The self does not retreat into the self-mediating safety of a clear conscience, but instead surrenders the question of its own goodness and justification to Christ in faith.

That said, even a minimally suspicious interlocutor could see how this appeal to faith might function as a cop-out. Is justification by grace and faith an excuse for irresponsibility? This is the problem Bonhoeffer (like Kierkegaard before him) addressed in terms of cheap grace. But Levinas compels us to ask whether *every* ontology of justification ends up being cheap grace. I am not (contra Dostoyevsky) more guilty than all the others, because I am justified by grace and faith. With this resolution, justification commits the same sin as theodicy: the latter justifies God and his ways in the world[24] while the former justifies the self, but both override the concrete reality of the vulnerable, suffering other who cannot be mediated by a system of thought.

First of all, we need to note how the *theologia crucis* differs from theodicy. The cross reveals a God who does not pay the price of his own justification out of the pockets of others, as in Hegel's theodicy.[25] The cross reveals a God who suffers in the world, who reconciles the world to himself at his own expense. The cross must therefore be a starting point for Christian thinking about suffering and responsibility. The cross is God's address to a suffering world, and as Hans Urs von Balthasar observes, numerous early Christian thinkers describe the cross as God opening his arms, as an invitation to enter his embrace.[26] At the cross God extends divine hospitality to the world.[27]

With that said, we must also insist that the reconciling word of the cross is an ultimate word and should not be introduced cheaply. On the one hand, it is the starting point for Christian thinking and acting in response to suffering. But this word should not be spoken prematurely. It is often appropriate to speak a penultimate rather than ultimate word (E 152–53). Furthermore, the appropriate response to the suffering of the other is not only a matter of speaking the right words, because, as Gabriel Marcel has argued, evil is not a "problem" for reflection to solve or resolve, to explain, or to synthesize in a higher unity.[28] It is a *mystery*,[29] which is not merely an absence of information that could be resolved by the presence of pertinent information; mystery resonates in the deeper recesses of one's participation in being, as a hiddenness that reflection cannot bring fully into view.[30] What the mystery of evil and suffering demands is therefore not a theoretical resolution, but a response of being-with others in "concrete communication of one person with another,"[31] in what

Marcel describes as availability and readiness (*disponibilité*),[32] and in what Bonhoeffer describes as identifying oneself and sharing in the suffering of others (LPP 389). This means forsaking the perspective of triumph and learning to see history from below, from the vantage point of those who *are not*—i.e., "the outcasts, the suspects, the maltreated, the powerless, the oppressed and reviled, in short from the perspective of the suffering" (LPP 52). It means living without reserve, taking up the demands, mysteries, and responsibilities that life brings our way. It also means throwing oneself into the outstretched arms of the God who suffers in the world. God's suffering in the world does not offer itself as a theoretical resolution; it calls us to participate in this suffering—to watch with Christ in Gethsemane (LPP 486). This is participation in "the messianic event" (LPP 480).

That said, we should not use these remarks to idealize or glorify some notion of redemptive suffering. To recall Bonhoeffer's point, we are not Christ and we should not assume the impossible task of redeeming the world through our own suffering. "We are not lords, but instruments in the hand of the Lord of history; and we can share in other people's sufferings only to a very limited degree." This might appear to be an excuse to shirk responsibility, but Bonhoeffer continues: "We are not Christ, but if we want to be Christians it means that we are to take part in Christ's greatness of heart, in the responsible action that in freedom lays hold of the hour and faces the danger, and in the true sympathy that springs forth not from fear but from Christ's freeing and redeeming love for all who suffer. Inactive waiting and dully looking on are not Christian responses" (LPP 49).

Responsibility, substitution, being-with and being-for others—these are penultimate actions that serve to prepare the way for the ultimate word. We cannot hear the ultimate word of the cross and its justification without some sense of its costliness. This is the context in which we must understand what it means to surrender our action in faith to God's judgment. We cannot really understand the ultimate if we do not have some sense of the gravity of the penultimate:

> Only when one knows that the name of God may not be uttered may one sometimes speak the name of Jesus Christ. Only when one loves life and the earth so much that without it everything seems to be lost and at its end may one believe in the resurrection of the dead and a new world. Only when one accepts the law of God as binding for oneself may one perhaps sometimes speak of grace. And only when the wrath and vengeance of God against God's enemies are allowed to stand can something of forgiveness and the love of enemies touch our hearts. (LPP 213)

By the same token, let me suggest that we need to hear what Levinas says regarding the proximity of the other. It is only after we have encountered the face of the other and been struck by the infinity of our responsibility that we can speak of responsibility being limited by justifying faith. We can only hear this ultimate word of justification after we have traversed the penultimate—after we have been confronted by the face of the other and have recognized the truth in

Levinas's description. We need to be accused by the law, to recognize our guilt and responsibility as infinite and unbearable, in order that we can recognize the costliness (and liberating power) of grace. This is what our interpretation of the cruciform self needs to take from Levinas. Only then can we suggest that the ontology of justification by faith is not a shirking of responsibility and that justifying faith really does set us free *for* (rather than *from*) responsibility.

9 Reflexivity, Intentionality, and Self-Understanding

In chapter 7 we saw how the category of the penultimate allows for a critical affirmation of human capability. This chapter employs a similar strategy regarding self-reflexivity and self-understanding, showing that the for-itself has a proper penultimate status in the life of faith and that the cruciform self is a self-interpreting animal. It is necessary to make this argument given our interpretation of sin as incurvature, which might seem to reinforce the Romantic-idealist interpretation of the fall as a *felix culpa,* a condition for the possibility of self-consciousness. Moreover, Bonhoeffer's claim that the intentionality of faith is an *actus directus* rather than an *actus reflexus* might lead us to suppose that faith and self-reflexivity are fundamentally at odds. In the first section I will argue that faith involves a proper self-understanding that is not reducible to the incurvature of sin. This leads into a brief examination of the intentionality of faith; in response to Levinas's argument that intentionality reduces the other to the aims of immanence, I propose that intentionality is a penultimate act that prepares the way for the coming of the ultimate word. But in order that intentional consciousness can recognize itself as *pen*ultimate, it must encounter the counter-intentionality of Christ, the counter-*Logos*.

In the second section I consider how faith can seek self-understanding in philosophical and theological reflection without turning into a closed circle of thought. Instead of faith finding consummation in a systematic understanding, the opposite is the case: faith seeks self-understanding, which must in turn seek faith in order to be justified and participate in the truth. As a result, reflective thinking (*Nachdenken*) takes the form of following-after (*Nachfolge*). The logic of the penultimate also provides a key for understanding the status of spiritual exercises and disciplines, since cruciform philosophy is not only theoretical reflection, but *a way of life.* The third section then focuses specifically on the practice of self-examination in the life of faith, arguing that self-examination is a vital yet penultimate practice. The quest for reflective certainty quickly leads into a crisis of intentionality, which I illustrate by contrasting Luther's description of spiritual trial (*Anfechtung*) with Descartes's attempt to escape radical doubt. Unlike the spiritual exercises of Descartes's *Meditations,* which result in the reflexive certainty of the cogito and the proof of God's existence, in *Anfechtung* the self cannot find consolation in a reflexive intuition of faith, nor in a philosophical proof for the goodness of God. Instead, God's grace and love are given in a word of promise—an external word that takes the self outside itself, to exist in faith and hope rather than intuited presence.

Reflexivity and the Intentionality of Faith

To begin, let us recall Ricoeur's definition of reflection, which we discussed in chapter 2: "Reflexion is that act of turning back upon itself by which a subject grasps, in a moment of intellectual clarity and moral responsibility, the unifying principle of the operations among which it is dispersed and forgets itself as subject."[1] This reflexive act makes possible a self-consciousness or self-understanding that is the locus of the humanity of the self. Whether it is interpreted in rationalist, idealist, or hermeneutical terms, human dignity lies in this reflexive self-responsibility.

But cruciform faith poses a serious rupture for reflexive philosophy because it cannot be illuminated and grasped in this way. Recall Bonhoeffer's description of being-in-Christ: "I am borne (*pati*), therefore I am (*esse*), therefore I believe (*agere*)." Each moment in this description frustrates reflexive thinking: *I am borne* by Christ in his body of believers, thus there is a prior passivity that my act cannot retrieve and re-present. *I am:* my being as a faithful self is hidden with Christ in God (Col. 3:3), so it has an ob-jectivity that stands over and against my act of consciousness, with a mystery that my reflexive act cannot illuminate and an opacity I cannot penetrate. *I believe:* my act of belief, which depends on this prior passivity and being, is similarly opaque for reflexive consciousness. As we saw in chapter 7, this act of believing is self-effacing; it is one of the operations in which the self "forgets itself." The aim of reflexive philosophy may be to retrieve this act "in a moment of intellectual clarity and moral responsibility," but this is precisely the point on which Bonhoeffer critiques reflexive philosophy, arguing that the intentionality of faith is an *actus directus* that cannot be re-presented in an *actus reflexus* (AB 133). The point is not that faith is some sort of exotic psychic act that eludes self-consciousness, since it is certainly possible to examine faith introspectively or classify it as a specific kind of religious act. What reflection cannot do is ground the authenticity or worth of this act before God. Reflexive philosophy's emphasis on moral self-responsibility is of utmost significance here: if I can grasp my act of faith reflexively, I can occupy my own *archē* and determine the merit of my act. Faith is thereby located as an act, a work through which I ground my own righteousness; I am self-mediating; I am autonomous; I call myself to unity as a subject (an act that reveals the intimate bond between conscience and reflexive consciousness). But faith entails that the question of my belief is not mine to ask. In that moment of reflexive "clarity," I remain locked in the closed circle of incurvature. By contrast, faith is an *actus directus* that does not see itself but only Christ.

Although this description of faith might seem to suggest that reflexivity is synonymous with the incurvature of sin, we must resist this conclusion, just as we must resist two related assumptions: (1) that innocence is immediacy and/or ignorance,[2] and (2) that sin is mediation and therefore the condition for the possibility of knowledge, freedom, and self-responsibility. These claims are particularly common in Romanticism and idealism. By interpreting the fall as mediation, we end up confusing the negativity of finitude with the destructive nothingness of fault (an error we discussed in chapter 4). This confusion leads to further problems: First, it obscures the sense in which finitude, mediation, and difference are part of the original goodness of creation.[3] Thus language, freedom, knowledge, and even human consciousness itself are interpreted as a consequence of sin, and we end up imagining prelapsarian innocence as a sort of dreamlike immediacy that bears little resemblance to anything we know as human consciousness.[4] This in turn leads to a misreading of sin as a happy fault that ultimately allows for a reconciliation that is greater than our original state—an idea that takes us back into the domain of theodicy and all its attendant problems. Another danger is that we recast Adam in the mold of Prometheus—as a tragic hero seizing knowledge, maturity, and self-responsibility from a God who desires that we remain in a state of infantile dependence.

In order to provide a counter-interpretation of this reading of the fall, let us return to *Creation and Fall*, where Bonhoeffer describes Adam's original condition as a *knowledge in ignorance* (CF 85–87). If prelapsarian innocence is "ignorance," this innocence also involves its own proper knowledge, as part of Adam's created being. Contra the Romantic-idealist view, God's prohibition regarding the forbidden tree was not simply to guard against human beings gaining knowledge or self-consciousness in general, but to prevent the human being from trying to become like God (*sicut Deus*), living out of its own resources with an autonomous knowledge of good and evil. The prohibition is therefore a word of address that gives Adam his proper self-understanding as a *human* being, and as a *creaturely* being[5]—that is, as a creature whose existence is defined by limits and boundaries. The prohibition speaks to Adam qua human and qua creature, and its meaning is this: "Adam, you are who you are because of me, your Creator; so now be what you are." Bonhoeffer observes that this address includes both an indicative and imperative, which are in fact one: "You are free creature, so now be that. You are free, so be free; you are a creature, so be a creature" (CF 85). Adam understands himself in this address, and this self-understanding depends on Adam remaining within his limits, as a creature addressed by his Creator.

Given our concerns here, two aspects of Bonhoeffer's reading are noteworthy. First, self-understanding (and thus an appropriate form of reflexive awareness) is a created good. Adam understands himself—not in an autonomous, self-sufficient way but as a truly free creature within his creaturely limits. This means, secondly, that finitude, limitation, and difference belong to the original goodness of creation. Prior to the fall Adam experiences these creaturely limits as grace, but after the fall he experiences his limits as frustration. He hates them. The incurved self wants to speak its own word of truth to itself, to internalize its own point of unity, to posit itself, to secure its identity and goodness through the mediation of its own reflexive act. Differentiation and otherness is precisely what the incurved self cannot bear, because it reveals the limits of the human as a finite, creaturely being. Only as a consequence of the fall does the awareness of difference become division and alienation.

Just as there is genuine self-understanding prior to the fall, so too is there a genuine self-understanding in faith. The intentionality of faith is an *actus directus* rather than an *actus reflexus,* yet there is a proper self-understanding in this encounter—indeed, this encounter is the place where true self-understanding is given. Through the word of address I discover my old being-in-Adam, but I also understand myself as justified by my being-in-Christ. In this encounter I am known by God, and I thereby know God and myself (AB 134). When Bonhoeffer describes faith as an *actus directus* he is not submitting a phenomenological description of intentionality in general. This is why his *Ethics* can make the startling claim that "the knowledge of Jesus is translated entirely into doing, without any self-reflection whatsoever." The right hand does not know what the left hand is doing.[6] As a psychological or phenomenological claim this is untenable, because we always have at least a tacit awareness of our bodily comportment in the world.[7] The point, however, is that in faith "one's own good remains hidden from oneself" (E 318). In other words, the self surrenders its reflexive attempt to grasp the unifying principle or *archē* of its action and thereby ground its moral worth autonomously. Christ overcomes the knowledge of good and evil, such that the Christian lives (pace Nietzsche) "beyond good and evil."[8]

Although the faithful self relinquishes the impulse to be self-mediating and autonomous, this does not preclude the self-understanding that is given in faith. The word of address enables me to say "I," to designate myself reflexively, to attest to myself. It answers a fundamental human question—*Who am I?* In faith I receive my identity as a gift. I am recognized and thereby enabled to recognize and understand myself. But this new self-understanding is always a penultimate reality, insofar as the self only has this new identity in faith and hope. The ultimate word appears in the horizon of the penultimate, one aspect of which is human self-understanding. It enters in and transforms one's self-understanding, but self-understanding never becomes the ultimate in itself. It is not a self-contained whole, because it always *is* in reference to a word beyond it. Faith depends at every moment on being addressed by this external word—by Christ, the counter-*Logos* who cannot be brought under the control of the immanent human *logos*. The cruciform self does not understand itself as a closed circle or totality, but as a genuinely ek-static identity in another, always outside of itself in faith and hope, in perpetual departure toward Christ and the neighbor.

Intentionality and Counter-Intentionality

If the penultimate provides a key for understanding self-reflexivity, it also provides a model for thinking about the intentionality of consciousness.

Intentionality has a teleological structure, since it aims at an intuition that would fulfill its intended meaning (*Sinn*).⁹ But the ultimate disrupts every immanent teleology. Instead of fulfilling our anticipations, it reveals a God whose thoughts are not our thoughts and whose ways are not our ways. The telos of God's coming kingdom is not naturally our intentional *telos*. Intentional consciousness is curved in on itself. Although the ego intends that which is other than itself, it tries to draw otherness back into its own projects, its own efforts to persist in being and to constitute its world as meaningful. On this point Luther and Levinas agree. But God's ultimate word does not fulfill our ethical or religious intentions; it is a surprise, a disruption. The ultimate cannot be anticipated or aimed at, and once it arrives the ultimate gives an excess of intuition that intending consciousness cannot master.

Finite intentionality is *incapax* regarding the infinite excess of intuition given by the other. This is a theme treated extensively by Levinas, who describes the approach of the other in terms that recall the Reformed *finitum non capax:* "The capacity of a being, and of consciousness, its correlate, is insufficient to contain the plot which forms in the face of another, trace of an immemorial past" (OB 97). The face of the other is a trace of infinity, which undoes reflexive philosophy and its goal of an autonomous transcendental unity. I am elected by a call that precedes me, my acts of intentionality, and my recognition; this election is prior to my assuming and initiating responsibility, in a passivity more passive than mere receptivity. This election is immemorial, which means no act of reflection could retrieve and re-present it within the clarity of consciousness. This is the sense in which responsibility is *an-archic:* reflection cannot grasp the *archē* of one's own responsibility. I am responsible not because I am the sovereign master of my acts, but because I am already elected to responsibility by the other. Responsibility is a departure without returning to self-reflection, because it is simply not a matter of reflective consciousness. It is an inversion of consciousness; the other "traverses consciousness countercurrentwise," escaping any representation or thematization. The glory of the infinite is a plot that cannot be narrated.¹⁰ With intentional consciousness, "[t]he given enters into a thought which recognizes in it or invests it with its own project, and thus exercises mastery over it" (OB 101), but it is impossible to capture the infinity of the other in this way. Hence Levinas's view: "No theme, no present, has a capacity for the Infinite" (OB 146). The only proper response of the self is that of ethical responsibility for the other, with no return to the transcendental unity of self-reflection.

Here it is instructive to recall Bonhoeffer's suggestion that the finite is capable of the infinite—not in itself, but through the infinite. What might this mean for the concept of intentionality? It does not mean that the thinking self is capable of capturing revelation, the ultimate, or the infinite within intentionality. There is always an excess that cannot be contained or mastered by the system of thinking. In this regard Bonhoeffer agrees with Kierkegaard, Barth, and Levinas, all of whom oppose the idealist interpretation of the *finitum capax*. No word, no *Sinn,* no act of reflection or intention is in itself *capax infiniti.* Likewise, no intention can determine the advent of the ultimate. The incurved self needs to be broken open by a new reality, by a new word it did not anticipate and a new meaning it did not intend. The human *logos* would like to be capable of intending the ultimate—such is the condition of the incurved *logos:* it wants to classify, to situate, to systematize, to constitute the meaning of every reality it encounters. But the ultimate word is a counter-*Logos,* exerting a counter-intentionality that puts the human *logos* in question: Who are *you,* that you presume to question me? The intending *logos* must be destroyed, crucified by the word of the cross, inverted by the counter-*Logos.*

Nevertheless, intentionality continues to have its place as a penultimate reality in relation to the ultimate. Intentional consciousness cannot constitute or control ultimate meaning, but it *can* play a vital penultimate role in "preparing the way" for the self-giving word of the ultimate. Prior to the moment of justification there is always "some action, suffering, movement, intention, defeat, recovery, pleading, hoping" (E 150). The penultimate is the intentional horizon within which the ultimate shows itself. Revelation is given to us through intentionality, just as the supernatural is given to us in the natural, the holy in the profane (E 59). This horizon needs to be *aufgehoben* by faith in this new word, and yet the horizon still plays a penultimate role in preparing the way. And once it has been broken open by this word of address, intentionality receives a new aim; it follows after this word in order to precede it again (cf. E 159).

A Non-Intentional Self-Relation?

Revelation is given in and through intentionality. Before we embrace this conclusion we must confront Michel Henry's critique of intentionality—a critique that is perhaps even more radical than that of Levinas. As we saw in chapter 7, Henry describes Christian life as a radical self-affection, in which one's life participates in the divine Life. This self-affection is a self-relation quite unlike the self-relatedness of incurvature; in fact, the two are mutually exclusive (IT 143). One of the merits of Henry's project is to recognize that not all self-relationality is incurvature. However, we need to question his description of the true self-relation as non-intentional. On this description, the self-affection of life consists in a sort of feeling or experience rather than thinking, because thinking involves an intentional relation to some object of intuition, which is given in the exteriority of the world (IT 147). Henry maintains that the phenomenality of the world is objectifying and ontologically monistic: everything given in the light of the world must conform to the world's one manner of appearing—i.e., as an inert thing. Life cannot appear in the world's light, so it remains both radically interior and radically non-intentional. The self therefore relates to itself in a pure unity, passively "submerged in itself without ever posing itself in front of itself, without proposing itself in some visible form (sensory or intelligible) or another" (IT 149). Consequently, there is no distance between the self and itself, no gap between intention and intuition, because the true self-relation is entirely non-intentional.

Henry thereby poses a significant challenge not only to the intellectualism of reflexive philosophy, but also to our hermeneutics of the self. From his perspective, one could only describe the human as a self-interpreting animal by forgetting the true nature of the self, which excludes any sort of self-interpretation: "Such a Self, foreign to any apparition of itself in the world, is what we are calling a radically immanent Self, a Self neither constituted by nor the object of thought, without an image of self, with nothing that might assume the aspect of its reality. It is a Self without a face, which never lets itself be envisaged. . . . [N]o Image of itself is interposed between it and itself" (IT 149). This self relates to itself in the non-intentional immanence of feeling, in its experience of itself as living in the divine Life. Whereas the hermeneutical model of the self maintains that the shortest distance from the self to itself is through the other, Henry rejects any external mediation of the self-relation. Granted, Henry maintains that Christ mediates between me and myself, but since Christ is not a transcendent *other* this mediation occurs within the immanence of Life rather than the exteriority of the world.

From a hermeneutical perspective it is the worldly mediation of other people, discourse, and images (symbols, texts, narratives, etc.) that makes self-understanding possible. There is a gap between me and myself, but I gain some degree of self-understanding through these forms of mediation. I recognize myself through the recognition of my significant others, in the texts that I read, and in the stories I tell about my life. Perhaps Henry would concede this point regarding the empirical self, but the true, transcendental self (i.e., *life*) has nothing to do with such worldly mediation. Moreover, even the idea of existential self-understanding is too intellectualist for Henry, since the self-affection of life is entirely non-intentional. But what sense can it make to propose that the true self—the self rightly related to God and to itself—is entirely disconnected from the concrete, historical self in this way? If we consider all that Henry's conception of life excludes, the implications are startling. This is yet another problematic consequence of Henry's dualism of life and world. The more fundamental question, then, is whether it is necessary to conceive of life and/or revelation (for Henry they are the same thing) in thoroughly non-intentional, nonworldly terms. Must intentionality necessarily violate the integrity of revelation?

As we have seen, Bonhoeffer argues that God discloses himself through inadequate, finite means. To paraphrase Luther, it is the honor of God to be handled in this dishonorable way; God is not allergic to phenomenality, to meaning, or to being. Instead God discloses himself deep in the flesh of the world, and deep in intentionality. In revelation, "unlike gives itself to be known by unlike" (AB 134), and yet this otherness is not overcome by a self-identical thinking I. Intentionality continues its penultimate operations in the encounter with the counter-*Logos,* who discloses himself in a way that the thinking I can never master. The ego must surrender itself as the master of meaning in order to become the disciple of the counter-*Logos,* who calls the self: *Take up your cross and follow after me.*

Faith Seeking Self-Understanding

This following-after (*Nachfolge*) provides a model for the meditative, reflective thinking-after (*Nachdenken*) that characterizes philosophy and theology. Can the cruciform self become a philosopher or theologian? How is it possible to remain open to the word of address—to the encounter with the counter-*Logos*—rather than appropriating this word and using it as a tool within its totality, an idea within its system of autonomous self-understanding? Hegel gives the most impressive philosophical expression of this systematic impulse,[11] but the self does not need the architectonic grandeur of Hegel's system in order to be totalizing. Bonhoeffer argues that incurved reason is driven by the impulse to systematic totality, and as such philosophical thinking inevitably leads to a closed circle.[12] Bonhoeffer makes sweeping claims like this on a number of occasions, and we might fault him for exhibiting the same lack of nuance as Levinas does in summing up all of Western philosophy as totalizing. But however unsubtle this pronouncement, it does make a legitimate point. Nietzsche may argue that "the will to a system is a lack of integrity,"[13] but we should not suppose that one can avoid the system by simply willing to have integrity. The desire for self-mediating closure is not only the goal of the notorious systematizers, because the will to a system can play out at varying degrees of sophistication.

The problem, then, is how faith can seek philosophical and theological self-understanding without falling back into the incurvature of systematic, totalizing thinking. First of all, no statement, claim, proposition, or intention is capable of bearing the infinite in itself—as if a mere utterance could, like an incantation, place one in the truth. Moreover, revelation is not reducible to static, manipulable information. It occurs in the concrete encounter with Christ, where reflection is continually broken open, without return to systematic closure. In itself, philosophical and theological reflection on faith remains a self-enclosed system. Theological anthropology, philosophical anthropology, even an *anthropologia crucis* remain self-enclosed systems (AB 135). No utterance, no datum of information, can in itself ensure self-transcendence. In itself, theoretical reflection is a dead work of the law. Simply put, no matter how much I think, write, or speak about Christ, the cross, and the forgiveness of sins, my reflective acts are not in themselves a living, existential encounter with these realities.

No act of reflection, no meaning, no word, and no intention is in itself *capax infiniti*. However, God nevertheless uses these humble finite media to disclose himself; through them "unlike gives itself to be known by unlike" (AB 134). But everything hinges on how we interpret this "through" (AB 106). As we have seen, it is a matter of reflection, speech, and discourse being *aufgehoben* in the encounter with the living Christ, and this encounter must be repeated again and again. Theological and philosophical reflection, as the activity of thinking-after (*Nachdenken*), is thereby justified and in the truth only insofar as it is also a following-after (*Nachfolge*) Christ. Talk is cheap, and like grace it is only costly when it surrenders its self-mediation and allows itself to be questioned by the counter-*Logos*. In the living encounter of following Christ and indwelling his body (the church), the thinker can proceed freely. Paraphrasing Luther's advice to "sin boldly," Bonhoeffer offers the following advice: "Reflect boldly, but more boldly still, believe and rejoice in Christ."[14] It is therefore not a matter of faith finding its consummation in conceptual understanding; understanding must in turn seek faith. And "faith" here does not mean a deficient epistemic act, a mere "believing that"; it is the encounter with the crucified and risen Christ. This encounter sets the theologian and the philosopher free to think reflectively, yet in a way that does not return to systematic closure.

Here we recall the question that opened our discussion in chapter 1: Is it possible for philosophy to confront the reality of the cross in such a way that allows its scandal to stand unresolved? The cross does not subvert the ultimacy of thinking consciousness by presenting an unthinkable thought, because the scandal would continue to be defined by the theoretical, albeit negatively. Rather, thinking consciousness is dethroned in the living, personal encounter with the crucified One, who calls me to take up the cross and follow after him in faith.

Cruciform Philosophy as a Way of Life?

With all of that said, we must also note well that philosophy is not solely a theoretical discourse. According to Pierre Hadot's influential thesis, the ancients understood philosophy as a *way of life*.[15] The love of wisdom is not merely a classroom discipline or strictly theoretical discourse; it encompasses one's full life, and integral to this life is the practice of philosophical *askēsis*—i.e., spiritual exercises and disciplines meant to transform the self.

In order to act upon oneself in a transformative way, the self must cultivate the right kind of self-consciousness. In Hadot's description, the exercises that cultivate self-consciousness generally involve two movements: (1) an inward movement, in which the self concentrates on itself through such exercises as meditation, memorization, reflecting on philosophical truths, examining one's conscience, and preparing for death; and (2) an outward movement of expansion, in which the self contemplates nature and the rational order of the cosmos, as well as the wisdom of the sage (who is the norm or ideal of the philosophical life). The outward expansion also involves relations with others—in moral education and in the relation between a philosophical master and his disciples. These relations allow the philosopher to engage in dialogue, to practice confession, and to receive instruction, exhortation, correction, and consolation.[16]

Given our present discussion of reflexivity and self-understanding, the inward movement Hadot describes is particularly salient. One of the recurring themes of these exercises, in which the self "concentrates itself upon itself," is the discovery that the self is not what it initially supposed. The self has previously identified itself with all sorts of foreign, accidental attributes and attachments. One of the most important philosophical exercises, then, is to isolate the true "I," purified of all false attachments.[17] We see this in Plato's *Phaedo,* where Socrates defines philosophy as practicing for dying and death by separating the soul from the confusion of the body and the senses.[18] The Stoics also commend this practice of purification, as in the advice of Marcus Aurelius to separate from oneself. This allows the "I" to circumscribe its consciousness within a pure present and to separate itself from concerns about past and future. By separating itself from whatever is outside of its control,[19] the I[20] thereby identifies itself with pure activity. This exercise strengthens the self to renew its choice of life at each instant.[21] Similarly, in the *Enneads* Plotinus commends the practice of turning to oneself (*epistrophē*) and attending to oneself (*prosokhē*) as a way to reveal the beauty of the soul:

> If you do not see your own beauty yet, do as the sculptor does with a statue which must become beautiful: he pares away this part, scratches that other part, makes one place smooth, and cleans another, until he causes a beautiful face to appear in the statue. In the same way, you too must pare away what is superfluous, straighten what is crooked, purify all that is dark, in order to make it gleam. And never cease sculpting your own statue, until the divine light of virtue shines within you.[22]

By clearing away all that is false, all that is accidental, and all that obscures the true beauty of the self, the truth of the soul can appear.

The exercises of inwardness have had a significant influence for the tradition of reflexive philosophy. Descartes implements this inward turn in his *Meditations,* which comprise a six-day regimen of philosophical exercises. We find one instance of the purification of the I in the opening lines of Meditation Three:

> I will now shut my eyes, stop up my ears, and withdraw all my senses. I will also blot out from my thoughts all images of corporeal things, or . . . regard these images as empty, false and worthless. And as I converse with myself alone and look more deeply into myself, I will attempt to render myself gradually better known and more familiar to myself.[23]

The result of this purification is that Descartes can identify himself as a pure cogito, a thinking thing distinct from extended things. This reflexive act aims at a pure self-transparency, devoid of any hiddenness. Commenting on Descartes's meditation, Arthur Danto observes that for Descartes "the limits of what I know about myself are the limits of the self, and if there are things true of me that I do not know, they do not belong to my essence."[24] In this reflexive act, the ego discerns clear and distinct limits of what is essential to itself.

The turn toward oneself (*epistrophē*) also became the paradigm for German Idealism's concept of reflection,[25] which seeks to distinguish the transcendental ego and the empirical ego and to enable the absolute *Ich* to absolve itself of all material and accidental conditions. The inward turn (whether *epistrophē* or *reflectio*) also aims to enable the self to determine its own unity, so that one can become truly self-responsible, autonomous, and free. Therein lies one's true humanity.

* * *

Having noted these influences, we should not conclude that there is a direct continuity from the ancient practices of self-attention to modern concepts of reflexivity. The Cartesian cogito, the transcendental ego, the absolute *Ich*—all of these concepts assume that true self-knowledge requires that one intuit oneself in an abstract objectivity rather than in one's concrete, historical subjectivity. Hence Kierkegaard's objection that the ancient saying "know thyself" has been misinterpreted by modern German philosophy so that it now connotes an ethereal self-consciousness, separate from one's existence. This is a major departure from Socrates, who recognized that truth engages the full scope of one's existential subjectivity and that philosophy is therefore a way of life. If the unexamined life is not worth living, it is also true that the unlived life is not worth examining. According to Kierkegaard, it is necessary to retrieve this original Greek sense of "know thyself"—yet as the Greeks would have understood it if they had Christian presuppositions (CA 79).

For ancient philosophy, the Delphic imperative (*know thyself*) was a call to existential commitment and an entire way of life. On this point Kierkegaard discerns strong parallels between ancient (especially Socratic) philosophy and Christianity,[26] insofar as Socrates and Christ both argue that truth requires subjective attachment rather than objective detachment. This emphasis on subjectivity does not entail subjectiv*ism*, however, since true self-knowledge requires conformity and devotion to the universal *logos*. At the same time, this attachment to the universal does not allow the thinking self to achieve self-certainty, nor to become absolute or self-grounding. The ancient *know thyself,* as well as the self-understanding of faith, both exhibit an epistemic modesty that is lacking in the ideals of modern reflexive philosophy. This is why Kierkegaard devotes so much attention to Socratic irony as a clue for thinking about Christian faith,[27] as well as for the challenge of communicating truth that can only be communicated indirectly.

If we acknowledge these parallels, what difference would "Christian presuppositions" make for a retrieval of the ancient *know thyself*? For Johannes Climacus, the fundamental difference is that Christianity introduces the scandalous presupposition that the eternal *logos* is a particular person who entered time. Therefore truth does not consist in a recollection (*anamnesis*) of the eternal *logoi* that are already in one's soul; truth comes in a word that is external to the self, in the person of the incarnate *Logos*. Unlike Socrates, Christ is not a midwife who aids in the recollection of the truth and can then disappear; Christ's role is not merely incidental, because this teacher is himself the truth. He therefore calls the self to take up the cross and follow after him.[28]

But what would Christian presuppositions mean for a retrieval of the ancient imperative *know thyself* as requiring spiritual exercises? If we presuppose the word of the cross in particular, what would this mean for a reinterpretation of these philosophical practices and their role in attaining self-knowledge? We have discussed the apostle Paul's point that the word of the cross is foolishness, a scandal for the philosopher because it conflicts with natural reason and its concepts of wisdom and power. But the word of the cross also pronounces a negative judgment on philosophy as a way of life, as a practice, discipline, or *askēsis* that strives to achieve one's true identity through one's own activity. This is why Luther so vehemently opposed medieval monasticism and asceticism, which appropriated many of the philosophical practices of antiquity.[29] As Hadot observes, the purpose of these practices was to be conformed to Christ and participate in his passion,[30] and as such they form a cross-centered spirituality. Yet according to Luther these practices misinterpret the cross by making it a self-devised means of grasping merit. No matter how extreme its emphasis on humility and however severe its means of mortification, the self-devised cross is actually another manifestation of the *theologia gloriae*.[31]

With that said, Luther's *theologia crucis* gave way to a distortion of its own, insofar as Lutheran Christendom secularized suffering and the cross. "It's my cross to bear" now designates the particular trials and misfortunes that characterize natural life in general. In response, Kierkegaard and Bonhoeffer both attempt to reinterpret the cross and suffering—not through a direct retrieval of asceticism, but by returning to the texts of the New Testament. *Take up your cross and follow after me.* This call has been obscured by the word of cheap grace, which entails neither cross nor suffering, but we cannot understand Christian faith without taking seriously what this call entails. The call itself initiates the first suffering when it tears us away from our attachments and puts the old self to death (D 87). This leads to rejection, spiritual trial, confrontation with sin and evil, suffering with others, and participation in God's suffering in the world.

There is therefore no need to seek or cultivate suffering under artificial conditions, because it will arise in due time as a result of following after Christ.[32] Thus Kierkegaard maintains that in retrieving the practice of following after Christ (*Christi Efterfølgelse*), this practice must be distinguished from the former errors. While *Efterfølgelse* involves imitation, this is quite another thing than "ascetic self-torturing,"[33] the practice of "fasting and flagellation,"[34] "scourging oneself, crawling on one's knees, standing on one leg,"[35] and the other "monkey antics" that came into practice in the name of imitation.[36] The error was to assume that these ascetic disciplines could provide a method of earning merit. Asceticism also created the illusion of a two-tiered Christianity, in which the ascetic lives an exceptional or extraordinary life in contrast to the average believer.³⁷ *Efterfølgelse* is not an exceptional exercise reserved for spiritual athletes; it is for everyone, because it is the hermeneutical context in which the word of grace can be meaningful.³⁸

Furthermore, spiritual exercises are vital to forming the habits and character of the self. True, the moment of justification gives the self an entirely new standing before God, but the self still requires time, continuity, and repetition in order that this word can work itself out in one's self-understanding and exert its transformative potency on one's character. Bonhoeffer elaborates on this point in his 1932 seminar course on theological anthropology. The new being of faith, the *esse*, is that of being a sinner and being forgiven. As we have seen, this *esse* is not a substance or static possession one has, but a reality one participates in. But just as the *esse* entails a proper acting (*agere*), so too does *esse* entail a proper having (*habere*), a habitus that is "the behavior of faith":

> The *habitus* must be explained from the *esse*. As, however, the *esse* cannot be had, the *habitus* cannot simply be formed from the *esse*. The *habitus* is formed in its awareness of the character of being had by the *esse*. Part of the nature of Christian *habitus* is that it continually annuls itself, i.e., it is part of its nature to be aware of being penultimate, compared to the finality of the *esse* of faith, and that it does not take itself so seriously. The *habitus* of Christian character distinguishes itself from that of individuality in that it is gained through practice. The practice that forms the Christian *habitus* must begin with [letting it find itself] in the penultimate. It is a practice of formed humans to look beyond themselves. Christian character therefore carries within it a basic element of neglecting itself. The knowledge of myself as sinner, this knowledge of my justification makes character formation into something secondary, penultimate, yet significant as practice.³⁹

The ultimate word imparts true self-understanding, disclosing me to myself as a justified sinner. I do not achieve this recognition and identity through spiritual exercises but through an external word, so there is no question of synergism here, and yet these exercises are a vital penultimate feature of faithful existence. One of the goals of this formation is to teach the self to look beyond itself; in this way, it is a penultimate practice that helps to prepare the way for and follow after the ultimate word. Without these practices the external word remains a pointlike event that does not take root and establish existential continuity in the self.⁴⁰

The cruciform self is called to a cruciform way of life, and this "way" involves exercises and disciplines, which have a penultimate significance insofar as they have their justification outside of themselves. They are self-effacing. In performing them, the self intends something beyond itself, surrendering its actions in faith and hope. By identifying character formation as penultimate, we can answer the radicalism that would view every such practice with suspicion as well as the compromise that would lead to the care of the self eclipsing the significance of the ultimate word. Character formation, spiritual exercises, and religious disciplines are not the ultimate, and they cannot compel its coming. The ultimate word relativizes the ethical-religious formation of the self,⁴¹ revealing it as vital yet *pen*ultimate. When religious projects become ends in themselves, faith is reduced to the care of the self. Religious practice is then determined by a self-ruled method. This could take the form of legalism, or pietism, or in its popular contemporary form, "spirituality"—a popular term to indicate a self-conscious religious cultivation of self or a lifestyle (often with an emphasis on social ethics and an overlay of self-articulated divinity). But despite its purported desire for self-transcendence, this spiritual self-cultivation ends up making selfhood an end in itself. The self-chosen way never truly surrenders its autonomy, and despite its attempts to overcome its natural egocentricity it is never truly decentered. It is a consumer approach to transcendence. At every step along its spiritual journey the self retains its sovereignty of choice (*hairesis*), heretically selecting the beliefs and practices that "work" for itself.

This self-styled interpretation of religion and spirituality follows from the attempt to accommodate the self-understanding of secular humanism. In his prison writings, Bonhoeffer provides an interpretation that moves in the reverse direction: rather than interpreting Christianity according to the secular and the humanistic, he interprets the secular and the human according to Christian faith. Christ does not address the human being in order to add a religious affiliation to an otherwise complete human being or to insert a religious word into the margins of the secular. Instead, Christ stands in the center of reality and therefore confronts the world in the center of its being, claiming the secular, the rational, and the humanistic for himself. This claim does not seek to install a radical theocratic or Christocratic rule, but to identify these realities as penultimate so that the world is free to be the world and the human free to be human. In this regard Christian faith is something otherwise than religion. "The 'religious act' is always something partial, whereas 'faith' is something whole and involves one's whole life." The call of Christ does not inaugurate a new religion or spirituality; it calls the self to a fully human life (LPP 482).

We will discuss Bonhoeffer's nonreligious interpretation of Christianity further in chapter 10, but I mention it now because it provides an important qualifier to our account of spiritual exercise and discipline. Christian *metanoia* is not conversion to a life of religious devotion and practice; it does not mean working on oneself as a sculpture, or becoming religious in a particular way in order "to make something of oneself (a sinner, a penitent, or a saint) on the basis of some method or other."[42] It means becoming human—not an ideal or type of humanity, "but the human being Christ creates in us." Spiritual exercises and disciplines have a proper place in the life of faith, but they are reoriented and reinterpreted in a nonreligious way. The call of Christ does not constitute us as religious selves, but as fully human beings.

Self-Attention and Self-Examination

A thorough discussion of spiritual exercises and disciplines would examine the varieties of religious practices, including prayer, confession, narration and testimony, mentorship, self-examination, memorization, reading and meditation on scripture, keeping a journal, etc. But I will not offer a catalogue of exercises nor presume to prescribe a rule for the cruciform self. Instead, given our concern with reflexivity and self-understanding, I will limit myself to commenting on the status of self-reflexivity in the practices of the cruciform self, focusing specifically on the tension that arises between self-examination and the external word.

The cruciform self looks beyond itself, even neglects itself, but this self-denial is not a matter of devising ascetic methods of mortification and self-martyrdom. Nor does it mean denying the false self that obscures the true or authentic self, because the self is incapable of adequately and ultimately discriminating between the authentic and the inauthentic self. The true self cannot be located directly, but is disclosed indirectly as one follows after Christ, and as the image of Christ in-forms and con-forms the self to his likeness. This conformation is not some sort of cloning procedure; it is a transformation by a word of love and grace, which liberates the self from the ontology of self-creation and self-justification to become uniquely itself.

Furthermore, if faith means self-neglect and self-forgetting, this does not mean that self-examination has no place in the life of faith—as though faith were thoughtless, naïve, or oblivious to itself. Self-examination has a proper, penultimate role in assuming responsibility,[43] as well as in the life of faith—as indicated by the apostle's admonition to test oneself, to examine oneself to see if one is in the faith, and to recognize Christ in oneself (2 Cor. 13:5).[44] But there are limits to what self-examination can disclose. It does not yield certainty regarding one's own faithfulness, which is why self-examination must surrender itself and its judgments to the justifying Word (E 325). On this point we discover the crucial difference between faithful self-examination and the *actus reflexus* of reflexive philosophy. When faith seeks the self-grounding certainty of the *cogito*, as a sort of *Credo, ergo sum*, it encounters a crisis of self-attention.

Anfechtung *as a Crisis of Intentionality*

In this section I would like to consider Luther's proto-phenomenological description of *Anfechtung* (*tentatio*, spiritual trial) as a crisis of intentionality. According to Luther's *theologia crucis*, the existential movement of faith means moving through from the hidden God (*deus absconditus*) to the revealed God (*deus revelatus*), from God's alien work of *destructio* (*opus alienum*) to God's proper, life-giving work (*opus proprium*). The spiritual trial of *Anfechtung* occurs when faith meets some mode of resistance and cannot access the revealed God of grace.[45] The self undergoes an experience of God-forsakenness—like the forsakenness of Christ on the cross, falling into darkness, despairing of God's promises and even God's goodness. The self is assailed by visions of God's wrath and only *destructio* is visible. There is no glimmer of grace on the other side of this dark storm. God's proper work of love is fully eclipsed by the threat of wrath and damnation. Luther goes so far as to describe God appearing as the devil, and then goes a step even further to suggest that God hides himself behind this diabolical mask, using the devil as his instrument in this trial. This terrifying description is spiritual trial at its most severe, which only strikes the "greatest of saints."[46] The only way through these depths of despair is to push through them in faith—to recognize that God's diabolical visage is a mask and that the reality of one's faith is hidden securely with Christ in God.

Anfechtung involves a crisis of intentionality: the self seeks to locate and grasp its object, but the intentional gaze founders on a twofold hiddenness. First, God is hidden; indeed, God *hides himself,* withdrawing from phenomenality. Second, faith is also hidden; reflection cannot verify it. In this regard it is illuminating to contrast Luther's description of *Anfechtung* with the threat of the evil genius in Descartes's *Meditations*. Descartes is seeking an indubitable foundation to prevent his radical methodological doubt from leading into an abyss of skepticism. He cannot rely on his senses; there is no guarantee that his waking life is not a dream, and he cannot be sure that an evil genius, or even God, is not deceiving him about the veracity of his judgment that 2+3=5. Descartes's solution comes with his discovery of the *cogito*. Even if he is deceived, he can be certain of one thing: *I think, I exist*. Here is a clear and distinct truth on which intentionality can feast, a plenitude of presence in which consciousness can bask. Yet this self-reflexive insight offers no consolation for the self undergoing *Anfechtung*. *Credo, ergo sum* offers little consolation because faith is hidden. I cannot verify my faith by turning inward in reflection, because it is hidden from view. In faith, I am borne (*pati*), therefore I am (*esse*), therefore I can believe (*agere*, i.e., *credere*). Thus the unified being of the self does not arise from an originary activity; the self of faith is constituted in a moment of passivity that the reflexive act cannot retrieve and re-represent. Moreover, if I seek confirmation in emotions, sincerity, conviction, or other psychological states, an abyss quickly opens up beneath me, because none of these states can withstand the suspicion that these psychic states are not elaborate self-deceptions. Self-attention therefore only deepens my anxiety, because I can never dig deep enough to strike bedrock. The *credo* of the faithful self is therefore anything but an Archimedean point.

Similarly, Descartes's conclusion regarding God's goodness also fails to provide consolation for the self in *Anfechtung*. In his third *Meditation* Descartes eliminates the threatening possibility that God is a deceiver: the ability to deceive is not truly an ability or power because it depends on some defect, and deficiency is incompatible with God's infinite nature.[47] At one level Descartes's description recognizes that God, or the idea of infinity, is a crisis for intentional consciousness; as Levinas and Marion have shown, the intuition of infinity exceeds the capacity of intentional consciousness.[48] But *Anfechtung* precipitates a crisis of a different sort. Although the idea of infinity exceeds or saturates intentionality, Descartes still finds resolution in the conclusion that this infinite God is *good*. But God's goodness is no consolation for the self in spiritual trial.

In fact, it is likely to sink the self even deeper into despair; if God were evil, or merely arbitrary or capricious, then spiritual trial would be a matter of tragedy, as in ancient Greek thought. But for the self before God's wrath, it is even more terrifying to recognize that God's judgment is good and just. As Merold Westphal observes, Luther's terror regarding the wrath of God and eternal punishment was not simply the threat of punishment: "What drove Luther . . . first to despair and then to grace was not a fear of suffering in hell, but the overwhelming sense that this is what he *deserved*. Not the mere fact of God's wrath, but its uncontestable rightness brought his existence to its crisis."[49] The only consolation after this recognition is God's word of grace. Yet there is no basis to hope for love and forgiveness from the idea of infinity, because grace is a contingent rather than necessary event. Such a hope arises from the promises that God has revealed to Abraham, Isaac, and Jacob, and in the incarnation, cross, and resurrection of Christ. Therefore faith must push through the dark hiddenness of God to the *deus revelatus*, the God who has revealed himself in his promises and will not forsake us. Faith must appeal to this God, against all appearance and experience, even to the point of struggling "with God against God." And if God appears to withdraw his promise? The self must fight with God against God himself.[50]

The word of revelation is given to faith and hope. It is not a clear and distinct idea, visible and manipulable for the thinking self. The self has its identity outside of itself, in promise rather than presence, and this gap is the opening by which *Anfechtung* enters. *Anfechtung* is therefore a crisis of intentionality because the faithful self must contend with the hiddenness of God as well as the hiddenness of the self's own identity and standing before God. But note well that this hiddenness is not only a deficient phenomenality, an absent aspect or a lack of intuition; the objects of faith are hidden *sub contrario*, under the aspect of their opposites. There are times when the faithful self examines itself and only sees sin, deception, and corruption. Self-examination leads to despair, because one's identity in Christ is not visible. Similarly, the God of love is hidden behind the mask of the devil; all that appears is a predestining God who has elected us to damnation. Yet faith must push through this hiddenness, clinging to the word of promise in faith and hope.

The External Word

Because self-examination can so easily fall into crisis, the exteriority of the word is of vital importance. We need to hear a word that does not originate from ourselves, because only an external word can prevent reflection from succumbing to the infinite regress of self-suspicion. From this it follows that the exercises of cruciform faith are primarily oriented toward the external word rather than unguided introspection. But the external word does make genuine self-examination possible, such that the word acts as a mirror (*speculum*) that discloses the truth about the self.

If the mirror of scripture is necessary for self-examination, then what does it disclose? How does it aid in my self-examination? According to Kierkegaard, the word requires that I examine myself and consider whether I am doing what it says (PC 234). The encounter with the word is therefore not primarily a discovery of new information about myself. Rather, it is directed toward the question of obedience, toward my existential engagement and action in the world. Self-examination does not have a primarily intellectual orientation, as a return to the closure of self-consciousness; it leads me to turn outward, following after Christ and serving my neighbor. Consequently, the mirror of the word is not the *speculum* of speculative philosophy—i.e., an external moment that I internalize as self-identity, a detour in the circuitous tour back to my self-mediating self.

Because it calls us into question, the external word is not only a discourse in the third person. It addresses us in the second person; it does not speak *about* us, but *to* us. According to Kierkegaard's description, the word has a counter-intentional character. It cannot be observed in a detached way, because in observing it I discover that I am being observed, in questioning it I am being questioned. The word addresses me, claims me, asks if I am doing what it says.[51] We see this counter-intentionality in *Practice in Christianity*, where Anti-Climacus describes the incarnate *Logos*, the God-man, as a sign of contradiction.[52] This is not a merely logical contradiction; it is a paradox—an *apparent* contradiction, a contradiction according to the normal logic of appearance. The notion of the eternal *Logos* entering time is paradoxical in itself, but the incarnation does not fulfill our expectations for such an event by appearing in glory. Here Luther's influence on Kierkegaard is evident: God hides himself *sub contrario*—under the opposite aspect. When Christ calls people to himself he does not call from the heights of glory, but from abasement (PC 24). Christ appears incognito, in a denial of immediacy, direct visibility, and direct communication. "He is the paradox that history can never digest or convert into an ordinary syllogism" (PC 30). As such, the external Word retains a perpetual exteriority, as the sign of contradiction and offense that continually conflicts with human reason (PC 26, 36).

To recall our discussion in the first section, the incarnate *Logos* is the counter-*Logos*—reversing the interrogation and inverting the intentionality of the classifying human *logos*. The sign of contradiction draws attention to itself; it fascinates the gaze, and so the classifying *logos* wants to identify this paradoxical phenomenon. What is it? How is it possible? But here the tables turn and intentions reverse: the counter-*Logos* puts the human *logos* in question: Who are *you*? As Anti-Climacus puts it, the sign of contradiction becomes a mirror that reflects the heart of the viewer. The self is confronted with a choice, and in choosing the self is disclosed. Who do you say that I am? This question discloses the truth about the self. But this question does not ask for an utterance of fact, a static *said*; it calls for a say*ing* that is always renewed in following after. Thus true self-understanding (the true *know thyself*) is not the reflective, meditative thinking (*Nachdenken*) of idealism, but the self-understanding of the disciple in the way of *Nachfolge*.

This cruciform self-understanding therefore entails a move, in Ricoeur's terms, *from text to action*. Self-understanding is manifest in the moment of appropriation, application, and obedience.[53] Hence the influence of the epistle of James on Kierkegaard: by merely hearing the word without *doing* the word, the self deceives itself. "For if anyone is a hearer of the word and not a doer, he is like a man who looks at his natural face in a mirror; for once he has looked at himself and gone away, he has immediately forgotten what kind of person he was" (James 1:22–24). This is not the good kind of self-forgetfulness, either. When the self stalls in hearing and never makes the transition to doing, the truth of the word does not take shape in one's concrete self-understanding. The self immediately forgets what the mirror has disclosed. True self-understanding, by contrast, consists in the transition from text to action.

But here a further question emerges: *What counts as action?* After all, hearing is an act. Saying is an act. Thinking is an act. Who can really distinguish between thinking and doing, between *theoria* and *praxis*? The Romantic and idealist ambition is to overcome this dichotomy by showing that theory *is* practice. From that perspective, it would therefore seem impossible for philosophy *not* to be a way of life. But Johannes Climacus rejects this equivocation as sophistry, insisting that there is a qualitative difference between thinking and acting. Thinking remains in disinterested detachment and possibility, but acting means that "the individual annuls possibility and identifies himself with what is thought in order to exist in it. This is action." Acting does not simply mean a certain way of thinking; it means the actuality and responsibility of existing subjectivity.[54]

There are a number of points to note here. First, Climacus argues that the movement (*kinesis*) from possibility to actuality is not necessarily an external action; the movement inheres in the interiority of the self's commitment. Second, this movement is a qualitative leap, but is not a voluntaristic "leap of faith." Faith is action, but also fundamentally *passion*, a gift of transcendence rather than an outworking of immanence.[55] Third, the act cannot be re-presented reflectively; it is a rupture of the incurved system of consciousness and cannot be brought into systematic closure without losing its character as faith.

We have seen that Bonhoeffer agrees with points two and three, but he differs over the description of faith as an interior movement. There is definitely truth to Climacus's argument: without the depths of inner formation, external action can simply be a matter of insincerely going through the motions, without really "meaning it." But the stress on earnestness becomes precarious when the self tries to determine the sincerity of its commitment; the further this self-examination goes, the more likely it is to find an abyss rather than a foundation. True, faith is an "objective uncertainty," but this insight alone is not sufficient to free the self from the labyrinth of self-reflection. This is why the self needs to encounter the word in its exteriority and corporeality, in the context of interlocution with other people[56] and in the physicality of the sacraments.

Moreover, interior actuality must take shape as exterior actuality. If external action without internal depth is meaningless, it is also true that interiority without external action is fruitless and prone to incurvature. We therefore need to balance Kierkegaard's emphasis on interiority with his emphasis on *Efterfølgelse*. This is what Bonhoeffer suggests when he describes the actuality of faith as taking up space in the world. Faith is not the cognition of a disembodied, Docetic truth; in the man Jesus, the incarnate *Logos* takes up space in the world and calls "actual, living human beings" to follow him *bodily*—to act, work, and suffer in community with him (D 226). This is not a pointlike event, but a reality that is extended in space and time.

* * *

If the new being, the new humanity, the Christ-reality (*Christuswirklichkeit*) takes up space in the world, it does not do so as a strictly religious phenomenality. It appears in the polyphony of life, in the fullness of human existence. For this reason we cannot uncritically identify faith with religious subjectivity. That is the topic of our next, and final, chapter.

10 Religion within the Limits of the Penultimate?

We have seen how the cruciform self fits and conflicts with a number of themes of philosophical anthropology, such that we can understand the sense in which the cruciform self is also a *homo capax*, a responsible self, and a self-reflexive, self-interpreting animal. In this final chapter we will see whether we should think of the cruciform self as a *homo religiosus*. Once again we will bring Ricoeur and Bonhoeffer into dialogue. Religion, and the sacred, is a significant aspect of Ricoeur's philosophical anthropology, since he argues that religion plays a pivotal role in the convergence of human capability and self-understanding. Religion is also a significant issue for Bonhoeffer, who famously argues for a *non-religious* interpretation of Christian faith. We will see that Ricoeur and Bonhoeffer complement each other in certain ways, but we will also highlight some fundamental differences, which become apparent in Ricoeur's interpretation of resurrection. By considering Christ's resurrection and its ontologically transformative potency, we will show the difference between Ricoeur's philosophical hermeneutics of religion and our own model of cruciform philosophy. In the final section I discuss the hope for one's own resurrection and respond to Ricoeur's critique of this hope, arguing (contra Nietzsche) that the promise of resurrection allows the world to be the world and the self to be fully human.

Interpreting Religion

A Post-Hegelian Kantian: Ricoeur's Hermeneutics of Religion

In this section I will argue that Ricoeur offers a *hermeneutics of religion within the limits of the penultimate*. The allusion to Kant here is deliberate, since Ricoeur articulates his project with explicit reference to Kant. First of all, Ricoeur exhibits a very Kantian caution regarding the limits of philosophical discourse, denying the impulse to make pronouncements about the ultimate and arguing instead that the eschatological horizon is one of hope rather than knowledge. In our introduction we noted that Ricoeur cites the *theologia crucis* in defense of this methodological asceticism, but his primary influence on this point is Kant rather than Luther. Like Kant, Ricoeur is self-consciously *not* a theologian, and for similar reasons Ricoeur refuses the label of "Christian philosopher." This is not, however, to say that Ricoeur's philosophy is devoid of theological presuppositions, for we will see that his account of religion is far from theologically neutral.

Ricoeur's debt to Kant is evident in his philosophy of religion. Kant gives a philosophical soteriology, in which conversion is a matter of moral regeneration. Where the self is bound by radical evil, the task of religion is to regenerate the self and restore its capacity to act in accord with moral obligation. Ricoeur follows Kant on this point, reading Kant's *Religion within the Limits of Reason Alone* as a proto-hermeneutics of religion. But Ricoeur takes Kant's nascent hermeneutics and gives it a more robust expression, arguing that Kant does not pay sufficient attention to the religious imagination. On this point Ricoeur echoes Hegel's view that we cannot bypass religious representations (*Vorstellungen*),[1] but after his appropriation of Hegel's point he returns to Kant, maintaining that faith and hope are not *aufgehoben* by knowledge, just as the religious imagination is not *aufgehoben* by the philosophical concept (*Begriff*). With Kant, we must respect the limits of human cognition and see that religious truth is given in the mode of hope rather than knowledge.

According to Ricoeur, the religious imagination acts as a schematism of hope, since religious discourse—i.e., symbols, metaphors, narratives—discloses new possibilities of meaning and action. In Ricoeur's words, "all religions are different attempts in different language games to recover the ground of goodness, to liberate, so to say, the enslaved freedom, the enslaved capability."[2] Although radical evil binds capability, it does not eliminate the human capacity for goodness altogether. Ricoeur appeals to an ontology of originary, created goodness that is "rooted in the ontological structure of the human being."[3] As the text of Genesis testifies, "God saw everything that he had made, and indeed, it was very good" (FS 298). Ricoeur argues that despite the reality of radical evil, this created goodness has not been completely erased. There is a theological wager here, with Ricoeur's emphasis on created goodness echoing his Reformed heritage and its notion of common grace.[4]

The purpose of religion is therefore to regain contact with this originary goodness.[5] Like Kant, for Ricoeur religion aims at moral regeneration and liberation of the corrupted will. Religious texts and images are effective and transformative because they penetrate to the deepest levels of our being. There is "an underlying connection between word and the active core of our existence."[6] This active core is the *conatus,* and Ricoeur maintains that the conatus is not identical with the sinful *homo incurvatus in se,* nor is it simply an indifference or allergy to alterity. Because of fault, or radical evil, the conatus curves in on itself in bondage, but the purpose of religion is to set the conatus free rather than to obliterate it altogether. According to Ricoeur, a proper desire to persist in being, along with a proper need for self-esteem, self-understanding, and self-recognition, is part of the created goodness of human being. We have a good, created desire to flourish and to live well.

Ricoeur's account of the conatus gives it a hermeneutical twist, insofar as the self strives to persist in its being in the world, which consists in understanding oneself and one's existential possibilities. Therein lies the transformative power of the word:

> Word has the power to change our understanding of ourselves. This power does not originally take the form of an imperative. Before addressing itself to the will as an order that must be obeyed, word addresses itself to what I have called our existence as effort and desire. We are changed, not because a will is imposed on our own will; we are changed by the "listening that understands." Word reaches us on the level of the symbolic structures of our existence, the dynamic schemes that express the way in which we understand our situation and the way in which we project ourselves into this situation. Consequently, there is something which precedes the will and the principle of obligation, which, according to Kant, is the *a priori* structure of this will. This something else is our existence insofar as it is capable of being modified by word.[7]

The power Ricoeur is talking about here is the imagination. On his account, the new being is first formed in the imagination, not in the will. "This is because the power of letting oneself be grasped by new possibilities precedes the power of deciding and choosing. Imagination is that dimension of subjectivity which responds to the text as *poem*."[8] The religious image has a poetic, regenerative potency, which is ontologically transformative because it penetrates to this active inner core and reconnects the self with an original goodness and capability.

With or without Religion?

But if the religious image is regenerative, it can also be repressive and destructive. And if the image can transform our being, it can also install self-deception and illusion. Thus Ricoeur argues that a viable religious faith must undergo a double critique. First, the idols and false consciousness of religion must be smashed by the external critique that comes from the hermeneutics of suspicion (Feuerbach, Marx, Nietzsche, and Freud). Second, this external critique must be extended into an internal critique. Here Ricoeur cites Bultmann's program of demythologization, which is inspired by Lutheran *destructio* and Heideggerian *Destruktion*. According to Ricoeur the purpose of demythologization is to smash false scandals so that religious symbols can disclose their true scandal.[9] Demythologization performs an alien work of destruction so religious symbols can perform their proper work of meaning. On the far side of the critique, the symbols still speak, but we hear them anew in what Ricoeur calls a second naiveté.

According to Ricoeur, Bonhoeffer provides another important example of this internal critique, as well as a promising example of the mature faith that could come after it.[10] As with his reading of such theologians as Barth, Bultmann, Ebeling, and Moltmann, Ricoeur's interest in Bonhoeffer is philosophical, as part of his larger project of a hermeneutics of religious language.[11] In particular, Ricoeur is interested in Bonhoeffer's provocative notion of a "nonreligious interpretation of Christianity."[12] But what is a nonreligious interpretation of Christianity, and why would this be preferable to a *religious* interpretation?

First of all, a nonreligious interpretation of Christianity is not a private, personal piety, nor is it social ethics with a dash of transcendence thrown in. Nor does Bonhoeffer advocate the abolition of prayer, worship, the reading of scripture, spiritual disciplines, and the communal life of the church. How then does he define *religion*? Bonhoeffer is not offering a general eidetic theory of religion (if an *eidos* of religion can even be discerned). In his account religion is a historically conditioned anthropological or psychological category, which describes human possibilities of thinking, acting, and feeling in response to such needs as finitude, weakness, and suffering. For Bonhoeffer the essential components of religion are (a) human weakness, (b) human dependence, and (c) a God of power. In religion, human weakness turns in dependence to a God of power.[13] Religion exalts the God of metaphysics; God is the highest, best, most powerful being around, and this God functions as a stopgap in human experience. Whenever human beings are weak, God is powerful; wherever human beings reach the limits of knowledge, God fills in as an explanatory hypothesis. Religion is also otherworldly; it negates life in this world in favor of an eternal *Hinterwelt*. Consequently, religion also cuts itself off from everyday, worldly existence, typically in favor of a private, interior piety.

Traditionally, Christian preaching and thinking has presupposed these religious impulses as an a priori point of contact, as the condition of being addressed by the ultimate word. But if these are historically effected presuppositions, what happens when they decline? Can we still speak of God after the cultural death of God? Can we proclaim the ultimate word "without religion," and thus without the "temporally conditioned presuppositions" of metaphysics and interiority (LPP 364)? For Bonhoeffer, the question of religion is analogous to the question of circumcision for Paul—namely, is it a condition of salvation (LPP 365–66)? What if the religious a priori is a dispensable rather than essential aspect of the penultimate? What if it is not essential to our *Menschsein* and *Gutsein*? Or what if the religious a priori is even detrimental to our penultimate being-in-the-world, insofar as religious apologetics seeks to "prepare the way" by attacking the human being in her maturity, strength, goodness, and happiness?

The religious interpretation of Christianity assumes that it must discredit (or more radically, *humiliate*) the penultimate in order to prepare the way for the ultimate. In order to make room for the ultimate, the religious apologist attacks the usual religious pressure points: the guilty conscience, anxiety, despair, fear, and weakness. Religion employs a hermeneutic of suspicion to expose hidden weakness and corruption, in order to show that the capable, mature human being does in fact need religion. Bonhoeffer is highly critical of the strategy that uses religion as a consolation when people are at their most desperate. By capitalizing on weakness, these tactics end up pushing God to the gaps, margins, and limits of human existence. By treating God as a stopgap, religion puts God into a mode of constant retreat (LPP 425–28). The overall result of these factors is that religion encourages intellectual dishonesty, cultivates immaturity, misery, and weakness, and undermines the wholeness and integrity of human existence.[14]

Bonhoeffer is highly sympathetic to the critiques that Feuerbach and Nietzsche level against religion. The problem with a religious interpretation of Christianity is that it depends on negation. It tears down the human being in order to create the sense that we need God. By contrast, a nonreligious interpretation of Christianity would thrive as an affirmation. God confronts human beings not merely in their weakness but in their penultimate strength and ability, so Christian faith is a Yes to the capable human being—to maturity, strength, knowledge, and goodness. It is also a Yes to the polyphony of life in this world, with all its joys, sorrows, and responsibilities. It recognizes that God is not threatened by our existence in this world (LPP 366–67, 405).

Moreover, authentic faith does not seek a *deus ex machina* to dissolve all of its problems. Rather than pointing to a God of power, scripture overturns our expectations by pointing us to God's powerlessness and suffering in the world. As Bonhoeffer famously writes, "only the suffering God can help." "The God who is with us is the God who forsakes us," as he forsook Christ on the cross. The *theologia crucis* entails an *anthropologia crucis*. God lets us live in the world *etsi deus non daretur*. The self-understanding of faith involves this recognition that we live as human beings without God as a working hypothesis. But this is not secular humanism *tout court*; it is a Christological, cruciform humanism. We recognize ourselves as God-forsaken, yet this recognition occurs *before God*. This gives a striking dialectical turn to the category of *coram Deo*: faith means living without God, yet *before* God and *with* God. It is a question of how we exist before God, and how we are with God. We encounter God in the cross, and that is how God is with us and helps us—not as a *deus ex machina* or as the omnipotent deity of metaphysics, but in his weakness and suffering in the world (LPP 479). Bonhoeffer is not describing a deistic removal from the world, but elaborating on the *theologia crucis*:[15] God discloses his power and wisdom in the weakness and folly of the cross; that is how God is present in the world, and that is how he helps us. God calls us to participate in his suffering by living a cruciform existence, which means living a "secular" life in the world, without appealing to the consolations of "religion." This kenotic being-in-the-world is how one becomes genuinely Christian, and thus human.

Bonhoeffer was only able to articulate this nonreligious interpretation in sketches and suggestions, so there are definite limitations to the sort of constructive work that one can do with them. Yet they are deeply provocative, and a large part of their appeal—and their promise—consists in showing that faith is not at odds with human maturity (*Mündigkeit*). Christianity means a robust affirmation of the capable human being. As we have seen, there is significant agreement between Ricoeur and Bonhoeffer on this point. But there are also significant differences between their respective projects, and in what follows I consider the most salient of them.

Meaning, Religious Figuration, and Ontological Transformation

According to Ricoeur, the second naiveté is vital for the hermeneutics of religion because religious truth is ineluctably figurative—contra the Enlightenment critique of positive religion. Just as Ricoeur does not want to reduce the figurative to a rationalized kernel, so he wants to preserve the alterity and prevenience of the text as a voice that precedes and constitutes the hearer.[16] The moment of hermeneutical appropriation requires a corresponding *dis*appropriation in which "I let the matter of the text be." By surrendering my interpretive sovereignty, "I exchange the *me, master* of itself, for the *self, disciple* of the text."[17] This break initiates a new relation to the text. I no longer approach the text trusting in my own interpretive works, but instead commit myself to the text in faith, in trust, in a confident yet uncertain step that Ricoeur characterizes as a wager. It is a wager that the text can still speak, that it can reconfigure my world by disclosing a new world in front of the text—a world charged with new existential possibilities, a world I might inhabit. Consequently, one's understanding of scriptural texts belongs to one's project of self-understanding and being-in-the-world.

Bonhoeffer would agree with Ricoeur that there is no getting around the figurative elements in scripture. For instance, in *Creation and Fall* he is clear regarding the need for figurative language in speaking about the things that Genesis addresses. Commenting on the Yahwist's description of the garden and the two trees, Bonhoeffer notes the need for "fantasy" (*Märchen*): "Who can speak of these things except in pictures?" Yet these pictures are not simply lies, since "they indicate things and enable the underlying meaning to shine through." This figurative language is historically and culturally contingent,[18] but we cannot simply step outside of it, nor can we penetrate to a rational core that can be directly stated, thereby rendering the figurative dispensable. Consequently, while Bonhoeffer writes of the need to translate the old "magical picture of the world" into the language of the technological age, this new language continues to be figurative, albeit in a different way. Either way, what really matters is that this figurative language is true "to the extent that human speech and even speech about abstract ideas can remain true at all—that is, to the extent that God dwells in them." This is the point we saw in chapters 6 and 9—namely, that revelation occurs in and through human words and meaning (*Sinn*), but everything depends on the meaning of this "through." In other words, what matters is that this figurative language addresses us as those who "can live only through Christ as people who have been lost and, whether in hope or in fulfillment, have been graciously pardoned" (CF 81–83). What matters is that I encounter the living Christ in and through this word, meaning, or image.

To some extent Bonhoeffer's remarks recall Bultmann's program of demythologization,[19] but there are important differences to recognize. In his prison letters Bonhoeffer writes that Bultmann's demythologization of the New Testament did not go "too far," as critics allege. The problem is that Bultmann did not go *far enough* (LPP 372). Bonhoeffer's point is not that Bultmann left too many myths untouched, because the problem is not "mythological" concepts like miracles, the resurrection, and the ascension. In a letter written a month later, Bonhoeffer writes that these concepts are indispensable because "the New Testament is not a mythological clothing up of a universal truth, but this mythology (resurrection and so forth) is the thing itself" (*"die Sache selbst!"*) (LPP 430). This is not to ignore the problems of historical knowledge, or to suggest a realism in which we have access to the thing in itself. Instead, Bonhoeffer's point is that these events are not manifestations of some more fundamental or transcendental meaning. Bultmann perpetuates liberal theology's typical reduction process (*Reduktionsverfahren*) that reduces Christianity to a religious essence, and in so doing remains beholden to a religious interpretation of Christianity (LPP 430).

Christianity proclaims the concrete reality of Christ, incarnate in history. This is pivotal to Bonhoeffer's critique of religion as well as his critique of Bultmann. In objecting that Bultmann did not go far enough, Bonhoeffer means that Bultmann was on the right track with his concern that the incarnation and cross of Christ be significant for us, here and now. Bonhoeffer's famous question "Who is Jesus Christ for us today?"[20] concerns the concrete, present reality of Christ, yet Bultmann's existential interpretation of the kerygma ends up abstracting from this concreteness[21] in favor of a Heideggerian ontology of Dasein's existential possibilities. As we saw in chapter 5, Bonhoeffer rejects this move in favor of a distinctly Christological ontology. What is at stake here is a question of how revelation alters the human being on an ontological level.

The Poetics of Religious Discourse: Transformation and the Truth For Me

According to Ricoeur's philosophical hermeneutics, the self is transformed through events of meaning. Through the encounter with words, images, and texts my self-understanding and being-in-the-world is changed. The text opens in front of itself a world charged with new possibilities for me—a world I might inhabit. The text is revelatory in a philosophical sense, since it enables a disclosure of being; it is a poem that discloses ontological possibilities. The text reveals new modes of being and forms of life, thereby giving new capacities of self-understanding and new possibilities of being-in-the-world. There is a genuine ontological *donation* here, since the text gives the self this new capacity for being.[22] In the event of appropriation, one's being is refigured.

Ricoeur's account of this poetic refiguration is profoundly illuminating, showing how deeply language and imagination penetrate into the ontological structure of the self. That said, we need to read Ricoeur's description as a description of penultimate rather than ultimate transformation. It is a transformation of my self-understanding as a human being in the world, my connection and commitment to the good, my responsibility for others, etc. This is the level at which Ricoeur's philosophical hermeneutics of religion proceeds: as an interpretation of religion within the limits of the penultimate. As philosophical, his hermeneutics will not draw an ultimate qualitative distinction between the transformative potency of religious texts and nonreligious texts, nor will it proclaim the theological truth of one religious text over others. What I would like to attempt at this point, then, is to demarcate some critical limits of philosophical hermeneutics and its account of poetic transformation.

First of all, the notion of poetic transformation must confront Kierkegaard's critique of the poetic, which parallels his critique of the imagination. On the one hand, imagination is vital to the existence of the self. According to Anti-Climacus, it "is the capacity *instar omnium*"—the capacity for all capacities. Thus "whatever of feeling, knowing, and willing a person has depends upon what imagination he has" (SUD 30–31). Imagination is the power of possibility; the self is addressed by possibilities (mundane and eschatological alike) in and through the imagination.[23] Given this central role, the imagination is "the power that is the first condition for what becomes of a person" (PC 186). Here Kierkegaard anticipates Ricoeur's point that new possibilities of being are first given in the imagination.

But if imagination is necessary, it is not a *sufficient* condition to move the self into truthful existence. If imagination is the first condition for what becomes of a person, the second condition is the will (PC 186). The self must venture forth from possibility into actuality; otherwise imagination [*Phantasie*] gives way to the fantastic [*Phantastiske*], and the self becomes lost in abstract possibilities rather than engaging in concrete existence. This is the basis for Kierkegaard's critique of the poetic as an aesthetic mode of being that stalls in possibility. Johannes Climacus will critique the speculative philosopher for much the same reason: philosophy trades in universals, which disclose truth as a universal possibility rather than a truth lived by an existing individual.[24] Thus Kierkegaard and several of his pseudonyms challenge the poet and the philosopher alike to take up the task of existence and move from abstract possibility to concrete actuality. This transition is the moment of becoming subjective, in which the truth becomes true *for me*.

Ricoeur's description of poetic transformation does not succumb to Kierkegaard's critique, since he offers neither a Romantic poetics nor an idealist philosophy, but a hermeneutical model in which self-understanding includes the moment of existential appropriation. What Kierkegaard describes as the subjective movement to actuality, Ricoeur describes as the movement from text to action. Self-understanding "is not something that just happens in one's head or in language. It is what the gospel calls 'putting the word to work.'" The self becomes a disciple of the text. The self does not properly understand the text if there is no movement into action, no transition from possibility to actuality. Consequently, "to understand the world and to change it are fundamentally the same thing."[25] Where Kierkegaard defines truth as subjectivity, Ricoeur defines understanding as being-in-the-world, but for both thinkers proper understanding means appropriation of the truth *for me* in living actuality.

We need to think carefully, however, about this notion of actuality as the subjective *for me*. There are two senses in which the truth is *for me*. The first is Luther's Christological *pro me*, which designates an actual, independent state of affairs in which Christ "stands there" for me, as a mediator between the self and God, others, and itself. However, with the modern turn to the subject Luther's notion of the *for me* assumed greater epistemological significance, indicating the fact that truth appears for me.[26] We see this *for me* in Kant's Copernican revolution, in post-Kantian German idealism, in existential philosophy, and in philosophical hermeneutics: I cannot access reality as unconditioned objectivity, as it is in itself, because truth is always the truth as it appears for me. In addition to this epistemological principle, the *for me* can also entail an ethics of belief, such as we find in Kierkegaard's definition of truth as subjectivity. As he writes at the end of *Either/Or*, only the truth that edifies me is true for me. It is therefore my responsibility to take hold of the truth subjectively, to live it in my own concrete existence rather than observing it in detached, disinterested objectivity.[27]

The word, image, or text is transformative because it is meaningful for me. I become the disciple of a text that names God and refigures my being-in-the-world. But does this interpretation of poetic *metanoia* fully account for the event of faith? Is there a difference between becoming a disciple of a religious text and becoming a disciple of Christ? Can we translate the Christological *pro me* into the epistemic, existential, or hermeneutical *for me* without remainder? I believe we must maintain the distinction between these two senses, yet without seeing them as mutually exclusive.

Let us recall Bonhoeffer's question: Who is Jesus Christ *for us* today? We need to read this Christological for us (*pro nobis*) in both senses of the phrase. Alongside Kant, Kierkegaard, and Ricoeur, Bonhoeffer argues that this is a question of truth *for us* and *for me*. The ultimate word is not a punctual, unextended event; it enters my horizon of self-understanding and appears as a phenomenon *for me*. Therefore we cannot retrieve a naïve realism or precritical objectivism. As we saw in chapter 6, Bonhoeffer argues that the being of revelation is not given in an unconditioned, positivistic way. Rather, being *is* in reference to the act of the thinking self. Revelation entails a hermeneutical horizon and it demands appropriation. The external word addresses the self, who hears and responds; it must become true for me and thereby transform my self-understanding.

That said, this appearance for me is neither identical nor coextensive with Christ's *promeity*, his being-there for me. In other words, appearance is not the thing in itself; the phenomenon is not the noumenon. Here Bonhoeffer sides with Kant[28] and Kierkegaard[29] against idealism and its denial of the thing in itself. Christ's being there *for us* must be distinguished from our subjective appropriation of this word. The ultimate word proclaims a truth we cannot know in itself, calling instead for faith and trust. We cannot achieve objective certainty about this, but at some point it will make an infinite qualitative difference whether or not Christ is actually there for us independent of our belief.

Too often in modern (and postmodern) thought the subjective *pro me* has eclipsed the ob-jective *pro me,* so that the emphasis falls on the subjective act of appropriation.[30] This leads to the faulty conclusion that truth is transformative because of *how* I appropriate and embody it, not because of an actuality external to my *how*. On this view, Christ alters me because I have appropriated his word or image in a meaningful or authentic way. But it also matters *what* I appropriate in this passionate, subjective, authentic way. Furthermore, in addition to the question of content, we must also confront the question of reference. Truth involves the subjective act *and* ob-jective (*Gegen-ständlich*) being, meaning for me *and* reference to the external reality of Christ being there for me.

As we saw in chapter 6, the faithful self discovers that its being in Christ is prior to its subjective act of faith. My act of faith, my self-understanding—these depend on my prior being, which depends on a prior passivity. "I am borne (*pati*), therefore I am (*esse*), therefore I believe (*agere*)." Prior to my appropriation or understanding of this reality, I have my being in Christ, which is neither identical nor coextensive with my act of faith. This being is a gift, given *for me* before I can appropriate its meaning *for me.* Moreover, one's being in Christ is *hidden,* and often the only thing that is apparent to oneself is one's fallenness in sin. Thus one's ongoing conformation to Christ is often not apparent to oneself—though it might be apparent to others.

The ultimate word reveals Christ there for me as a reality that is already actual prior to my act of appropriation. Despite the importance of subjective appropriation, the word of cross and resurrection do not reveal an ethico-religious ideal or possibility that I must actualize. Thus in *Ethics* Bonhoeffer describes the one Christ-reality (*Christuswirklichkeit*), in which God and the world have already been reconciled.[31] This *already* is qualified by a crucial *not yet,* since the kingdom is still coming. We do not inhabit a realized eschaton. Contra Hegel, the actuality of God's reconciliation with the world is hidden, and we attest to it in faith and hope rather than sight. But this adds an important clarification to our discussion of eschatological possibility in chapter 3, where I argued that for the cruciform self possibility is prior to actuality, because the self is given a possibility that has no basis in its present actuality. This gift of possibility is unconditioned by a demand for an actuality already achieved by the self. However, this eschatological promise is a possibility for me only because the incarnate, crucified, and resurrected Christ is already and actually there *for me.* The self believes that the promise of the eschatological *not yet* is trustworthy because of the Christological *already.*

Resurrection and Faith at the Limit of Poetics

For Christian faith, both of the previous examples depend on the resurrection of Christ. If Christ has not already and actually risen in bodily form, then we cannot maintain the distinction between the two senses of the *for me*. Christ can only be there for me as a symbol, image, idea, example, or some other semantic figure. As such he can only be there for me insofar as he enters my horizon of understanding. But if Christ is risen as living flesh and blood, then philosophical hermeneutics is confronted with an other that transcends self-understanding. How then should our philosophical-hermeneutical anthropology interpret the resurrection?

The resurrection marks a limit of Ricoeur's hermeneutics of religion, as well as a limit of poetic transformation. For Ricoeur, the resurrection is a *meaning-event*.[32] To be sure, it is not just any old meaning-event; it has an excess of meaning because the name of God has been bound to this Christological event. The name *Christ*, like the name *God*, takes us beyond philosophical language about Being. The word "God" says more than the word "being," because it has a semantic abundance that presupposes the polyphony of biblical discourse—stories, prophecies, laws, hymns, etc.[33] And by naming God as "Christ," there is a further semantic gain insofar as this name

> adds the power to incarnate all the religious significations in one fundamental symbol, the symbol of a sacrificial love, of a love stronger than death. It is the function of the preaching of the cross and the resurrection to give to the word "God" a *density* which the word "being" does not possess. In its meaning is contained the notion of *its* relation to us as gracious, and of *our* relation to it as "ultimately concerned" and as fully "re-cognizant" of it.[34]

The biblical texts proclaim this name as inaugurating a new being, which is "bound up with the *meaning-event* preached as resurrection." The resurrection is a meaning-event that is given textually. It proclaims the new being in a meaningful form, in a text among other texts. Consequently, even if this new being claims any unique or privileged status, it only does so by speaking textually and addressing us as beings who must follow the movements of the hermeneutical circle in order to understand.[35]

In an interview from 1995, Ricoeur elaborates on his interpretation of the resurrection. On his reading, the meaning of the resurrection originates in the quality of Jesus' death, not in his bodily resurrection. Ricoeur admits that the philosopher in him is tempted by the Hegelian interpretation, according to which the resurrection is completed not in a physical body, but as a historical body "in the other of the crucified"—the Christian community. The spirit of Jesus "now animates the handful of disciples, transformed, from the deserters they were, into an *ecclesia*." The resurrection is a victory over death, but this victory does not consist in a literal bodily resurrection. It consists in Jesus' sacrifice, service, and his laying down his life for others—showing that love is truly stronger than death.[36] As Ricoeur argues in *Living Up to Death,* Jesus triumphs over death through service to others; his death exemplifies "the idea of service" that Ricoeur describes as a "positive ethics of detachment."[37] For Ricoeur, then, the cross and resurrection are in some sense the same thing.[38]

According to Ricoeur's interpretation, the resurrection is ontologically transformative because it is an event of refigured meaning. It profoundly transforms the disciples' self-understanding and their being in the world, disclosing unforeseen possibilities and constituting a new community of faith. The resurrection narratives have a second-order reference: their referent is not an empirical body, as in ostensive, first-order reference; their referent is the new possibility of faithful being-in-the-world as a follower of Christ. The resurrection narratives redescribe reality, giving it a poetic refiguration that discloses new, unforeseen possibilities of the *I can*. The resurrection narrative regenerates the self by interrupting its radical corruption and reconnecting it to its created capacity for goodness. According to Ricoeur's philosophical hermeneutics of religion, then, cruciform selfhood would be constituted by the event of crucifixion and resurrection, which enables the self to be for others, even to the point of laying down one's life in service for others.

What should we make of this interpretation of the resurrection as a *meaning-event*? And what should we make of this unification of the cross and resurrection? To be sure, the resurrection is saturated with significance; it is a meaning-event *par excellence.* But are poetics and the category of *meaning* sufficient to account for the transformative potency of the resurrection?

Ricoeur argues that the resurrection, like the exodus narrative in the Old Testament, is a liberating event that discloses "the utmost possibilities of my own freedom," thereby becoming "for me the Word of God."[39] But if this *for me* of appropriation is necessary for understanding the biblical text, it is not *sufficient* to account for the new being inaugurated by the resurrection. The new being—the new humanity (*deuteros anthropos*) of Christ—does not only transform my self-understanding and being-in-the-world. It does that, to be sure, but the ontological transformation depends on the fact that the risen Christ is actually there *for me*—not only as a semantic innovation and refigured meaning, but in flesh and blood. If the category of meaning-event is sufficient to account for the resurrection and its transformative potency, then it does not ultimately matter whether Christ is actually risen and there for me. Perhaps my belief in the bodily nature of the resurrection gives me a different hope than if I understood it strictly symbolically, but the efficacy nevertheless consists in the passion of my imaginative appropriation. The word "Christ is risen" would therefore function as a placebo. The narrative of Christ's resurrection would not have an efficacy that is ultimately different from the myth of the Phoenix, the cult of Mithras, or any other narrative of dying and rising gods. Granted, the Christian narrative might have a pre-eminent status because of its historical and cultural influence; it might even possess some structural uniqueness or superior meaning—perhaps it discloses more compelling ideas, images, or richer possibilities for self-understanding and being for others. But these are all relative differences that can be evaluated within the limits of the poetic. In Kierkegaard's terms, there would ultimately be no qualitative difference between the poetic genius and the apostle.

On this point Ricoeur departs from the apostle Paul, who argues that if Christ has not been raised, our faith is worthless and we are still in our sin (1 Cor. 15:17). It is not enough to argue that the narrative of the resurrection transforms our understanding of ourselves and our world. Following Paul's logic, Kevin Vanhoozer poses this question for Ricoeur: "Would not the world continue to 'lie in evil' even if we saw it through resurrection-tinted spectacles?"[40] But if Christ *has* risen, then this entails a transformation of reality that is not coextensive with our self-understanding and being in the world. This transformation occurs in and through meaning, but it is also *otherwise than meaning*, since Christ is there for us independent of us, risen in bodily form and not only in the communal spirit or self-understanding of the church.[41]

Here we encounter the limits of religious poetics. Christ's resurrected body is not reducible to a metaphor or analogy, a parable or figure of the rhythms of life or the cycles of nature. It must be his body in all of its scandalous corporeality—his hands, his feet, his side. Here one thinks of Caravaggio's painting *The Incredulity of St. Thomas,* the naturalism of which offers a similarly stark confrontation with Christ's corporeality. We see Thomas placing his finger in Jesus' side, and a small roll of skin folds back as Thomas probes the wounded, now risen flesh.[42]

* * *

As with the word of the cross, the risen body of Christ presents philosophy with a *skandalon* it cannot resolve. Philosophy and kerygma stand in confrontation. Can philosophy proceed according to this incarnate, crucified, and risen *Logos,* following after him in faith, thereby remaining broken open? This cruciform philosophy would not, however, be a radicalism in which faith provides a trump card; it would allow philosophical discourse its relative autonomy within the limits of the penultimate, and in many aspects might look very similar to Ricoeur's philosophy. But it would differ from Ricoeur's philosophy in its interpretation of the ultimate. First of all, it will let the scandal of Christ's bodily resurrection remain. According to Ricoeur, the internal critique of religion aims to remove the false scandal so that religious symbolism can speak the true scandal. But what counts as the true scandal? Ricoeur's reading of the cross and resurrection succeeds in articulating some crucial aspects of the scandalous nature of Christ's crucifixion—as a sacrifice without remainder, a complete surrendering of oneself for others. But even if we concede that this meaning-event is necessarily incarnate in a particular historical person, this interpretation still flirts with Docetism because "resurrection" seems to be separable from the risen one. Christ lives on as a meaning rather than a body. But this is not the resurrection that Paul proclaimed at the Areopagus in Athens; had Paul interpreted the resurrection in this way, his philosophical interlocutors would not have been as likely to sneer at his proclamation (Acts 17:32). Paul could have compared the cross and resurrection of Christ with the death of Socrates, since the *Phaedo* too has a profound power for poetic transformation, and has refigured many selves and their way of being in the world.[43]

Perhaps our appeal to kerygma against philosophy results in a critique more transcendent than immanent. To be sure, the resurrection is an object of faith rather than knowledge, and we cannot conclusively prove it is true. But if we cannot demonstrate philosophically that Ricoeur's interpretation is simply false, we can critique his interpretation on hermeneutical grounds. Ricoeur aims at a philosophical engagement with religious scandal, suggesting that his hermeneutical retrieval of the cross and resurrection will preserve their true scandal. Yet despite this admirable goal, Ricoeur loses the true scandal. Ricoeur identifies the resurrection as a triumph over death, insofar as Jesus endured this death for the sake of others. But even if Jesus was the living embodiment of this sacrifice, it is difficult to avoid the implication that he embodies some more fundamental meaning or existential possibility, and that we are transformed by our appropriation and enactment of this new possibility of meaningful being-in-the-world. As such, resurrection would ultimately (and not just *pen*ultimately) be a matter of refigured meaning.

Ricoeur's philosophical hermeneutics provides brilliant descriptions of the religious imagination and its power to transform our self-understanding, our being in the world, and our capacities for being human and being good. In many ways it is exemplary as a philosophy of religion within the limits of the penultimate. But there is also a danger that his hermeneutics follows the way of compromise, such that immanence ends up domesticating transcendence. As a result, its character as *pen*ultimate is in danger. After all, the penultimate only recognizes itself as such following the encounter with the ultimate. True, Ricoeur's scrupulous insistence on Kantian limits guards against a totality that would reduce the ultimate to the penultimate. Like Kant, and contra Hegel, Ricoeur wants to leave room for faith and hope rather than seeking closure and fulfillment. But faith does not refer to an empty placeholder; it must intend more substantive content. This is why Kant turns to the postulates of practical reason, and why Ricoeur turns to the poetics of the religious imagination, and yet both thinkers in their own ways compromise the transcendence of the kerygma, and in such a way that philosophy cannot avoid encroaching on theology, so that philosophy of religion ends up looking a lot like a philosophical religion.[44] It is not self-evident that this is a bad thing; perhaps philosophy makes for a better religion. But we must then ask whether this philosophical religion allows revelation to have an ultimate exteriority.

As we have seen, Bonhoeffer argues that philosophy cannot be truly self-critical and cannot set a genuine limit for itself, because it can only set these limits by overstepping them. Likewise, philosophy cannot of itself establish the *a priori* possibility of a revelation that is genuinely exterior, because this move determines in advance *how* revelation can appear and *what* revelation can be or mean. When philosophy begins with critical reflection on its own limits and possibilities, it seeks to cut revelation to the measure of these conditions. Philosophy cannot determine the conditions of possibility for revelation a priori, because these conditions only appear a posteriori, after revelation has been given in actuality. Nor can philosophy recognize this *im*possibility prior to the actuality of revelation, since it has no reason to suppose that something might not fit its expectations. Hence Bonhoeffer's remarks in *Act and Being*: "*Per se*, a philosophy can concede no room for revelation unless it knows revelation and confesses itself to be Christian philosophy in full recognition that the place it wanted to usurp *is* already occupied by another—namely, by Christ" (AB 76–78). In order to proceed according to genuine limits, then, philosophy must begin with the actuality of revelation.

This outcome is starkly evident in Fichte's *Attempt at a Critique of All Revelation*,[45] as well as Kant's *Religion within the Limits of Reason Alone*. We have also noted Bonhoeffer's critique of Heidegger along similar lines. In the name of preserving its limits and protecting itself from the illicit influence of theology and kerygma, philosophy ends up positing a philosophy of religion (or a philosophical religion) that is more of a competitor than a complement to kerygmatic faith. Heidegger's later thought, with its emphasis on the piety of philosophical-poetic thinking, is one case in point.[46] But what about Ricoeur's hermeneutics of religion? Ricoeur offers a much richer and more robust interpretation of kerygmatic faith than any of these thinkers, but while he describes himself as a philosopher who is also a hearer of the kerygma, his interpretation of the cross and resurrection suggests that philosophy retains the prerogative to judge the true scandal from the false. Unless we begin with the presupposition of Christ's bodily resurrection as an actuality, there is no reason why philosophy should concede the possibility of such a kerygma a priori.[47] Thus when philosophy seeks to interpret the resurrection, it ends up reducing it to a refiguration of meaning. However profound this semantic innovation is, it is difficult to avoid the hermeneutically crude and infelicitous conclusion that at some point the resurrection is "*just* a symbol" or "*just* a story."

I do not advance this criticism as a dismissal of the category of meaning, but to highlight its limits. If we fail to recognize the penultimate character of meaning, it will eclipse the ultimate. Then resurrection cannot avoid being reduced to refiguration, and Christology, staurology, and soteriology cannot avoid being reduced to anthropology and ethics—thereby confirming Feuerbach's suspicion that theology is ultimately anthropology. In order to retrieve and affirm the discourse of faith after Feuerbach, we must resist this reduction to meaning. To be sure, we need to recognize that meaning is vital as a penultimate, anthropological category. The ultimate word is indeed meaningful *for me*, since it enters my hermeneutical horizon and reconstitutes my self-understanding by allowing me to recognize myself as a human being before God. God discloses himself in and through meaning, *as* meaningful. But as Bonhoeffer argues in

Act and Being: "It is not because the word of God is in itself 'meaning' [*Sinn*] that it affects the existence of human beings, but because it is *God's* word, the word of the creator, reconciler, and redeemer" (AB 134–35). The word of the cross addresses me and transforms me, not only because it is meaningful *for me*, but because of the actuality of the risen Christ there *for me*.[48]

Final Things: Resurrection and Faithful Dwelling in the World

Our discussion of meaning and resurrection leads into the final section of this chapter, and of this book as a whole. I will examine the hope of the faithful self for individual resurrection—a hope that several of our interlocutors criticize. How should we interpret this desire for one's own resurrection, and how does this impact the way we think about meaning, justification, and existence in the world?

* * *

According to Ricoeur, for post-Nietzschean humanity the basic existential problem is no longer that of one's own salvation or damnation, as it was in the Middle Ages and for Luther. Nietzsche diagnosed the threat of nihilism as a crisis of meaning and value in this world. We must confront the question of "sense" and "non-sense," and this question "can no longer be expressed solely in terms of guilt, of sin, or of Redemption."[49] In Ricoeur's view justification is not a question of sin and forgiveness, but a question of the meaning of existence.[50] Thus justification is not about God forgiving sin; it's about God giving *Sinn*. Moreover, according to Nietzsche the crisis of meaning is a consequence of the Christian preoccupation with guilt, sin, and redemption, since Christianity defers meaning here and now in favor of a world beyond, an afterlife, a truth behind the scenes, a thing in itself.

Following our discussion earlier in the chapter, allow me to suggest that the question of justification should not be subordinated to the question of meaning. Instead, the question of meaning needs to be affirmed in its proper penultimate status. This means it must be teleologically suspended or *aufgehoben* by the question of justification. As Jüngel observes, justification does in fact address the loss of meaning that characterizes the fallen world, but it does not respond to this crisis through a religious *Sinngebung*—that is, by giving or establishing a religious meaning.[51] By granting primacy to the question of meaning, we remain in an anthropocentric framework. It might seem that the question of justification is similarly anthropocentric, but there is a crucial difference: meaning concerns how things stand before the self (*coram seipso*) while justification concerns how things ultimately stand before God (*coram Deo*). Justification takes me out of my closed circle of sense-giving by relocating the question of meaning *for me* and *for us* within the larger question of *truth*.[52] Christ is there for me, and he is there for us. As Bonhoeffer argues in his Christology lectures,

Christ stands in the center of human existence, but also in the center of history, nature, and all reality. Thus when God recognizes us in Christ and claims us as his own, we are taken out of ourselves and our sense of what is meaningful, since we inhabit a reality that is larger than our own egocentric or anthropocentric cares.

With this in mind we can understand Bonhoeffer's comment that the "unbiblical" (albeit not *anti*biblical) concept of meaning is "only one translation" of the biblical concept of promise (LPP 515). Promise does not only concern my own need for meaning nor my own salvation, but resituates me within a coming kingdom and a new creation.

That said, it has been objected that an orientation toward promise turns faith into a project of egoism. According to Levinas, the desire for a promised land or personal salvation is an obstacle to responsibility. True religion, like true humanity, is a departure from the egoistic concern for one's own being—whether in this life or an afterlife. Levinas argues for a religion within the limits of ethics alone, which excludes any self-seeking piety. In an interview from 1986, he suggests that we might be entering a new moment in history, in which "the good must be loved without promises." This would mean "a new form of faith"—a faith without triumph, but with a devotion to the proximity of the other, since this is where God breaks in and reverberates in being.[53] Similarly, in his essay "Signification and Sense" Levinas argues that the responsible self "acts without entering the Promised Land." Such responsible action is directed toward a future that is "indifferent to my death"; it means working for triumph "in a *time without me,*" with an orientation toward an "eschatology without hope for self or liberation with regard to my time."[54] The egoistic projects of the self are thereby surpassed. It is, however, rather surprising to discover that Ricoeur too critiques the desire for personal resurrection, in his view because it stems from an egocentric or infantile desire to survive one's own death. Ricoeur maintains that we need to learn to accept death, to recognize that the negativity of death is not the hostile nothingness of evil, but rather one aspect of the negativity that defines us as finite beings.[55] In the fragments and sketches that make up *Living Up to Death*, Ricoeur is seeking the basis for a joyful, even "cheerful" process of "living to the end."[56] This is not a call for inauthenticity or naïve optimism, though, since genuine hope requires a journey through what Freud calls the work of mourning, and it is necessary to carry this work through to its end. Ricoeur also draws on Meister Eckhart's notion of *detachment*—that is, relinquishing "any *attachment to self.*" This means living up to death without imaginary projections of an afterlife; it means renouncing the consolations of an eternity that continues, or runs parallel to, our current lived temporality; and it means surrendering one's desire for personal survival.

It is rather surprising that Ricoeur argues that the self must be disinterested when it comes to the question of personal resurrection, because at the level of philosophical and ethical discourse he defends the inter*est*edness of the self against Levinas, wagering that the *conatus essendi* belongs to the original goodness of creation. Yet Ricoeur proposes that in religious discourse the self must lose itself and give up the question of identity ("Who am I?"). This requires detachment from concern for one's own personal resurrection.[57]

With the question of personal resurrection in brackets, Ricoeur suggests a reinterpretation of resurrection that is "in complete accord" with his interpretation of Christ's resurrection.[58] The cross shows us that life and love are stronger than death, because the crucifixion is Jesus' triumph over death through service and sacrifice for others. But to put it in Levinasian terms, Ricoeur's view is that Jesus surrenders his life for the sake of a triumph in a *time without him,* that is, without him in personal, bodily form. The victory consists in the manner of Jesus' sacrificial and self-giving death, which allows Jesus to be resurrected as Christ in the spirit of the church community. The word of the cross and resurrection continues to speak, and thereby refigures the self and its being-in-the-world. Christ incarnates the true word that life is stronger than death. This means saying Yes to the polyphony of life. In contrast to Heidegger's theme of authentic being-towards-death, Ricoeur describes a being *until* death, a living *up to* death in such a way that the act of dying becomes an act of life.[59]

The self overcomes death through the character of its act of dying, but also through the memory of others. Just as Christ was resurrected in the life of the church community, I hope that my life will be "extended horizontally" in the lives of the others who continue to live after my death. This is an eschatological hope—albeit an eschatology without hope for myself: I do not hope for my own survival or self-identity after death, because my desire to be is directed toward those who will live on after me. By renouncing my concern for my own *ipseity,* I am able to transfer my love of life to the *other.*[60] According to Ricoeur, this transfer finds expression in a saying of Jesus: "The one who wants to save his existence will lose it. But the one who will lose his existence will save it."[61] The salvation in question, however, lies in the ethical transfer, in which my desire to be is directed toward the future of those who will survive me.[62]

Ricoeur also hints at the possibility of a vertical dimension—the possibility that my life may be "transcended vertically in the 'memory of God.'"[63] To be remembered by God is to have one's existence justified, in the sense that its meaning is inscribed in God's memory. Ricoeur describes this with an allusion to Irenaeus's notion of recapitulation (*anacephalaeosis*): "Nothing is lost of what has been." I have not existed in vain.[64] That is the vertical dimension of hope. Yet Ricoeur only suggests this possibility on the far side of detachment, and he is hesitant to assert too much—not only because his fragmentary meditations on these themes are "purely exploratory,"[65] but also because they threaten to undermine the work of mourning and detachment. I cannot be truly detached if I am holding on to the consolation of an imaginary model of survival. So Ricoeur appeals to a certain conception of grace: "Nothing is owed to me. I expect nothing for myself; I ask for nothing. I have renounced—I try to renounce!—claiming, demanding. I say: God, you will do as you will with me. Maybe nothing at all. I accept no longer being."[66]

Some may find Ricoeur's meditation on death noble in its own way, but it is surprising that he is so adamant about bracketing the desire for personal resurrection. Why is the *conatus essendi* suddenly inadmissible when asking the question of resurrection? Why is the desire to *be* only legitimate for life here and now? What if the goodness of creation includes a desire to flourish in the new creation? What if the catechism is correct and the chief end of the human being is to glorify God and fully enjoy him forever?[67] One might object that this enjoyment is still incurved and egoistic, but in response we recall that this enjoyment is only possible once the self is broken out of its incurvature. The incurved self is incapable of enjoying God *as God*. The self needs to be liberated from its incurvature in order to enjoy God, and (dare we suggest?) to enjoy oneself and others in their creaturely being, as human beings who no longer hate their limits but flourish within them.

The promise of resurrection is a scandal; it is offensive to our self-understanding. It does not fit with the culturally available schema of belief of our scientifically disenchanted world. It also conflicts with the dualism of so much popular spirituality and religiosity, which anticipates an afterworld populated by disembodied souls. But the promise of resurrection is also offensive to a significant trend in Continental philosophy, which assumes that religion and ethics must be detached and disinterested. Allied with a strong hermeneutic of suspicion, this demand for ethical disinterestedness exposes every gesture of faith and responsibility as egoistic. We cannot dispense with questions of ethics, and since a pure ethical gesture is impossible, the discourse of ethics resigns itself to a state of aporia. These ethical sensibilities have also informed the philosophical assumption that faith requires a state of detached, disinterested purity. But here again philosophy determines the a priori limits of what revelation can disclose. What if there is more to the promise of resurrection than an egoistic and narcissistic project of self-preservation? As Bonhoeffer puts it, we should "find and love God in what he actually gives us," including those times of earthly enjoyment and happiness as well as (we might add) the promise of resurrection. If we insist on rejecting this possibility for the sake of some superior ethical seriousness, we risk falling into a religious vanity of our own—as Bonhoeffer puts it, that of trying to be "more pious than God" (LPP 228).

With all of that said, we must still confront the other major objection to hoping for one's own personal resurrection. This objection is put most sharply by Nietzsche, who sees this hope as a nihilistic denial of this world. On his account Christianity deserves a large part of the blame for the development of nihilism, since it proclaims redemption from the world and the body for the sake of a heavenly nothingness and an illusory soul substance. From a Nietzschean perspective, our cruciform interpretation of the self would be complicit in this problem. A self defined by the cross is a self pierced by the nails of nihilism. In response to the cross, Nietzsche presents a Dionysian religiosity. In one of his last writings, he distinguishes two types of *homo religiosus:* the pagan versus the Christian. These two ways of life and devotion are constituted by two very different figures: Dionysus and the Crucified.[68] Both figures suffer and die as martyrs, but they embody starkly different interpretations of the meaning of suffering. "The god on the cross is a curse on life, a signpost to seek redemption from life." By contrast, Dionysus exhibits a tragic interpretation of suffering—namely, that "being is counted as *holy enough* to justify even a monstrous amount of suffering." The tragic human being is strong, capable, and has the abundance of spirit to affirm life even amidst the harshest suffering. Dionysian suffering pronounces an unqualified affirmation of life: "Dionysus cut to pieces is a *promise* of life: it will be eternally reborn and return again from destruction." The true promise of meaning and value does not lie in redemption from the world, but in the eternal recurrence of the same. To overcome nihilism would be to say an unequivocal Yes to this eternal return, thereby affirming life in all of its diverse aspects and moments.[69]

Bonhoeffer's nonreligious interpretation of Christian faith is in many ways a response to Nietzsche's objections. This is not surprising, since his reading of Nietzsche is one reason why he is so attuned to the worldly, embodied character of faith.[70] Feuerbach's emphasis on the wholeness of the human being is also an influence here,[71] but the theme of the *totus homo* did not arise with these nineteenth-century thinkers. According to Bonhoeffer, the religious opposition between inner and outer is not biblical. Scripture concerns the human being as a whole (*anthropos teleios*); thus when it speaks of the heart it does not mean an intimate, inner life, but rather the whole human being in relation to God. Human beings "live as much from their 'outer' to their 'inner' selves as from their 'inner' to their 'outer' selves" (LPP 457). To borrow Merleau-Ponty's terms, scripture understands human being as a chiasmic intertwining between the inner and outer.[72]

The relegation of faith to religious interiority typically goes hand in hand with a dualistic account of the self, in which the soul is the locus of salvation while body (*Soma*) is mistakenly identified with flesh (*Sarx*).[73] But faith is not a retreat from the outer, the physical, and the sensible into an inner, disembodied spiritual realm. On the contrary, our embodied being is the very possibility of existing before God. In *Creation and Fall*, Bonhoeffer observes that the human being who is created in God's image is a creature taken from the earth and bound to the earth in the very heart of its being. The physical body is not a dispensable shell or instrument of the spirit, and it is certainly not the external prison of an internal soul. The human being does not *have* a body and soul, but rather *is* body and soul. The human is an embodied being, and therefore those "who reject their bodies reject their existence before God the Creator" (CF 76–77). It is the body that bears the image of God and enables us to exist as relational beings:

Religion within the Limits of the Penultimate? 195

> Humankind created in this way is humankind as the image of God. It is the image of God not in spite of but precisely in its bodily nature. For in their bodily nature human beings are related to the earth and to other bodies, they are there for others and are dependent upon others. In their bodily existence human beings find their brothers and sisters and find the earth. As such creatures human beings of earth and spirit are "like" God, their creator. (CF 79)

This is why Christ calls embodied human beings not to a life of interior piety, but to follow after him in the world. Faith is not an escape from the body, but a redemption *in and as* body: "Because Adam is created as body, Adam is also redeemed as body." Moreover, God effects this redemption by coming as body, as the Word incarnate in flesh and blood—in the concreteness of the man Jesus and in the sacrament of the Lord's Supper (CF 79).

Furthermore, it is *as* bodies that we trust and hope in the promise of resurrection. In this regard Christian faith differs fundamentally from myths and cults of redemption, which stem from a desire to escape the body and the burdens, responsibilities, and suffering of this world. By contrast, the promise of resurrection sends the human being back into worldly existence in an entirely new way. "Unlike believers in the redemption myths, Christians do not have an ultimate escape route out of their earthly tasks and difficulties into eternity. Like Christ ('My God . . . why have you forsaken me?'), they have to drink the cup of earthly life to the last drop, and only when they do this is the Crucified and Risen One with them, and they are crucified and resurrected with Christ" (LPP 447–48). This means that this world is not to be disregarded or condemned. Faith means living without remainder in this world, without seeking an afterworldly escape. As Bonhoeffer writes, it is only "when one loves life and the earth so much that without it everything seems to be lost and at its end may one believe in the resurrection of the dead and a new world" (LPP 213).

Redemption myths arise at human limit-experiences (*Grenzerfahrungen*), but Christ confronts us at the center of our lives as human beings in the world (LPP 447–48). With this point Bonhoeffer responds to Nietzsche's celebration of the Dionysian figure who "takes into itself and *redeems* the contradictions and questionable aspects of existence!" For Nietzsche, this is a "religious affirmation of life, life whole and not denied or in part."[74] A central premise in Bonhoeffer's nonreligious interpretation of Christianity is that the "religious act" is something partial, fragmentary, on the margins, in the gaps. But Christ stands in the center of our existence as human beings and calls us to life (LPP 482). Faith is not about making the self into a *homo religiosus,* but into a human being in the fullest sense. Faith is not about interiority, but about the whole human being—the *anthropos teleios*—in relation to God (LPP 456).

This is not, however, simply an affirmation of the status quo, because the promise of resurrection entails a new creation, a promise of healing and liberation—and this is something that Nietzsche will not countenance because it requires the recognition that there might be something wrong with the world. We can highlight this conflict of interpretations by contrasting Nietzsche's theme of eternal recurrence with the theme of recapitulation. Like Ricoeur, Bonhoeffer appropriates this theme from Irenaeus; yet in Bonhoeffer's use its significance is much more robust. In the Incarnation, Christ sums up all things in himself, so that in the fullness of time all of creation will be gathered together and reconstituted in Christ.[75] In Bonhoeffer's words, "nothing is lost" (LPP 229). This hope is not for an escape from the world, but instead reinvests the self in the world with the promise that Christ will give the world back—not as the eternal return of the same, but with a genuine newness. Similar to Kierkegaard's category of repetition, the world is given back the same, and yet different.[76] As Bonhoeffer puts it, in being taken up in Christ, all things are reconstituted and restored as they were meant to be (LPP 230–31).

The promise of resurrection and recapitulation makes Kierkegaardian repetition possible. The self receives the world back, but in a new way, so that the self is now free for the world in a way that Nietzschean *amor fati* cannot allow—despite the various figures Nietzsche uses to affirm the world. For example, Nietzsche's Zarathustra points to the child as a figure of new creation. In the first of his speeches, Zarathustra describes the three metamorphoses: from spirit to camel, from camel to lion, and from lion to the child. The lion opposes the old values of "Thou shalt" by asserting "I will." The lion represents the creation of a new freedom, but the creation of new values—this magnificent, terrifying task—falls to the child. Only the child can lead the way, because "the child is innocence and forgetting, a new beginning, a game, a self-propelled wheel, a first movement, a sacred 'Yes.'"[77] For Zarathustra the child is a quasi-eschatological figure of new creativity and a hope for Nietzsche's new humanity, which will overcome humanity as it currently is. Just as Nietzsche opposes Dionysus to the Crucified, so his *Übermensch* stands opposed to the new humanity (*deuteros anthropos*) of Christ. Both are eschatological figures.[78] Nietzsche's eschatology depends on the paradoxical struggle for self-overcoming, and along with it the tragic heroism that joyfully embraces the eternal recurrence of the same. But at root this circular eschatology is another instance of the *homo incurvatus in se*—a despairing gesture that refuses the possibility of salvation, insisting instead on a willed affirmation of fate. If we turn the hermeneutic of suspicion back on Nietzsche, we recognize Anti-Climacus's description of the demonic despair in which the self refuses to be healed or have its suffering alleviated. According to Anti-Climacus's diagnosis, in demonic despair the self spitefully clings to its misery as evidence against the goodness of existence (SUD 72–74). Yet here Nietzsche introduces a further dialectical turn that Anti-Climacus does not quite anticipate: rather than embracing suffering in protest against of existence, he insists that the goodness and holiness of existence consists in precisely this misery. Everything depends on affirming the world as it is. The eternal recurrence of the same must be the ultimate, because if there is a point beyond this closed circle, it devalues this world. One can only overcome nihilism through the will to meaning; the meaning and value of this world depend on my willing it to be so. As a result, the self and the world both remain bound to the ontology of self-justification.

One problem with the Nietzschean view is that the world is not free to be the world, nor is the human being free to be human. Consider Zarathustra's remark: If there were Gods, how could I bear not to be God? Thus there is no God. Likewise, if the world and the human being are justified by an ultimate word (an affirming *Yes*), how could I bear not to be the one who speaks this word of affirmation? How could I stand to be dependent on a word from outside of myself? Thus there is no external, justifying Word. These conclusions betray the condition of a self and a world curved in on themselves, locked into the burden of self-justification.

By contrast, the promise of resurrection follows the logic of the gift: it is unconditional, and it opens a genuine futurity and new creativity in a way that Nietzsche's tragic *amor fati* simply cannot. The world is set free to be the world, and the human being to be human, because they recognize themselves as penultimate. They are no longer bound to the tragic burden of self-justification. They have their identity in reference to the ultimate. However, this reference to an outside does not devalue the world because it is not dualistic. The ultimate and the penultimate, like the sacred and profane, the revelational and rational, are not dualistically opposed; they have their unity in the one Christ-reality (*Christuswirklichkeit*). In Christ the world finds its true identity. Consequently, the eschatological word of justification does not devalue the world; it pronounces a polemical No against the world's false self-understanding, but only for the sake of a *better* worldliness (E 60). By recognizing itself as penultimate, the world is free to flourish as the world, and the cruciform self is free to flourish as a human being.

Notes

1. Philosophy, the Cross, and Human Being

The epigraph is from G. W. F. Hegel, *Lectures on the Philosophy of Religion, Volume III: The Consummate Religion*, ed. Peter C. Hodgson, trans. R. F. Brown, P. C. Hodgson, and J. M. Stewart, with H. S. Harris (Berkeley: University of California Press, 1985), p. 346.

1. According to Kant, this is one of the four primary philosophical questions. The first question is that of metaphysics: *What can I know?* The second concerns morals: *What should I do?* The third raises the concerns of religion: *What may I hope for?* Finally, Kant adds the anthropological question: *What is the human being?* Kant presents this in his *Logic*, cited in Manfred Kuehn's introduction to *Anthropology from a Pragmatic Point of View*, trans. and ed. Robert B. Louden (Cambridge: Cambridge University Press, 2006), pp. xi–xii. Kuehn also argues that Kant did not approach this question with fundamentally ontological concerns, contra Heidegger's reading in *Kant and the Problem of Metaphysics*. Instead, Kant proceeds "from a pragmatic point of view"—not concerning a given human nature or essence, but what the human being "as a free-acting being makes of himself, or can and should make of himself" (p. 3).

2. Hannah Arendt, *The Human Condition* (Chicago: University of Chicago Press, 1958).

3. See Jean Greisch, *Qui sommes-nous? Chemins phénoménologiques vers l'homme* (Louvain: Peeters, 2009).

4. George Herbert, *Poems* (New York: Alfred A. Knopf, 2004), p. 213.

5. Søren Kierkegaard, *Concluding Unscientific Postscript to Philosophical Fragments*, trans. and ed. Howard V. Hong and Edna H. Hong (Princeton, N.J.: Princeton University Press, 1992), p. 15.

6. "Gott selbst liegt tot / Am Kreuz ist er gestorben." From Johannes Rist's 1641 hymn "O Traurigkeit, O Herzeleid." Hegel cites this hymn in his *Lectures on the Philosophy of Religion*, pp. 125, 326.

7. Nietzsche, *Beyond Good and Evil*, #46, in *The Basic Writings of Nietzsche*, ed. and trans. Walter Kaufmann (New York: Modern Library, 1968), p. 250. Cf. Oswald Bayer, "The Word of the Cross," trans. John R. Betz, *Lutheran Quarterly* 9 (1995), p. 53 n. 3.

8. Martin Hengel, *Crucifixion in the Ancient World and the Folly of the Message of the Cross*, in *The Cross of the Son of God*, trans. John Bowden (London: SCM Press, 1986), p. 102.

9. *Pro Rabirico* 5:16, quoted in Alexandra R. Brown, *The Cross and Human Transformation: Paul's Apocalyptic Word in 1 Corinthians* (Minneapolis: Fortress Press, 1995), p. 159 n. 20.

10. J. Louis Martyn, quoted in Alexandra R. Brown, *The Cross and Human Transformation: Paul's Apocalyptic Word in 1 Corinthians* (Minneapolis: Fortress Press, 1995), p. 159 n. 20.

11. Hengel, *Crucifixion in the Ancient World*, p. 110. Hengel quotes Walter Bauer's observation regarding Christianity's Jewish and pagan critics: "The enemies of Christianity

always referred to the disgraceful death of Jesus with great emphasis and malicious pleasure. A god or son of god dying on the cross! That was enough to put paid to the new religion" (p. 111). Hengel cites numerous sources such as Pliny, Tacitus, Minicius Felix, and Suetonius regarding the evident perversity of this new superstition (pp. 93ff.).

12. As Hengel notes, in many Greco-Roman documents one finds "the idea that offensive happenings should not be ascribed to revered divine beings or demi-gods themselves, but only to their 'representations.'" *Crucifixion in the Ancient World*, p. 108.

13. Hengel, *Crucifixion in the Ancient World*, p. 110.

14. This excess of signification is compounded by the fact that the cross, more than almost any other religious symbol, is so widely dispersed throughout so many different cultures, and conveys so many diverse and conflicting meanings. Thus understanding the cross requires an endless hermeneutic. In addition to evoking sacrifice, suffering, shame, burden, redemption, grace, and love, the cross has also been detached from specifically religious understandings—as with its use as a symbol in medicine and fashion. Moreover, the cross connotes for some people such destructive forces as racism (in the burning cross of the Ku Klux Klan and as a locus of accusation in anti-Semitism) and nationalist aggression. See the preface to *Cross-Examinations: Readings on the Meaning of the Cross Today*, ed. Marit Trelstad (Minneapolis: Augsburg Fortress Press, 2006), p. xiii.

15. Søren Kierkegaard, *Philosophical Fragments*, ed. and trans. Howard V. Hong and Edna H. Hong (Princeton, N.J.: Princeton University Press, 1985), p. 37.

16. G. W. F. Hegel, *Faith and Knowledge*, trans. Walter Cerf and H. S. Harris (Albany: State University of New York Press, 1977), p. 190.

17. Ibid., p. 191.

18. G. W. F. Hegel, *Phenomenology of Spirit*, trans. A. V. Miller (Oxford: Oxford University Press, 1977), p. 475 (translation slightly altered).

19. Alan E. Lewis, *Between Cross and Resurrection: A Theology of Holy Saturday* (Grand Rapids, Mich.: Eerdmans, 2001), p. 241.

20. It is telling that, as Eberhard Jüngel observes, the name Jesus Christ never appears in the entire *Phenomenology of Spirit*. See *God as the Mystery of the World: On the Foundation of the Theology of the Crucified One in the Dispute between Theism and Atheism*, trans. Darrell L. Guder (Grand Rapids, Mich.: William B. Eerdmans, 1983), p. 89.

21. Hegel, *Phenomenology of Spirit*, p. 476.

22. For a detailed discussion of Hegel's thinking of the cross, showing what theology can learn from Hegel and where it must part ways with him, see Jüngel's *God as the Mystery of the World*, esp. pp. 63–100.

23. Bayer charges Kierkegaard, and even Barth, with this sort of compromise ("The Word of the Cross," pp. 49–50). Whether these allegations are warranted is a question for another discussion.

24. To paraphrase 2 Timothy 3:5.

25. "Too much: because it makes bold with words and concepts at a point where the Word of God is silent, suffers and dies, in order to reveal what no philosophy can know, except through faith, namely God's ever greater Trinitarian love; and in order, also, to vanquish what no philosophy can make an end of, human dying so that the human totality may be restored in God. Too little, because philosophy does not measure that abyss into which the word sinks down, and, having no inkling of it, closes the hiatus, or deliberately festoons the appalling thing with garlands." *Mysterium Paschale: The Mystery*

of Easter, trans. Adain Nichols, O.P. (San Francisco: Ignatius Press, 1990), p. 65 (emphasis mine).

26. See von Balthasar's *Mysterium Paschale*, p. 66: "If philosophy is not willing to content itself with, either, speaking abstractly of being, or with thinking concretely of the earthly and worldly (and no further), then it must at once empty itself in order to 'know nothing . . . except Jesus Christ and him crucified' (I Corinthians 2, 2). Then it may, starting out from this source, go on to 'impart a secret and hidden wisdom of God, which God decreed before the ages for our glorification' (ibid., 2, 7). This proclamation, however, rises up over a deeper silence and a darker abyss than pure philosophy can know."

27. For a helpful treatment of Luther's (early) anthropology see Steven E. Ozment's *Homo Spiritualis: A Comparative Study of the Anthropology of Johannes Tauler, Jean Gerson and Martin Luther (1509-16) in the Context of Their Theological Thought* (Leiden: E. J. Brill, 1969).

28. In one of his earliest books, Jaroslav Pelikan calls for a distinctly Lutheran philosophy, arguing that Kierkegaard provides the best model for such an undertaking. *From Luther to Kierkegaard: A Study in the History of Theology* (St. Louis, Mo.: Concordia Publishing House, 1950), pp. 119-20.

29. I borrow this term from Oswald Bayer, "The Doctrine of Justification and Ontology," trans. Christine Helmer, *Neue Zeitschrift für Systematische Theologie und Religionsphilosophie* 43, issue 1 (2001): p. 49.

30. Eberhard Jüngel, *Justification: The Heart of the Christian Faith. A Theological Study with an Ecumenical Purpose*, trans. Jeffrey F. Cayzer (Edinburgh: T & T Clark, 2001), p. 54.

31. Kierkegaard, JP 143.

32. Louis Mackey, "From Autobiography to Theology: Augustine's *Confessiones*," in *Peregrinations of the Word: Essays in Medieval Philosophy* (Ann Arbor: University of Michigan Press, 1997), p. 55.

33. Barth, *The Humanity of God* (Atlanta: John Knox Press, 1960), p. 40. Barth's concern was with liberal Protestant theology, which was its own sort of *theologia gloriae*; Barth issued his early dialectical/*Krisis* theology as a sharp challenge to his theological milieu, which confined theological inquiry to the questions of human religious consciousness.

34. Matthew 16:25. This is the translation quoted in Ricoeur's text.

35. Ricoeur, "Whoever Loses Their Life for My Sake Will Find It" (FS 288).

36. Ibid.

37. Later in his life, however, Ricoeur claimed to feel a greater freedom to explore the overlap between philosophy and theology, even characterizing his work in *Thinking Biblically* as "philosophical theology or theological philosophy." See Ricoeur's interview with Richard Kearney in *Debates in Continental Philosophy: Conversations with Contemporary Thinkers* (New York: Fordham University Press, 2004), p. 43. Cf. Ricoeur, "Ethics and Human Capability," in *Paul Ricoeur and Contemporary Moral Thought*, ed. John Wall and William Schweiker (New York: Routledge, 2002), p. 283.

38. Thus for Hegel, philosophy is theology. "It presents the reconciliation of God with himself and with nature, showing that nature, otherness, is implicitly divine, and that the raising of itself to reconciliation is on the one hand what finite spirit implicitly is, while on the other hand it arrives at this reconciliation, or brings it forth, in world history."

Note the last point, namely that this philosophical theology, or theological philosophy, achieves this reconciliation in history. *Lectures on the Philosophy of Religion*, p. 347.

39. Ricoeur, "Religion, Atheism, and Faith," in *The Conflict of Interpretations: Essays in Hermeneutics*, ed. Don Ihde, p. 460 (Evanston, Ill.: Northwestern University Press, 1974).

40. Barth, *Evangelical Theology: An Introduction*, trans. Grover Foley (Grand Rapids, Mich.: William B. Eerdmans, 1963), p. xiii.

41. Mackey, "From Autobiography to Theology," p. 55.

42. Plantinga makes this point in response to Pope John Paul II's encyclical *Fides et Ratio*, in *Books & Culture*, July/August 1999, p. 35. Also see Charles Taylor's essay "A Philosopher's Postscript: Engaging the Citadel of Secular Reason," in *Reason and the Reasons of Faith*, ed. Paul J. Griffiths and Reinhard Hütter, pp. 343-44 (New York and London: T & T Clark, 2005).

43. Ricoeur, "Approaching the Human Person," *Ethical Perspectives* 6, no. 1 (1999): p. 45.

44. Ibid.

45. See the essays in John D. Zizioulas, *Communion and Otherness: Further Studies in Personhood and the Church*, ed. Paul McPartlan (New York and London: T & T Clark, 2006).

46. John Macmurray, *Persons in Relation* (Amherst, N.Y.: Humanity Books, 1961).

47. Robert Spaemann, *Persons: The Difference Between "Someone" and "Something,"* trans. Oliver O'Donovan (Oxford: Oxford University Press, 2007).

48. See chapters 10 and 11 in Robert Sokolowski, *Christian Faith and Human Understanding: Studies on the Eucharist, Trinity, and the Human Person* (Washington, D.C.: The Catholic University of America Press, 2006).

49. In his essay cited above, "Approaching the Human Person," Ricoeur goes on to explain what the term "self" adds to the discussion of personhood. The notion of self-esteem is central to Ricoeur's account of the human person, because self-esteem is the recognition of oneself as capable of acting intentionally and responsibly ("according to reflective reasons") in the events and institutions of the world. Having said that, Ricoeur carefully distinguishes self-esteem from egoism or solipsism; there is a crucial difference between the *self* and the *ego* that centers on itself (p. 46).

50. Heidegger, "Letter on Humanism," in *Basic Writings*, rev. ed., ed. David Farrell Krell (San Francisco: HarperCollins, 1977, 1993), pp. 220, 224-26, 233, 237.

51. Martin Heidegger, *Ontology—The Hermeneutics of Facticity*, trans. John van Buren (Bloomington: Indiana University Press, 1999), pp. 21, 23-24.

52. In his *Soliloquies*, Augustine thematizes the task of faith seeking understanding as a search to understand God and the soul. Asked by a personified Reason what he wills to know, Augustine answers: "I desire to know God and the soul. R.—Nothing more? A.—Nothing at all. R.—Then begin your seeking." *Soliloquies*, 1.2.7. in *Augustine: On the Inner Life of the Mind*, ed. Robert E. Meagher (Indianapolis: Hackett, 1998), p. 36. What becomes clear in the course of Augustine's *oeuvre* is that knowledge of God and knowledge of the soul are inseparably connected. Cf. Book I of Augustine's *Confessions*.

53. Bernard of Clairvaux, *The Two-Fold Knowledge: Readings on the Knowledge of Self and the Knowledge of God. Selected and Translated from the Works of Saint Bernard of Clairvaux*, trans. and ed. Franz Posset (Milwaukee: Marquette University Press, 2004).

54. Thesis 17 of Luther's *Disputation Concerning Man*: "Nor is there any hope that man in this principle part can himself know what he is until he sees himself in his origin

which is God" (LW 34 p. 138). Also see Bernard Lohse, *Martin Luther's Theology: Its Historical and Systematic Development,* trans. and ed. Roy A. Harrisville (Minneapolis: Fortress Press, 1999), pp. 39–41. For an excellent discussion of Luther on reason's inability to define itself, see Ernstpeter Maurer's essay "The Perplexity and Complexity of Sinful and Redeemed Reason," in *Reason and the Reasons of Faith,* ed. Paul J. Griffiths and Reinhard Hütter, pp. 194–220 (New York and London: T & T Clark, 2005).

55. Calvin's *Institutes* opens with the same Augustinian point. Cf. Jens Zimmermann, *Recovering Theological Hermeneutics: An Incarnational-Trinitarian Theory of Interpretation* (Grand Rapids, Mich.: Baker Academic, 2004), p. 30.

2. The Hermeneutics of the Self

1. Saint Augustine, *Confessions,* XI. xiv (17), trans. Henry Chadwick (Oxford: Oxford University Press, 1991), p. 230.

2. Taylor, "The Moral Topography of the Self," in *Hermeneutics and Psychological Theory: Interpretive Perspectives on Personality, Psychotherapy, and Psychopathology,* ed. Stanley B. Messer, Louis A. Sass, and Robert L. Woolfolk, pp. 298–99 (New Brunswick, N.J.: Rutgers University Press, 1988).

3. Taylor charts this development in great detail in his *Sources of the Self: The Making of the Modern Identity* (Cambridge, Mass.: Harvard University Press, 1989).

4. Heidegger, *Ontology—The Hermeneutics of Facticity,* trans. John van Buren (Bloomington: Indiana University Press, 1999), p. 11.

5. Benjamin Crowe offers a helpful Heideggerian definition of philosophical theology along these lines in his essay "On the Track of the Fugitive Gods: Heidegger, Luther, Hölderlin," *The Journal of Religion* 87, issue 2 (2007): p. 185.

6. Ricoeur, "On Interpretation," TA 12.

7. Ibid.

8. Nietzsche, "On Truth and Lie in an Extra-Moral Sense," in *The Portable Nietzsche,* ed. and trans. Walter Kaufmann (New York: Viking Penguin 1968, 1982), p. 44.

9. Ricoeur, "The Critique of Religion," in *The Philosophy of Paul Ricoeur: An Anthology of His Work,* ed. Charles E. Reagan and David Stewart (Boston: Beacon Press, 1978), pp. 213–14.

10. Nietzsche, "On Truth and Lie," p. 46.

11. Ibid., p. 45.

12. The famous passage goes as follows: "What, then, is truth? A mobile army of metaphors, metonyms, and anthropomorphisms—in short, a sum of human relations, which have been enhanced, transposed, and embellished poetically and rhetorically, and which after long use seem firm, canonical, and obligatory to a people: truths are illusions about which one has forgotten that this is what they are; metaphors which are worn out and without sensuous power; coins which have lost their pictures and now matter only as metal, no longer as coins" ("On Truth and Lie," pp. 46–47).

13. See nos. 475, 476, 477 in Nietzsche, *The Will to Power,* trans. Walter Kaufmann and R. J. Hollingdale (New York: Vintage, 1967), pp. 263–64.

14. See OA 15.

15. Nietzsche, *On the Genealogy of Morals,* First Essay, Section 13, in *Basic Writings of Nietzsche,* ed. and trans. Walter Kaufmann (New York: The Modern Library, 1968), p. 481.

16. Ricoeur agrees with Nietzsche regarding the linguistic mediation of self-reflection. He disagrees, however, with Nietzsche's reduction of language, concepts, and truth to ar-

bitrary convention. See, for instance, Ricoeur's engagement with Nietzsche's account of metaphor in Study 8 of *The Rule of Metaphor: Multidisciplinary Studies of the Creation of Meaning in Language,* trans. Robert Czerny (Toronto: University of Toronto Press, 1977). Ricoeur insists on the potency of language (including figurative language) to refer to reality. In particular, figurative language has the ability to disclose being in the mode of possibility—disclosing possible worlds, along with the ability to inhabit those possibilities. We will return to this point below.

17. Nietzsche, *The Will to Power,* no. 492. "The danger of the direct questioning of the subject *about* the subject and of all self-reflection of the spirit lies in this, that it could be useful and important for one's activity to interpret oneself *falsely.* That is why we question the body and reject the evidence of the sharpened senses: we try, if you like, to see whether the inferior parts themselves cannot enter into communication with us."

18. For Ricoeur's phenomenology of *l'homme capable,* the capable human being, see *The Course of Recognition,* trans. David Pellauer (Cambridge, Mass.: Harvard University Press, 2005), pp. 89–109.

19. Maurice Merleau-Ponty, *Phenomenology of Perception,* trans. Colin Smith (London: Routledge & Kegan Paul, 1962), pp. 137–39. With *Freedom and Nature* Ricoeur envisioned a practical extension of Merleau-Ponty's *Phenomenology of Perception.* Ricoeur later viewed this goal as naïve, since he had underestimated the degree to which Merleau-Ponty's text was already occupied with the question of the practical and how thoroughly it was influenced by Heidegger's analyses of care and being-in-the-world. "Intellectual Autobiography," in *The Philosophy of Paul Ricoeur,* The Library of Living Philosophers, p. 11.

20. Charles Taylor, "Embodied Agency," in *Merleau-Ponty: Critical Essays,* ed. Henry Pietersma, pp. 1, 4–5 (Washington, D.C.: University Press of America, 1989).

21. Marcel is another important influence in *Freedom and Nature.* From Marcel, Ricoeur inherits the themes of incarnate freedom and the *corps propre*—i.e., the mystery of one's own body (FN 14, 15, 17). My own body is a mystery; it is not a problem to be solved. The first-person perspective of incarnate being is irreducible to a third-person perspective—a thing that can be accounted for in objective, impersonal terms.

22. Ricoeur cites *Cartesian Meditations* and the 1930 afterword to *Ideas* as the most developed account of Husserl's idealist moments. "Phenomenology and Hermeneutics," TA 26.

23. Ricoeur, "On Interpretation," TA 13–14.

24. See Edmund Husserl, *The Crisis of European Sciences and Transcendental Phenomenology,* trans. David Carr (Evanston, Ill.: Northwestern University Press, 1970), pp. 103–89.

25. Ibid., pp. 173–74.

26. Ricoeur, "On Interpretation," TA 14.

27. Ibid., TA 19. Ricoeur identifies his notion of participatory belonging with Heidegger's *being-in-the-world*: "Phenomenology and Hermeneutics," TA 30.

28. Ricoeur, "On Interpretation," TA 14–15.

29. Taylor, "Embodied Agency," pp. 1–2.

30. Michael Polanyi, *Personal Knowledge: Towards a Post-Critical Philosophy* (Chicago: University of Chicago Press, 1958, 1962), p. 59. Note that equipment is not limited to hammers and other things we normally think of as tools. As Polanyi observes, when we use language to speak, read, and write, we "extend our bodily equipment and become

intelligent human beings. We may say that when we learn to use language, or a probe, or a tool, and thus make ourselves aware of these things as we are of our body, we *interiorize* these things and *make ourselves dwell in them*. Such extensions of ourselves develop new faculties in us; our whole education operates in this way; as each of us interiorizes our cultural heritage, he grows into a person seeing the world and experiencing life in terms of this outlook. Interiorization bestows meaning." "The Logic of Tacit Inference," in *Knowing and Being: Essays by Michael Polanyi*, ed. Marjorie Grene (Chicago: University of Chicago Press, 1969), p. 148.

31. BT, §§31–32. Cf. Ricoeur, "On Interpretation," TA 14–15.

32. That is, the fore-having, fore-sight, and fore-conception we bring to any interpretation (BT 192–94).

33. Hans-Georg Gadamer, *Truth and Method*, 2nd rev. ed., trans. Joel Weinsheimer and Donald G. Marshall (New York: Continuum, 1989), pp. 270–80.

34. It is therefore a mistake to suggest, as Bruce Reichenbach does, that the hermeneutical circle is something to which interpretation "falls prey," and which is in need of "a solution." See his essay "Divine Revelation: Discernment and Interpretation," in *For Faith and Clarity: Philosophical Contributions to Christian Theology*, ed. James K. Beilby, pp. 109–10 (Grand Rapids, Mich.: Baker Academic Books, 2006).

35. Gadamer, *Truth and Method*, p. 97.

36. Ricoeur, "On Interpretation," TA 13.

37. For example, in "On Interpretation" Ricoeur writes that "the shortest path from the self to itself lies in the speech of the other" (TA 16).

38. Ricoeur, "Philosophical and Theological Hermeneutics," *Sciences Religieuses/Studies in Religion* 5 no. 1 (Summer 1975): p. 30. (Cf. "Philosophical Hermeneutics and Biblical Hermeneutics" in TA 89–101.)

39. In his words, "there is no self-understanding that is not *mediated* by signs, symbols, and texts." "On Interpretation," TA 15.

40. Ricoeur supports this claim by pointing to Hegel, whose *Phenomenology of Spirit* showed that perception and desire are both articulated linguistically. Freud deepened this insight by showing that language allows for the revelation and clarification of experience that is buried, concealed, and distorted. This belief grounds the practice of psychoanalysis as a talking cure. And, Ricoeur adds, "since speech is heard before it is uttered, the shortest path from the self to itself lies in the speech of the other, which leads me across the open space of signs" ("On Interpretation," TA 16).

41. Ricoeur will later describe this as a second-order reference. See "Imagination in Discourse and Action," TA 175.

42. "Meaning does not originate in the conscious, reflecting subject but comes to him from the outside, from his encounter with certain thought-provoking symbols mediated by his culture. Meaning is the result, not of a work of constitution, but of an effort of appropriation." G. B. Madison, "Ricoeur and the Hermeneutics of the Subject," in *The Philosophy of Paul Ricoeur*, The Library of Living Philosophers, vol. XXII, ed. Lewis Edwin Hahn, p. 78 (Chicago and LaSalle, Ill.: Open Court, 1995). Of course, individual poets, novelists, and thinkers certainly do create new symbols, metaphors, and meanings. These semantic innovations are genuinely innovative, but they are not created *ex nihilo* by a sovereign, self-grounding ego. The innovation occurs within the current of a preceding linguistic tradition, which provides the framework of meaning within which any creativity is possible.

43. Cf. Madison, "Ricoeur and the Hermeneutics of the Subject," p. 79.

44. Paul Ricoeur, *Time and Narrative*, 3 vols., trans. Kathleen McLaughlin and David Pellauer (Chicago: University of Chicago Press, 1984–88).

45. Ricoeur, *Time and Narrative*, vol. 1, p. ix.

46. Richard Kearney provides many concrete illustrations of this relationship in his book *On Stories* (London and New York: Routledge, 2002).

47. Ricoeur, "On Interpretation," TA 17.

48. Ibid., TA 18.

49. See *The Symbolism of Evil* (SE 348).

50. It is also worth noting that Barth's commentary came out several years prior to *Being and Time*. See Jens Zimmermann, *Recovering Theological Hermeneutics: An Incarnational-Trinitarian Theory of Interpretation* (Grand Rapids, Mich.: Baker Academic, 2004), p. 23. Of course, behind both Barth and Heidegger was Kierkegaard's existential critique of the absolute ego.

51. See Ricoeur's interview with Richard Kearney, "The Poetics of Language and Myth," in *Debates in Continental Philosophy*, p. 109. On more than one occasion Ricoeur identified himself as a Barthian. See "The Demythization of Accusation," in *The Conflict of Interpretations: Essays in Hermeneutics*, ed. Don Ihde, p. 344 (Evanston, Ill.: Northwestern University Press, 1974); "The Critique of Religion," in Reagan and Stewart, eds., *The Philosophy of Paul Ricoeur*, p. 219. Whether Ricoeur's hermeneutics remained truly Barthian is a point of debate. See David E. Klemm's "Ricoeur, Theology, and the Rhetoric of Overturning," *Journal of Literature & Theology* 3 no. 3 (1989): pp. 274–75. For a more recent study of Ricoeur and Barth, see Boyd Blundell's *Paul Ricoeur between Theology and Philosophy: Detour and Return* (Bloomington: Indiana University Press, 2010). Ricoeur later saw himself as departing from "the antimetaphysical Protestant lineage of Karl Barth," which was more prominent in his earlier works. See "The Power of the Possible," with Kearney in *Debates in Continental Philosophy*, p. 42. Ricoeur developed a greater commitment to metaphysics and the project of working out a philosophical ontology, which is why he also resists the descriptor "postmetaphysical" as a characterization of his thinking. See his "Reply to G. B. Madison," in *The Philosophy of Paul Ricoeur*, The Library of Living Philosophers, pp. 93–95. We will return to the question of Ricoeur's ontology in chapter 10. It is an open question just how much of a Barthian Ricoeur really is, but whatever the case, this Barthian emphasis on the decentering effect of the text is a central rather than peripheral insight in Ricoeur's hermeneutics.

52. Karl Barth, *The Epistle to the Romans*, trans. Edwyn C. Hoskyns (London: Oxford University Press, 1933), p. 38.

53. Karl Barth, *The Word of God and the Word of Man*, trans. Douglas Horton (New York: Harper, 1957), p. 34.

54. "The question, What is within the Bible? has a mortifying way of converting itself into the opposite question, Well, what are you looking for, and who are you, pray, who make bold to look?" *The Word of God and the Word of Man*, p. 32.

55. Lao Tse and Goethe are Barth's examples. *The Epistle to the Romans*, p. 12.

56. Barth, *Church Dogmatics* 1/2, trans. G. T. Thomson and Harold Knight (Edinburgh: T & T Clark, 1956), p. 471. For a fuller discussion of Barth on engaging *die Sache*, and commentary on some of the Barth quotations cited here, see Kevin Vanhoozer's "Discourse on Matter: Hermeneutics and the 'Miracle' of Understanding," in *Hermeneutics at the Crossroads*, ed. Kevin J. Vanhoozer, James K. A. Smith, and Bruce Ellis Benson, pp. 8-13 (Bloomington: Indiana University Press, 2006).

57. Ricoeur, "Phenomenology and Hermeneutics," TA 37.
58. See Taylor's essay "Self-Interpreting Animals," in *Human Agency and Language: Philosophical Papers I* (Cambridge: Cambridge University Press, 1985), pp. 45–76.
59. Taylor, *Sources of the Self*, pp. 106, 112, 185.
60. Taylor, "Responsibility for Self," in *The Identity of Persons*, ed. Amélie Oksenberg Rorty, p. 282 (Berkeley: University of California Press, 1976).
61. Taylor, "Self-Interpreting Animals," p. 66.
62. Taylor, "Responsibility for Self," p. 282.
63. Charles Taylor, *The Ethics of Authenticity* (Cambridge, Mass.: Harvard University Press, 1991), pp. 37–39.
64. Taylor, "The Moral Topography of the Self," p. 302. Cf. *Sources of the Self*, chapter 5.
65. "Self-Interpreting Animals," pp. 67–68.
66. See Taylor's introduction to *Human Agency and Language: Philosophical Papers I* (Cambridge: Cambridge University Press, 1985), p. 10.
67. This is an important theme in Ricoeur (see his three-volume *Time and Narrative* as well as chapters 5 and 6 in *Oneself as Another*), Taylor (see *Sources of the Self*, pp. 47, 96, 288–89), as well as Alasdair MacIntyre's influential treatment of the narrative unity of life. See *After Virtue: A Study in Moral Theory*, 2nd ed. (Notre Dame, Ind.: University of Notre Dame Press, 1984), pp. 217–19.
68. Taylor, *Sources of the Self*, p. 47.
69. MacIntyre, *After Virtue*, p. 218.
70. On the givenness of horizons, see Taylor, *The Ethics of Authenticity*, p. 39.
71. SUD 79; cf. Jüngel, *Justification*, p. 6.
72. Taylor, *The Ethics of Authenticity*, p. 47.
73. *The Presocratic Philosophers: A Critical History with a Selection of Texts*, 2nd ed., ed. G. S. Kirk, J. E. Raven, and M. Schofield (Cambridge: Cambridge University Press, 1983), p. 118.
74. Jüngel, *Justification*, p. 57.
75. Bayer, "The Doctrine of Justification and Ontology," trans. Christine Helmer, *Neue Zeitschrift für Systematische Theologie und Religionsphilosophie* 43, issue 1 (2001): pp. 50–51. Cf. Bayer, *Living by Faith: Justification and Sanctification*, trans. Geoffrey W. Bromiley (Grand Rapids, Mich.: William B. Eerdmans, 2003), p. 6.
76. Emmanuel Levinas, *Is it Righteous to Be? Interviews with Emmanuel Levinas*, ed. Jill Robbins (Stanford, Calif.: Stanford University Press, 2001), p. 163.
77. Ibid., p. 113.
78. This passage by Pascal appears as an epigram at the start of Levinas's *Otherwise than Being or Beyond Essence*.
79. Levinas, *Is it Righteous to Be?* p. 128.
80. Ibid., p. 105.
81. Ibid., p. 129.
82. Levinas, *Humanism of the Other*, trans. Nidra Poller (Urbana: University of Illinois Press, 2003).
83. Levinas, *Is it Righteous to Be?* p. 107.
84. On Levinas's critique of Hegelian recognition, see Robert R. Williams, *Hegel's Ethics of Recognition* (Berkeley: University of California Press, 1997), pp. 408–12.
85. Levinas opens the Preface to *Totality and Infinity* as follows: "Everyone will readily agree that it is of the highest importance to know whether we are not duped by mo-

rality." *Totality and Infinity: An Essay on Exteriority,* trans. Alphonso Lingis (Pittsburgh: Duquesne University Press, 1969), p. 21.

86. "[T]he handling of everyday objects is interpreted as their comprehension. But in this example, broadening of the notion of knowledge is justified by the overcoming of known objects. . . . At the heart of such handling, the being (*l'etant*) is *overcome* in the very movement that grasps it." Emmanuel Levinas, "Is Ontology Fundamental?" in *Emmanuel Levinas: Basic Philosophical Writings,* ed. Adriaan Peperzak, Simon Critchley, and Robert Bernasconi (Bloomington: Indiana University Press, 1996), pp. 6–7, 9.

87. Emmanuel Levinas, *Alterity and Transcendence,* trans. Michael B. Smith (New York: Columbia University Press, 1999), p. 49.

88. Ricoeur prefers to present the circle of understanding as a spiral, "an endless spiral that would carry the meditation past the same point a number of times, but at different altitudes." *Time and Narrative vol. 1,* p. 72.

89. Levinas, *Alterity and Transcendence,* p. 49.

90. There are many versions of the critique of onto-theology, some better than others. One of the most helpful treatments of this critique can be found in Merold Westphal's work. See *Overcoming Onto-Theology: Toward a Postmodern Christian Faith* (New York: Fordham University Press, 2001).

91. See chapter 1 in Merold Westphal's *Transcendence and Self-Transcendence: On God and the Soul* (Bloomington: Indiana University Press, 2004).

92. Levinas, *Is it Righteous to Be?* p. 107.

93. Emmanuel Levinas, *Of God Who Comes to Mind,* trans. Bettina Bergo (Stanford, Calif.: Stanford University Press, 1998).

3. Faith, Substance, and the Cross

1. Thus Anti-Climacus writes: "There is so much talk about being offended by Christianity because it is so dark and gloomy, offended at it because it is so rigorous etc., but it would be best of all to explain for once that the real reason that men are offended by Christianity is that it is too high, because its goal is not man's goal, because it wants to make man into something so extraordinary that he cannot grasp the thought" (SUD 83).

2. Reiner Schürmann has even argued that Luther is one of the originators of the modern conception of transcendental self-consciousness. See David J. Kangas, "Luther and Modernity: Reiner Schürmann's Topology of the Modern in *Broken Hegemonies.*" *Epoché* 14, issue 2 (Spring 2010): pp. 431–52.

3. In the words of Bernard Lohse, the disputation is "a battle cry." *Martin Luther's Theology,* p. 38.

4. *Martin Luther's Basic Theological Writings,* 2nd ed., ed. Timothy F. Lull (Minneapolis: Fortress Press, 2005), p. 49.

5. Bayer, *Living by Faith,* pp. 24–25. B. A. Gerrish suggests that the theology of glory encompasses a threefold path, including the ladders of rational speculation and legalism, as well as mysticism. *Grace and Reason: A Study in the Theology of Luther* (London: Oxford University Press, 1962), p. 103.

6. Walther von Loewenich, *Luther's Theology of the Cross,* trans. Herbert J. A. Bouman (Minneapolis: Augsburg Publishing House, 1976), pp. 18–19.

7. Luther's main target in his criticisms of mysticism is Pseudo-Dionysius, whose descriptions of mystical ascent Luther accuses of being more Platonic than Christian (LW 36:109). It should be noted, however, that there is some precedent for Luther's

Christocentric and cross-centered critique of Dionysius in such earlier theologians as Bonaventure, Maximus the Confessor, and John of Scythopolis. See Paul Rorem's "Martin Luther's Christocentric Critique of Pseudo-Dionysian Spirituality," *Lutheran Quarterly* XI (1997): pp. 291–307.

8. Aristotle, *Nicomachean Ethics*, 1103a30–1103b2, trans. Hippocrates G. Apostle (Grinnell, Iowa: Peripatetic Press, 1984), p. 21.

9. Gerrish, *Grace and Reason*, p. 96.

10. LW 26, p. 256.

11. LW 31, p. 12, Thesis 40.

12. Luther, "Two Kinds of Righteousness," *Martin Luther's Basic Theological Writings*, p. 135.

13. Ibid., pp. 136–37.

14. Ibid., p. 135.

15. LW 31, p. 9, Thesis 4. See Matthew 7:17–18.

16. LW 31, p. 12, Thesis 41.

17. Paraphrasing Luther, Gerrish writes that reason "goes insane in spiritual matters," since "it 'fools around with works' (*narret mit den werken*)—fasting, praying, building churches, ringing bells, burning incense, intoning, singing, wearing cowls, shaving heads, burning candles, and unending silly works." *Grace and Reason*, pp. 92, 94.

18. "Disputation Against Scholastic Theology," LW 31, p. 11, Thesis 30.

19. One recalls here the words of Nietzsche's Zarathustra: "*if* there were gods, how could I endure not to be a god? *Hence* there are no gods." *Thus Spoke Zarathustra*, in *The Portable Nietzsche*, ed. and trans. Walter Kaufmann (New York: Viking Penguin, 1968, 1982), p. 198.

20. Gerrish, *Grace and Reason*, p. 78.

21. Deuteronomy 4:24, Hebrews 12:29, etc.

22. Von Loewenich, *Luther's Theology of the Cross*, p. 33.

23. LW 31, Comments on Thesis 20, pp. 52–53.

24. LW 34, p. 139, Thesis 32.

25. See Jüngel's essay "The World as Possibility and Actuality: The Ontology of the Doctrine of Justification," in *Theological Essays* I, trans. J. B. Webster (Edinburgh: T & T Clark, 1989), pp. 95–123.

26. Jüngel, "Humanity in Correspondence to God: Remarks on the Image of God as a Basic Concept in Theological Anthropology," in *Theological Essays* I, pp. 124–25, 150–52.

27. LW 31, p. 44, Thesis 4.

28. As Gerrish describes it, "[t]he law is a 'Hercules' sent by God to destroy the savage monster of human pride; it is the 'hammer' of God, shattering all human righteousness; it is the 'thunder' and 'lightning' of God's wrath against the obstinate; it is a dazzling light that reveals God's judgment upon the works of men" (*Grace and Reason*, p. 109).

29. Gerrish, *Grace and Reason*, p. 111.

30. *Apology*, 23a–b.

31. Gerrish, *Grace and Reason*, pp. 94, 110.

32. Aristotle, *Metaphysics*, 1029a.

33. Aristotle, *Categories*, 2a.

34. E. J. Lowe, "Substance," in *An Encyclopaedia of Philosophy*, ed. G. H. R. Parkinson (New York and London: Routledge, 1988), p. 259. For example, in *De ente et essentia* Aquinas divides substance into divine, spiritual, and material.

35. Boethius, *A Treatise Against Eutyches and Nestorius*, in *The Theological Tractates*, trans. H. F. Stewart, E. K. Rand, and S. J. Tester (Cambridge, Mass.: The Loeb Classical Library / Harvard University Press, 1973), p. 85.

36. For instance, see the *Summa Theologica* First Part, Q.29, where Aquinas defines the person as a special name for individual substances of a rational nature (cf. the note in Boethius, *A Treatise Against Eutyches and Nestorius*, pp. 84-85).

37. *Principles of Philosophy*, Part One, 51-54. In *The Philosophical Writings of Descartes*, vol. I, trans. John Cottingham, Robert Stoothoff, and Dugald Murdoch (Cambridge: Cambridge University Press, 1985), pp. 210-211.

38. Lowe, "Substance," pp. 263-64.

39. Robert Jenson, *On Thinking the Human: Resolutions of Difficult Notions* (Grand Rapids, Mich.: William B. Eerdmans, 2003), p. 61.

40. Lowe, "Substance," p. 258.

41. Jenson, *On Thinking the Human*, pp. 68-69; Eric W. Gritsch and Robert W. Jenson, *Lutheranism: The Theological Movement and its Confessional Writings* (Philadelphia: Fortress Press, 1976), pp. 65-68.

42. Zizioulas, *Communion and Otherness*, pp. 70, 213.

43. Ibid., pp. 106ff. Also see John D. Zizioulas, *Being as Communion: Studies in Personhood and the Church* (Crestwood, N.Y.: St. Vladimir's Seminary Press, 1985), pp. 27-65.

44. Zizioulas, *Communion and Otherness*, pp. 213-14.

45. See the editor's footnote in *Basil: Letters and Select Works*, ed. Philip Schaff (Edinburgh: T & T Clark, 1895), p. 132 n. 735.

46. *Basil: Letters and Select Works*, Letters xxxviii, ccxiv, ccxxxvi (pp. 376, 587-88, 630-31).

47. Zizioulas, *Communion and Otherness*, pp. 162-64.

48. It should also be noted that there are distinguished contemporary Catholic accounts that emphasize the relationality of personhood rather than individual substance. For example, Hans Urs von Balthasar's "On the Concept of Person," *Communio* 13 (Spring 1986): pp. 18-26; and Joseph Ratzinger's "Retrieving the Tradition: Concerning the Notion of Person in Theology," *Communio* 17 (Fall 1990): pp. 439-54. Michael Baur has also suggested that Aquinas's concept of human being is not as much an instance of the metaphysics of presence as one might expect. "Heidegger and Aquinas on the Self as Substance," in *Postmodernism and Christian Philosophy*, ed. Roman T. Ciapalo, pp. 38-57 (Mishawaka, Ind.: American Maritain Association, 1997).

49. LW 10, 355-56. This is not to say that Jerome recognized this or reflected it in his translation. His Vulgate often employs *substantia* in the traditional sense, for example Genesis 7:4, where God vows to destroy every living thing—every "substance" (*omnem substantiam*), removing it from the face of the earth.

50. LW 10, 356.

51. Luke 12:15.

52. LW 10, 384.

53. Ozment, *Homo Spiritualis*, p. 202.

54. Having said that, we must also stress that while one's life is hidden with Christ, it is also true that Christ is really present in the life of faith, indwelling the life of the believer. This is not, however, a static or visible presence. The existentialist interpretation of Luther (e.g., Ebeling, Joest) has overemphasized Luther's ek-static, relational ontology and underemphasized the fact that Christ is really present in faith. This is the complaint

of the recent Finnish school of Luther interpretation, which has argued that Luther advances a concept of participatory theosis. See *Union with Christ: The New Finnish Interpretation of Luther,* ed. Carl E. Braaten and Robert W. Jenson (Grand Rapids, Mich.: William B. Eerdmans, 1998). This is not, however, a debate we can host in the present context.

55. Ozment, *Homo Spiritualis,* p. 121.

56. The central passage in view here is Romans 8:18–25: "For I consider that the sufferings of this present time are not worthy to be compared with the glory that is to be revealed to us. For the anxious longing of the creation waits eagerly for the revealing of the sons of God. For the created was subjected to futility, not willingly, but because of Him who subjected it, in hope that the creation itself also will be set free from its slavery to corruption into the freedom of the glory of the children of God. For we know that the whole creation groans and suffers the pains of childbirth together until now. And not only this, but also we ourselves, having the first fruits of the Spirit, even we ourselves groan within ourselves, waiting eagerly for our adoption as sons, the redemption of our body. For in hope we have been saved, but hope that is already seen is not hope; for who hopes for what he already sees? But if we hope for what we do not see, with perseverance we wait eagerly for it."

57. Von Loewenich, *Luther's Theology of the Cross,* p. 69.

58. See LW 25, pp. 360–61. Perhaps most famously: "whoever searches into the essences and actions of creation rather than its groanings and expectations is without doubt a fool and blind man, for he does not know that creatures are also a creation of God" (p. 362).

59. Von Loewenich, *Luther's Theology of the Cross,* p. 69.

60. The object of faith and hope belongs to "things not seen," but anticipated. "Now the one who expects sees nothing and has nothing on which to rest, except the word of promise itself." "Scholia on Psalm 5: On Hope," in *Luther's Spirituality,* ed. and trans. Philip D. W. Krey and Peter D. S. Krey (New York: Paulist Press, 2007), p. 63. Cf. Ozment, *Homo Spiritualis,* p. 108.

61. Quoted in Ozment, *Homo Spiritualis,* pp. 132–33.

62. This must be understood dialectically; it is not a matter of an either/or, such that one is either righteous or sinner, nor is it a matter of being partly righteous and partly sinner. At each moment the self is both justified and sinner. Ozment, *Homo Spiritualis,* p. 138. Daphne Hampson, *Christian Contradictions: The Structures of Lutheran and Catholic Thought* (Cambridge: Cambridge University Press, 2001), pp. 117ff.

63. Ozment, *Homo Spiritualis,* pp. 110–11.

64. Aristotle, *Nicomachean Ethics,* 1103a14–35.

65. Hampson, *Christian Contradictions,* p. 12.

66. Gritsch and Jenson, *Lutheranism,* p. 65.

67. Ibid. Rudolf Bultmann also makes this point in defense of his appropriation of Heidegger. "The Historicity of Man and Faith," in *Existence and Faith: Shorter Writings of Rudolf Bultmann,* trans. Schubert M. Ogden (Cleveland: The World Publishing Company, 1960), p. 98.

68. Robert Kolb, "Confessional Lutheran Theology," in *The Cambridge Companion to Reformation Theology,* ed. David Bagchi and David C. Steinmetz, p. 75 (Cambridge: Cambridge University Press, 2004). Cf. Jürgen Moltmann, *God in Creation,* trans. Margaret Kohl (Minneapolis: Fortress Press, 1993), pp. 231–34. Also see Jenson, *On Thinking the Human,* p. 62.

69. Kolb, "Confessional Lutheran Theology," p. 75; Jenson, *On Thinking the Human*, p. 63; Gritsch and Jenson, *Lutheranism*, p. 61.

70. Jenson, *On Thinking the Human*, pp. 63-65.

71. See R. R. Reno, *Redemptive Change: Atonement and the Christian Cure for the Soul* (Harrisburg, Pa.: Trinity Press International, 2002), pp. 203-207.

72. As Stephen Mulhall observes, Heidegger has difficulty determining whether inauthenticity is ontic or ontological. Does it have the necessity of an ontological structure, or the contingency of an ontic fact? If inauthenticity is an ontological structure, then Dasein would be inauthentic by necessity; *authenticity* would therefore be "inconceivable." *Philosophical Myths of the Fall* (New York: Routledge, 2005), pp. 52-53. But if it is ontic, then it is not the proper concern of Heidegger's *Daseinanalytik*. It therefore seems that inauthenticity is "more than a fact but less than a necessity" and "more than an error and less than a fate," and thus "neither ontic nor ontological." But this disturbs the ontological difference that is pivotal to Heidegger's entire project in *Being and Time* (p. 55). By succumbing to this ambiguity, Heidegger repeats the fundamental ambiguity of "the Christian perception of human beings as at once irremediably lost and open to redemption" (p. 56).

73. Martin Heidegger, "Phenomenological Interpretations in Connection with Aristotle: An Indication of the Hermeneutical Situation," in *Supplements: From the Earliest Essays to* Being and Time *and Beyond,* ed. John van Buren (Albany: State University of New York Press, 2002), p. 125.

74. See chapter 5 in Pelikan's early book, *From Luther to Kierkegaard*.

4. The Incurved Self

The epigraph is from Whit Stillman, *The Last Days of Disco, with Cocktails at Petrossian Afterwards* (New York: Farrar, Straus, and Giroux, 2000), p. 299.

1. Madison, "Ricoeur and the Hermeneutics of the Subject," p. 79.

2. With that in mind, a word on demythologization is in order. A common assumption is that "myth" denotes a fable or allegory, in which an underlying rational core finds figurative expression. Demythologization would therefore seem to imply that once one has penetrated to this rational insight, the external symbolic vessel can be discarded. Ricoeur wants to challenge this characteristically modern view of symbol and myth, in which the elements of figurative discourse (i.e., symbol, metaphor, myth, narrative) are expendable adornments for insights that are ultimately reducible to direct, literal discourse. Much to the contrary, Ricoeur maintains that religious discourse is inescapably figurative. Demythologization is therefore not demythicization. In order to understand religious phenomena, we cannot dispense with figurative discourse. No matter how far reflection goes, a fundamental opacity remains. See "The Hermeneutics of Symbols," in *The Conflict of Interpretations*, p. 299.

3. Barth, *The Epistle to the Romans*, p. 168.

4. Barth, *Church Dogmatics* IV/1, p. 419.

5. Barth, *The Epistle to the Romans*, p. 172.

6. Cf. Barth, *Church Dogmatics* IV/1, p. 419, cited in Matt Jenson, *The Gravity of Sin: Augustine, Luther, and Barth on* homo incurvatus in se (New York and London: T & T Clark, 2006), p. 159.

7. Jüngel, *Justification*, p. 95.

8. Commenting on this passage from *The Sickness Unto Death,* Jüngel points out that "only God can discern the difference between human nature and its corruption." *Justification,* p. 95.

9. Ricoeur, "'Original Sin': A Study in Meaning," in *The Conflict of Interpretations,* p. 282.

10. Sin is not given immediately, and it always slips away from observation. How is it possible to discern the origin of one's sin? How is it possible to ensure that sin is not infecting one's decisions or actions? The opacity and elusiveness of sin is enough to lead the conscience into anguish. As one theologian observes, "[i]f one attempts to determine one's status in the presence of God by an empirical sifting of the evidence, by an honest examination of conscience and rigorous self-scrutiny, one enters a labyrinth from which one cannot always escape, a maze in which the evidence is ambiguous and the possibilities of self-deception are endless." David C. Steinmetz, *Luther and Staupitz: An Essay in the Intellectual Origins of the Protestant Reformation* (Durham, N.C.: Duke University Press, 1980), p. 118, quoted in Jenson, *The Gravity of Sin,* p. 73 n. 138.

11. Ricoeur, "Evil, a Challenge to Philosophy and Theology," FS 250.

12. Ricoeur, "Two Encounters with Kierkegaard: Kierkegaard and Evil, Doing Philosophy after Kierkegaard," trans. David Pellauer, in *Kierkegaard's Truth: The Disclosure of the Self,* ed. J. H. Smith (New Haven, Conn.: Yale University Press, 1981), p. 333.

13. For further comparison of Kierkegaard and Ricoeur on indirect communication and figurative discourse, see my "Selfhood and the Three Rs: Reference, Repetition, and Refiguration," *International Journal for Philosophy of Religion* 58 (2005): pp. 63–94.

14. Augustine, *Confessions,* IV.xv (24) and VII.xii (18) and xiii (19) (pp. 67, 124–25).

15. Ibid., VII.xvi (22) (p. 126).

16. Augustine, *On the Free Choice of the Will,* Book Two, 19–20, trans. Thomas Williams (Indianapolis: Hackett, 1993), pp. 68–69.

17. Matt Jenson has discussed this theme in Augustine, stressing that relationality is an important part of Augustine's view of the goodness of creation and his participatory ontology. It is also central to Augustine's distinction between the heavenly city, which is characterized by *amor Dei,* and the earthly city, which is characterized by *amor sui. The Gravity of Sin,* pp. 6, 8–13, 14–15.

18. Jenson, *The Gravity of Sin,* p. 21.

19. Paul Ricoeur, "Original Sin: A Study in Meaning," in *The Conflict of Interpretations: Essays in Hermeneutics,* ed. Don Ihde, p. 275 (Evanston, Ill.: Northwestern University Press).

20. Ibid., pp. 280–81, 282–83, 286.

21. Ibid., p. 280.

22. Ibid., p. 285.

23. Ricoeur does not use the word "deconstruct," but the French verb *défaire.* However, the English translation "deconstruct" is an apt rendering, since it connotes not only the destructive work but also the more constructive interpretive work that Ricoeur undertakes in unpacking the meaning of the symbol and exposing its inner tensions.

24. Ricoeur, "Original Sin," pp. 269–70.

25. Ibid., pp. 282–83.

26. Bonhoeffer is also influenced by Hegel's concept of *Geist* as social/corporate. This notion, though, dates back further than Scheler or Hegel. As John Zizioulas shows, the notion of corporate personality appears in the Cappadocian Fathers, who opposed

this to the platonic model of participating in an ideal human nature (*ousia hyperkeimenon*) and the Aristotelian model of participating in a nature (*ousia hypokeimenon*). But Zizioulas also observes that this hearkens back to the Hebrew perspective, which offers a third sort of ontology, one of corporate personality, in which a particular person is the cause of particular beings (*Communion and Otherness*, pp. 104–106). Zizioulas observes that this is deeply perplexing for philosophical reflection because it runs counter to the tradition and the concepts it has at its disposal. Cf. Bonhoeffer's interpretation of Israel as collective ethical person (SC 118).

27. Max Scheler, *Formalism in Ethics and Non-Formal Ethics of Values: A New Attempt Toward the Foundation of an Ethical Personalism*, trans. Manfred S. Frings and Roger L. Funk (Evanston, Ill.: Northwestern University Press, 1973), p. 520.

28. Ibid., p. 522.

29. Ricoeur, "Original Sin," p. 269.

30. *Thus Spoke Zarathustra*, in *The Portable Nietzsche*, p. 206. Cf. Stephen Bax's altered translation of this passage, which explicitly connects this with Luther's and Bonhoeffer's notion of the *cor curvum in se*: "The circle's thirst is within you; every circle curves and turns in order to catch itself up again." CF, p. 26 n. 7.

31. LW 25, p. 291.

32. LW 25, p. 345.

33. LW 25, p. 345.

34. Cf. Gerrish, *Grace and Reason*, p. 101.

35. Jenson, *The Gravity of Sin*, pp. 48–49.

36. This is not, however, to say that he spurns the insights of historical-critical methodology altogether. For instance, see his discussion of the sources of the two trees in the garden (CF 83). See John de Gruchy's introduction to *Creation and Fall*, CF, pp. 5–7.

37. CF 32, pp. 50–51.

38. Ricoeur evokes the imagery of incurvature throughout *Freedom and Nature*. See FN 14–15, 18, 21, 33, 189. "[T]he self as radical autonomy, not only moral but ontological, is precisely the fault. The Self—written with a capital S—is a product of separation" (FN 29). Also see SE, p. 356.

39. Ricoeur, "The Unity of the Voluntary and the Involuntary . . . ," in Reagan and Stewart, eds., *The Philosophy of Paul Ricoeur*, p. 9.

40. André LaCocque and Paul Ricoeur, *Thinking Biblically: Exegetical and Hermeneutical Studies*, trans. David Pellauer (Chicago, Ill.: University of Chicago Press, 1998), p. 51.

41. "If we adopt the point of view of present consciousness, the paradox of the after the fact gets caught in the aporia of an unlocatable beginning. This beginning is intended on the horizon of a regressive movement that retraces time and gets lost in a maze of relative beginnings that in turn lead back to a first beginning, which is, as I have said, ungraspable." LaCocque and Ricoeur, *Thinking Biblically*, p. 50.

42. "But this rock hardly surfaces for a moment in the sea, before the sea, roused to a furious storm by the sight of one who is immovable, covers over it again. What does it mean that in the beginning God is? Which God? Your God, whom you make for yourself out of your own need because you need an idol, because you do not wish to live without the beginning, without the end, because being in the middle causes you anxiety?" (CF 29).

43. LaCocque and Ricoeur, *Thinking Biblically*, pp. 52–54.

44. Ricoeur makes this point in *The Symbolism of Evil* (SE 356), though with regard to symbols rather than narrative. For Ricoeur, figurative discourse in general decenters

reflection in this way, giving reason to believe "that the *Cogito* is within being, and not vice versa."

45. Which is quite another thing from saying that this temptation *introduces* the hermeneutical situation. See James K. A. Smith, *The Fall of Interpretation: Philosophical Foundations for a Creational Hermeneutic* (Downers Grove, Ill.: InterVarsity Press, 2000), which argues that interpretation is part of the created goodness of finite existence. My point here is that the serpent exploits the fact that even in the prelapsarian goodness of creation, meaning is not given as pure presence, and the serpent exploits this hermeneutical condition.

46. LaCocque and Ricoeur, *Thinking Biblically*, p. 42.

47. Bonhoeffer does not use the term *gnosis* here, but his reading is certainly pertinent to a critique of Gnosticism. Note his suggestion that the serpent presents itself as "the dark root from which the visible tree of God . . . stems" (CF 106).

48. LaCocque and Ricoeur, *Thinking Biblically*, p. 43.

49. Ibid., p. 43.

50. Barth, *The Epistle to the Romans*, p. 168.

51. "Human beings make themselves the defendant, they appeal to their better selves. But the cries of conscience only dull the mute loneliness of a desolate 'with-itself' ['Beisich']; they ring without echo in the world that the self rules and explains" (AB 139).

52. This is one of Ricoeur's theses in *Freedom and Nature*—namely, that human freedom is not a sheer unconditioned voluntary, nor the exertion of a pure potency; it occurs in the reciprocal relation of the voluntary and the involuntary.

53. See Charles Taylor's essay "What's Wrong with Negative Liberty?" in *Philosophy and the Human Sciences. Philosophical Papers Volume 2* (Cambridge: Cambridge University Press, 1985), pp. 211-29.

54. Barth, *The Epistle to the Romans*, p. 262.

55. Luther, *The Bondage of the Will*, in *Discourse on Free Will*, ed. Ernst F. Winter (New York and London: Continuum, 1961, 1989), p. 113.

56. Cf. Allan Bloom's (in)famous critique in *The Closing of the American Mind* (New York: Simon and Schuster, 1987). Also note his critique of America's "nihilism without the abyss" (p. 155).

57. Friedrich Nietzsche, *The Gay Science*, 125, trans. Walter Kaufmann (New York: Vintage, 1974), p. 181.

58. See Part I of Taylor's *Sources of the Self*.

59. Cf. Taylor's point that the need for recognition has also become more urgent in modernity, as opposed to premodern society. *The Ethics of Authenticity*, p. 48.

60. See Jüngel's work on the distinction between person and works. "On Becoming Truly Human: The Significance of the Reformation Distinction Between Person and Works for the Self-Understanding of Modern Humanity," in *Theological Essays II*, trans. Arnold Neufeldt-Fast and J. B. Webster (Edinburgh: T & T Clark, 1995), pp. 216-40. Also see Mark C. Mattes, *The Role of Justification in Contemporary Theology* (Grand Rapids, Mich.: William B. Eerdmans, 2004), pp. 47-49.

61. Miroslav Volf, *Free of Charge: Giving and Forgiving in a Culture Stripped of Grace* (Grand Rapids, Mich.: Zondervan, 2005).

62. Bayer suggests that this modern account of self-justification has become "more terrifying than at the time of Luther, when the Aristotelian understanding of justice had been imported into the doctrines of sin and grace. In Aristotle's own time, the dilemma of a self-justifying ontology was even less obvious, for he conceived his metaphysics of

the world of action (energeia) in which the human being was cushioned within a stable polis and cosmos, not naked as modern man" ("The Doctrine of Justification and Ontology," p. 49).

63. Jean-Paul Sartre, *Existentialism and Human Emotions*, trans. Bernard Frechtman and Hazel E. Barnes (New York: Philosophical Library, 1957), p. 23. Cf. Mattes, *The Role of Justification in Contemporary Theology*, p. 156.

64. Paraphrasing Bayer, Mattes writes: "There is no Sabbath rest for this human. The onus of the entire world rests on his or her shoulders. One is thus doomed to be an Atlas." *The Role of Justification in Contemporary Theology*, p. 156.

65. Jüngel, "On Becoming Truly Human," pp. 221-22.

66. Jüngel, "Living Out of Righteousness," in *Theological Essays II*, pp. 254-55; Jüngel, "On Becoming Truly Human," pp. 238-39.

67. Jüngel, "Living Out of Righteousness," pp. 256-58.

68. On the ultimate and penultimate, see chapter 6.

69. G. K. Chesterton, *Orthodoxy* (Garden City, N.Y.: Image/Doubleday, 1959), p. 15.

70. Quoted by Martin E. Marty in "Reinhold Niebuhr: Public Theology and the American Experience," *The Journal of Religion* 54, no. 4 (October 1974): p. 338.

71. For a helpful summary, see Joy Ann McDougall's "Sin—No More? A Feminist Re-Visioning of a Christian Theology of Sin," *Anglican Theological Review* 88, no. 2 (2006): pp. 215-35. Also see Daphne Hampson, "Luther on the Self: A Feminist Critique," *Word & World* VIII, no. 4 (1988): pp. 334-42. Several of the essays in *Cross Examinations: Readings on the Meaning of the Cross Today* also address these concerns. See, for instance, Rosemary P. Carbine's "Contextualizing the Cross for the Sake of Subjectivity," pp. 91-107.

72. Daphne Hampson, as cited by McDougall in "Sin—No More?" p. 227.

73. McDougall, "Sin—No More?" p. 218.

74. In *Eighteen Upbuilding Discourses*, ed. and trans. Howard V. and Edna H. Hong (Princeton, N.J.: Princeton University Press, 1990), pp. 353-75, Kierkegaard observes that cowardice is in fact a form of pride, which refuses to venture forth when a situation demands resolution.

75. See Matt Jenson's discussion of sloth as incurvature, and his more thorough response to Daphne Hampson's critique of incurvature, in chapters 3 and 4 of *The Gravity of Sin*.

76. The incurved self cannot but break the commandment against coveting, which means "turn nothing in on yourself and seek nothing for yourself, but live, do, and think all things for God alone" (LW 25, p. 345).

77. Deanna A. Thompson, *Crossing the Divide: Luther, Feminism, and the Cross* (Minneapolis: Fortress Press, 2004), p. 151.

5. The Anthropological Question

1. "*Die Frage nach dem Menschen in der gegenwärtigen Philosophie und Theologie*," translated as "The Anthropological Question in Contemporary Philosophy and Theology" (cited in the text as AQ).

2. See Marion's trilogy: *Reduction and Givenness: Investigations of Husserl, Heidegger, and Phenomenology*, trans. Thomas A. Carlson (Evanston, Ill.: Northwestern University Press, 1998); *In Excess: Studies of Saturated Phenomena*, trans. Robyn Horner and Vincent Berraud (New York: Fordham University Press, 2002); *Being Given: Toward a*

Phenomenology of Givenness, trans. Jeffrey L. Kosky (Stanford, Calif.: Stanford University Press, 2002). Jean-Louis Chrétien, *The Call and the Response,* trans. Anne A. Davenport (New York: Fordham University Press, 2004).

3. In an interview Marion provides some helpful examples that illuminate this point without the usual phenomenological terminology. "Consciousness is the result of the call. Human beings are traditionally described as the creatures endowed with the *logos,* and this has usually been glossed as a capacity to reason and speak. But in fact our first experience of speech is not because *we* speak; it's because we hear other people speak. It always starts that way. And it is not even that we are conscious before we speak; we are conscious of ourself because first we listen to other people speaking to each other and to us. To talk of a call does not imply that I understand it, or that it is what I think it is. When you speak to a baby, you don't say anything. What is very striking is that the baby knows you are saying something to him or to her, and this is the beginning of their self-consciousness. What is important is not the content of the call, it is that it comes before me." "God and the Gift: A Continental Perspective," in Rupert Shortt, *God's Advocates: Christian Thinkers in Conversation* (Grand Rapids, Mich.: William B. Eerdmans, 2005), p. 148.

4. Bayer, "Luther as an Interpreter of Holy Scripture," in *The Cambridge Companion to Martin Luther,* ed. Donald K. McKim, pp. 75–76 (Cambridge: Cambridge University Press, 2003). Cf. Jüngel's *God as the Mystery of the World,* pp. 10ff.

5. Bonhoeffer does not interpret the formless earth as a pre-existing, unformed matter to be formed by creation. The Hebrew term *tohu* in Genesis 1:1 can mean either "desert" or "chaos." Bonhoeffer uses the latter translation and follows Augustine and Luther by interpreting the formless chaos as the first phase in creation (CF 25 n. 1).

6. On justification as creation *ex nihilo,* see Barth, *The Epistle to the Romans,* pp. 102, 121, 141–42, 166. "The universal challenge of faith is the creative word which calls men into existence out of the chaos of independent personality" (p. 114).

7. Bayer, "Luther as an Interpreter of Holy Scripture," p. 76.

8. Ibid., p. 77.

9. Gritsch and Jenson, *Lutheranism,* pp. 67–68.

10. This is what Marion attempts with his phenomenology of the call.

11. As Jüngel writes, this "invective spoken against me repudiates my being by coming too close to me, in a sense, by intervening between me and myself. Invective thus gathers together the existence of the person around itself. If it really hits me, then it penetrates deeply into me and has a profound effect on me." This illustrates the point that the word of address is not merely a signification of a separate reality, but an act or event in which the word effects what it denotes. Thus Jüngel continues: "If the word were only a sign, a denominating, then the person who was cursed could respond, 'Wrong signification!'" But this is not what usually happens, indicating that the word has a more intimate impact: "its effect consists in the fact that the person addressed and the result of what is said are both drawn into the act of speaking." *God as the Mystery of the World,* pp. 10–11.

12. Gritsch and Jenson, *Lutheranism,* p. 68.

13. Brown, *The Cross and Human Transformation,* pp. 105, 139, 165.

14. Ibid., p. 167.

15. On the relation between the indicative and imperative moods, see Jüngel, *Justification,* pp. 259, 261; also Derek Nelson, "The Indicative of Grace and the Imperative of Freedom: An Invitation to the Theology of Eberhard Jüngel," *Dialog: A Journal of The-*

ology 44, no. 2 (Summer 2005): p. 174. Also see the final chapter of Bonhoeffer's *Discipleship*, which locates the participatory being-in-Christ prior to the activity of the imitation of Christ (D 281–88).

16. Gritsch and Jenson, *Lutheranism*, p. 68; Bayer, "The Doctrine of Justification and Ontology," pp. 46–47.

17. Brown, *The Cross and Human Transformation*, pp. 163–64.

18. Gritsch and Jenson, *Lutheranism*, p. 68.

19. John van Buren, *The Young Heidegger: Rumor of the Hidden King* (Bloomington: Indiana University Press, 1994), p. 166.

20. Van Buren, *The Young Heidegger*, p. 167.

21. See the foreword to *Ontology—The Hermeneutics of Facticity*, p. 4. For Heidegger's phenomenological engagement with the epistles of Paul and Augustine's *Confessions*, which he took as examples of concrete religious existence, see his *Phenomenology of Religious Life*, trans. Matthias Fritsch and Jennifer Anna Gosetti-Ferencei (Bloomington: Indiana University Press, 2004).

22. Heidegger, "Phenomenological Interpretations in Connection with Aristotle," p. 125.

23. Van Buren, *The Young Heidegger*, pp. 165–66.

24. Ibid., p. 136.

25. John van Buren's *The Young Heidegger* is one of the most important accounts of this influence. Also see his "Martin Luther, Martin Heidegger," in *Reading Heidegger from the Start: Essays in His Earliest Thought*, ed. Theodore Kisiel and John van Buren (Albany: State University of New York Press, 1994). In the same volume see Theodore Kisiel, "Heidegger (1920–21) on Becoming a Christian: A Conceptual Picture Show." Kisiel's book *The Genesis of Heidegger's* Being and Time (Berkeley: University of California Press, 1993) is also an important document in this research. More recently, Benjamin D. Crowe has focused specifically on the transition from Lutheran *destructio* to Heideggerian *Destruktion* and its importance for Heidegger's concept of authenticity. See *Heidegger's Religious Origins: Destruction and Authenticity* (Bloomington: Indiana University Press, 2006).

26. Van Buren, *The Young Heidegger*, p. 166.

27. In his 1927/28 lecture "Phenomenology and Theology" [*Pathmarks*, ed. William McNeill (Cambridge: Cambridge University Press, 1998)], Heidegger argues for the absolute difference between philosophy (the ontological science) and all other ontic, positive sciences (including theology). Philosophy is not a regional, ontic science because it does not investigate particular beings; it investigates the Being of beings. Although theology should be faithful to its own calling, allowing revelation to determine its course, Heidegger argues that theology nevertheless needs philosophy. Philosophy can be of service because it is the *ontological* science. Every ontic science proceeds with an understanding of being; it carries ontological presuppositions regarding what and how beings *are*. Often this may be a tacit, unthematized understanding, but ontological understanding underwrites specific ontic interpretation (pp. 42, 50). Ontological assumptions shape the way science conducts its investigations. Protestant scholasticism is a case in point: a better ontology might have preserved the radical implications of Luther's insight and prevented the fall back into substance metaphysics. This is one reason why Heidegger thinks philosophy can help theology by giving it ontological guidance.

28. A few years earlier Heidegger describes this process as "dismantling" (*Abbau*), calling for "a regress to Greek philosophy, to Aristotle, in order to see how a certain

original dimension came to be fallen away from and covered up and to see that we are situated in this *falling away.*" *Ontology—The Hermeneutics of Facticity,* p. 59.

29. Crowe, *Heidegger's Religious Origins,* pp. 230, 247, 263.

30. Heidegger, "Phenomenology and Theology," in *Pathmarks,* ed. William McNeill (Cambridge: Cambridge University Press, 1998), pp. 51–52.

31. Heidegger, "Phenomenology and Theology," p. 51.

32. Paraphrasing 2 Timothy 3:5.

33. Van Buren, *The Young Heidegger,* pp. 151, 167.

34. A hermeneutical ontology uses ontic models as the starting point and raw material for its investigations. Thus in the early years leading up to *Being and Time,* Heidegger drew heavily from Paul, Augustine, Luther, and Kierkegaard, since each of these thinkers provided rich interpretations of primal Christian existence. Aristotle's practical philosophy was also an important influence on Heidegger during this time, just as in the 1930s Heidegger shifted his focus to the experience of Being in pre-Socratic poetry and philosophy. See van Buren, *The Young Heidegger,* pp. 151–52.

35. Ozment, *Homo Spiritualis,* p. 105. Cf. Jenson, *The Gravity of Sin,* p. 60.

36. Cf. my essay "Formal Indication, Philosophy, and Theology: Bonhoeffer's Critique of Heidegger," *Faith and Philosophy* 24, no. 2 (April 2007): p. 195.

37. Or as Heidegger puts it in "Phenomenology and Theology": "One can allow 'faithless' science to run up against and be shattered by faith only if one already holds fast to the truth of faith. But faith misconceives itself if it thinks that it is first proven right or even thereby fortified when the other sciences shatter against it" (pp. 49–50).

38. Bonhoeffer acknowledges that Heidegger's ontology achieves an "enormous expansion through its discovery of the existential sphere," but ultimately concludes that its concept of finitude remains that of a self-enclosed, incurved finitude. As such, it "remains unsuitable for theology" (AB 72–73).

39. BT §53.

40. "[W]e must learn to experience the fact that the Being of the human first determines itself on the basis of the happening of the essential belonging together of Being and apprehension" (IM 149).

41. "The Being of all beings is what is most seemly (*das Scheinendste*)—that is, what is most beautiful, what is most constant in itself. What the Greeks meant by 'beauty' is discipline" (IM 140).

42. In this regard Heidegger can be a strong ally against many aspects of the modern ontology of self-justification. Nevertheless, his use of these themes needs critical evaluation as well. See the analysis of Jens Zimmermann ["Dietrich Bonhoeffer and Martin Heidegger: Two Different Visions of Humanity," in *Bonhoeffer and Continental Thought: Cruciform Philosophy,* ed. Brian Gregor and Jens Zimmermann (Bloomington: Indiana University Press, 2009), pp. 102–33] and Richard Kearney [*Strangers, Gods, and Monsters: Interpreting Otherness* (London and New York: Routledge, 2003), pp. 213–26].

43. IM 168–69, emphasis mine.

44. "As the breach for the opening up of Being in beings—a Being that has been set to work—the Dasein of historical humanity is an *in-cident,* the incident in which the violent powers of the released excessive violence of Being suddenly emerge and go to work as history" (IM 174).

45. Gadamer, *Truth and Method,* p. 344. "That the other must be experienced not as the other of myself grasped by pure self-consciousness, but as a Thou—this prototype of

all objections to the infiniteness of Hegel's dialectic—does not seriously challenge him" (p. 343).

46. On the development of Bonhoeffer's thought regarding the problem of otherness and self-mediation, see Charles Marsh, *Reclaiming Dietrich Bonhoeffer: The Promise of His Theology* (Oxford: Oxford University Press, 1994), pp. 83, 90.

47. Cf. Marsh, *Reclaiming Dietrich Bonhoeffer*, p. 83.

48. We will return to this point below.

49. Specifically, Bonhoeffer is referring to Christ's claim "I am the life" (John 14:26, 11:25), which overturns every attempt to formulate the essence of life. "While we are still living and are thus ignorant about the limit of our life, namely, death, how could we be able to say what life is in itself? We can only live life, but not define it. The saying of Jesus binds every thought about life to his own person. I am the life. No question about life can reach behind this 'I am.' The question of *what* life is changes here into the answer of *who* life is. Life is not a thing, an essence, or a concept, but a person" (E 249).

50. In the language of Bonhoeffer's *Ethics*, Christ is the center of reality. As we see in Colossians 1:15–20: "For by Him all things were created, both in the heavens and on earth, visible and invisible, whether thrones or dominions or rulers or authorities—all things have been created through Him and for Him. He is before all things, and in Him all things hold together" (16–17).

51. As one scholar observes, Bonhoeffer's Christology lectures, and later his *Ethics*, expand his *theologia crucis* toward a vision of the *Christus Pantocrator*. See Larry L. Rasmussen, *Dietrich Bonhoeffer: Reality and Resistance* (Louisville, Ky.: Westminster John Knox Press, 2005), pp. 21–22. In this regard Bonhoeffer goes beyond the Lutheran tradition of the *theologia crucis*, moving closer to a patristic conception of Christ and reality. Charles Marsh argues that Bonhoeffer's notion of Christ as the center of reality is less a Hegelian theme than it is the influence of Irenaeus's notion of recapitulation, "in which the whole of creation is conceived to be re-constituted, 'gathered together, included and comprised' in Christ." Marsh, *Reclaiming Dietrich Bonhoeffer*, pp. 104–105.

52. For another comparison of Bonhoeffer and Anti-Climacus, see Paul Janz, *God, The Mind's Desire: Reference, Reason and Christian Thinking* (Cambridge University Press, 2004), pp. 207–13.

53. Bonhoeffer, *Christ the Center*, trans. Edwin H. Robinson (New York: Harper & Row, 1978), p. 104.

54. Bayer critiques Kierkegaard on this point. "The Word of the Cross," p. 50.

55. It is worth noting how this formulation of the Christological question differs from that of Anti-Climacus: "What do you think of Christ?" (SUD 131), which does not highlight the "Who?" question as clearly, and is still susceptible to a theoretical posture.

56. Jeffrey Bloechl, "Being and the Promise," in *Phenomenology and Eschatology: Not Yet in the Now*, ed. Neal DeRoo and John Panteleimon Manoussakis (Burlington, Vt.: Ashgate, 2009), p. 129.

57. Emphasis his. See Auden's very Kierkegaardian essay "Purely Subjective," in *Prose. Volume II. 1939-1948*, ed. Edward Mendelson (Princeton, N.J.: Princeton University Press, 2002), pp. 196–97.

58. Kierkegaard describes this logic in a journal entry titled "How Did It Happen That Christ Was Put to Death?" Christianity requires that one die to the world, but this is so foreign to the natural human being that it seems worse than simply dying. "The natural man can tolerate it for an hour when it is introduced very guardedly at the distance of imagination—yes, then it even pleases him. But if it is moved any closer to him,

so close that it is presented in dead earnestness as a demand upon him, then the self-preservation instinct of the natural life is aroused to such an extent that it becomes a regular fury, as happens through drinking, or as they say, a *furor uterinus*. In this state of derangement he demands the death of the man of spirit or rushes in upon him to slay him" (JP 4360). Cf. Charles K. Bellinger, *The Genealogy of Violence: Reflections on Creation, Freedom, and Evil* (Oxford: Oxford University Press, 2001), p. 64.

59. On this point Heidegger is highly instructive.

60. Lesslie Newbigin, *The Gospel in a Pluralist Society* (Grand Rapids, Mich.: William B. Eerdmans, 1989), pp. 203-10.

61. Jüngel writes that Jesus' resurrection from the dead "means that God has identified himself with this dead man" (*God as the Mystery of the World*, p. 363; cf. §13 in ibid., "God's Unity with Perishability as the Basis for Thinking God"). Alan E. Lewis's language is even more striking: in the church's story of the crucifixion and burial of Jesus, God is united with "a human corpse." *Between Cross and Resurrection*, pp. 25, 27, 83.

62. See Thomas Torrance, *Theological Science* (Oxford: Oxford University Press, 1969), pp. 48-49: the Incarnate One reveals—i.e., uncovers and arouses—our hostility toward God.

63. This is how Bonhoeffer puts it in his prison writings, in the outline for a book he was never able to write. See LPP 501; Cf. *Widerstand und Ergebung. Briefe und Aufzeichnungen aus der Haft*, ed. Christian Gremmels, Eberhard Bethge, et al. (Gütersloh: Christian Kaiser Verlag, 1998), p. 558.

64. As Luther writes in commenting on Galatians: "And that is the reason why our theology is certain: it snatches us away from ourselves and places us outside ourselves, so that we do not depend on our own strength, conscience, experience, person, or works but depend on that which is outside ourselves, that is, on the promise and truth of God, which cannot deceive" (LW 27, p. 387). Cf. Bayer, "Luther as an Interpreter of Holy Scripture," p. 77. Likewise, in *The Freedom of a Christian* Luther writes "that a Christian lives not in himself, but in Christ and in his neighbor. Otherwise he is not a Christian. He lives in Christ through faith, in his neighbor through love. By faith he is caught up beyond himself into God. By love he descends beneath himself into his neighbor. Yet he always remains in God and in his love" (LW 31, p. 371).

65. Bonhoeffer, *Life Together*, trans. Daniel Bloesch and James H. Burtness (Minneapolis: Fortress Press, 1996), pp. 42-44.

66. John Zizioulas notes the individualism that predominates in so much Christian worship, noting that "the cosmic dimension of man is missing; man in his relation to God singles himself out from nature as the autonomous self, as if his capacities and incapacities had nothing to do with those of the entire cosmos." *Communion and Otherness*, p. 211 n. 9.

67. Ephesians 1:22-23.

68. "The church is church only when it is there for others" (LPP 503). "Die Kirche ist nur Kirche, wenn sie für andere da ist." *Widerstand und Ergebung*, p. 560.

69. Newbigin, *The Gospel in a Pluralist Society*, pp. 209-10.

70. We should also question the assumption that pre-Socratic thought—or post-Socratic thought, for that matter—is clearly philosophical rather than theological and thus wields a "natural" or "rational" authority that Christian thinking lacks. What would the text of Parmenides, for instance, be without revelation? Moreover, as Pierre Hadot observes, in Greek philosophy there is "an entire tradition of systematic theology" that follows from Plato's *Timaeus*, Book Ten of the *Laws*, and Book 12 of Aristotle's *Meta-*

physics [Pierre Hadot, *What Is Ancient Philosophy?* trans. Michael Chase (Cambridge, Mass.: Harvard University Press, 2002), p. 240]. As Robert Jenson observes, the church fathers had a better sense that the doctrines of the philosophers were not purely secular, but were in fact theologoumena of a different faith; insofar as it exhibits a secular or rationalistic impulse, this thinking simply shows its roots in "Olympian religion itself, which pursued a divinity purged of mystery." Consequently, "[i]nsofar as Western philosophy is not now reduced to the pure study of logic, it is still in fact theology, Christian or Olympian-Parmenidean," both of which "are engaged in the *same* sort of enterprise." Jenson, *Systematic Theology, Volume I: The Triune God* (Oxford: Oxford University Press, 1997), pp. 9-10. It is important to recognize that Heidegger's way of bracketing Christian revelation has theological implications of its own, since his retrieval of the early Greek understanding of *logos* is an alternative to the Christian understanding of the *Logos*. He presents us with an either/or.

71. "We no longer claim any full understanding of human reality—but we now understand why such a complete self-understanding is not necessary and not even desirable." Ernstpeter Maurer, "The Perplexity and Complexity of Sinful and Redeemed Reason," in *Reason and the Reasons of Faith*, ed. Paul J. Griffiths and Reinhard Hütter, p. 215 (New York and London: T & T Clark, 2005).

6. The Concreteness and Continuity of Faith

1. Taylor, *Sources of the Self*, pp. 171-72.
2. Barth, *The Epistle to the Romans*, p. 111.
3. Ibid., p. 10.
4. Ibid., p. 30.
5. See James M. Robinson, "Hermeneutic Since Barth," in *The New Hermeneutic*, ed. James M. Robinson and John H. Cobb, Jr., pp. 57-58 (New York: Harper & Row, 1964).
6. Ricoeur cites Moltmann and the theology of hope as a critique of this tendency. See "Freedom in the Light of Hope," in *The Conflict of Interpretations*, pp. 407, 409.
7. This is the question Robert Jenson poses for Rudolf Bultmann, who remained too mired in existentialist eschatology to give the robustly Christian answer: "a future determined as fellowship with Jesus." Jenson criticizes Bultmann and the "new hermeneutic" (Fuchs, Ebeling) insofar as they prioritize word-events but fail to appreciate the indispensable role of the biblical narrative in allowing us to identify the eschaton that these word-events proclaim. *Systematic Theology* I, pp. 170-71.
8. This is John Webster's concern regarding Jüngel. See "Systematic Theology after Barth," in *The Modern Theologians*, ed. David Ford and Rachel Muers, p. 253 (Oxford: Blackwell, 2005). That said, Jüngel also anticipates critique along these lines by noting that "[e]vent is more than a momentary happening. Events can have their history and can make it. The accusation of 'existentialistic punctualism' would simply miss entirely" what and how such an event is. *God as the Mystery of the World*, p. 324. Likewise, Jüngel also insists on the need for narrative continuity in order to understand the event of God's life in the world (ibid., pp. 302-303).
9. Bonhoeffer uses this expression in LPP 303. Or to change the metaphor, such an emphasis is monochrome or even colorless, failing to reflect the full spectrum of faithful existence. As John Dillenberger observes, this treatment of language results in an account in which "the contours of faith have little color or pulse." "On Broadening the New Hermeneutic," in *The New Hermeneutic*, p. 151. Cf. Miikka Ruokanen, *Hermeneutics as*

an Ecumenical Method in the Theology of Gerhard Ebeling (Helsinki: Luther-Agricola Society, 1982), p. 99: "[Ebeling's] ontology is an expression of his close link with the principles of transcendental anthropology and the duality it contains: matter, nature or the ontology of negative existence have no place in Ebeling's personalistic-verbal conception of reality." Ruokanen also notes the criticism (articulated by American critics such as Dillenberger and Wilder) that "Ebeling's existential ontology leads to a colourless, unreal and non-cultural interpretation" of faith and reality (p. 99 n. 77).

This was not, note well, the case with Barth, who later recognized that his early reflections were still too determined by a formal, philosophical reflection on eternity and time. As a result, Barth concluded, this "wholly other" God bore a stronger resemblance to the God of the philosophers than the God of Abraham, Isaac, and Jacob. See *The Humanity of God,* p. 45. Barth later sought to orient his theology as explicitly as possible according to biblical narrative rather than an abstract philosophical theology. Garrett Green, "Introduction: Barth as Theorist of Religion," in *On Religion: The Revelation of God as the Sublimation of Religion,* trans. Garrett Green (New York and London: T & T Clark, 2006), p. 10. Barth's narrative orientation provides a point of departure for Ricoeur as well as for Hans Frei; the latter two thinkers' disparate appropriations of Barth are central to the Yale-Chicago debate in theology. See Mark I. Wallace, *The Second Naiveté: Barth, Ricoeur, and the New Yale Theology,* 2nd ed. (Macon, Ga.: Mercer University Press, 1995).

10. Barth, *The Epistle to the Romans,* p. 29.

11. See Barth's famous debate with Brunner and his emphatic essay "No!" in *Natural Theology: Comprising "Nature and Grace" by Professor Dr. Emil Brunner and the Reply "No!" by Dr. Karl Barth,* trans. Peter Fraenkel (Eugene, Ore.: Wipf & Stock, 2002).

12. Barth, *The Humanity of God,* p. 39.

13. Ibid., p. 40. In a personal letter, Barth recounts: "'It was like the twilight of the gods when I saw the reaction of Harnack, Hermann, Rade, Eucken and company to the new situation', and discovered how religion and scholarship could be changed completely, 'into intellectual 42 cm cannons'." Quoted in Eberhard Busch's *Karl Barth: His Life from Letters and Autobiographical Texts,* trans. John Bowden (Grand Rapids, Mich.: William B. Eerdmans, 1976), p. 81.

14. In the present discussion we are concerned with Barth primarily insofar as Bonhoeffer read him, and not with providing a full account of developments in Barth's own thinking about revelation, divine activity, and being. Charles Marsh points to Barth's book on Anselm (*Fides Quaerens Intellectum*) and *Church Dogmatics* II/1 as developments in Barth's thought that help to answer Bonhoeffer's objections (*Reclaiming Dietrich Bonhoeffer,* pp. 15–20). It is also worth noting Barth's attempt to think through the vital and internal relation between justification (*Rechtfertigung*) and justice (*Recht*) in his 1938 essay, translated into English as "Church and State," in *Community, State, and Church: Three Essays,* ed. Will Herberg (Gloucester, Mass.: Peter Smith, 1968), p. 101. Andreas Pangritz suggests that Barth's concern with the connection between justification and justice was an important influence on Bonhoeffer's account of the penultimate in *Ethics.* See *Karl Barth in the Theology of Dietrich Bonhoeffer,* trans. Barbara and Martin Rumscheidt (Grand Rapids, Mich.: William B. Eerdmans, 2000), pp. 64–65.

15. "[T]his preaching is not fundamentally rooted in our experience, has no correspondence in our experience; it cannot justify itself, prove itself by something about which we could say we truthfully await; it is the eruption of something from the other side, from the totally other into our culture." "The Critique of Religion," p. 219.

16. Ricoeur, "The Critique of Religion," p. 220.

17. Ricoeur, "Manifestation and Proclamation," FS 57–60.

18. Ricoeur, "The Canon between the Text and the Community," in *Philosophical Hermeneutics and Biblical Exegesis*, ed. Petr Pokorný and Jan Roskovec, p. 9 (Tübingen: Mohr Siebeck, 2002).

19. "We are not dealing with a rupture, but a circle between the spoken word as an event and language as a system." "The Canon between the Text and the Community," p. 9. Also see "Structure, Word, Event," in *The Conflict of Interpretations*, pp. 79ff.

20. "The Summoned Subject in the School of the Narratives of the Prophetic Vocation," FS 274.

21. "From Existentialism to the Philosophy of Language," in *The Rule of Metaphor*, p. 320.

22. Adolf von Harnack made a similar objection to Barth's early dialectical theology, accusing him of Marcionism, of condemning all Christian education, and severing "every link between faith and what is human." "An Open Letter to Professor Karl Barth," in *The Beginnings of Dialectical Theology*, vol. 1, ed. James M. Robinson, trans. Keith R. Crim, p. 172 (Richmond, Va.: John Knox Press, 1968).

23. Bonhoeffer was particularly concerned with the implications of faith for ethics. See Eberhard Bethge's *Dietrich Bonhoeffer: A Biography*, trans. Eric Mosbacher, rev. and ed. Victoria J. Barnett (Minneapolis: Fortress Press, 2000), pp. 183–86.

24. Dietrich Bonhoeffer, *The Young Bonhoeffer: 1918–1927*, trans. Mary C. Nebelsick and Douglas W. Stott (Minneapolis: Fortress Press, 2003), p. 338.

25. AB 99–100. Cf. *The Young Bonhoeffer*, p. 343.

26. Barth, *The Epistle to the Romans*, pp. 157–58: "He is invisible, outside the continuity of the visible human subject and beyond all psychological analysis. He creates the new subject of the man who stands upright in the presence of God. He is the subject of faith, which 'religious experience' reaches after and longs for, but never finds."

27. The debate concerns the interpretation of the Definition of Chalcedon, which describes the hypostatic union of the two natures in the one person (or *hypostasis*) of Christ. How are divinity and humanity related in the person of Jesus Christ? Wanting to preserve the integrity of both natures, the Reformed position emphasized their distinctness, arguing that this distinction is crucial to preserving the integrity of both natures; otherwise one risks a divinization of humanity or a loss of divine majesty. Wanting to stress the unity of the two natures, the Lutheran position borrows the concept of *perichoresis* from Trinitarian debates to speak of an interpenetration of the divine and human natures. The Reformed and Lutheran positions also disagree regarding the nature of the *communicatio idiomatum*—the communication of properties between the divine and human natures. The crux of this disagreement is the *genus maiestaticum*, which argues that the human nature partakes of the divine attributes (while retaining its human properties, but without conferring them on the divine nature). Consequently, Christ's human nature partakes of the divine omnipresence. The ubiquity of Christ then plays out in the Lutheran interpretation of Christ's ascension as well as Christ's real presence in the sacraments. [See Richard A. Muller, *Dictionary of Latin and Greek Theological Terms* (Grand Rapids, Mich.: Baker Books, 1985), p. 73.] Further, the Lutheran position insists that the *Logos*, the second person of the Trinity, is fully contained in the incarnate Christ. In becoming flesh, the *Logos* does not withhold a reserve of existence outside of the fleshly humanity of Jesus Christ (contra the Reformed view, which the Lutherans dubbed the *extra calvinisticum*). The finite is capable of bearing the infinite.

28. Martin J. Heinecken, "Christology, the Lord's Supper, and its Observance in the Church," in *Marburg Revisited: A Reexamination of Lutheran and Reformed Traditions*, ed. Paul C. Empie and James I. McCord, p. 90 (Minneapolis: Augsburg, 1966). The spatial language employed here indicates another complexity in the debate: What does it mean to speak of Christ "in" the church and the sacraments? (Or for our concerns, what does it mean to speak of the believer's being "in" Christ?) As Heinecken notes, Heidegger has helped to show that prepositions like "in" and "with" apply to personal reality in a way quite different from inanimate objects. A person is *in* community in a quite different way than a match is in a box, and persons are *with* each other in quite a different way than a chair is with a table (p. 97). The question of spatiality also becomes more complicated after Einstein, though it is a matter of dispute whether the Lutheran or Reformed position better accords with modern developments in physics. Thomas F. Torrance argues that Luther's *finitum capax* proceeds with a flawed assumption of space as a receptacle. See his *Space, Time and Incarnation* (Oxford University Press, 1969), pp. 35–37. Robert Jenson, on the other hand, proposes that the Lutheran position in fact challenges received ways of conceiving space and embodiment. See, for instance, "Autobiographical Reflections on the Relation of Theology, Science, and Philosophy; or, You Wonder Where the Body Went," in *Essays in Theology of Culture* (Grand Rapids, Mich.: Eerdmans, 1995), pp. 216–24.

29. Torrance, *Space, Time and Incarnation*, p. 41.

30. "With ingenious overemphasis, Luther himself urged us to seek deity not in heaven but on earth, in *man, man,* the *man* Jesus; and for him the bread of the Lord's supper had to *be* the glorified body of the Exalted One. This emphasis is crystallized in the orthodox Lutheran doctrine of the 'communication of idioms' with its sovereign genus (*genus maiestaticum*), according to which the predicates of the divine majesty really belong to the *humanity* of Jesus as such and *in abstracto*. With great elation people triumphantly turned away (and are still turning away) from the Reformed *Finitum non capax infiniti* (a finite thing is not capable of the infinite). All this clearly suggests the possibility of an inversion of above and below, of heaven and earth, of God and man—the possibility of forgetting the eschatological limit. Indeed, Hegel (by his own confession) showed himself perhaps only too good a Lutheran in his exploitation of this possibility. It is certain that Luther and the old-Lutherans with their heaven-storming Christology have left their followers in a somewhat exposed and defenseless situation, in face of the speculative anthropological consequences that have irresistibly developed." From Barth's introduction to Feuerbach's *The Essence of Christianity,* trans. George Eliot (New York: Harper, 1957), p. xxiii.

31. "[S]o long as the relation to God is not unconditionally inconvertible for us, and does not remain so under all circumstances, we shall have no rest in this matter." Ibid., p. xxiv.

32. "My Speech to the Graduates," in *The Complete Prose of Woody Allen* (New York: Wings Books, 1991), p. 363.

33. "The finite is capable of the infinite, not by itself, but only through the infinite." C 346; AB 178.

34. See *Philosophical Fragments*, p. 14. Kierkegaard's pseudonym in this text, Johannes Climacus, is a speculative philosopher trying to confront that which ruptures the system and exceeds the limits of thinking. He recognizes that if the truth is a person, then the teacher and the teaching coincide, and truth cannot be reduced to an idea. But the question is how the thinking subject can recognize the teacher as the truth. If the learner

already possesses the condition, then all that is necessary is recollection (*anamnesis*), and the problem of learning has already been treated adequately by Socrates. According to Climacus the new condition is faith, but beyond this he does not go. He finds himself confronted with the paradox of the God-man. But how does one recognize this teacher as the truth? Why this teacher and not another teacher (or messiah)? There is no absolutely reliable criterion. Too often, however, philosophers of religion overlook the fact that according to Christian thinking, the Holy Spirit is present and active in the life of the self and is a necessary condition of recognizing Christ (see I Corinthians 2:10-16). (The notable exception here is Hegel, but the problem with his account of receiving divine truth is that it ultimately identifies the Holy Spirit with the human spirit.) It is not insignificant that while Climacus has broached the second person of the Trinity, he has not broached the third person. On the Holy Spirit, see Brown, *The Cross and Human Transformation*, p. 160; note that the Holy Spirit is also not merely a condition of *cognition*, but also the agent of transformation in the self. Furthermore, the Holy Spirit is not simply an activating agent that brings the self to Christ. Instead, we participate in Christ in and through the Holy Spirit. Also see Zizioulas, *Communion and Otherness*, p. 244. One of Bonhoeffer's weaknesses is his underdeveloped pneumatology.

35. Marsh, *Reclaiming Dietrich Bonhoeffer*, p. 127.

36. In chapter 5 we discussed Gadamer's argument that appealing to the immediacy of the Thou is futile, since this encounter is always still mediated. For Bonhoeffer, the critical point is that this mediation is not self-mediation, but rather *Christological* mediation.

37. See, for instance, Kierkegaard's reading of Nathan's confrontation with King David. David was aware of his guilt, "yet someone from the outside was needed, someone who said to him: You." *For Self-Examination/Judge For Yourself!* ed. and trans. Howard V. Hong and Edna H. Hong (Princeton, N.J.: Princeton University Press, 1990), p. 39. Merold Westphal discusses Kierkegaard's emphasis on the transcendent address in the chapter "Inverted Intentionality: Being Addressed," in his *Levinas and Kierkegaard in Dialogue* (Bloomington: Indiana University Press, 2008), pp. 138-51.

38. Quoted by Bonhoeffer in AB 82 n. 1.

39. Gritsch and Jenson, *Lutheranism*, pp. 100, 108-109.

40. "This being is not dependent on faith; on the contrary, faith knows that this being is wholly independent of faith itself and faith's own being or nonbeing. Everything hinges on faith's knowing itself not as somehow conditioning or even creating this being, but precisely as conditioned and created by it" (AB 117-18).

41. Likewise the ontological continuity of revelation: "The continuity of revelation means that it is always present (in the sense of 'what is in the future'). For that reason, it can be a question today only of the Christ preached in the church, of Christ's death and resurrection. If the individual were the hearer of the sermon, the continuity would still be in danger. But it is the church itself that hears the word of the church, even if I did not hear in each instance. In this manner preaching is always heard. It is outside me that the gospel is proclaimed, that Christ 'is' in Christ's community. And so the continuity does not lie in human beings, but rather it is guaranteed suprapersonally [*überpersönlich*] through a community of persons" (AB 113-14).

42. See Luther's lectures on Galatians: "[T]he Christian person is righteous and sinner at the same time, holy and profane, an enemy of God and a child of God. None of the Sophists will admit this paradox, because they do not understand the true meaning

of justification." *Luther's Spirituality,* p. 168. The paradox is that the new self includes two aspects that are "diametrically opposed: that a Christian is righteous and loved by God and nevertheless at the same time is a sinner" (p. 170).

43. Janz, *God, the Mind's Desire,* pp. 11–14.

44. For Tillich, ultimate concern is the "spiritual center" that grounds the meaning of one's existence; it is the "meaning which gives meaning to all meanings." *The Courage to Be* (New Haven, Conn.: Yale University Press, 1952, 1980), p. 47.

45. As Barth puts it the ultimate, "the last thing, the ἔσχατον, the synthesis, is *not* the continuation, the result, the consequence, the next step after the penultimate, so to speak, *but,* on the contrary, is forever a radical break with everything penultimate." *The Word of God and the Word of Man,* p. 324 (translation altered).

46. 2 Corinthians 6:2. Bonhoeffer cites this verse in the text (E 151).

47. See especially chapter 8 in Lacoste's *Experience and the Absolute: Disputed Questions on the Humanity of Man,* trans. Mark Raftery-Skehan (New York: Fordham University Press, 2004).

48. Cf. section XXVI of *The Bondage of the Will,* where Luther remarks that heaven was not made for geese.

49. Here we see Bonhoeffer's resolute resistance to the view that revelation requires fundamental transcendental conditions for its possibility—in this case, which would determine justification as a fulfillment of an a priori religious structure of the human being. Bonhoeffer maintains this Barthian conviction throughout his authorship. He treats this issue extensively in *Act and Being,* and it also appears in his last writings, which he wrote in the two years of imprisonment prior to his execution. There too he resists the notion of a religious a priori.

50. Cf. E 306.

51. Cf. E 167: "Christ alone creates faith. Nevertheless, there are situations that make it either harder or easier to have faith."

52. I recently read a striking story that illustrates the exigency of these penultimate concerns. In Paraguay, Dr. Jorge Gomez-Frey and his wife Gloria established a health clinic to work with the residents of the poor and remote village of Encarnación. Gloria also became involved with families who live in the Vertedero, the local garbage dump. The people who live there try to earn a meager living by finding recyclable materials in the garbage. Through the support of her church, Gloria and some volunteers bought a small piece of land and erected a building to serve lunch and provide bathing facilities. They also built a treehouse for the children. What is striking about this story is that the children from the Vertedero had to be taught *how to play,* because previously their only mode of interaction was fighting. Play is also a penultimate good—part of being human. Kathi Bates, "Encarnación, Paraguay: Finding Ministry Work in Unlikely Places," *Luke Society News* 30, no. 1 (March 2008): pp. 4–5.

53. "To bring bread to the hungry is preparing the way for the coming of grace." Feeding the hungry is not yet the proclamation of the ultimate, just as being fed is not the same as standing in faith. "But for the one who does something penultimate for the sake of the ultimate, this penultimate thing is related to the ultimate. It is a *pen*-ultimate, before the last" (E 163).

54. Thus Bonhoeffer critiques the traditional Lutheran doctrine of the two kingdoms.

55. For example: "In the name of a better Christianity Luther used the worldly to protest against a type of Christianity that was making itself independent by separating itself

from the reality of Christ. Similarly, Christianity must be used polemically today against the worldly in the name of a better worldliness; [but] this polemical use of Christianity must not end up again in a static and self-serving sacred realm" (E 60).

56. It is worth noting the alleged Kierkegaardianism of *Brand*. Whatever Kierkegaard's influence on Ibsen, we cannot reduce his complex and nuanced authorship to the radicalism of Brand. That said, there are radical tendencies in Kierkegaard's oeuvre. See, for instance, his journal entry on "The Night of the Unconditioned": "By nature man dreads walking in the dark—no wonder, then, that he by nature dreads the unconditioned, getting involved with the unconditioned, of which it holds true that no night and 'no darkness is half so black' as this darkness and this night in which all relative goals (the ordinary milestones and road markers), in which all considerations (the lights we generally use to help ourselves), in which even the most sensitive and warmest feelings of devotion—are extinguished, for otherwise it is not unconditionally the unconditioned" (JP 4908).

57. "Even to ask about the ultimate is regarded as radicalism, as a lack of love toward the given orders of the world and toward those who are dependent on them. Freedom from the world, which is Christ's gift to Christians, and renunciation of the world (1 John 2:17) are accused of being unnatural and opposed to creation, an estrangement from, or even hostility toward, the world and humanity" (E 156).

58. See Barth's *Protestant Theology in the Nineteenth Century: Its Background and History*, new ed., trans. Brian Cozens and John Bowden (Grand Rapids, Mich.: Eerdmans, 2002). Also cf. Kierkegaard, who writes in his journal: "We have completely abolished imitation [i.e., the imitation of Christ], and at most we hold to the paltriness called social morality. In this way men cannot become properly humbled so that they genuinely feel the need of 'grace,' because the requirement is no more than 'social morality,' which they fulfill tolerably well" (JP 1902).

7. The Capable Human Being as a Penultimate Good

1. Ricoeur, "Capabilities and Rights," in *Transforming Unjust Structures: The Capability Approach*, ed. Séverine Deneulin, Mathias Nebel, and Nicholas Sagovsky, pp. 17-18 (Dordrecht: Springer, 2006).

2. DBWE 10, p. 403, Bonhoeffer, *The Young Bonhoeffer*, p. 440—Thesis 4, also SC 126-30.

3. If this were a study of Luther, we would need to discuss in detail his debate with Erasmus regarding the freedom (or bondage) of the will. For our task of philosophical anthropology, however, it is sufficient to understand that when Luther identifies the will as bound rather than free, he is denying the possibility of the fallen human being freely contributing to her own salvation. According to Luther, it is only because justification is an unconditional gift given prior to any act that the self is in turn able to love God and the neighbor freely. If self-justification is a possibility within reach, then one's action will always be corrupted by the possibility of getting something out of it, so to speak. See Kyle A. Pasewark, "Predestination as a Condition of Freedom: Reconsidering the Reformation," in *Human and Divine Agency: Anglican, Catholic, and Lutheran Perspectives*, ed. F. Michael McLain and W. Mark Richardson, pp. 49-66 (Lanham, Md.: University Press of America, 1999). Also, it is important to recognize that according to Luther, the self is not free before God, but she is free before other human beings and capable of

making progress according to civil and moral law. See *The Bondage of the Will*, #767. Also see #638 for Luther's distinction between freedom for what is above and freedom for what is below.

4. Nietzsche, *Beyond Good and Evil*, #46, in *Basic Writings of Nietzsche*, p. 250.

5. In a journal entry on "Cunning Humility," Kierkegaard writes: "Lutheran religiosity, especially in the next generation after Luther and following, is undeniably the kind we human beings like best of all, the kind that whines and whimpers to us and to God—and then everything is all right. 'What is man, a miserable wretch, unable to accomplish anything, etc.' O, but I get another impression reading the New Testament; I get the impression that according to God's idea man is a giant—but he is to be stretched, not spared. Otherwise, does not Luther's position easily become a cunning swindle?" (JP 2682).

6. To be sure, this was not Luther's intent—something Kierkegaard laments: "O, Luther, who more than you has been used by adherents [*Tilhængere*] for the very opposite of what he intended?" (JP 1923). According to Kierkegaard, Luther enabled the world to call itself Christian, but at the cheapest price possible. Hearing Luther once, then listening again (just to be sure, since this proclamation seemed too good to be true!), people said to themselves: "Excellent! This is something for us. Luther says: It depends on faith alone. He himself does not say that his life expresses works, and since he is now dead it is no longer an actuality. So we take his words, his doctrine—and we are free from all works—long live Luther!" *For Self-Examination*, p. 16.

7. "Under no circumstances must one count on or wait for unmediated inspirations, lest all too easily one fall prey to self-deception" (E 324).

8. Responsible action remains penultimate since it relinquishes its impulse for autonomous self-justification. "As responsible action, the good takes place without knowing, by surrendering to God the deed that has become necessary and is nevertheless (or because of it!) free, surrendering it to God, who looks upon the heart, weighs the deeds, and guides history. Thus a profound mystery of history is disclosed to us. Precisely those who act in the freedom of their very own responsibility see their activity as flowing into God's guidance. Free action recognizes itself ultimately as being God's action, decision as God's guidance, the venture as divine necessity. In freely surrendering the knowledge of our own goodness, the good of God occurs. Only in this ultimate perspective can we speak about good in historical action" (E 284–85).

9. "Lectures on Galatians 3:6—'Thus Abraham Believed God,'" in *Luther's Spirituality*, pp. 163–64.

10. Luther's objection concerns the presumption of autonomous reason to be the final authority and judge in divine matters. For a classic study of Luther's surprisingly subtle view of reason, see Gerrish, *Grace and Reason*. For Bonhoeffer's account of incurved reason and the development of his view of reason from *Act and Being* to *Ethics*, see Christiane Tietz's essay "Bonhoeffer on the Uses and Limits of Philosophy," in *Bonhoeffer and Continental Thought*, pp. 31–45.

11. Cf. our discussion of the counter-*Logos* in chapter 5.

12. Bonhoeffer observes that facile contempt for "rationalism" often betrays a deficient desire for truth (E 115).

13. Some of Bonhoeffer's remarks might even be taken as programmatic for Henry. For example: "Ever since Jesus Christ said of himself, 'I am the life' (John 14:6; 11:27), no Christian thinking or indeed philosophical reflection can any longer ignore this claim

and the reality it contains" (E 249). One certainly cannot accuse Henry of ignoring this claim; indeed, it is central to his entire project. Likewise Bonhoeffer's subsequent words: "This statement of Jesus about himself declares every attempt to formulate the essence of life in itself as futile and doomed from the start.... We can only live life, but not define it. The saying of Jesus binds every thought about life to his own person. I am the life. No question about life can reach behind this 'I am.' . . . Jesus posits this I in sharpest contrast to all thoughts, concepts, and approaches that claim to capture the essence of life. He also does not say I have life, but I am the life. Life can thus never again be separated from this I, from the person of Jesus" (E 249–50). The similarity between Bonhoeffer and Henry on this point is due primarily to the common influence of the Gospel and epistles of John. It becomes quickly apparent upon reading the two thinkers that their interpretation of these texts is significantly different.

14. Henry, "Material Phenomenology and Language (or, pathos and language)," *Continental Philosophy Review* 32 (1999): p. 346.

15. Ibid., p. 347.

16. Ibid., p. 346.

17. Ibid. For more on this theme, see Jeffrey Hanson, "Michel Henry's Critique of the Limits of Intuition." *Studia Phænomenologica* IX (2009): pp. 97–111.

18. Henry, "Material Phenomenology and Language," p. 352.

19. For example, in *Ethics* Bonhoeffer writes: "My life is outside myself, beyond my disposal. My life is another, a stranger, Jesus Christ.... 'I am the life'—this is the word, the revelation, the proclamation of Jesus Christ. The statement that our life is outside ourselves and in Jesus Christ is in no way the result of our own self-understanding. Instead, it is a claim that encounters us from outside" (E 250).

20. While Christ is the "First Living," he is nonetheless consubstantial with the Father. As Henry writes: "Although he is himself generated in the self-affection of absolute Life, Christ co-belongs to the process of this absolute self-affection as the essential Ipseity and the First Living, without which no self-affection of this kind could be accomplished. Thus he is 'consubstantial' with the Father, sharing in the power of this process in which, embracing itself, Life makes itself Life" (IT 109).

21. Here I am paraphrasing Henry, who describes the human Son as "him who in his self-enjoyment is nothing other than Christ's self-enjoyment as the Father's self-enjoyment" (IT 189).

22. To cite just a few examples, Henry's inexplicable neglect of the third person of the Trinity, which results in a theology more binitarian than Trinitarian; his Gnostic tendencies; his neglect of the Judaic sources of Christianity; his neglect of the cross; and the absence of an eschatology. For critical discussion of these and other issues, see the following articles: Rudolf Bernet, "Christianity and Philosophy," *Continental Philosophy Review* 32 (1999): pp. 325–42; Michael Kelly, "Dispossession: On the Untenability of Michel Henry's Theory of Self-Awareness," *Journal of the British Society for Phenomenology* 35, no. 3 (October 2004): pp. 261–82; Kevin Hart, "Phenomenality and Christianity," *Angelaki* 12, no. 1 (April 2007): pp. 37–53; Kevin Hart, "'Without World': Eschatology in Michel Henry," in *Phenomenology and Eschatology: Not Yet in the Now*, ed. Neal DeRoo and John Panteleimon Manoussakis, pp. 167–92 (Burlington, Vt.: Ashgate, 2009); Jeffrey Hanson, "Phenomenology and Eschatology in Michel Henry," in *Phenomenology and Eschatology: Not Yet in the Now*, ed. Neal DeRoo and John Panteleimon Manoussakis, pp. 153–66 (Burlington, Vt.: Ashgate, 2009); Christoph Moonen, "Touching from a Distance: In Search of the Self in Henry and Kierkegaard," *Studia Phænome-*

nologica IX (2009): pp. 147–56; Anthony Steinbock, "The Problem of Forgetfulness in Michel Henry," *Continental Philosophy Review* 32 (1999): pp. 271–302.

23. It is therefore quite surprising when Henry suggests there is still a sense in which life speaks in the world—i.e., "in the world which secretly speaks the language of life to us. *Coeli enarrant gloriam Dei.* The world is the speech of God" ("Material Phenomenology and Language," p. 363). But as Jeffrey Hanson observes, "to validate this point, which seems to run counter to Henry's fundamental commitment, would require significant modification of his position that God or life appears nowhere in the world. . . . By consistently maintaining that the world is powerless to embody life, as he does with greater and greater intensity especially in the later work, it is possible that Henry in effect denigrates that which he is most eager to preserve, the truth of life." "Michel Henry's Critique of the Limits of Intuition," p. 109.

24. For more discussion of this point in Bonhoeffer, see our discussion in chapter 10.

25. Drew Leder, *The Absent Body* (Chicago: University of Chicago Press, 1990), p. 6.

26. This dualism is also evident in Henry's sharp distinction between the Jesus of history and the Christ of faith. See his introduction to *I Am the Truth.*

27. Leder, *The Absent Body,* pp. 6–7.

28. For a helpful and influential treatment of this theme, see Kathryn Tanner's *God and Creation in Christian Theology: Tyranny or Empowerment?* (Minneapolis: Fortress Press, 1988).

29. Kierkegaard, *Works of Love,* ed. and trans. Howard V. Hong and Edna H. Hong (Princeton, N.J.: Princeton University Press, 1995), pp. 9–10. Cf. Kierkegaard's opening prayer: "How could one speak properly about love if you were forgotten, you God of love, source of all love in heaven and on earth; . . . you who are love, so that one who loves is what he is only by being in you!" (p. 3).

30. Hart, "'Without World,'" p. 191.

31. Ibid.

32. It is also significant that Henry, despite his elaborate distinction between law and gospel, argues that the self "achieves his salvation" by performing acts of mercy out of the power of Life within itself (IT 167).

33. Which for Henry is quite different from *life.*

34. See Steinbock, "The Problem of Forgetfulness in Michel Henry," p. 297.

35. Hart, "'Without World,'" p. 192.

36. Isaiah 6:8.

37. Ricoeur, "Experience and Language in Religious Discourse," in *Phenomenology and the "Theological Turn": The French Debate,* ed. Dominique Janicaud et al., p. 131 (New York: Fordham University Press, 2000). Ricoeur provides a hermeneutics of the call and response in his essay "The Summoned Subject in the School of the Narratives of the Prophetic Vocation," where he interprets the call-and-response structure through a series of scriptural and theological figures: the prophetic call, the call to conformity with the Christ figure, the Augustinian figure of the inner teacher, and the testimony of conscience (FS 262–75).

38. See Matthew 16:24, which I am transposing from the third person ("If anyone wishes to come after me, he must deny himself, and take up his cross and follow Me") to an address in the second person, in the mode of the calling of the disciples in Matthew 4:19 ("Follow me, and I will make you fishers of men"); cf. Mark 1:17.

39. *Judge For Yourself!* ed. and trans. Howard V. Hong and Edna H. Hong (Princeton, N.J.: Princeton University Press, 1990), p. 191.

40. Mark 1:16-18.

41. Matthew 14:28. It is interesting to observe that Peter will not step out of the boat of his own initiative; he asks Christ to call or command him to step out and come to him (D 66).

42. "Because we are justified by faith, faith and obedience have to be distinguished. But their division must never destroy their unity" (D 64).

43. See Roy A. Harrisville's distinction between "conversion" and "call" as models of understanding the transformation of faith. *Fracture: The Cross as Irreconcilable in the Language and Thought of the Biblical Writers* (Grand Rapids, Mich.: William B. Eerdmans, 2006), pp. 39-53.

44. BT 206-207. But as we saw in chapter 5, Bonhoeffer and Heidegger nevertheless differ over the notion of Dasein's ownmost potentiality-for-Being. The call creates a new situation, which comes from beyond Dasein's ownmost possibilities.

45. Karl Rahner, *Hearer of the Word: Laying the Foundation for a Philosophy of Religion*, trans. Joseph Donceel (New York: Continuum, 1994), p. 92.

46. Ibid., p. 23.

47. LaCoste, *Experience and the Absolute*, pp. 105, 108.

48. Ibid., p. 199 n. 20. This ambiguity is a problem with Rahner's transcendental deduction of a possible openness to revelation. Lacoste writes that "however laudable the efforts made by the Maréchalian Thomists to set down the roots of the relation of man to God in the basic givens of experience might be, they nevertheless come up against unforeseen ambivalences. We are told that 'transcendental experience' has to do with God—but does it not rather have to do only with the sacred proper to the world? We are told (by Karl Rahner in *Hörer des Wortes*) that it has to do with God's silence—but is it not rather a question of the muteness of Being?" *Experience and the Absolute*, p. 200 n. 9.

49. The problem with Heidegger's philosophy is not its failure to find an immanent capacity for revelation; the problem, as we noted above in chapter 5, lies with Heidegger's refusal to consider the proclamation of the ultimate word, deliberately opting for a pagan piety devoted to the thinking of Being.

50. On this distinction see Ricoeur's essay "Manifestation and Proclamation" (FS 48-67).

51. LaCoste, *Experience and the Absolute*, p. 103.

52. This is another reason why Bonhoeffer rejects possibility as a theological category.

53. While it is not clear that Bonhoeffer is offering a phenomenology of intentionality in general, one could easily read his epistemological discussions in *Act and Being* this way; a clarification is therefore required.

54. Michael Polanyi, *The Tacit Dimension* (Garden City, N.Y.: Doubleday, 1966), pp. 10-16.

55. Leder, *The Absent Body*, p. 20.

56. Cf. Leder, *The Absent Body*, p. 22.

57. "If we take the first step with the intention of putting ourselves into the situation of being able to believe, then even this ability to believe is itself nothing but works. It is but a new possibility for living within our old existence and thereby a complete misunderstanding" (D 65).

58. Bonhoeffer takes care to point out that the Lutheran confessions also recognize the need for this first step—even if this recognition is often downplayed, "almost as if they were ashamed of it" (!) because of their concern to defuse the threat of "a synergistic misunderstanding." In a sketch from 1940, Bonhoeffer interprets Paul's notion of be-

ing God's coworkers (1 Cor. 3:9—the same epistle where Paul describes the word of the cross) in an intersubjective context: we do not work with God for our own salvation, but for the salvation of the other. *Conspiracy and Imprisonment: 1940–1945*, trans. Lisa E. Dahill (Minneapolis: Fortress Press, 2006), p. 485.

8. The Call to Responsibility

1. Ricoeur carries these points into his description in "The Summoned Subject," FS 271.
2. OB 113–14, 89, 109.
3. OB 48–49, 140–41.
4. Ricoeur, "Emmanuel Levinas: Thinker of Testimony," FS 126.
5. Cf. OA 191.
6. See Ricoeur's interlude, "Tragic Action," in *Oneself as Another*, OA 241ff.
7. This book was also significant for Bonhoeffer. See Bethge, *Dietrich Bonhoeffer: A Biography*, pp. 562–63.
8. OA, p. 24 n. 31.
9. Ricoeur, "Ethical and Theological Considerations on the Golden Rule," FS 298.
10. I discuss this theme at greater length in "Bonhoeffer's 'Christian Social Philosophy': Conscience, Alterity, and the Moment of Ethical Responsibility," in *Bonhoeffer and Continental Thought*, pp. 201–25.
11. OB 15.
12. See OA, chapters 7 and 8.
13. Bonhoeffer makes this point in his essay "After Ten Years," which he circulated among his fellow conspirators in early 1943. The fact that "a bad conscience may be stronger and more wholesome than a deceived one is something that the man whose sole support is his conscience can never comprehend" (LPP 39).
14. Ricoeur, "The Summoned Subject," FS 271–72, 274.
15. Ibid., FS 272.
16. Ibid., FS 273.
17. As we saw in chapter 6, this is Ricoeur's critique of the New Hermeneutic of Ebeling and Fuchs.
18. Ricoeur, "The Summoned Subject," FS 274–75.
19. Ibid., FS 274.
20. Or "between the verdict of conscience and the christomorphism of faith" ("The Summoned Subject," FS 275).
21. Ricoeur, "The Summoned Subject," FS 271–72.
22. Ricoeur anticipates something of this problem and sees resources in Ebeling's account of conscience as having a triadic structure in which care for self, attention to the world, and hearing God intersect. This means that the activity of conscience does not require the self to be a solitary individual ("The Summoned Subject," FS 273).
23. In the working notes for *Ethics*, Bonhoeffer writes: "Voice of the heart | in principle | self-deception" (E 321, n. 77).
24. G. W. F. Hegel, *Introduction to The Philosophy of History*, trans. Leo Rauch (Indianapolis: Hackett, 1988), p. 18.
25. Hegel, *Introduction to The Philosophy of History*, p. 35.
26. Cyril of Jerusalem writes: "God has opened wide his arms on the Cross in order to span the limits of the earth's orb." Likewise Lactantius: "So God in his suffering spread

out his arms and gathered in the circle of the earth, so as to announce that, from the rising of the sun to its setting, a future people would be gathered under his wings." God extends himself as a human being, distinguishing himself from animals by his ability to stand upright and "spread out his hands" (Justin). Von Balthasar, *Mysterium Paschale: The Mystery of Easter,* pp. 129-30.

27. Hans Boersma, "Redemptive Hospitality in Irenaeus: A Model for Ecumenicity in a Violent World." *Pro Ecclesia* XI, no. 2 (Spring 2002): pp. 207-26; Hans Boersma, "Irenaeus, Derrida and Hospitality: On the Eschatological Overcoming of Violence," *Modern Theology* 19, no. 2 (April 2003): pp. 163-80.

28. Gabriel Marcel, *Tragic Wisdom and Beyond,* trans. Stephen Jolin and Peter McCormick (Evanston, Ill.: Northwestern University Press, 1973), pp. 141, 145.

29. Gabriel Marcel, "Concrete Approaches to Investigating the Ontological Mystery," in *Gabriel Marcel's Perspectives on the Broken World,* trans. Katharine Rose Hanley (Milwaukee: Marquette University Press, 1998), p. 179.

30. Thus "anyone who attempts to reflect on evil philosophically without taking into account the irreducible fact of the encounter with evil condemns himself to remaining outside the subject he claims to be dealing with." Apart from this concrete encounter, "we are perhaps no longer speaking of evil but of something else, from which it would be very simple to liberate ourselves." Marcel, *Tragic Wisdom and Beyond,* pp. 140, 133.

31. Marcel, *Tragic Wisdom and Beyond,* p. 140. Moreover, this sort of concrete availability is crucial to save particular manifestations of evil and suffering from the abstraction of "causes," in which self-consciousness eclipses the needs of concrete others. Thus our causes and commitments can quickly become an occasion for self-righteousness. I recently saw a flyer stapled to a telephone pole in my neighborhood, announcing a high school concert to raise funds for relief work in Darfur. What was so striking about the poster was the large text on the lower half of the page: "COME CELEBRATE THE POWER OF ACTION!" The danger is that such a posture is more a celebration of one's status as a socially-ethically-politically aware agent than a concern for the actual people in need of help.

32. Sam Keen, *Gabriel Marcel* (Richmond, Va.: John Knox Press, 1967), p. 33.

9. Reflexivity, Intentionality, and Self-Understanding

1. Ricoeur, "On Interpretation," TA 12.

2. This is the way Hegel interprets the individual Self as it is originally and immediately posited: it "is not yet Spirit *for itself;* it does not *exist* as Spirit; it can be called 'innocent' but hardly 'good.'" In order to become Self and/or Spirit, it is necessary to become "other" to oneself; this "othering" of oneself is "the withdrawal into itself, or self-centredness, of knowing as such. Immediate existence suddenly turns into thought, or mere sense-consciousness into consciousness of thought." This turn inward occurs in the event that religion represents as eating the forbidden fruit from the tree of the knowledge of good and evil. *Phenomenology of Spirit,* pp. 467-68. From a speculative perspective, then, the "Fall" is truly a *felix culpa* insofar as it is a step forward in the development of Spirit.

3. See Smith, *The Fall of Interpretation,* which argues for the created goodness of finitude, mediation, and interpretation.

4. Even Nietzsche falls into this tendency. With his description of the noble blond beasts in *Beyond Good and Evil,* Nietzsche envisions a prelapsarian state prior to the

"fall" into slave morality, with its bad conscience and its distinction between good and evil. In this quasi-Edenic existence, these unfallen nobles give the will to power a direct expression, without reflection, self-doubt, or bad conscience. But as Stephen Mulhall observes, it is difficult to see how Nietzsche's description resembles anything like human subjectivity. How would life in any society be possible without some distinction between the instinctual action and the self-evaluation of conscience, between impulse and its expression, or between the inner and outer life? *Philosophical Myths of the Fall*, p. 41.

5. The prohibition is an address by which Adam understands himself as a human being. "[I]t is Adam, the human being, who is addressed concerning Adam's own human existence, and Adam understands this. . . . It is about being human . . . that Adam is addressed" (CF 85).

6. Matthew 6:3.

7. See our discussion in chapter 7. Bonhoeffer acknowledges this point explicitly: "Psychologically speaking, it is indeed impossible for the left hand not to know what the right hand is doing" (E 319).

8. On Bonhoeffer's interest in this phrase from Nietzsche, see Peter Frick's essay "Friedrich Nietzsche's Aphorisms and Dietrich Bonhoeffer's Theology," in *Bonhoeffer's Intellectual Formation*, ed. Peter Frick, pp. 193–96 (Tübingen: Mohr Siebeck, 2008).

9. See Levinas: "Signification is signifying out of a lack, a certain negativity, an aspiration which aims emptily, like a hunger, but in a determinative way, at the presence which is to satisfy it. Whether it be an expectation for a representation or a listening for a message, the intuitive fulfillment is the accomplishing of a teleological intention" (OB 96).

10. OB 145, 166.

11. See Hegel's *Encyclopaedia Logic*, trans. T. F. Geraets, W. A. Suchting, and H. S. Harris (Indianapolis: Hackett, 1991), §17: Philosophy is a circle that returns to its first act, such that its beginning turns out to be its goal, the initial concept becomes the Concept, and *Geist* thereby achieves closure and contentment (p. 41).

12. "Thinking as such is boundless, it pulls all transcendent reality into its circle" (DBWE 10, 472). Cf. Christiane Tietz, "Bonhoeffer on the Uses and Limits of Philosophy," in *Bonhoeffer and Continental Thought*, ed. Brian Gregor and Jens Zimmermann, p. 36 (Bloomington: Indiana University Press, 2009).

13. Nietzsche, *Twilight of the Idols*, #26, in *The Portable Nietzsche*, p. 470.

14. "Reflecte fortiter, sed fortius fide et gaude in Christo" (AB 135).

15. See Part Two of Hadot's *What Is Ancient Philosophy?*

16. Hadot, *What Is Ancient Philosophy?* pp. 188–233.

17. Ibid., pp. 109–91.

18. *Phaedo*, 64a–c, 65b, 66a–e.

19. See Epictetus, *The Handbook (The Encheiridion)*, Section 1.

20. Hadot, *What Is Ancient Philosophy?* p. 191.

21. Ibid., pp. 192–93.

22. Quoted in ibid., p. 191.

23. Descartes, *Meditations on First Philosophy*, trans. Donald A. Cress (Indianapolis: Hackett, 1998), pp. 69–70.

24. Arthur C. Danto, "The Body/Body Problem," in *The Body/Body Problem: Selected Essays* (Berkeley: University of California Press, 2001), p. 193.

25. Dieter Henrich, *Between Kant and Hegel: Lectures on German Idealism*, ed. David S. Pacini (Cambridge, Mass.: Harvard University Press, 2003), pp. 247–48.

26. For more on Kierkegaard and Hadot regarding the ancient practice of philosophy as a way of life, see my essay "The Text as Mirror: Kierkegaard and Hadot on Transformative Reading," *History of Philosophy Quarterly* 28, no. 1 (January 2011): 65–84.

27. On Kierkegaard's interpretation of Socratic irony against the systematic closure of thinking, see David J. Kangas, *Kierkegaard's Instant: On Beginnings* (Bloomington: Indiana University Press, 2007), ch. 1.

28. See chapter IV of Kierkegaard's *Philosophical Fragments*.

29. Hadot makes the intriguing case that early Christianity (namely, the early apologists and several church fathers) presented itself as a philosophical way of life. As a discourse Christian philosophy is the *true* philosophy, because it had received the revelation of the divine *Logos* that other philosophers had sought. But Christianity is also a way of life, they argued, because the believer seeks to live in conformity with Reason, i.e., the *Logos*, i.e., the incarnate Christ (Hadot, *What Is Ancient Philosophy?* p. 239). Christian philosophy also included its own spiritual exercises. This tradition led to the development of asceticism and monasticism, which provided a context in which to practice exercises of thought, such as attention to oneself and the examination of the conscience, scriptural exegesis, and the cultivation of humility, self-mortification, and preparation for death.

30. Hadot, *What Is Ancient Philosophy?* p. 248.

31. See Luther on "the fanatics" who "choose their own suffering" and "pick their own crosses." "Sermon at Coburg on Cross and Suffering," in *Luther's Spirituality*, p. 153.

32. Two points of clarification are in order: *First*, we should not conclude that these distortions characterize medieval monasticism and asceticism as a whole. Just as a reading list limited to Nietzsche would suggest that all asceticism is world-denying, life-hating nihilism, so an exclusive focus on Luther could suggest that all monasticism was unrepentant Pelagianism. If we pay attention to Josef Pieper's arguments in *Leisure, the Basis of Culture*, trans. Gerald Malsbary (South Bend, Ind.: St. Augustine's Press, 1998), we can see how the monastic life (particularly the philosophical contemplation for which it allowed) provides a potent challenge to the ontology of self-justification, particularly as this self-justification is expressed in what Pieper describes as the world of "total work," which is indeed a culture devoid of grace (p. 4). In this regard philosophy is allied with worship, the festival, and the Sabbath. *Second*, we should not conclude that Luther discarded spiritual exercises and disciplines from faithful existence. See Luther's preface to his German writings for his account of the three rules—*oratio, meditatio, tentatio* (*Luther's Spirituality*, pp. 122–23); on the imitation of Christ (p. 163); and on the daily reading of the catechism (pp. 129–30).

33. JP 1902.

34. JP 1905.

35. Kierkegaard, *Judge for Yourself!* p. 192.

36. Ibid., p. 193.

37. JP 1914.

38. Cf. JP 1902.

39. DBWE 12, pp. 231–32. For more on this passage, see Peter Frick, "The *Imitatio Christi* of Thomas à Kempis and Dietrich Bonhoeffer," in *Bonhoeffer's Intellectual Formation*, p. 47.

40. This emphasis on the continuity developed in spiritual exercises helps to expand Bonhoeffer's earlier emphasis on the church as the basis of the ontological continuity of faith, which we discussed in chapter 6.

41. Frick, "The *Imitatio Christi* of Thomas à Kempis and Dietrich Bonhoeffer," pp. 47–48.

42. LPP 480. "If one has completely renounced making something of oneself—whether it be a saint or a converted sinner or a church leader (a so-called priestly figure!), a just or an unjust person, a sick or a healthy person—then one throws oneself completely into the arms of God, and this is what I call this-worldliness" (LPP 486).

43. Bonhoeffer argues that there are criteria for self-examination regarding the call of Christ to assume responsibility: "if, according to my character traits, I know that I tend to be a reformer, a know-it-all, a fanatic, one who does not heed any limits, there I run the risk of expanding my responsibility arbitrarily, and confusing my natural desire with the call of Jesus; if I know myself to be cautious, anxious, insecure, and legalistic, there I must be careful not to equate the call of Jesus Christ with my limiting responsibility to a narrow domain." These criteria for self-examination are, however, only guidelines; they cannot provide certainty: "I am never set free to act in genuine responsibility by looking at myself, but only by attending to Christ's call" (E 294).

44. According to Bonhoeffer, because Christ "really is and wants to be in *us*," this self-examination is significant (E 325–26). In self-examination, the faithful self attends to Christ present within oneself—not as a Gnostic inner voice or a New Age sense of one's own "Christ nature," nor as a stable mechanism, but as the Christ who now lives in the self, after the autonomous ego has been crucified with him (Gal. 2:20). Thus self-examination attends to Christ and his being and activity within oneself.

45. Von Loewenich, Luther's Theology of the Cross, p. 136.

46. Ibid., p. 136. Also see Craig Hinkson, "Luther and Kierkegaard: Theologians of the Cross," *International Journal of Systematic Theology* 3, no. 1 (March 2001), pp. 35f.

47. Descartes, *Meditations on First Philosophy*, p. 80.

48. Levinas, "The Idea of Infinity," in *Collected Philosophical Papers*, trans. Alphonso Lingis (Dordrecht: Martinus Nijhoff, 1987), pp. 53–54. Marion, "The Saturated Phenomenon," in *Phenomenology and the "Theological Turn": The French Debate*, ed. Dominique Janicaud, trans. Thomas A. Carlson, p. 213 (Bronx, N.Y.: Fordham University Press, 2000).

49. Merold Westphal, *God, Guilt, and Death: An Existential Phenomenology of Religion* (Bloomington: Indiana University Press, 1984), p. 42.

50. Von Loewenich, *Luther's Theology of the Cross*, pp. 136–37.

51. Thus Kierkegaard writes in *Works of Love*: "Divine authority . . . is as if all eyes; it first constrains the person being addressed to see who it is with whom he is speaking and then fastens its piercing look upon him and with this look says: It is to you to whom this is said" (p. 97; cf. pp. 46, 96). Similarly, in *Practice in Christianity* Anti-Climacus writes that Christian truth cannot be observed in a detached way; in observing it, I discover that I am being observed, that it makes a claim on me, questions me, asking if I am doing what it says I should do (PC 234, 241).

52. First of all, a *sign* is a denial of immediacy. The sign mediates; it means something other than what it immediately is. Secondly, the sign of contradiction contains a contradiction within itself (PC 124–25).

53. Ricoeur distinguishes this hermeneutical self-understanding from the self-consciousness of idealism. Whereas idealism will emphasize the self-responsibility of the reflexive act, this outward movement consists in a "*response to*." The *moi*, master of itself, becomes the *soi*, disciple of the text. "Phenomenology and Hermeneutics," TA 37–38.

54. Kierkegaard, *Concluding Unscientific Postscript*, pp. 338–39.

55. This is the crucial difference between the Kierkegaardian category of repetition and Platonic recollection, Aristotelian *kinesis,* and Hegelian mediation.

56. At his best Kierkegaard recognizes this (see his writings on imitation, and *Works of Love*), but he tends in the direction of inwardness and interiority. His interpretation of Nathan's rebuke of David is telling in this regard. After David has committed adultery with Bathsheba and murdered her husband Uriah, Nathan's story was meant to compel David to take responsibility for his sin. But when David altogether failed to see how the story applied to him, it was necessary for Nathan to say "You are the man!" This interlocution "was the transition to the subjective." Thus Kierkegaard recognizes that "someone from outside was needed, someone who said to him: You" (*For Self-Examination*, pp. 38-39). Unfortunately, though, Kierkegaard does not spell out the full significance of intersubjectivity in the practice of self-examination; instead, his recurring point is that self-examination in the mirror of the word requires that "during the reading you must incessantly say to yourself: 'It is I to whom it is speaking, it is I about whom it is speaking'" (p. 40). This is true as far as it goes, but it fails to appreciate that I also need someone else to say this to me—whether it is the word of conviction, or the word of grace and forgiveness. This practice also inherits the dangers of conscience, i.e., self-justification and self-deception. I want to be the one to tell myself "I am the man." Here again Kierkegaard's undernourished ecclesiology is evident. Cf. my discussion in "The Text as Mirror."

10. Religion within the Limits of the Penultimate?

1. Ricoeur, "The Status of *Vorstellung* in Hegel's Philosophy of Religion," in *Meaning, Truth, and God,* ed. Leroy S. Rouner, p. 86 (Notre Dame, Ind.: University of Notre Dame Press, 1982).

2. Ricoeur, "Ethics and Human Capability," p. 284. "The regeneration, which is at issue in this philosophy of religion, happens at the level of the fundamental disposition, at the level of what I am here calling 'the capable self.' This restoration, this regeneration, this rebirth of the capable self, stands in a close relation to the economy of the gift which I celebrate in the study 'Amour et justice'" ("Experience and Language in Religious Discourse," p. 146 n. 4).

3. Ricoeur, "Ethics and Human Capability," p. 284.

4. Mark I. Wallace makes a similar observation in his introduction to *Figuring the Sacred* (FS 31).

5. Ricoeur, "Ethics and Human Capability," p. 284; "Ethical and Theological Considerations on the Golden Rule," FS 297-98.

6. Ricoeur, "Religion, Atheism, and Faith," p. 454.

7. Ibid.

8. Ricoeur, "Philosophical and Theological Hermeneutics," p. 33.

9. Ricoeur, "The Critique of Religion," p. 221.

10. Ibid., p. 219.

11. Consequently, Ricoeur maintains that his discussions of Barth, Bultmann, and Bonhoeffer are "situated entirely on the periphery of (his) *philosophical* field of investigation of religious thematics." "Reply to David Stewart," in *The Philosophy of Paul Ricoeur,* Library of Living Philosophers, p. 446. We noted Barth's influence on Ricoeur in chapter 2. The influence of Bultmann is also evident in Ricoeur's work, most obviously in his appropriation of demythologization. Ricoeur did not embrace the Bultmannian

program uncritically, but he was committed to demythologization as a necessary step of smashing idols in order to allow religious symbols to speak. See "Preface to Bultmann," in *The Conflict of Interpretations*, pp. 381–401.

12. To my knowledge Ricoeur's only extended discussion of Bonhoeffer appears in his 1966 lecture titled "The Non-Religious Interpretation of Christianity in Bonhoeffer," which appears in *Bonhoeffer and Continental Thought*, pp. 156–76.

13. See Clifford Green's analysis in *Bonhoeffer: A Theology of Sociality*, rev. ed. (Grand Rapids, Mich.: Wm. B. Eerdmans, 1972/1999), p. 261. According to Green, Bonhoeffer's concept of religion is an operational/behavioral concept, not a morphological/institutional one. Thus he is not critiquing church institution and its forms of life, such as prayer, worship, the reading of scripture, formation of doctrine, etc. (p. 262). This is why it is possible for the church to face two options: either a *religious* or *nonreligious* interpretation of Christianity. A nonreligious Christianity would not repudiate the church and the elements of its common life. Rather, it would direct the psychic posture of Christianity away from that of weakness depending on a God of power.

14. Bonhoeffer was highly critical of the way theologians and pastors sought to use existentialist philosophy and psychotherapy as a means of preparing the way for the gospel. See LPP 326. Bonhoeffer writes quite harshly about modern pastoral workers hunting, like "the dirtiest gutter journalists," for some detail to use in "religious blackmail" of the human being (LPP 344). Thus, "we should give up all our clerical tricks, and not regard psychotherapy and existentialist philosophy as God's pioneers" (LPP 346). Bonhoeffer argues that a nonreligious interpretation of Christianity must not cultivate and capitalize on the weakness and misery of humanity. The religious apologist uses these tools to highlight anxiety, misery, despair, and other human problems, so that people feel the need for a divine answer. In an essay from the 1970s, Ricoeur writes that "Bonhoeffer has said all that needs to be said against the God of the gaps, whether it be a question of explaining things or of understanding humanity." "Toward a Hermeneutic of the Idea of Revelation," *Harvard Theological Review* 70, no. 1/2 (January–April 1977): p. 20.

15. It is worth noting that Luther also uses this expression in his exposition of Psalm 127:1: "Unless the Lord builds the house, those who build it labor in vain. Unless the Lord guards the city, the watchman stays awake in vain." What does this mean for human activity? "Are we to provide no supplies, leave our gates and windows open, make no effort and become lifeless corpses?" Not at all, argues Luther. Those with responsibilities should in general "proceed *as if there were no God* and they had to rescue themselves and manage their own affairs" (LW 45, p. 331, emphasis mine). Cf. Bayer, *Living by Faith*, p. 37.

16. "The exegete is not his own master; to understand is to place himself under the object which is at stake in the text; thus, the Christian hermeneutics must be placed in motion by the Announcement which is at stake." Ricoeur, "The Critique of Religion," p. 222.

17. Ricoeur, "Phenomenology and Hermeneutics," p. 37.

18. For example, "the pictures of a child differ from those of an adult, and those of a person from the desert differ from those of a person from the city" (CF 81).

19. Note, however, this is not exclusively Bultmann's territory. Barth too writes of the need for mythological language when speaking of the mystery of the fall. See Barth's *The Epistle to the Romans*, pp. 246–48.

20. LPP 279.

21. See Janz, *God, The Mind's Desire*, pp. 181-83.

22. Ricoeur, "Appropriation," in *Hermeneutics and the Human Sciences*, ed. and trans. John B. Thompson (Cambridge: Cambridge University Press, 1981), p. 192.

23. Cf. Garrett Green's argument that imagination is the point of contact or locus of revelation. *Imagining God: Theology and the Religious Imagination* (Grand Rapids, Mich.: Wm. B. Eerdmans, 1989/1998), p. 43.

24. Kierkegaard, *Concluding Unscientific Postscript*, pp. 318ff.

25. "Naming God," FS 234.

26. Kathryn Tanner, "Jesus Christ," in *The Cambridge Companion to Christian Doctrine*, ed. Colin E. Gunton (Cambridge: Cambridge University Press, 1997), pp. 246, 252-55.

27. Kierkegaard, *Either/Or* II, ed. and trans. Howard V. Hong and Edna H. Hong (Princeton, N.J.: Princeton University Press, 1987), p. 354. In a journal entry, Kierkegaard expresses his delight at discovering the "for you" in one of Luther's sermons. "Wonderful! The category 'for you' (subjectivity, inwardness) with which *Either/Or* concludes (only the truth that builds up [*opbygge*] is truth for you) is Luther's own. I have never really read anything by Luther. But now I open up his sermons — and right there in the Gospel for the First Sunday in Advent he says 'for you,' on this everything depends" (JP 2463).

28. For an excellent treatment of the Kantian influences in *Act and Being*, see Janz, *God, The Mind's Desire*, chapter 5.

29. Despite Kierkegaard's emphasis on the subjective *pro me*, he does not argue that the subjective is all that matters. In addition to the subjective *how*, it is also vital to recognize the priority of the objective *what*. In *The Book on Adler* he argues against the idealist synthesis of the subjective and objective, writing, "The essentially Christian exists before any Christian exists; it must exist in order for one to become a Christian. It contains the qualification by which a test is made of whether someone has become a Christian; it maintains its objective continuance outside all believers, while it also is in the inwardness of the believer. In short, here there is no identity between the subjective and the objective. If the essentially Christian enters into the hearts of ever so many believers, every believer realizes that it did not arise in his heart.... It is therefore a volatization of the concept, a dislocation of the essentially Christian, when one admits the wordplay that a revelation is a qualification belonging to subjectivity, or is the direct identity of subject-object, is an apparently objective something that nevertheless is subjective in the same way as erotic love *qua* an objective something is an illusion and falling in love is the reality. No, even if no one had become aware that God revealed himself in human form in Christ, he still had revealed himself; indeed, this is also why every contemporary (in the immediate sense) retains a responsibility if he did not become aware." *The Book on Adler*, ed. and trans. Howard V. Hong and Edna H. Hong (Princeton, N.J.: Princeton University Press, 1998), pp. 17-18.

Moreover, Kierkegaard is resolutely opposed to the idea that consciousness could achieve systematic closure in its account of reality. The existing individual never occupies this absolute standpoint. There is, however, such a standpoint, and it is occupied by God. Merold Westphal has written on this theme extensively in his work. See, for instance, "Theological Anti-Realism," in *Realism and Religion: Philosophical and Theological Perspectives*, ed. Andrew Moore and Michael Scott, pp. 132-45 (Burlington, Vt.: Ashgate, 2007).

30. It should be noted that Luther's own writings contribute to this confusion. In his lectures on Galatians, he notoriously suggests that faith creates God's divinity in us (*Luther's Spirituality*, p. 162). Barth seizes on this passage, arguing that this opens the door for idealism, and with it Feuerbach's reduction of theology to anthropology. See Barth's introduction to Feuerbach's *The Essence of Christianity*, pp. xxii–xxiii.

31. E 55, 67, 400. Cf. Bayer, "The Being of Christ in Faith," *Lutheran Quarterly* X (1996): p. 143: "The forgiveness of sins is not only what Schleiermacher interprets to be a clarification and strengthening of God-consciousness, but it is the victory over powers at enmity with God and humankind, powers that in their reality reach far beyond consciousness."

32. Ricoeur, "Philosophical and Theological Hermeneutics," p. 29.

33. Ibid., p. 28; cf. "Naming God," FS 227.

34. Ricoeur, "Philosophical and Theological Hermeneutics," p. 28 (translation slightly altered).

35. Ibid., p. 29. Faith, hope, ultimate concern, the feeling of absolute dependence would be empty and mute if they were not imaginatively figured by religious symbols, images, and narratives (p. 32).

36. Ricoeur, *Critique and Conviction: Conversations with François Azouvi and Marc de Launay*, trans. Kathleen Blamey (New York: Columbia University Press, 1998), pp. 152–54, 158.

37. Ricoeur, *Living Up to Death*, trans. David Pellauer (Chicago: University of Chicago Press, 2009), p. 51.

38. Ricoeur, *Critique and Conviction*, pp. 152–54. Ricoeur makes a similar identification of the cross and resurrection in his much earlier essay on Bonhoeffer, "The Non-Religious Interpretation of Christianity in Bonhoeffer," in *Bonhoeffer and Continental Thought: Cruciform Philosophy*, ed. Brian Gregor and Jens Zimmermann, p. 172 (Bloomington: Indiana University Press, 2009). In *Living Up to Death*, Ricoeur points toward a short circuit of Cross-Pentecost, which does not necessarily pass through a corporeal resurrection (p. 53).

39. Ricoeur, "Philosophical and Theological Hermeneutics," p. 32.

40. Vanhoozer, *Biblical Narrative in the Philosophy of Paul Ricoeur: A Study in Hermeneutics and Theology* (Cambridge: Cambridge University Press, 1990), p. 248.

41. Ricoeur's Hegelian interpretation has similarities with Bonhoeffer's definition of the church as Christ existing as church-community, which has strong Hegelian features of its own, but Bonhoeffer stresses the empirical, bodily presence of Christ in a way Ricoeur does not. I am indebted to Paul Janz's book *God, the Mind's Desire* for helping me to appreciate the degree to which Bonhoeffer's thought stresses the concrete empirical presence of Christ here and now. (See pp. 180, 183–84, 220–21.)

42. Of course, if we interpret this empirical body as an unconditioned, positivistic given, we are vulnerable to Hegel's critique of sense-certainty. But we have already distanced ourselves from that view through Bonhoeffer's point that being *is* in reference to act. At the same time, act is also in reference to ob-jective being, which has a crucial exteriority and independence of the mediation of reflection and self-understanding.

43. See Gadamer's essay "The Proofs of Immortality in Plato's *Phaedo*," in *Dialogue and Dialectic: Eight Hermeneutical Studies on Plato*, trans. P. Christopher Smith, p. 22 (New Haven, Conn.: Yale University Press, 1980). "As Nietzsche has so aptly put it, the figure of the dying Socrates became the new ideal to which the noblest of the Greek

youth now dedicated themselves instead of to that older heroic ideal, Achilles. Thus the *Phaedo*'s poetic power to convince is stronger than its arguments' logical power to prove." This is not to deny that there are differences between the death of Socrates and that of Christ, since Christ exemplifies a sacrificial death for others, embodying an other-orientation beyond what we see in Socrates. But as with the comparison with the dying and rising gods, this would be a relative difference, within the limits of poetics.

44. See Kevin Hart's comments in "Mystic Maybes," in *After God: Richard Kearney and the Religious Turn in Continental Philosophy*, ed. John Panteleimon Manoussakis, pp. 220–21 (New York: Fordham University Press, 2006).

45. J. G. Fichte, *Attempt at a Critique of All Revelation*, trans. Garrett Green (Cambridge: Cambridge University Press, 1978).

46. This is all the more interesting given Heidegger's famous critique of onto-theology, which only allows the deity to enter on philosophy's own terms. The god of philosophy is the cold, lifeless *causa sui*, before whom human beings "can neither pray nor sacrifice," nor fall to their knees in awe, nor play music or dance. Heidegger suggests that the "god-less thinking" that abandons this philosophical god might be closer to the genuinely divine God. "The Onto-Theo-Logical Constitution of Metaphysics," in *Identity and Difference*, trans. Joan Stambaugh (Chicago: University of Chicago Press, 1969), p. 72. Heidegger's critique of onto-theology needs to be taken seriously, but here again we must view with suspicion the purported openness of his god-less philosophical thinking. Despite the occasional reverent remark about preserving the integrity of Christian faith and theology, Heidegger shows little interest in seriously facing up to the claims of Christian revelation. Instead, the "openness" of his philosophical-poetic piety allows for an ongoing deferral of Christian revelation in favor of a pagan alternative.

47. It is, however, the case that philosophy can concede such possibilities when it proceeds in the hypothetical mode: e.g., "if Christian faith is true, this is what it is and what it means." Similarly, the phenomenology of religion can also proceed in the mode of the possible when it describes the practices and beliefs of particular religions without proclaiming them as true. See, for instance, Westphal, *God, Guilt, and Death*.

48. Theologically, we cannot do justice to this notion of encountering Christ as there for us unless we consider that the Spirit is also there for us, quickening faith in us and testifying to Christ, making it possible for us to understand the word, and interceding for us with groanings too deep for words (Rom. 8:26). On this point there is a clear difference between theological hermeneutics and Ricoeur's philosophical hermeneutics, which focuses on the imagination and gives surprisingly little attention to the grace of the Spirit. Theologically, the imagination is indeed a locus of the Holy Spirit's activity, but for a theological hermeneutics imagination must not supplant the activity of the Spirit.

49. Ricoeur, *Critique and Conviction*, p. 166.

50. Ricoeur, *Living Up to Death*, pp. 44, 46–47.

51. Jüngel, *Justification*, p. 263.

52. Ibid., p. 264.

53. Levinas, *Is it Righteous to Be?* p. 218.

54. Levinas, *Humanism of the Other*, p. 27.

55. Ricoeur, "Evil, A Challenge to Philosophy and Theology," FS, p. 261.

56. Ricoeur, *Living Up to Death*, p. 11.

57. Ricoeur, *Critique and Conviction*, p. 156.

58. Ibid., p. 158.

59. Ibid., p. 156.
60. Ricoeur, *Living Up to Death*, p. 42.
61. Ibid., p. 50.
62. Ibid., p. 159.
63. Ibid., p. 161.
64. Ibid., pp. 46–47.
65. Ibid., p. 43.
66. Ibid., p. 44. Or as he puts it in *Critique and Conviction:* "Let God, at my death, do with me as he wills. I demand nothing, I demand no 'after.' I cast upon others, my survivors, the task of taking up again my desire to be, my effort to exist, in the time of the living" (p. 158). This seems to be the only sense in which Ricoeur would be willing to speak of death being swallowed up in victory (I Cor. 15:54).
67. See Q.1 of the Larger Catechism of the Westminster Confession of Faith.
68. Cf. *Ecce Homo*, "Why I Am a Destiny," 9, in *Basic Writings of Nietzsche*, p. 791. "Have I been understood?—*Dionysus versus the Crucified.*"
69. Nietzsche, *The Will to Power*, #1052, pp. 542–43.
70. See Frits de Lange, "Aristocratic Christendom: On Bonhoeffer and Nietzsche," in *Bonhoeffer and Continental Thought*, pp. 73–83; and Frick, "Friedrich Nietzsche's Aphorisms and Dietrich Bonhoeffer's Theology."
71. Bonhoeffer suggests that Nietzsche takes over Feuerbach's doctrine of the whole (rather than partial) human being. Cf. Frick, "Friedrich Nietzsche's Aphorisms and Dietrich Bonhoeffer's Theology," p. 179.
72. See Merleau-Ponty, *The Visible and the Invisible*, ed. Claude Lefort, trans. Alphonso Lingis (Evanston, Ill.: Northwestern University Press, 1964), pp. 130–55.
73. The sinfulness of the *sarx* is not a matter of materiality or physicality, but rather the incurred orientation of the human being that seeks itself rather than God. *Sarx* is a sinful *how*, not an ontic *what*; this is why it is possible to undertake spiritual and intellectual pursuits in a fleshly manner.
74. Nietzsche, *The Will to Power*, #1052, p. 542.
75. Marsh, *Reclaiming Dietrich Bonhoeffer*, p. 104.
76. Cf. Walter Lowrie's introduction to Kierkegaard's *Stages on Life's Way* (New York: Schocken Books, 1967), p. 7.
77. *Thus Spoke Zarathustra*, First Part, in *The Portable Nietzsche*, p. 139.
78. For a comparison of Nietzsche's *Übermensch* with Bonhoeffer's Christology, see Frick, "Friedrich Nietzsche's Aphorisms and Dietrich Bonhoeffer's Theology," pp. 197–99.

Select Bibliography

Augustine. *Augustine: On the Inner Life of the Mind.* Edited by Robert E. Meagher. Indianapolis: Hackett, 1998.
———. *Confessions.* Translated by Henry Chadwick. Oxford: Oxford University Press, 1991.
———. *On Free Choice of the Will.* Translated by Thomas Williams. Indianapolis: Hackett, 1993.
Barker, H. Gaylon. "Bonhoeffer, Luther, and *Theologia Crucis*." *Dialog* 34, no. 1 (Winter 1995): pp. 10–17.
Barth, Karl. *The Epistle to the Romans.* Translated by Edwyn C. Hoskyns. London: Oxford University Press, 1933.
———. *The Humanity of God.* Atlanta: John Knox Press, 1960.
———. *On Religion: The Revelation of God as the Sublimation of Religion.* Translated by Garrett Green. New York: T & T Clark, 2006.
———. *Protestant Theology in the Nineteenth Century: Its Background and History,* new ed. Translated by Brian Cozens and John Bowden. Grand Rapids, Mich.: Eerdmans, 2002.
Baur, Michael. "Heidegger and Aquinas on the Self as Substance." In *Postmodernism and Christian Philosophy,* ed. Roman T. Ciapalo, pp. 38–57. Mishawaka, Ind.: American Maritain Association, 1997.
Bayer, Oswald. "The Being of Christ in Faith." Translated by Christine Helmer. *Lutheran Quarterly* X (1996): pp. 135–50.
———. "The Doctrine of Justification and Ontology." Translated by Christine Helmer. *Neue Zeitschrift für Systematische Theologie und Religionsphilosophie* 43, issue 1 (2001): pp. 44–53.
———. "Does Evil Persist?" Translated by Christine Helmer. *Lutheran Quarterly* XI (1997), pp. 143–50.
———. "Hermeneutical Theology." In *Philosophical Hermeneutics and Biblical Exegesis,* ed. Petr Pokorný and Jan Roskovec, pp. 103–20. Tübingen: Mohr Siebeck, 2002.
———. *Living by Faith: Justification and Santification.* Translated by Geoffrey W. Bromiley. Grand Rapids, Mich.: William B. Eerdmans, 2003.
———. "Luther as an Interpreter of Holy Scripture." Translated by Mark Mattes. In *The Cambridge Companion to Martin Luther,* ed. Donald K. McKim, pp. 73–85. Cambridge: Cambridge University Press, 2003.
———. "The Modern Narcissus." Translated by Christine Helmer. *Lutheran Quarterly* 9 (1995): pp. 301–13.
———. "Theology in the Conflict of Interpretations—Before the Text." Translated by Gwen Griffiths-Dickson. *Modern Theology* 16, no. 2 (October 2000): pp. 495–502.
———. "The Word of the Cross." Translated by John R. Betz. *Lutheran Quarterly* 9 (1995): pp. 47–55.
Bellinger, Charles K. *The Genealogy of Violence: Reflections on Creation, Freedom, and Evil.* Oxford: Oxford University Press, 2001.

Bernet, Rudolf. "Christianity and Philosophy." *Continental Philosophy Review* 32 (1999): pp. 325-42.
Bethge, Eberhard. *Dietrich Bonhoeffer: A Biography*. Translated by Eric Mosbacher. Revised and edited by Victoria J. Barnett. Minneapolis: Fortress Press, 2000.
Bloechl, Jeffrey. "Ethics as First Philosophy and Religion." In *The Face of the Other and the Trace of God: Essays on the Philosophy of Emmanuel Lévinas*, ed. Jeffrey Bloechl, pp. 130-51. New York: Fordham University Press, 2000.
Boersma, Hans. "Irenaeus, Derrida and Hospitality: On the Eschatological Overcoming of Violence." *Modern Theology* 19, no. 2 (April 2003): pp. 163-80.
―――. "Redemptive Hospitality in Irenaeus: A Model for Ecumenicity in a Violent World." *Pro Ecclesia* XI, no. 2 (2002): pp. 207-26.
Bonhoeffer, Dietrich. *Act and Being: Transcendental Philosophy and Ontology in Systematic Theology*. Translated by H. Martin Rumscheidt. Minneapolis: Fortress Press, 1996.
―――. *Barcelona, Berlin, New York: 1928-1931*. Translated by Douglas W. Stott. Minneapolis: Fortress Press, 2008.
―――. *Christ the Center*. Translated by Edwin H. Robinson. New York: Harper & Row, 1978.
―――. *Conspiracy and Imprisonment: 1940-1945*. Translated by Lisa E. Dahill. Minneapolis: Fortress Press, 2006.
―――. *Creation and Fall: A Theological Exposition of Genesis 1-3*. Translated by Douglas Stephen Bax. Minneapolis: Fortress Press, 1997.
―――. *Discipleship*. Translated by Martin Kuske and Ilse Tödt. Minneapolis: Fortress Press, 2001.
―――. *Ethics*. Edited by Clifford J. Green. Translated by Reinhard Krauss, Charles C. West, and Douglas W. Stott. Minneapolis: Fortress Press, 2005.
―――. *Letters and Papers from Prison*. Enlarged edition. Edited by Eberhard Bethge. New York: Simon & Schuster, 1971.
―――. *Letters and Papers from Prison*. Edited by John W. de Gruchy. Translated by Isabel Best, Lisa E. Dahill, Reinhard Krauss, and Nancy Lukens. Minneapolis: Fortress Press, 2010.
―――. *Life Together / Prayerbook of the Bible*. Translated by Daniel Bloesch and James H. Burtness. Minneapolis: Fortress Press, 1996.
―――. *Sanctorum Communio: A Theological Study of the Sociology of the Church*. Translated by Reinhard Krauss and Nancy Lukens. Minneapolis: Fortress Press, 1998.
Braaten, Carl E., and Robert W. Jenson, eds. *Union with Christ: The New Finnish Interpretation of Luther*. Grand Rapids, Mich.: William B. Eerdmans, 1998.
Breton, Stanislas. *The Word and the Cross*. Translated by Jacquelyn Porter. New York: Fordham University Press, 2002.
Busch, Eberhard. *Karl Barth: His Life from Letters and Autobiographical Texts*. Translated by John Bowden. Grand Rapids, Mich.: William B. Eerdmans, 1976.
Busch, Thomas W. "Perception, Finitude, and Transgression: A Note on Merleau-Ponty and Ricoeur." In *Merleau-Ponty, Hermeneutics, and Postmodernism*, ed. Thomas W. Busch and Shaun Gallagher, pp. 25-35. Albany: State University of New York Press, 1992.
Chrétien, Jean-Louis. *The Call and the Response*. Translated by Anne A. Davenport. New York: Fordham University Press, 2004.
Crites, Stephen. "*The Sickness Unto Death*: A Social Interpretation." In *Søren Kierke-

gaard: *Critical Assessments of Leading Philosophers*. Volume IV, Social and Political Philosophy: Kierkegaard and the "Present Age." Edited by Daniel W. Conway with K. E. Grover, pp. 51–66. London and New York: Routledge, 2002.

Crowe, Benjamin D. *Heidegger's Religious Origins: Destruction and Authenticity*. Bloomington: Indiana University Press, 2006.

———. "On the Track of the Fugitive Gods: Heidegger, Luther, Hölderlin." *The Journal of Religion* 87, issue 2 (2007): pp. 183–205.

Dahill, Lisa. "Reading from the Underside of Selfhood: Dietrich Bonhoeffer and Spiritual Formation." *Spiritus* 1 (2003): pp. 186–203.

Desmond, William. *Is There a Sabbath for Thought? Between Religion and Philosophy*. New York: Fordham University Press, 2005.

Dupré, Louis. *Religious Mystery and Rational Reflection*. Grand Rapids, Mich.: William B. Eerdmans, 1998.

Elshtain, Jean Bethke. *Who Are We? Critical Reflections and Hopeful Possibilities*. Grand Rapids, Mich.: William B. Eerdmans, 2000.

Empie, Paul C., and James I. McCord, eds. *Marburg Revisited: A Reexamination of Lutheran and Reformed Traditions*. Minneapolis: Augsburg Publishing House, 1966.

Erasmus, Desiderius, and Martin Luther. *Discourse on Free Will*. Edited by Ernst F. Winter. New York and London: Continuum, 1961, 1989.

Evans, C. Stephen. "Who Is the Other in *Sickness Unto Death*? God and Human Relations in the Constitution of the Self." *Kierkegaard Studies*, Year Book 1997. Berlin: Walter de Gruyter, 1997: pp. 1–15.

Ferreira, M. Jamie. "Kierkegaardian Faith: The 'Condition' and the Response." *International Journal for Philosophy of Religion* 28 (1990): pp. 63–79.

———. "Kierkegaardian Transitions: Paradox and Pathos." *International Philosophical Quarterly* XXXI, no. 1, issue no. 121 (March 1991): pp. 65–80.

———. *Love's Grateful Striving: A Commentary on Kierkegaard's* Works of Love. Oxford: Oxford University Press, 2001.

Feuerbach, Ludwig. *The Essence of Christianity*. Translated by George Eliot. New York: Harper, 1957.

Fichte, J. G. *Attempt at a Critique of All Revelation*. Translated by Garrett Green. Cambridge: Cambridge University Press, 1978.

Ford, David. *Self and Salvation: Being Transformed*. Cambridge: Cambridge University Press, 1999.

Forde, Gerhard O. *On Being a Theologian of the Cross: Reflections on Luther's Heidelberg Disputation, 1518*. Grand Rapids, Mich.: William B. Eerdmans, 1997.

Gadamer, Hans-Georg. *A Century of Philosophy: A Conversation with Riccardo Dottori*. Translated by Rod Coltman with Sigrid Koepke. New York and London: Continuum, 2003.

———. *Philosophical Hermeneutics*. Translated and edited by David Linge. Berkeley: University of California Press, 1976.

———. *Truth and Method*. 2nd rev. ed. Translated by Joel Weinsheimer and Donald G. Marshall. New York: Continuum, 1989.

Gerrish, B. A. *Grace and Reason: A Study in the Theology of Luther*. London: Oxford University Press, 1962.

Green, Clifford J. *Bonhoeffer: A Theology of Sociality*, rev. ed. Grand Rapids, Mich.: William B. Eerdmans, 1972/1999.

Green, Garrett. *Imagining God: Theology and the Religious Imagination*. Grand Rapids, Mich.: William B. Eerdmans, 1989/1998.

———. *Theology, Hermeneutics, and Imagination: The Crisis of Interpretation at the End of Modernity*. Cambridge: Cambridge University Press, 2000.

Gritsch, Eric W., and Robert W. Jenson. *Lutheranism: The Theological Movement and its Confessional Writings*. Philadelphia: Fortress Press, 1976.

Hadot, Pierre. *Philosophy as a Way of Life: Spiritual Exercises from Socrates to Foucault*. Edited by Arnold I. Davidson. Translated by Michael Chase. Malden, Mass.: Blackwell, 1995.

———. *What Is Ancient Philosophy?* Translated by Michael Chase. Cambridge, Mass.: Harvard University Press, 2002.

Hall, Douglas John. *The Cross in Our Context: Jesus and the Suffering World*. Minneapolis: Fortress Press, 2003.

Hampson, Daphne. *Christian Contradictions: The Structures of Lutheran and Catholic Thought*. Cambridge: Cambridge University Press, 2001.

———. "Luther on the Self: A Feminist Critique." *Word & World* VIII, no. 4 (1988): pp. 334–42.

Hanson, Jeffrey. "Michel Henry's Critique of the Limits of Intuition." *Studia Phænomenologica* IX (2009): pp. 97–111.

———. "Phenomenology and Eschatology in Michel Henry." In *Phenomenology and Eschatology: Not Yet in the Now*, ed. Neal DeRoo and John Panteleimon Manoussakis, pp. 153–66. Burlington, Vt.: Ashgate, 2009.

Hart, Kevin. "Phenomenality and Christianity." *Angelaki* 12, no. 1 (April 2007): pp. 37–53.

———. "'Without World': Eschatology in Michel Henry." In *Phenomenology and Eschatology: Not Yet in the Now*, ed. Neal DeRoo and John Panteleimon Manoussakis, pp. 167–92. Burlington, Vt.: Ashgate, 2009.

Hegel, G. W. F. *The Encylopaedia Logic*. Translated by T. F. Geraets, W. A. Suchting, and H. S. Harris. Indianapolis: Hackett, 1991.

———. *Introduction to* The Philosophy of History. Translated by Leo Rauch. Indianapolis: Hackett, 1988.

———. *Lectures on the Philosophy of Religion Volume III: The Consummate Religion*. Edited by Peter C. Hodgson. Translated by R. F. Brown, P. C. Hodgson, and J. M. Stewart, with H. S. Harris. Berkeley: University of California Press, 1985.

Heidegger, Martin. *Being and Time*. Translated by John Macquarrie and Edward Robinson. San Francisco: Harper & Row, 1962.

———. *Introduction to Metaphysics*. Translated by Gregory Fried and Richard Polt. New Haven, Conn.: Yale University Press, 2000.

———. *Ontology—The Hermeneutics of Facticity*. Translated by John van Buren. Bloomington: Indiana University Press, 1999.

———. "Phenomenology and Theology." In *Pathmarks*, ed. William McNeill. Cambridge: Cambridge University Press, 1998.

———. *Supplements: From the Earliest Essays to* Being and Time *and Beyond*. Edited by John van Buren. Albany: State University of New York Press, 2002.

Henrich, Dieter. *Between Kant and Hegel: Lectures on German Idealism*. Edited by David S. Pacini. Cambridge, Mass.: Harvard University Press, 2003.

Henry, Michel. "Material Phenomenology and Language (or, pathos and language)." *Continental Philosophy Review* 32 (1999): p. 346.

Hinkson, Craig. "Luther and Kierkegaard: Theologians of the Cross." *International Journal of Systematic Theology* 3, no. 1 (March 2001): pp. 27-45.
Houston, Sam. "Possibility and Identity: Ricoeur and Frei on the Resurrection." *Journal of Philosophy and Scripture* 4, issue 2 (Spring 2007): pp. 16-31.
Hunsinger, George. *Disruptive Grace: Studies in the Theology of Karl Barth*. Grand Rapids, Mich.: William B. Eerdmans, 2000.
Janz, Paul D. "Bonhoeffer, This-Worldliness, and the Limits of Phenomenology." In *Bonhoeffer and Continental Thought: Cruciform Philosophy*, ed. Brian Gregor and Jens Zimmermann, pp. 46-69. Bloomington: Indiana University Press, 2009.
———. *God, The Mind's Desire: Reference, Reason and Christian Thinking*. Cambridge: Cambridge University Press, 2004.
———. "Revelation as Divine Causality." In Oliver Davies, Paul D. Janz, and Clemens Sedmak, *Transformation Theology: Church in the World*. London: T & T Clark, 2007, pp. 63-88.
Jeanrond, Werner G. *Theological Hermeneutics: Development and Significance*. New York: Crossroad, 1991.
Jenson, Matt. *The Gravity of Sin: Augustine, Luther, and Barth on* homo incurvatus in se. New York and London: T & T Clark, 2006.
Jenson, Robert W. *On Thinking the Human: Resolutions of Difficult Notions*. Grand Rapids, Mich.: William B. Eerdmans, 2003.
———. "An Ontology of Freedom in the *De servo arbitrio* of Luther." *Modern Theology* 10, no. 3 (July 1994): pp. 247-52.
———. *Systematic Theology, Volume I: The Triune God*. Oxford: Oxford University Press, 1997.
———. *Systematic Theology, Volume II: The Works of God*. Oxford: Oxford University Press, 1999.
Jüngel, Eberhard. *God as the Mystery of the World: On the Foundation of the Theology of the Crucified One in the Dispute between Theism and Atheism*. Translated by Darrell L. Guder. Grand Rapids, Mich.: William B. Eerdmans, 1983.
———. *Justification: The Heart of the Christian Faith. A Theological Study with an Ecumenical Purpose*. Translated by Jeffrey F. Cayzer. Edinburgh: T & T Clark, 2001.
———. *Theological Essays* I. Translated by J. B. Webster. Edinburgh: T & T Clark, 1989.
———. *Theological Essays* II. Translated by Arnold Neufeldt-Fast and J. B. Webster. Edinburgh: T & T Clark, 1995.
Kangas, David J. *Kierkegaard's Instant: On Beginnings*. Bloomington: Indiana University Press, 2007.
———. "Luther and Modernity: Reiner Schürmann's Topology of the Modern in *Broken Hegemonies*." *Epoché* 14, issue 2 (Spring 2010): pp. 431-52.
Kant, Immanuel. *Anthropology from a Pragmatic Point of View*. Edited by Robert B. Louden. Cambridge: Cambridge University Press, 2006.
———. *Religion and Rational Theology*. Translated and edited by Allen W. Wood and George Di Giovanni. Cambridge: Cambridge University Press, 1996.
Kearney, Richard. *Debates in Continental Philosophy: Conversations with Contemporary Thinkers*. New York: Fordham University Press, 2004.
———. *The God Who May Be: A Hermeneutics of Religion*. Bloomington: Indiana University Press, 2001.
———. *On Paul Ricoeur: The Owl of Minerva*. Burlington, Vt.: Ashgate, 2004.

———. *On Stories*. London and New York: Routledge, 2002.
———. *Poetics of Imagining: Modern to Post-Modern*. Edinburgh: Edinburgh University Press, 1998.
———. *Strangers, Gods, and Monsters: Interpreting Otherness*. London and New York: Routledge, 2003.
Kelly, Michael. "Dispossession: On the Untenability of Michel Henry's Theory of Self-Awareness." *Journal of the British Society for Phenomenology* 35, no. 3 (October 2004): pp. 261–82.
Kempis, Thomas à. *The Imitation of Christ*. Edited and translated by Joseph N. Tylenda, S.J. New York: Vintage, 1998.
Kierkegaard, Søren. *The Concept of Anxiety*. Edited and translated by Reidar Thomte and Albert B. Anderson. Princeton, N.J.: Princeton University Press, 1980.
———. *Concluding Unscientific Postscript to* Philosophical Fragments. Edited and translated by Howard V. Hong and Edna H. Hong. Princeton, N.J.: Princeton University Press, 1992.
———. *Either/Or,* vols. I and II. Edited and translated by Howard V. Hong and Edna H. Hong. Princeton, N.J.: Princeton University Press, 1987.
———. *Fear and Trembling/Repetition*. Edited and translated by Howard V. Hong and Edna H. Hong. Princeton, N.J.: Princeton University Press, 1983.
———. *For Self-Examination / Judge For Yourself!* Edited and translated by Howard V. Hong and Edna H. Hong. Princeton, N.J.: Princeton University Press, 1990.
———. *Philosophical Fragments*. Edited and translated by Howard V. Hong and Edna H. Hong. Princeton, N.J.: Princeton University Press, 1985.
———. *Practice in Christianity*. Edited and translated by Howard V. Hong and Edna H. Hong. Princeton, N.J.: Princeton University Press, 1991.
———. *The Sickness Unto Death*. Edited and translated by Howard V. Hong and Edna H. Hong. Princeton, N.J.: Princeton University Press, 1980.
———. *Works of Love*. Edited and translated by Howard V. Hong and Edna H. Hong. Princeton, N.J.: Princeton University Press, 1995.
Klemm, David E. "Ricoeur, Theology, and the Rhetoric of Overturning." *Journal of Literature & Theology* 3, no. 3 (1989): pp. 267–84.
Kotsko, Adam. "Objective Spirit and Continuity in the Theology of Dietrich Bonhoeffer." *Philosophy & Theology* 17, nos. 1 & 2 (2005): pp. 17–31.
LaCocque, André, and Paul Ricoeur. *Thinking Biblically: Exegetical and Hermeneutical Studies*. Translated by David Pellauer. Chicago: University of Chicago Press, 1998.
Leder, Drew. *The Absent Body*. Chicago: University of Chicago Press, 1990.
———. "Flesh and Blood: A Proposed Supplement to Merleau-Ponty." In *The Body: Classic and Contemporary Readings*, ed. Donn Welton, pp. 200–210. Oxford: Blackwell, 1999.
———. "A Tale of Two Bodies: The Cartesian Corpse and the Lived Body." In *Body and Flesh: A Philosophical Reader*, ed. Donn Welton, pp. 117–29. Malden, Mass.: Wiley-Blackwell, 1998.
Levinas, Emmanuel. *Alterity and Transcendence*. Translated by Michael B. Smith. New York: Columbia University Press, 1999.
———. *Emmanuel Levinas: Basic Philosophical Writings*. Edited by Adriaan Peperzak, Simon Critchley, and Robert Bernasconi. Bloomington: Indiana University Press, 1996.

———. *Existence and Existents*. Translated by Alphonso Lingis. Pittsburgh: Duquesne University Press, 1969.
———. *Humanism of the Other*. Translated by Nidra Poller. Urbana: University of Illinois Press, 2003.
———. *Is it Righteous to Be? Interviews with Emmanuel Levinas*. Edited by Jill Robbins. Stanford, Calif.: Stanford University Press, 2001.
———. *Otherwise than Being or Beyond Essence*. Translated by Alphonso Lingis. Pittsburgh: Duquesne University Press, 1981, 1997.
———. *Time and the Other*. Translated by Richard A. Cohen. Pittsburgh: Duquesne University Press, 1987.
———. *Totality and Infinity: An Essay on Exteriority*. Translated by Alphonso Lingis. Pittsburgh: Duquesne University Press, 1969.
Lewis, Alan E. *Between Cross and Resurrection: A Theology of Holy Saturday*. Grand Rapids, Mich.: William B. Eerdmans, 2001.
Lowe, E. J. "Substance." In *An Encyclopaedia of Philosophy*, ed. G. H. R. Parkinson, pp. 255–78. New York: Routledge, 1988.
Lowe, Walter James. "The Coherence of Ricoeur." *The Journal of Religion* 61, no. 4 (October 1981): pp. 384–402.
Luther, Martin. *Martin Luther's Basic Theological Writings*, 2nd ed. Edited by Timothy F. Lull. Minneapolis: Fortress Press, 2005.
———. *Luther's Spirituality*. Edited and translated by Philip D. W. Krey and Peter D. S. Krey. New York: Paulist Press, 2007.
———. *Luther's Works*. 55 vols. Edited by Jaroslav Pelikan. St. Louis, Mo.: Concordia Publishing House / Philadelphia: Fortress Press, 1955–86.
Mackey, Louis. "From Autobiography to Theology: Augustine's *Confessions*." In *Peregrinations of the Word: Essays in Medieval Philosophy*. Ann Arbor: University of Michigan Press, 1997, pp. 7–55.
Marcel, Gabriel. *Gabriel Marcel's Perspectives on the Broken World*. Translated by Katharine Rose Hanley. Milwaukee: Marquette University Press, 1998.
———. *Tragic Wisdom and Beyond*. Translated by Stephen Jolin and Peter McCormick. Evanston, Ill.: Northwestern University Press, 1973.
Marion, Jean-Luc. *Being Given: Toward a Phenomenology of Givenness*. Translated by Jeffrey L. Kosky. Stanford, Calif.: Stanford University Press, 2002.
———. *In Excess: Studies of Saturated Phenomena*. Translated by Robyn Horner and Vincent Berraud. New York: Fordham University Press, 2002.
Marsh, Charles. "In Defense of a Self: The Theological Search for a Postmodern Identity." *Scottish Journal of Theology* 55, no. 3 (2002): pp. 253–82.
———. *Reclaiming Dietrich Bonhoeffer: The Promise of His Theology*. Oxford: Oxford University Press, 1994.
Mattes, Mark C. "Hegel's Lutheran Claim." *Lutheran Quarterly* XIV (2000): pp. 249–79.
———. *The Role of Justification in Contemporary Theology*. Grand Rapids, Mich.: William B. Eerdmans, 2004.
———. "The Thomistic Turn in Evangelical Catholic Ethics." *Lutheran Quarterly* XVI (2002): pp. 65–100.
McDougall, Joy Ann. "Sin—No More? A Feminist Re-Visioning of a Christian Theology of Sin." *Anglican Theological Review* 88, no. 2 (2006): pp. 215–35.
Meilaender, Gilbert C. "The Examined Life Is not Worth Living: Learning from Luther."

In *The Theory and Practice of Virtue*. Notre Dame, Ind.: University of Notre Dame Press, 1984, pp. 100–26.

Menacher, Mark D. "Gerhard Ebeling in Retrospect." *Lutheran Quarterly* XXI (2007): pp. 163–96.

Merleau-Ponty, Maurice. *Phenomenology of Perception*. Translated by Colin Smith. London: Routledge & Kegan Paul, 1962.

Minear, Paul Sevier. "The Crucified World: The Enigma of Galatians 6,14." In *Theologia Crucis—Signum Crucis: Festschrift für Erich Dinkler zum 70. Geburtstag*, ed. Carl Andresen and Günter Klein, pp. 395–407. Tübingen: J. C. B. Mohr, 1979.

Moonen, Christoph. "Touching from a Distance: In Search of the Self in Henry and Kierkegaard." *Studia Phænomenologica* IX (2009): pp. 147–56.

Mulhall, Stephen. *Philosophical Myths of the Fall*. New York: Routledge, 2005.

Nelson, Derek. "The Indicative of Grace and the Imperative of Freedom: An Invitation to the Theology of Eberhard Jüngel." *Dialog: A Journal of Theology* 44, no. 2 (Summer 2005): pp. 164–80.

Newbigin, Lesslie. *The Gospel in a Pluralist Society*. Grand Rapids, Mich.: William B. Eerdmans, 1989.

Nietzsche, Friedrich. *Basic Writings of Nietzsche*. Edited and translated by Walter Kaufmann. New York: The Modern Library, 1968.

———. *The Portable Nietzsche*. Edited and translated by Walter Kaufmann. New York: Viking Penguin, 1968, 1982.

———. *The Will to Power*. Edited and translated by Walter Kaufmann and R. J. Hollingdale. New York: Vintage, 1967.

Ochs, Peter. "From Phenomenology to Scripture: A Response." *Modern Theology* 16, no. 3 (July 2000): pp. 341–45.

Ozment, Stephen E. *Homo Spiritualis: A Comparative Study of the Anthropology of Johannes Tauler, Jean Gerson and Martin Luther (1509–16) in the Context of Their Theological Thought*. Leiden: E. J. Brill, 1969.

Pangritz, Andreas. *Karl Barth in the Theology of Dietrich Bonhoeffer*. Translated by Barbara and Martin Rumscheidt. Grand Rapids, Mich.: William B. Eerdmans, 2000.

Pasewark, Kyle A. "Predestination as a Condition of Freedom: Reconsidering the Reformation." In *Human and Divine Agency: Anglican, Catholic, and Lutheran Perspectives*, ed. F. Michael McLain and W. Mark Richardson, pp. 49–66. Lanham, Md.: University Press of America, 1999.

Pelikan, Jaroslav. *From Luther to Kierkegaard: A Study in the History of Theology*. St. Louis, Mo.: Concordia Publishing House, 1950.

Pieper, Josef. *Leisure, the Basis of Culture*. Translated by Gerald Malsbary. South Bend, Ind.: St. Augustine's Press, 1998.

Polanyi, Michael. *Knowing and Being: Essays by Michael Polanyi*. Edited by Marjorie Grene. Chicago: University of Chicago Press, 1969.

———. *Personal Knowledge: Towards a Post-Critical Philosophy*. Chicago: University of Chicago Press, 1958, 1962.

———. *The Study of Man*. Chicago: University of Chicago Press, 1959.

———. *The Tacit Dimension*. Garden City, N.Y.: Doubleday, 1966.

Rahner, Karl. *Hearer of the Word: Laying the Foundation for a Philosophy of Religion*. Translated by Joseph Donceel. New York: Continuum, 1994.

Rasmussen, Larry L. *Dietrich Bonhoeffer: Reality and Resistance*. Louisville, Ky.: Westminster John Knox Press, 2005.
Reno, R. R. *Redemptive Change: Atonement and the Christian Cure for the Soul*. Harrisburg, Pa.: Trinity Press International, 2002.
Ricoeur, Paul. "Approaching the Human Person." *Ethical Perspectives* 6, no. 1 (1999): pp. 45–54.
———. "The Canon between the Text and the Community." In *Philosophical Hermeneutics and Biblical Exegesis*, ed. Petr Pokorný and Jan Roskovec, pp. 7–26. Tübingen: Mohr Siebeck, 2002.
———. "Capabilities and Rights." In *Transforming Unjust Structures: The Capability Approach*, ed. Séverine Deneulin, Mathias Nebel, and Nicholas Sagovsky, pp. 17–26. Dordrecht: Springer, 2006.
———. *The Conflict of Interpretations: Essays in Hermeneutics*. Edited by Don Ihde. Evanston, Ill.: Northwestern University Press, 1974.
———. *The Course of Recognition*. Translated by David Pellauer. Cambridge, Mass.: Harvard University Press, 2005.
———. *Critique and Conviction: Conversations with François Azouvi and Marc de Launay*. Translated by Kathleen Blamey. New York: Columbia University Press, 1998.
———. "Ethics and Human Capability." In *Paul Ricoeur and Contemporary Moral Thought*, ed. John Wall and William Schweiker. New York: Routledge, 2002, pp. 279–90.
———. "Experience and Language in Religious Discourse." In *Phenomenology and the "Theological Turn": The French Debate*, ed. Dominique Janicaud et al., pp. 127–46. New York: Fordham University Press, 2000.
———. *Fallible Man*. Translated by Charles A. Kelbley. New York: Fordham University Press, 1986.
———. *Figuring the Sacred: Religion, Narrative, and Imagination*. Translated by David Pellauer. Edited by Mark I. Wallace. Minneapolis: Fortress Press, 1995.
———. *Freedom and Nature: The Voluntary and the Involuntary*. Translated by Erazím V. Kohak. Evanston, Ill.: Northwestern University Press, 1966.
———. *From Text to Action: Essays in Hermeneutics II*. Translated by Kathleen Blamey and John B. Thompson. London: The Athlone Press, 1991.
———. "The Human Being as the Subject Matter of Philosophy." In *The Narrative Path: The Later Works of Paul Ricoeur*, ed. T. Peter Kemp and David Rasmussen, pp. 89–101. Cambridge, Mass.: MIT Press, 1989.
———. *Oneself as Another*. Translated by Kathleen Blamey. Chicago: University of Chicago Press, 1992.
———. "Otherwise: A Reading of Emmanuel Levinas's *Otherwise than Being or Beyond Essence*." *Yale French Studies* no. 104 (2003): pp. 82–99.
———. *The Philosophy of Paul Ricoeur: An Anthology of His Work*. Edited by Charles E. Reagan and David Stewart. Boston: Beacon Press, 1978.
———. "Philosophical and Theological Hermeneutics." *Sciences Religieuses / Studies in Religion* 5, no. 1 (Summer 1975): pp. 14–33.
———. "Religion and Symbolic Violence." Translated by James Williams. *Contagion* 6 (1999): pp. 1–11.
———. "A Response by Paul Ricoeur." In *Paul Ricoeur and Narrative: Context and Contestation*, ed. Morny Joy, pp. xxxix–xliv. Calgary: University of Calgary Press, 1997.
———. "The Self in the Mirror of the Scriptures." In *The Whole and Divided Self*, ed.

David E. Aune and John McCarthy, pp. 201-20. New York: The Crossroad Publishing Company, 1997.

———. "The Status of *Vorstellung* in Hegel's Philosophy of Religion." In *Meaning, Truth, and God*, ed. Leroy S. Rouner, pp. 70-88. Notre Dame, Ind.: University of Notre Dame Press, 1982.

———. *The Symbolism of Evil*. Translated by Emerson Buchanan. Boston: Beacon Press, 1967.

———. "Toward a Hermeneutic of the Idea of Revelation." *Harvard Theological Review* 70, no. 1/2 (January-April 1977): pp. 1-37.

———. "Two Encounters with Kierkegaard: Kierkegaard and Evil; Doing Philosophy after Kierkegaard." Translated by David Pellauer. In *Kierkegaard's Truth: The Disclosure of the Self.* Vol. 5, Psychiatry and the Humanities, ed. Joseph H. Smith, pp. 313-42. New Haven, Conn., and London: Yale University Press, 1981.

Rorem, Paul. "Martin Luther's Christocentric Critique of Pseudo-Dionysian Spirituality." *Lutheran Quarterly* XI (1997): pp. 291-307.

Ruin, Hans. "The Moment of Truth: *Augenblick* and *Ereignis* in Heidegger." *Epochē: A Journal for the History of Philosophy* 6, no. 1 (1998): pp. 75-88.

Simms, Karl. *Paul Ricoeur.* London and New York: Routledge, 2003.

Smith, James K. A. *The Fall of Interpretation: Philosophical Foundations for a Creational Hermeneutic.* Downers Grove, Ill.: InterVarsity Press, 2000.

Smith, Michael B. *Toward the Outside: Concepts and Themes in Emmanuel Levinas.* Pittsburgh: Duquesne University Press, 2005.

Steinbock, Anthony. "The Problem of Forgetfulness in Michel Henry." *Continental Philosophy Review* 32 (1999): pp. 271-302.

Stock, Brian. *Augustine the Reader: Meditation, Self-Knowledge, and the Ethics of Interpretation.* Cambridge, Mass.: Harvard University Press, 1996.

Stiver, Dan R. *Theology After Ricoeur: New Directions in Hermeneutical Theology.* Louisville, Ky.: Westminster John Knox Press, 2001.

Tanner, Kathryn. *God and Creation in Christian Theology: Tyranny or Empowerment?* Minneapolis: Fortress Press, 1988.

———. "Jesus Christ." In *The Cambridge Companion to Christian Doctrine*, ed. Colin E. Gunton, pp. 245-71. Cambridge: Cambridge University Press, 1997.

Taylor, Charles. "The Dialogical Self." In *Rethinking Knowledge: Reflections Across the Disciplines*, ed. Robert F. Goodman and Walter F. Fisher, pp. 57-66. Albany: SUNY Press, 1995.

———. "Embodied Agency." In *Merleau-Ponty: Critical Essays*, ed. Henry Pietersma, pp. 1-21. Washington, D.C.: University Press of America, 1989.

———. *The Ethics of Authenticity.* Cambridge, Mass.: Harvard University Press, 1991.

———. "From Philosophical Anthropology to the Politics of Recognition: An Interview with Charles Taylor." *Thesis Eleven* 52 (1998): pp. 103-12.

———. *Human Agency and Language: Philosophical Papers I.* Cambridge: Cambridge University Press, 1985.

———. "The Moral Topography of the Self." In *Hermeneutics and Psychological Theory: Interpretive Perspectives on Personality, Psychotherapy, and Psychopathology*, ed. Stanley B. Messer, Louis A. Sass, and Robert L. Woolfolk, pp. 298-320. New Brunswick, N.J.: Rutgers University Press, 1988.

———. "A Philosopher's Postscript: Engaging the Citadel of Secular Reason." In *Reason*

      and the Reasons of Faith, ed. Paul J. Griffiths and Reinhard Hütter, pp. 339-53. New York and London: T & T Clark, 2005.
———. *Philosophical Arguments.* Cambridge, Mass.: Harvard University Press, 1995.
———. *Philosophy and the Human Sciences. Philosophical Papers Volume 2.* Cambridge: Cambridge University Press, 1985.
———. "Responsibility for Self." In *The Identity of Persons,* ed. Amélie Oksenberg Rorty, pp. 281-99. Berkeley: University of California Press, 1976.
———. *Sources of the Self: The Making of the Modern Identity.* Cambridge, Mass.: Harvard University Press, 1989.
———. "Taylor-made Selves." *The Philosopher's Magazine* 12 (Autumn 2000): pp. 37-40.
———. "What Is Secularity?" In *Transcending Boundaries in Philosophy and Theology: Reason, Meaning and Experience,* ed. Kevin Vanhoozer and Martin Warner, pp. 57-76. Burlington, Vt.: Ashgate, 2007.
Tietz, Christiane. "Bonhoeffer on the Uses and Limits of Philosophy." In *Bonhoeffer and Continental Thought,* ed. Brian Gregor and Jens Zimmermann, pp. 31-45. Bloomington: Indiana University Press, 2009.
Tödt, Heinz Eduard. *Authentic Faith: Bonhoeffer's Theological Ethics in Context.* Edited by Ernst-Albert Scharffenorth. Translated by David Stassen and Ilse Tödt. Grand Rapids, Mich.: William B. Eerdmans, 2007.
Torrance, Thomas F. *Space, Time and Incarnation.* Oxford: Oxford University Press, 1969.
———. *Theological Science.* Oxford: Oxford University Press, 1969.
van Buren, John. *The Young Heidegger: Rumor of the Hidden King.* Bloomington: Indiana University Press, 1994.
van den Hengel, John. "Between Philosophy and Theology: Ricoeur's Testimony of the Self." In *Between the Human and the Divine: Philosophical and Theological Hermeneutics,* ed. Andrzej Wierciński, pp. 122-37. Toronto: The Hermeneutic Press, 2002.
Vanhoozer, Kevin J. *Biblical Narrative in the Philosophy of Paul Ricoeur: A Study in Hermeneutics and Theology.* Cambridge: Cambridge University Press, 1990.
———. "Discourse on Matter: Hermeneutics and the 'Miracle' of Understanding." In *Hermeneutics at the Crossroads,* ed. Kevin J. Vanhoozer, James K. A. Smith, and Bruce Ellis Benson, pp. 3-34. Bloomington: Indiana University Press, 2006.
———. "The Spirit of Understanding: Special Revelation and General Hermeneutics." In *Disciplining Hermeneutics: Interpretation in Christian Perspective,* ed. Roger Lundin, pp. 131-65. Grand Rapids, Mich.: William B. Eerdmans, 1997.
von Loewenich, Walther. *Luther's Theology of the Cross.* Translated by Herbert J. A. Bouman. Minneapolis: Augsburg Publishing House, 1976.
Wall, John. *Moral Creativity: Paul Ricoeur and the Poetics of Possibility.* Oxford: Oxford University Press, 2005.
Wallace, Mark I. "From Phenomenology to Scripture? Paul Ricoeur's Hermeneutical Philosophy of Religion." *Modern Theology* 16, no. 3 (July 2000): pp. 301-13.
———. *The Second Naiveté: Barth, Ricoeur, and the New Yale Theology,* 2nd ed. Macon, Ga.: Mercer University Press, 1995.
———. "The Summoned Self: Ethics and Hermeneutics in Paul Ricoeur in Dialogue with Emmanuel Levinas." In *Paul Ricoeur and Contemporary Moral Thought,* ed. John Wall, William Schweiker, and W. David Hall. New York: Routledge, 2002.

Watson, Natalie K. "*Theologia Incurvata In Se Ipse?* One Feminist Theologian's Reading of Eberhard Jüngel's Theology." *Reviews in Religion and Theology* 9, no. 3 (2002): pp. 201-205.

Webster, John. "Systematic Theology after Barth." In *The Modern Theologians*, ed. David Ford and Rachel Muers, pp. 249-64. Oxford: Blackwell, 2005.

———. "'The Grammar of Doing': Luther and Barth on Human Agency." In *Barth's Moral Theology*, pp. 151-78. New York: Continuum, 2004.

Westphal, Merold. *Becoming a Self: A Reading of Kierkegaard's* Concluding Unscientific Postscript. West Lafayette, Ind.: Purdue University Press, 1996.

———. *God, Guilt, and Death: An Existential Phenomenology of Religion*. Bloomington: Indiana University Press, 1984.

———. *Levinas and Kierkegaard in Dialogue*. Bloomington: Indiana University Press, 2008.

———. *Overcoming Onto-Theology: Toward a Postmodern Christian Faith*. New York: Fordham University Press, 2001.

———. *Suspicion and Faith: The Religious Uses of Modern Atheism*. New York: Fordham University Press, 1998.

———. "Theological Anti-Realism." In *Realism and Religion: Philosophical and Theological Perspectives*, ed. Andrew Moore and Michael Scott, pp. 132-45. Burlington, Vt.: Ashgate, 2007.

———. *Transcendence and Self-Transcendence: On God and the Soul*. Bloomington: Indiana University Press, 2004.

Wicks, Jared, S.J. "Luther and 'This Damned, Conceited, Rascally Heathen' Aristotle: An Encounter More Complicated than Many Think." *Pro Ecclesia* XVI, no. 1 (Winter 2007): pp. 90-104.

Wüstenberg, Ralf K. *A Theology of Life: Dietrich Bonhoeffer's Religionless Christianity*. Translated by Doug Stott. Grand Rapids, Mich.: William B. Eerdmans, 1998.

Zimmermann, Jens. "Dietrich Bonhoeffer and Martin Heidegger: Two Different Visions of Humanity." In *Bonhoeffer and Continental Thought: Cruciform Philosophy*, ed. Brian Gregor and Jens Zimmermann, pp. 102-33. Bloomington: Indiana University Press, 2009.

———. *Recovering Theological Hermeneutics: An Incarnational-Trinitarian Theory of Interpretation*. Grand Rapids, Mich.: Baker Academic, 2004.

Zizioulas, John D. *Being as Communion: Studies in Personhood and the Church*. Crestwood, N.Y.: St. Vladimir's Seminary Press, 1985.

———. *Communion and Otherness: Further Studies in Personhood and the Church*. Edited by Paul McPartlan. New York and London: T & T Clark, 2006.

Index

act, intellectual, 24, 26, 28, 31, 32, 90, 91, 109, 164, 165, 171
action, 4, 21, 25, 28, 42, 57, 69, 105, 114, 123–25, 130, 135–36, 137, 140, 144, 161, 166, 168, 177, 183–84, 229n8, 237n15; Henry's Christian philosophy of, 125–35; internal and external, 174–75; responsible, 144, 146, 149, 152, 153, 154, 159, 173, 192, 229n8
activity, 167, 204n17, 218n32; divine, 43, 46, 107, 223n14, 229n8, 237n44, 242n48; meritorious, 16, 42–45, 50, 52, 72, 113, 228n3, 234n31; practical, 25, 26, 36, 103, 123, 167
actuality, 3, 4, 9, 12, 44–46, 51, 52, 57, 59, 60, 72, 80, 81, 139, 174–75, 183–85, 190–91, 211n58, 216n62, 229n6. *See also* possibility; potency; potentiality
actus directus and *actus reflexus*, 110, 139–40, 156–57, 170, 189
agency, 10, 26, 57, 122–24, 136, 139; divine and human, 132–33, 228n3. *See also* action; capability; freedom
Anaximander, 34
Anselm, 11
anthropologia crucis, 7, 10, 11, 16, 40, 41, 51, 74, 119, 122, 163, 180
anthropologia gloriae, 8, 16
Aquinas, 14
Aristotle, 34, 42–43, 46, 51, 52, 82, 218n28, 219n34, 221n70
atheism, 5, 12, 16, 99–100, 108, 138–39
Auden, W. H., 95
Augustine, Saint, 16, 21, 61–63, 82
Aurelius, Marcus, 165

Barth, Karl, 10, 12, 30, 31, 58, 64, 67, 70, 92, 104–108, 111, 113, 119, 160, 178, 200n23, 201n33, 206n50, 206n51, 223n9, 223n13, 223n14, 227n45, 239n19, 241n30
Basil of Caesarea, 48
Bayer, Oswald, 8, 34, 79, 200n23, 201n29, 215n62, 241n31
Bernard of Clairvaux, 16
Bloechl, Jeffrey, 95
body, 23, 26, 60, 130–31, 139–40, 165, 194–96, 204n17, 204n21, 205n30, 211n56; of Christ, 96, 98, 157, 164, 175, 186–88, 225n30, 241n42
Boethius, 14, 47
Bonhoeffer, Dietrich, 8–10, 12, 74, 77–99, 103–21, 122–25, 127, 129–30, 134, 136–37, 139–40, 144–49, 151–60, 162–64, 167–69, 174–75, 176, 178–82, 184–85; actuality of revelation, 12, 190; being addressed, 77–79, 88, 103, 111, 137, 159, 179; being for others, 68, 76, 77, 97, 99, 123, 144–46, 154, 196; being in Adam, 60–63, 67–68; being in Christ, 86, 96, 112, 114, 119, 145, 157, 159, 185, 218n15; critique of Heidegger, 81, 85–92, 99, 219n38, 219n42, 232n44; fall into sin, 60, 64–69; limit(s), 12, 67–69, 90–91, 94, 97–98, 100, 114, 118, 145–46, 149, 151–52, 154, 158–59, 179, 189–90, 194, 196, 220n49, 237n43; new humanity, 10, 16, 81, 86, 98, 100, 112, 116, 125, 175, 187, 197; radicalism and compromise, 117–19; religion, 169, 175–76, 178–82, 195–97, 239n13, 239n14; responsibility, 144–49, 152–55; revelation, 103–14, 189–90, 227n49; self-understanding, 77–78, 90–91, 158–59, 163–64, 168, 180, 198
Bultmann, Rudolf, 9, 78, 104, 106, 178, 181–82, 222n7, 238n11

call, 10, 25, 35, 37, 40, 68, 72, 78–81, 84, 87, 95, 100, 114, 122, 123, 127, 129, 135–41, 142–55, 157, 160, 163, 164, 166–68, 169, 173, 175, 180, 196, 217n3, 217n6, 231n37, 231n38, 232n41, 232n44, 237n43
Calvin, John, 16
capability, capable human being, 4, 10, 25, 27, 43, 44, 53, 57, 70, 77, 87, 113, 119, 120–21, 122–41, 142–44, 146, 150, 170, 177–80, 195, 238n2. *See also finitum capax/incapax* debate
Cappadocian Fathers, 14, 48, 213n26
Caravaggio, 188
Chesterton, G. K., 73
Chrétien, Jean-Louis, 78
church, 6, 63, 79, 86, 98, 99, 110–13, 114, 147, 164, 179, 186, 187, 188, 193, 226n41, 239n13, 241n41

Cicero, 3
community, 25, 32, 39, 62, 75, 79, 98, 117, 148, 225n28. *See also* church
conscience, 34, 35, 36, 68, 81, 84, 87, 110, 125, 142–44, 146–52, 153, 157, 164, 179, 213n10, 215n51, 231n37, 233n13, 233n22, 235n4, 238n56
cor curvum in se. *See* incurvature
counter-Logos. *See* logos
creation, 15, 42, 51, 61, 64–69, 73, 87, 93, 96, 99, 107, 115–16, 118, 130, 131–32, 144, 158, 177, 187, 193, 197, 211n58, 213n17, 215n45, 217n5, 220n51, 221n56, 228n57; *ex nihilo*, 46, 119, 132–33, 143, 147, 217n6; new creation, 10, 46, 79, 87, 100, 106, 113, 192, 194, 196–97
creative word, 79–81, 86, 99, 170, 217n6. *See also* call

Darwin, Charles, 130
death, 1, 44, 50, 67–69, 97, 124, 164, 165, 186–87, 189, 192–94, 220n49, 236n29, 243n66; Being-towards, 84, 87, 89, 91, 100, 193; of God, 4, 5, 71, 179
demythologization, 178, 181–82, 212n2, 238n11
Descartes, 8, 22, 24, 47, 156, 165, 171; Cartesianism, 15, 26, 130–31, 166
Destructio/Destruktion, 1, 3, 7, 9, 16, 21, 25, 37, 42, 45–46, 50, 54, 61–62, 74, 80–85, 87, 95, 97, 110, 114, 119–20, 122, 123, 145–46, 161, 170, 178, 209n28, 210n49, 218n25
Dionysus, 195
discipleship. *See* following after
discipline, 32, 43, 89, 117, 156, 164–70, 172, 179, 219n41, 236n29, 236n32, 236n40. *See also* formation
docetism, 4, 6, 12, 92, 94, 106, 175, 188

Ebeling, Gerhard, 9, 78, 104, 106, 150, 178, 210n54, 222n7, 223n9, 233n22
ek-stasis, 9, 10, 48, 82, 85, 97–98, 121, 127, 137, 140, 159, 210n54
embodiment. *See* body
eschatology, 7, 9, 10, 16, 30, 51, 64, 82, 87, 103–105, 112–14, 118–19, 121, 125, 134, 176, 183, 185, 192–93, 197, 198, 222n7, 225n30, 230n22
exercises, spiritual. *See* discipline
extra se, 53, 79, 81, 127

felix culpa, 79, 156, 234n2
feminism, 74–75, 123

Feuerbach, Ludwig, 24, 37, 108, 130, 178, 180, 190, 195, 225n30, 241n30, 243n71
Fichte, Johann Gottlieb, 8, 22, 26, 78, 92, 126, 127, 138, 142
finitum capax/incapax debate, 106–109, 160–61, 163, 224n27, 225n28, 225n30
Flacius, Matthias, 53, 73
following after, 81, 109, 114, 120, 135–36, 151, 152, 156, 161, 163, 164, 167, 168, 170, 173, 175, 187, 188, 196, 231n38
formation, 41, 113, 118, 125, 143, 148, 168, 170, 174. *See also* discipline
for me, 23, 37, 80, 91, 93, 97, 98, 106, 109, 110, 111, 145, 182–87, 190–91
freedom, 54, 57–58, 67–72, 117, 123, 124, 130, 133, 137, 145, 147–48, 154, 158, 177, 187, 197, 215n52, 228n3, 229n8; divine, 94, 111, 117
Freud, Sigmund, 24, 178, 192, 205n40
Fuchs, Ernst, 9, 78, 104, 106, 222n7

Gadamer, Hans-Georg, 7, 9, 13, 27–28, 31, 90, 106, 138, 219n45, 241n43
Gnosticism, 67, 215n47, 230n22, 237n44
Green, Clifford, 239n13
Green, Garrett, 223n9, 240n23

Hadot, Pierre, 164–65, 167, 221n70, 236n26, 236n29
Hanson, Jeffrey, 231n23
Harnack, Adolf von, 223n13, 224n22
Hart, Kevin, 134
Hegel, Georg Wilhelm Friedrich, 1, 5–6, 8, 12, 22, 36, 37, 54, 90, 92, 94, 146, 153, 163, 176, 177, 185, 186, 189, 201n38, 205n40, 213n26, 220n45, 220n51, 225n30, 226n34, 234n2, 235n11, 238n55, 241n41, 241n42
Heidegger, Martin, 1, 7, 8, 9, 12, 15–17, 22, 26, 27, 30, 31, 35, 36, 37, 41, 46, 54, 77, 78, 81–91, 93–96, 99–100, 104, 108, 126, 131, 138, 142, 144, 178, 182, 190, 193, 199, 204n19, 204n27, 212n72, 218n27, 218n28, 219n34, 219n37, 219n38, 219n42, 222n70, 225n28, 232n49, 242n46
Hengel, Martin, 3
Henry, Michel, 122, 125–35, 137–38, 161–62, 229n13, 230nn20–22, 231n23, 231n32
Heraclitus, 59, 88–89, 93, 96
hermeneutics, 22, 30–31, 35–37, 56, 60, 85, 87, 91, 106, 125, 139, 162, 183–84, 186, 189, 205n34, 215n45, 219n34, 237n53; of the cross, 4, 6, 7, 9, 123, 189, 200n14; New Hermeneutic, 9, 104, 150, 222n7, 222n9; and

phenomenology, 14, 26–28, 30, 56–58, 63, 92, 135; of religion, 135, 176–78, 181, 183, 186–87, 190; of the self, 2, 7, 9, 11, 21–38, 143, 162, 182, 237n53; of suspicion, 24–25, 66, 74, 108, 178, 179, 194, 197
Holy Spirit, 106–107, 226n34, 242n48
Husserl, Edmund, 8, 22, 26, 78, 92, 126, 127, 138, 142
hypostasis, 48, 224n27

Ibsen, Henrik, 118
imagination, 4, 7, 45, 177–78, 182–83, 189, 220n58, 240n23, 242n48
imago dei, 53, 67, 69
incarnation, 11, 43, 68, 81, 86, 93, 94, 106, 114, 119, 130, 145, 172, 173, 182, 197
incurvature, 9, 28, 38, 54–55, 56–76, 77, 79–81, 87–92, 95–98, 114, 119, 124, 125, 128–29, 130, 138, 143, 145, 146, 149, 150–51, 156–61, 163, 174–75, 177, 194–97, 198, 214n30, 214n38, 216n75, 216n76
indirect communication, 28, 44, 54, 60, 166, 170
intentionality, 28, 110, 113, 121, 127, 134, 139–40, 156, 157–63, 170–73, 232n53. See also *actus directus* and *actus reflexus*
Irenaeus, 193, 197, 220n51

Janz, Paul D., 241n41
Jenson, Matt, 213n17, 216n75
Jenson, Robert W., 8, 54, 79, 81, 222n70, 222n7, 225n37
Jüngel, Eberhard, 8, 9, 11, 34, 45, 59, 71, 72, 78, 191, 200n20, 213n8, 217n11, 221n61, 222n8
justification, 34–36, 40, 42, 44, 53, 89, 103–104, 107, 113–16, 118, 123, 125, 140, 142, 149, 156, 159, 164, 168, 191, 193, 195, 198, 227n49, 228n3; and ethical responsibility, 36, 37, 123, 146–49, 152–55; ontology of justification by faith, 9–10, 40, 44–45, 51, 52, 81, 112, 150; ontology of self-justification, 9, 40, 44–46, 50, 68, 69–73, 79–81, 87–90, 97, 100, 110, 111, 113, 119, 130, 136, 140, 151–52, 170, 198, 215n62, 219n42, 236n32, 238n56

Kant, Immanuel, 2, 8, 12, 22, 41, 54, 72, 126, 138, 148, 176–78, 184, 185, 189, 190, 199n1
Kearney, Richard, 59, 206n46
kenosis, 6, 7, 11, 43, 68, 74, 81, 99, 180
Khora, 79
Kierkegaard, Søren, 2, 3, 4–5, 8, 10, 16–17, 33, 37, 41, 54–55, 59, 60, 69, 82, 95, 104, 108–109, 110, 111, 113, 123, 124, 132–33, 134, 136, 153, 160, 166, 167, 173–75, 183–85, 188, 197, 200n23, 201n28, 206n50, 216n74, 219n34, 220n54, 220n58, 225n34, 226n37, 228n56, 228n58, 229n5, 229n6, 237n51, 238n56, 240n27, 240n29
know thyself, 2, 16, 21, 166–67, 173

Lacoste, Jean-Yves, 114, 138–39, 232n48
Leder, Drew, 131, 139–40
Leibniz, Gottfried Wilhelm, 47
Levinas, Emmanuel, 35–37, 40, 78, 90–92, 108, 122, 137, 142–47, 152–55, 156, 160–61, 163, 171, 192–93, 208n86, 235n9
limit(s), 4, 67–68, 90–92, 152, 158, 165, 225n30; of communication, 60; death as, 84, 89, 90; human, 58, 158–59, 179, 194, 196; other person as, 67, 90–91, 94, 96–98, 100, 151; and the penultimate, 114, 118, 176–98; of philosophy, 4, 9, 11, 12, 176–77, 183, 189–90, 194, 225n34; of poetics, 186–91, 242n43; of responsibility, 145–46, 149, 164, 237n43
logos, 85, 88, 89, 92–97, 99, 100, 109, 110, 120, 151, 159, 161, 166, 173, 175, 188, 217n3, 222n70, 224n27, 236n29; counter-Logos, 95, 96–97, 120, 151, 156, 159, 162–64, 173
love, 1, 6, 11, 16, 17, 34, 42, 61, 67, 68, 79, 80, 81, 94, 95, 97, 124–25, 133–34, 144, 148, 154, 170, 172, 186, 192–93, 196, 221n64, 228n3, 231n29
Luther, 7, 8, 9, 11, 16, 41–46, 51, 53, 54, 59, 63, 64, 67, 70, 71, 75, 78, 81–85, 87, 91, 106–108, 110–11, 113, 115, 123, 125, 135, 142, 148, 156, 160, 162, 164, 167, 170–73, 176, 178, 184, 191, 202n5, 208n2, 209n17, 210n54, 215n62, 217n5, 218n25, 218n27, 219n34, 221n64, 225n30, 226n42, 227n48, 227n55, 228n3, 229n6, 229n10, 236n31, 236n32, 239n15, 240n27, 241n30
Lutheran, Lutheranism, 3, 5, 8, 9, 53–54, 107–108, 110, 123, 135, 167, 201n28, 220n51, 224n27, 225n28, 225n30, 227n54, 229n5, 232n58. See also *finitum capax/incapax* debate

Marcel, Gabriel, 26, 153–54, 204n21, 234n30, 234n31
Marion, Jean-Luc, 78, 171, 217n3
Marx, Karl, 24, 178
meaning, 4, 5, 6, 7, 8, 22, 23, 26–30, 98, 152, 160–63, 181–91; of Being, 15, 82, 88, 98, 205n42; of existence, 34, 36, 37, 40, 53, 71, 80, 191–98, 227n44; meaning-event, 186–88; revelation and, 108, 109; of sin, 62, 70

mediation, 25, 28, 29, 44, 60, 63, 65, 86, 92, 135, 137, 143, 146–47, 158, 162, 205n42, 237n52, 241n42; Christological mediation, 97–98, 127, 153, 162, 184, 226n36; self-mediation, 23, 38, 77, 81, 90, 91, 92, 99, 107, 110, 149, 151–53, 157, 159, 163, 164, 173, 205n42, 220n46, 237n52, 241n42

Meister Eckhart, 127, 192

Merleau-Ponty, Maurice, 25, 139, 195, 204n19

Moltmann, Jürgen, 178, 222n7

moment, 22, 36, 37, 42, 50, 52, 82, 103–107, 113–14, 116, 148, 157, 161, 168, 171, 173, 174, 183, 222n8

narrative, 14, 28, 29–30, 32–33, 58, 62, 64, 65, 66, 98, 112, 162, 177, 187–88, 212n2, 222n7, 222n8, 223n9, 241n35

Niebuhr, Reinhold, 73

Nietzsche, Friedrich, 1, 3, 10, 23–25, 67, 71, 72, 75, 123–24, 159, 163, 176, 178, 180, 191, 194–98, 203n16, 204n17, 209n19, 214n30, 234n4, 236n32, 241n43, 243n71

nihilism, 1, 10, 69, 71, 123, 124, 125, 191, 194, 195, 197, 215n56, 236n32

non-religious interpretation of Christianity, 169, 178–80, 195–97, 239n13, 239n14

nothing, nothingness, 58, 61, 79, 80, 99, 100, 129, 132–33, 158, 192, 194. *See also* creation

ontologia crucis, 7, 77, 81–88

onto-theology, 37, 40, 64, 65, 92, 99, 153, 208n90, 242n46

Parmenides, 88–89, 221n70

participation, 4, 31, 72, 153, 168, 213n17; being-in-Adam, 61, 62; being-in-Christ, 109, 113, 114, 126, 145, 218n15, 226n34; in God, 134, 161, 211n54; in God's suffering, 154, 167, 180; Platonic, 62, 214n26; in truth, 16, 109, 156; in the world, 25, 26–27, 204n27

Pascal, Blaise, 32, 35, 59

Paul, the Apostle, 1, 3–4, 8, 41, 44, 51, 58, 70, 80, 82, 84, 96, 98, 132, 135, 149, 167, 179, 188–89, 232n58

Pelagianism, 61, 236n32

penultimate, 10, 96, 113–21, 124, 137, 180, 183, 188, 198, 227n45, 227n52, 227n53; character formation as, 168–69; intentionality, 156, 159, 161, 162; meaning as, 190, 191; possibility and capability, 122, 138–39, 142, 144; reason as, 125; religion and, 179, 189; responsibility, 144, 147–48, 151, 153, 154, 229n8; self-examination, 170

person, 14, 42, 47, 48–49, 62, 72–73, 75, 109–10, 202n49; Christ as person, 92–94, 97, 100, 164, 166, 188, 220n49, 225n28, 225n34; collective person, 62–63, 75, 213n26

personalism, 14, 90–91, 223n9

phenomenology, 22, 26, 27, 30, 57, 60, 126, 130, 131, 134; of the call, 78, 137; of capability, 128, 142, 170; of conscience, 142–49; of the Crucified Logos, 92–95; of the person, 14; of religion, 107, 135, 242n47

philosophy: Christian, 11–12, 51, 99–100, 125–35, 176, 190, 236n29; and the cross, 1, 3, 4–6, 7, 12, 41, 44, 45, 51, 84–86, 92, 94, 100, 120, 164, 186, 188–89, 200n25, 201n26; cruciform, 1, 7, 12, 14, 51, 99–100, 156, 164, 176, 188; reflexive, 8, 22–23, 25, 90, 157, 160, 162, 170; relative autonomy of, 13; of religion, 1, 138, 176, 177, 183, 187, 189–90, 194, 226n34, 238n2; and theology, 11–13, 14, 30, 45, 70, 99–100, 176, 201n37, 201n38, 218n27, 221n70; as a way of life, 156, 164–70, 174, 236n29

phusis, 34, 88–89, 96, 97

Plato, Platonism, 34, 48, 57, 62, 165, 208n7, 214n26, 221n70, 238n55

pneumatology. *See* Holy Spirit

poetics, 6, 7, 57, 58, 89–90, 178, 182–91, 242n43, 242n46

Polanyi, Michael, 27, 139, 204n30

polyphony of life, 105, 175, 180, 193

possibility, 4, 33, 44–46, 52, 57, 59, 66, 79, 80, 90, 122, 125, 174, 183–85, 193–95, 197, 228n3, 232n52, 232n57; of death, 84, 87; eschatological, 4, 9, 10, 45, 51, 52, 72, 80, 81, 87, 119, 185; of revelation, 12, 139, 189, 190, 227n49; of understanding, 9, 22, 77, 83, 84, 87, 187, 189, 204n16. *See also* potency; potentiality

potency, 138, 168, 176, 178, 183, 187, 204n16, 215n52. *See also* possibility; potentiality

potentiality, 52, 83, 87, 113, 119, 122, 143. *See also* possibility; potency

pro me / pro nobis. See for me

Prometheus, 158

Pseudo-Dionysius, 208n7

Rahner, Karl, 138, 232n48

recognition, 25, 32, 33–36, 39–46, 49, 59, 67–68, 69, 71, 72–75, 80–81, 94, 98, 112, 124, 139, 143, 146, 155, 159, 160, 162, 168, 170, 177, 180, 190, 192, 198, 202n49, 215n59, 226n34

reflexivity, 15, 22–31, 32, 51, 52, 87, 129, 139, 140, 142, 156–75, 237n53

religion, 10, 12, 43, 169, 176–98; critique of, 24, 104–105, 178–81, 183, 194–95
responsibility, 14, 22, 23, 25, 32, 33, 39, 40, 68, 72, 75, 83, 89, 94, 98, 123, 125, 142–55, 157–58, 166, 170, 174, 180, 183, 184, 192, 194, 196, 229n8, 237n43, 237n53, 239n15; Levinas on, 35–37, 137, 142–47, 152–55, 160, 192; for sin, 60–63, 238n56
resurrection, 4, 5, 6, 17, 52, 79, 81, 86, 104, 106, 112, 119, 130, 134, 145, 154, 172, 176, 182, 185, 186–98, 221n61, 241n38
revelation, 4, 5, 12, 13, 30, 41, 43, 44, 59, 73–74, 81, 86, 91, 92, 93, 99, 103, 105–11, 113, 114, 118, 125, 130, 134, 138, 139, 160–63, 172, 181, 182, 184, 189–90, 194, 198, 218n27, 221n70, 226n41, 227n49, 232n48, 232n49, 236n29, 240n23, 240n29, 242n46
Ricoeur, Paul, 1, 4, 7–9, 11–12, 14, 22, 24–26, 28–31, 37, 55–67, 70, 78, 90, 104–106, 112, 122, 131, 135, 137, 142–44, 146–51, 157, 174, 176–78, 180–84, 186–94, 197, 201n37, 202n49, 203n16, 204n19, 204n21, 204n27, 205n37, 205n40, 205n42, 206n51, 208n88, 212n2, 213n23, 214n41, 214n44, 215n52, 223n9, 231n37, 233n22, 237n53, 238n2, 238n11, 239n14, 239n16, 241n38, 241n41, 242n48, 243n66

sacraments, 4, 63, 78, 107, 110–12, 175, 196, 224n27, 225n28
Sartre, Jean-Paul, 67, 72, 74
Scheler, Max, 62, 213n26
Schelling, Friedrich Wilhelm Joseph, 54
secularity, 167, 169, 180; of philosophy, 13, 222n70
self-examination, 156, 169–75, 237n43, 237n44, 238n56
self-interpretation, 22, 23, 25, 31–38, 156, 162
self-understanding, 2, 3, 4, 7–11, 15, 16, 22, 23, 25, 27–30, 32, 33, 36–38, 40, 45, 63, 77, 78, 80, 81, 86, 87, 90–92, 103, 106, 114, 115–20, 130, 150, 152, 156–75, 176, 177, 180, 181, 182–90, 194, 230n19, 237n53
sicut deus, 58, 67–68, 149, 151, 158
simul justus et peccator, 52, 113, 221n62, 227n42
sin, 28, 40, 42, 44, 45, 46, 47, 50, 52, 56–76, 81, 83–87, 97, 116, 134, 158, 191, 213n10, 243n73; feminist critique of, 73–76; original, 53–54, 60–73; as substance or accident, 53–54, 60–63. *See also* incurvature
Socrates, 2, 7, 49–50, 133, 165, 166, 189, 226, 241n43
spiritual trial, 156, 167, 170–72
Strigel, Victorinus, 53
strong evaluation, 32–34, 39, 70, 71, 89, 148
substance, 41, 46–55, 60, 61, 63, 79, 81–82, 84, 85, 87, 88, 168, 194
symbol, 3–4, 11, 28–30, 57–58, 60, 62, 120, 150, 162, 177–78, 186–88, 190, 200n14, 205n42, 212n2, 239n11, 241n35

Taylor, Charles, 7, 21, 31–34, 39, 69, 71, 103, 115, 215n59
time, 21, 34, 43, 46–47, 82, 84, 103–104, 109, 111, 113–14, 148, 166, 168, 173, 175, 192–93, 194, 197, 223n9
totality, 5, 26, 36–37, 84, 88, 91, 159, 163, 189
Trinity, 14, 48, 134, 224n27, 230n22

Vanhoozer, Kevin, 188
Varro, Marcus Terentius, 3
virtue, 42, 51, 52, 74, 148, 165
Volf, Miroslav, 72

Westphal, Merold, 172, 208n90, 226n37, 240n29

Zizioulas, John, 14, 48–49

Index 261

Brian Gregor is a postdoctoral teaching fellow in the Department of Philosophy at Fordham University. He is the author of several articles on philosophy of religion, ethics, and aesthetics and is the co-editor of *Bonhoeffer and Continental Thought: Cruciform Philosophy* (2009) and *Being Human, Becoming Human: Dietrich Bonhoeffer and Social Thought* (2010).

www.ingramcontent.com/pod-product-compliance
Lightning Source LLC
Chambersburg PA
CBHW031804220426
43662CB00007B/516